D1135881

The Backpacker

John Christopher Harris

summersdale

Reprinted 2003, 2005.

Copyright © John Harris 2001

All rights reserved.

No part of this book may be reproduced by any means, nor transmitted, nor translated into a machine language, without the written permission of the publisher.

Summersdale Publishers Ltd
46 West Street
Chichester
West Sussex
PO19 1RP
UK

www.summersdale.com

Printed and bound by J H. Haynes & Co. Ltd., Sparkford.

ISBN 1 84024 161 6

Cover design: Blue Lemon, Brighton.

Special thanks to Tang Pui Wah Elise.

To *everyone* on the 08.15 to Charing Cross.

CONTENTS

THE END

' . . . Big Balls is number one!' he shouted over the noise of the road. He had to shout, because even though we were riding in a Rolls Royce, the smoothest and most luxurious car on that road, it was a convertible, and even the world's best engineers could do nothing about the sound of rubber rolling against tarmac. Nor could they redirect the air as it ricocheted off the windscreen and blasted around the ears, which, like the rest of the human anatomy, were designed in the days when aerodynamics weren't a consideration.

'I know he's number one,' I shouted, sliding forward on the back seat and resting my forearms on the leather headrest in front. His long blond hair was flying horizontally in the wind and I had to crane my neck, pushing my head between him and the driver to see his face.

'I'm not disputing that. Big Balls is number one. Fact! What I want to know is: who was number two?' The Triad lookalike who was driving us glanced quickly sideways at me, as though about to offer the answer to my question, before returning his gaze to the road ahead. 'Don't know do you? You don't fucking remember!' I slid noiselessly back on the animal skin and folded my arms.

'Course I fooking do.' He bent forward to light a cigarette in the footwell, momentarily disappearing from view, before reappearing in a mass of hairy smoke. 'Joost give me time.' He paused, puffing vigorously to keep the cigarette alight, and looked at his watch. 'Fooking hell, can't this thing go any faster? I'm gonna be late.'

'Well it'll be your own fault if you are,' I said, and left a moment's silence for my statement to sink in before turning to my girlfriend. 'Apple, can you tell the driver to go faster, please?'

She leaned forward, one hand holding her long black hair against the wind, the other holding down her mini-skirt, and said something in Cantonese. The hum of the engine went up a pitch, throwing her back into the seat, and we rose on to the elevated carriageway into the full glare of the bright morning sunshine. Each of us turned on cue, as though attached to the same strings, and squinted at the shimmering harbour.

'Woo-hoo!' He stood up on his seat, one hand holding on to the top of the windscreen for support, sparks flying from his cigarette as the wind buffeted his face. 'Woo-hoo! This is it John, this is the day!'

'Wow,' I gasped, picking up my camcorder and starting to film. 'I've seen it a thousand times but it never looked like that before.' The harbour glistened in the sunlight causing me to blink against the magnified image in the viewfinder. As usual, the solitary government-sponsored junk was there, plying up and down for the benefit of tourists' cameras, but it failed to spoil the scene. The harbour was to our right, and the shining steel and glass skyscrapers on our left. It felt like we were sitting on a speeding, metallic-blue bullet that had been fired between the two. A bullet with beige upholstery.

'Woo-hoo! What a day it's gonna be!' He sat down, much to the driver's relief, and turned to face me. 'This is it, John,' he said breathlessly, sweeping his hair from his face, 'this is the day.'

I pressed the *STOP* button and lowered the camera. 'Are you sure you're doing the right thing?'

He hesitated, using one hand to shield his face from the sunlight, then nodded. 'Yeah, the compass says so.'

Afraid to show my emotion to my best friend, I turned away from him and looked out over the other side of the flyover. Below us, in a tennis court, a perfectly synchronised group of old ladies stood on one leg as part of their morning t'ai chi class like a well-groomed flock of grey-haired flamingos. My head turned slowly, pretending to be interested in the display, as we sped past one group and then another, before they were replaced by another blinding skyscraper and I turned back.

'You'd better have this then,' I said, reaching into my jacket pocket and pulling out the little mahogany box. The sunlight caught its brass corners and made them wink. 'Even though you can't remember who was number two, I'm gonna let you have it. But don't open it until after!'

He took it from my palm and shook his head pensively. 'It's been a long time John.'

'Mmm, and a long way.'

'"To Sir William George Garthrick Jenner",' he read from the gift label, '"From Lord John".'

I wasn't born with a title, no one from south-east London ever has been, and he had never been knighted, as far as I'm aware they don't knight ex-North Sea fishermen, but we still have them, and no one can take them away. Even though the rules that tell us whether we'll be a worker or a player are made before we are born, some of us learn to jump from one to the other.

Nobody told me how to jump but I'm going to tell you because I've learned and broken free, in the same way that the other man in that car did. There is no way of telling his story without telling my own because they are the same. And if that sounds like a cliché then so be it; I don't know how else to say it.

We had come a long way. I don't know how many miles or countries; I lost count. It all started when I went on a three-week holiday to India.

That was four years ago . . .

REWIND

THE BEGINNING

ONE

'Beep, beep, beep, beeeep. This ... is London ...'

By the time the BBC World Service intro had started its signature tune I was already standing at the bedroom window with my camcorder, finger poised over the *RECORD* button. I pulled aside one end of the dusty curtains and looked through the viewfinder, closing one eye and squinting the other against the bright, early morning sunshine.

It was still only 01.00 Greenwich Mean Time according to the man on the radio, which made it six o'clock in the morning, I reasoned, Indian Time. I could have been wrong, I'd had virtually no sleep all night, but even through the electronically-relayed phosphorous image in my camera it looked like early morning outside.

On the street beneath me Indians were starting their day. I let my eyes wander down the road: from the two children directly beneath my third-floor window who were mercilessly teasing a half-starved kitten, past the Sikh man meticulously polishing his rickshaw, to the point where the road curved out of sight. The narrow street looked like a perfectly-formed concrete canyon, the brilliant blue sky a snaking band above the rooftops.

'This is *Goa*,' I mumbled, 'dum-tee dum-tee dum-tee-dum ...'

'What are you doing John? It's so early.'

I didn't look around; instead ruffling the curtains and sending a small fog of dust into the air making me gag and cough slightly.

My girlfriend sighed again, more tiresomely this time. Opening my eyes and looking across at her briefly and then over to the corner of the room, I studied my surfboard, tucked into its protective travel bag. The words, *Fragile! Top Load Only!* written on a label and stuck on to the bag were peeling off like a wilting petal in the hot, humid air.

Sanita turned her head towards me wearily, looked at the surfboard and then back to me. 'I don't know why you brought that with you, I didn't know there was any surf in India.' She turned and rolled back on to her stomach with a huff, and buried her face in the damp pillow. I pressed the *STOP* button and lowered the camera. I was beginning to think she was right. Well, not beginning, I already thought she was right. Two minutes after stepping off the plane at Goa's International Airport it was crystal clear that she was right.

The airport in Goa was a mess, a joke. The previous Monday evening at about six o'clock I had arrived on a flight from London with Sanita, my fiancée, one surfboard and minimal cabin baggage.

The first thing that hits you when you step off the plane in India is the heat. The first thing should be the smell but that has already penetrated the welded joints of the aeroplane long before the doors have even been opened. The second thing that hits you when the doors do open is the sight of what appears to be complete mayhem. Not the usual airport sight: people boarding and disembarking planes. No. What you get in Indian airports is London Underground station in rush hour meets Third World Armageddon. There were at least a dozen different modes of transport available, from clapped-out trucks to rickshaws to cow-driven baggage cars. God knows what they were all doing on the runway.

Once we'd managed to get off the plane and fight our way through to collect my surfboard we discovered that all the cash Sanita had so cleverly put into her shoulder bag, which she had equally cleverly checked in as luggage, was gone. We tried to get some help to recover the money but it was hopeless. 'You put cash in luggage, no lock?' said the man at the information counter wobbling his head. 'Ohdearohdear.' I immediately saw his point of view and told Sanita to forget it. I had a Visa card anyway – an essential part of every traveller's kit. We picked up our gear and trudged off in search of transport into Umta Vaddo and a place to stay.

Umta Vaddo is a half-mile square area of Calangute beach that houses wall-to-wall guest houses, food-stalls and trinket shops. There's an Umta Vaddo in every Asian town: in Calcutta it's Sudder Street, Bangkok has

Khao San Road, and Jakarta has Jalan Jaksa. All of them are different, in that it's a different country and language, but all of them are the same: serving the same variety of backpacker food, selling the same tie-dye baggy pants, and are home to the same variety of charmless concrete guest houses. We chose the Palmtops Hotel.

I let the dusty curtains fall limply back across the window, walked across the dark room and opened the door to the small fridge, retrieving my underpants from the icebox. This I looked forward to in the morning. In anticipation I kicked the fridge door shut with my foot and steadied myself, letting out a steady puff of air. Counting to three I jumped into them, both feet at once, gasping as they came into contact with my groin. 'Ahh, lovely.'

Sanita clucked loudly.

'You should put your knickers in there at night,' I said. 'It's brilliant.'

She sat up in bed, the damp sheet sticking to her back with sweat, and eyed me vacantly.

I don't know how, but I knew exactly what she was about to say. Maybe it was the way her eyes dropped slightly and then came up to meet mine; maybe it was the shape of her mouth, drooping unhappily at the corners. She leaned over on to one elbow and ran a single finger between her breasts, like a windscreen wiper on a car, wiping off a layer of sweat and studying the water dripping from her finger. 'John,' she said, looking up at me, 'I want to go home.'

If the airport was a joke the train station was worse. Sanita, upon seeing the mayhem, had refused to even go into the station building and had decided to wait outside. The place was full of beggars, thousands of them, in various stages of collapse and decay. I found the way in which they spotted a target, a potential source of funds, from far across the station hall and then moved in for the kill was quite amusing, and while I queued for the tickets south I had plenty of time to watch exactly how they operated.

As soon as a tourist entered the station concourse they would pounce from all four corners, steadily bearing down on their prey. It was essentially a race. It reminded me of a scene from the film *Aliens*. In it the creatures are steadily moving in on two of the commandos who are hemmed-in inside the ventilation ducts. The rest of the frantic crew are watching the appalling events unfold on a TV monitor which shows a dozen or so luminous green dots converging on the unlucky victims.

I watched through the fuzzy image in my camcorder as another tourist, oblivious to the impending danger, studied his guidebook for some clue as to how or where to buy the correct train ticket. The resultant look of shock on their faces was always the same: one minute they would be calmly thumbing through the pages, the next they would jump back with fright as they felt the stump of a beggar stroking their bare legs.

Amongst the beggars at the station there was a sub-group who always got to the subject first and therefore won the race. These were the skaters. Without legs, or at least without the use of their legs, they had constructed small four-wheeled trolleys, a bit like square skateboards, on which they propelled themselves along with their hands or stumps. While most other beggars had to be content with dragging themselves laboriously from one side of the concourse to the other, the skaters would fly across, bobbing and weaving in and out of pedestrians as they went, steel wheels screaming against the concrete floor as they shot towards the intended target.

'Sir?'

I was so engrossed that I couldn't place the loud knocking sound in my ears.

'Sir? Please, sir.'

I lowered the camera and turned to face the clerk.

'Your tickets please, sir.' He rapped on the glass screen that separated us and pointed at the counter.

'What?'

Sliding the two tickets under the chipped glass, he wobbled his head. 'Two tickets. Please, sir, there are many people waiting, thank you.'

I glanced behind me at the snaking line of angry faces. 'Oh, yeah, thanks.' Sliding the tickets off the greasy counter I checked them, flapping the hem of my shirt with one hand to dry the sweat. The heat in the concourse was stifling, sticking my shirt to me like an extra skin. I'd drunk two bottles of water at breakfast and had mostly sweated them out already but I still needed to go to the toilet. I figured I could kill two birds with one stone: freshen up and pee.

'Is there a toilet in here?' I asked, turning back to the counter. The clerk, without looking up from his timetable, lazily raised an arm and pointed to the right.

Slipping the two damp tickets into my pocket, I pushed though the crowd and walked towards the corner of the building. I didn't need a sign to know where the toilet was situated; the rank smell of sour piss and shit, and the cloud of flies hovering over a stagnant pool in the doorway were all the direction I needed. I would have turned away and waited until we were back at the guest house but I was desperate. 'Hold your breath,' I told myself, 'and go in.'

As I walked towards the entrance of the toilet a small turbaned man who had been standing in the doorway moved slightly to one side, and seemed to nod to someone. He could have been dislodging a particularly annoying fly from a nostril, anything's possible, but with the benefit of hindsight I choose to record it as a nod. Hindsight's like that: one always remembers tiny details, even if they didn't exist. I think the brain must invent them subconsciously to fill in the gaps.

Anyway, he nodded and I walked past him into the stinking concrete box. The floor was four inches deep in water, which came dribbling from a waste pipe in one corner where a man stood washing a tin bowl. I tiptoed in and turned into one of the cubicles, stopping at the entrance. There was no door, and I figured that I could probably aim the jet from three feet, thus avoiding stepping in the piles of shit that had been dropped all around the hole in the floor like bombs that had missed their intended target. I was just about to undo my zip when I felt a tap on the shoulder. I quickly pulled my hand away and turned around.

I remember gasping and sucking in a fly as soon as I saw the knife. A knife!

'What?'

The man who held it to my chin was the same one who'd been washing the bowl. I know that because as soon as I jumped back in shock and stepped in shit he dropped the tin bowl on the floor with a loud *clang*. He moved forward to cover the step back that I'd just taken and pushed the six-inch blade back into my throat. I couldn't breath! I tried to swallow but my Adam's apple got stuck on the knife edge. 'Ah, ah, ah . . . '

Instinctively I tilted my head up, but I could still see his face.

And I can still see it now, writing this. He had a small, almost spherically round head, like a little football. He had wispy black hair that was greased down and clung to his forehead like running ink, almost as though someone had spilt a pot of it on to his head and turned him on his side so that each run became a thick black curl. The smallness of his head was accentuated by bulbous eyes, ping-pong balls rammed into his sockets, each one blood-red from years of alcohol abuse. As he opened his mouth to speak I got a whiff of booze and saw his few rotten teeth, stained red by betel.

'*Money! Money!*' he screamed, holding out a shaking hand and tapping the fingers against the palm.

The room swam as I came to the brink of passing out. A droplet of sweat trickled backwards along my hairline before running down the back of my neck. Tilting my head higher as he pushed the blade in and looking down my nose at him, partly because my movement was restricted and partly because I was a foot taller than him, I swallowed carefully and put both hands into my shorts pockets. The money I had in them seemed to jump into my palms, and I clenched each fist and pulled them out slowly.

If anyone ever says that they were held at knife or gunpoint and refused to give up their money, they're either crazy or it's bullshit. The fear of the moment is so intense that it's impossible to speak, or even move, or do anything other than what's instructed. Even then it's hard to move a muscle. It would be easy for me to waffle on now about how my mind was torn between giving him the cash and giving him a swift kick in the bollocks, but those thoughts only come after the event. I didn't even register the stink of shit any more. The only reason I know I stepped in it was because it squeezed into my sandal and I found it later. My life didn't even flash before my eyes!

What happened next is engrained on my memory.

The image of a white leg, with a leather sandal on the foot, flying through the air and striking the Indian on the side of the head is imprinted on my mind like a single frame from a film. My brain's camera froze the picture in the split second before the foot came into contact with the side of the Indian's head.

The poor guy didn't know what hit him. His head went over like a boxer's punch-ball on a spring as the foot struck his face and he was sent tumbling to one side. He was immediately followed by the body of the person attached to the leg: a mixture of tie-dye shirt and hair that went sailing past the doorway and landed with a splash on top of the Indian.

I stood, stiff and totally unmoving except for my eyes, both fists clenched in front of me, still holding out the money.

'*Go!*' ordered a voice.

'Eh?'

He picked himself up off the Indian and grabbed my shirt collar. 'Come on, go!'

Still incapable of making a decision I stumbled forward, dragged by the man, and splashed my way out of the room, back on to the station concourse. Only then did I hear my heart pounding as the blood rushed back into my ears and surged through my body. I opened my parched month and filled my lungs with warm air, coughing out the fly.

'*Fooking* Indians!' the man said angrily, wringing out his T-shirt. '*Fooking* India! You OK?'

'I, um, yeah ... think so.' I blinked, and suddenly seemed to come round.

'Yes, I-I'm OK,' I said, unclenching my fists and staring down at the crumpled rupees.

'Not worth being mugged for, huh?'

'No,' I said blankly, 'it's not. Thanks. I-I don't know what ...'

'It's OK.' He waved a hand through the air. 'Listen, I've got to go to pick up my plane ticket. Don't hang around in here. Follow the compass ...'

Plane ticket? This is a railway station! Compass? What compass? I was just about to ask him what he meant when he started to walk away.

'Maybe see you later,' he called back. 'You're staying at the Palmtops, right?'

I nodded vacantly.

'Me too. Catch you there later.'

I watched the lurid orange tie-dye circle on the back of his T-shirt merge into the crowd as he jogged away and shouted, 'What's your name?'

But he was already gone.

TWO

When I finally got back outside to where I had left Sanita, she was gone. Shit, I thought, why does she always have to wander off at the wrong fucking time? I stood on the spot for a few minutes, perspiring and trying to steady my heartbeat. Just down the entrance steps from the station stood an ice cream vendor who'd been there when we arrived an hour earlier, and was still shouting at the top of his voice. Beside the vendor a small group of people had gathered, apparently looking at the ground. Curious, I walked over to take a look.

Sanita was sitting on the floor in the middle of the group, holding her head. She saw me and started crying.

'What happened?' I asked, bending down and putting my arm around her back but at the same time scanning the crowd for any sign of a tie-dye shirt.

'John,' she cried, sobbing harder and self-consciously pushing her skirt down below her knees, 'I fainted.'

'You haven't seen a traveller around here wearing ...'

'John!'

'Fain– How?'

'How'd you think?' She glared at me, tensing her jaw to hold back the tears. 'It's too hot!'

Ten minutes later we were riding through the streets in a clapped-out old rickshaw, Sanita at one end of the back seat, sulking, me at the opposite end. We arrived back at the hotel but she wanted to go into the centre of town to get 'something nice to eat'. I leaned forward and spoke though the perspex sheet that separated the driver from the passengers.

The driver looked over his shoulder briefly, told us that he knew just the place, and floored it. We sped forward with a jerk. 1 ... 2 ... 3 ... 4: four gears, four seconds. The handlebar clutch depressions were a blur to the human eye, the only way to detect the gear changes was from the glint of the driver's ringed fingers in the sunshine each time he clenched and then straightened his chubby hand. Every time we cornered, one of the two rear wheels left the road momentarily and we were thrown from one side of the tin box to the other.

The driver's view, front and rear, was almost completely blocked by trinkets, deities and other objects dangling from mirrors, and the windscreen contained a stick-on, blue-tinted sun-strip top and bottom, so that only a pillbox-sized area of clear glass could actually be seen through. He may as well have had his eyes closed.

'How much you pay?' the driver barked, and at the same time took a corner, leaning into the bend the way a motorcycle racer leans his bike over when cornering.

I thought quickly, calculating the distance in my mind. 'Twenty,' I said, leaning with him as we came out of the corner.

He shook his head. 'No-no-no, pay twenty-five.'

'No, it only costs–'

Sanita sighed loudly. 'John, just pay the man, for Christ's sake. Five rupees!'

I thought for a moment and then agreed, slumping back into the seat, sulking.

We screeched to a halt outside a Western-style restaurant that served, I'd learned a few days earlier, the best ice cream, milk shakes and burgers in town. Another reason for being dropped here was to change money. I had established over the past week that the best black market exchange rate for foreign currency was obtainable right outside the bookstall just up from the restaurant.

Changing money on the black market was easy and, despite the guidebook's advice to the contrary, was not a risky business. At least ten percent could be gained over and above the current bank exchange rate by simply pretending to be interested in one of the books on sale on the bookstall next door to the restaurant. I gave Sanita my food order and walked off to pretend to buy a book.

'Change money? Dollar, pound, yen, what you have?'

'Pound Sterling,' I said to the man loitering around the paperbacks. 'Fifty.'

We haggled a little, went through the obligatory laugh at each other's audacity routine and finally agreed a price.

The restaurant was crowded, as usual, and the air conditioning was freezing heaven. The sweat chilled and then dried, leaving my T-shirt stuck to my body. If the weather outside was ever cold the restaurant would have no business; most people would eat Indian food from the street stalls. Customers often lingered there for hours, taking outrageously small sips from their milk shakes just to stay out of the heat. It always looked like booming business, but for all I know the same people had been sitting there since breakfast-time.

Sanita had already ordered when I entered, and was sitting in one corner, idly flicking through her food tickets. She hadn't seen me walk in so I decided to stand to one side for a while in an attempt to collect my thoughts. I was hidden from her by the few people queuing at the ice cream counter, and when they shuffled forward every time a customer was served, I ambled alongside, pretending to be interested in ice cream.

Sanita looked shattered, utterly exhausted. Her face looked pale against the brightly coloured vest she wore, and her hair, usually one of her physical charms, was hanging limply across her face, stuck to her forehead and cheeks with dried sweat.

She hadn't even wanted to come to India in the first place, but had finally agreed just to be with me. I had convinced her by bombarding her with pictures from tourist brochures at our high street travel agent, and I think my enthusiasm eventually just wore her down and she succumbed to the unrelenting pressure.

Since arriving in Goa the previous week she had suffered from an upset stomach almost from day one, constantly needing to go to the toilet. At one point she had spent almost the whole day in the room, only leaving once to buy some medicine from a nearby chemist. Even that short errand across the street to the shop outside the hotel had turned into an ordeal, in which she rushed out fitfully into the burning midday sun, bought the goods and then ran back, sweating and clutching her stomach, to the safety of our toilet.

I had always imagined that she would feel completely at home once we arrived in India, and that all her fears would be put to the back of her mind. After all, I reasoned, she was of Indian descent. My reasoning was ridiculous. Although her parents were originally from India she had been born and bred in London, and, to make matters worse, had never even been on holiday abroad before.

The ice cream queue shortened again, and I stood still to look across at my fiancée. As the teller called out another food order number and Sanita blinked and wearily stood up to collect the food, I moved from my statuesque poise and walked over to the table and sat down.

I waited for her to return with the food and start eating, before saying, 'I got fifty to the pound, not bad huh?'

'Great', she said flatly, and didn't look up from her meal. 'What about the train south tonight? What time do we need to be at the station?'

I hesitated, stuffing half a dozen chips into my mouth.

'John?'

'Bit of a problem there,' I said, swallowing and looking nervously around for the ketchup.

'What problem? Don't tell me you couldn't get the tickets ...'

'No, I got the tickets all right. They're just not on tonight's train; that's all. You saw that station San – packed out.'

She looked up, her eyes wide with alarm. 'What then?'

I still hadn't told her what had happened to me in the station. I don't know why. Maybe her fainting; maybe the look on her face now, I don't know. A wave of resentment towards Sanita suddenly washed over me. Resentment at having to explain about the tickets, resentment at her fainting, at her inability to cope with the filth. Resentment at everything. 'All the trains are full,' I finally said, concentrating on the ketchup to avoid her stare. 'The next available sleeper is tomorrow night.' I paused before dropping the bombshell. 'They only had third-class, so I bought them.'

'You what? Oh God, no, third-class! You're joking?' She put her knife and fork down on the table and sighed, rolling her head back. 'No!'

Here we go, I thought. 'What else was I supposed to do, San?' I screwed the top back on to the sauce bottle. 'So I bought two tickets to that place with the temple as well, for tomorrow morning, to kill time. We can go and see the temple in the morning, come back, pick up our gear and get the night-train south. Sorted!' I beamed.

'Temple! Fucking hell, John, that's all I need!'

I'd never heard Sanita swear before, ever, and was taken aback. I looked around sheepishly to see if anyone had heard her. Indians may forgive foreigners and their strange behaviour while in India, but I knew that the sight and sound of a bare-shouldered Indian girl swearing her head off would freak them out. Nobody seemed to notice.

'I've got the runs twice every ten minutes, and now I've got to go on a bloody four-hour train ride, probably without toilets, to look at some . . . Arrgh!' She put her head in her hands. 'Jesus, John, what were you thinking of?'

'I thought it'd be a laugh,' I said, shrugging innocently.

'A laugh?' She looked through her fingers. 'I can't think of anything less funny.' Lowering her hands and placing them on her stomach, she winced and closed her eyes. 'What about the train south? How long does it take to get to . . . wherever we're going?'

I'd been dreading this question. 'T-two days,' I said nervously.

Silence.

' . . . About.'

She opened her eyes again. 'By *two* days, do you mean we leave tomorrow night and arrive the next day, or we leave tomorrow night and arrive forty-eight hours later?'

'Yeah,' I said, nodding.

'*Yeah* what?'

'Yeah we arrive forty-eight hours after leaving here.' I quickly put up a reasoning hand. 'Don't worry, you'll feel better tomorrow. And by the time we leave for Trivandrum tomorrow night you'll be back to normal.'

'You said that a week ago John.'

I leaned back in the chair, relieved at having told her. 'We haven't even been here a week, San. Anyway, see how you feel tomorrow. We'll go back to the hotel now and you can have a rest. How'd that be?'

She put her head back into her hands and sat in silence for the rest of the meal, occasionally picking at the food and briefly flicking through her guidebook. I noticed that she concentrated mostly on the *Getting Away* section.

THREE

The next morning found me standing alone on the platform of the railway station waiting for the train to the temple. Despite my optimism Sanita had not improved overnight, and by the time I had left the room she still didn't even want to eat breakfast. We had changed rooms and moved upmarket to a new room with air conditioning so that we could both get a decent night's sleep, but it had done nothing to ease her stomach.

Having air conditioning in the room was all well and good while you were inside, but once you stepped outside you felt twice as bad as you did when leaving a room with no air con. Air conditioning, I believed, was the reason that I was sweating so heavily now, and I silently cursed Sanita.

When the train finally pulled into the station, I jumped into the air conditioned first-class car along with two middle-aged American tourists, and settled in for the ride to the temple.

The two women sat opposite me and talked constantly during the train journey, about India and its people, analysing every single thing that passed by the train window. When they saw a village they wondered how the people in the village made a living, when they heard someone speaking Hindi at a station they talked about the spread of the English language throughout the world. At one point, when they saw a cow grazing on a rubbish tip, they even began a long discussion on the quality of beef in India – no mean feat when you consider that beef is not even eaten due to the religion.

I spoke to them only briefly and found out that they were sisters from Wyoming, and they said that I could join them in a tour of the temple if I wanted to. But I declined; my thoughts were elsewhere. I had woken early, and the rocking motion of the train was sending me into a dream-like haze. Half awake, half asleep, I began to think about the guy at the train station and the conversation, if you can call it that, that we had had the day before. 'Follow the compass'. What the hell did that mean? Follow the compass to find what? And besides, I didn't have a compass!

The train juddered to a halt, causing me to bang my head against the side and wake up. Blinking against the harsh sun, I looked out of the window to see if there was a station sign on the platform. Just as I pushed my face up against the glass, one of the American women pushed her head in from the other direction.

'We're here! Better get off, young man,' she said.

I left the station and walked wearily down a long road to get a rickshaw ride to the temple. On the pavement about halfway along was what, at first glance, looked like a bundle of rags piled on the ground. As I drew closer I realised it was in fact an animal: a huge vulture. It stood about a metre tall, but its head was bowed and almost touched the floor, as if dead. I picked up a long stick and, standing beside it at a safe distance, gave it a prod. Its head and long spindly neck lifted slowly to eye me. Then, just as slowly, it lowered again. I repeated the move and the bird did exactly the same: up ... then down ... The two Americans, who had been arguing with a rickshaw driver, saw what I had found.

'Oh God, Kathy, look! Ooh, young man, what is it?'

I looked up as they came closer. 'It's a vulture. I think it's dying.'

'Oh God, Kathy, did you ever see that programme? The one where—'

'Maybe see you at the temple later,' I said, breaking her off in mid-sentence. I began to walk away.

'OK, see you later. Have a nice day!' She picked up my stick and gingerly poked the bird.

I didn't see them at the temple later and, after spending almost an hour at the site, decided to move on to a Portuguese fort. I wasn't particularly interested in sightseeing at that point but my return train wasn't due to leave for over three hours and I didn't think that I could string out lunch that long.

The fort turned out to be more boring than the temple, with one notable exception. As I walked down from the fort's entrance and crossed the bridge that led to the road outside, I noticed that a lone beggar boy I'd seen on the way in was still sitting on the ground, his hand and one humongous foot outstretched. Big Foot's whole body was completely normal as far as I could tell, with the exception of his right foot, which was about ten times bigger than his left. I stood next to him, on the pretext of giving him some money, and was able to study him. His right foot was bigger than his left in all aspects: length, breadth, depth, and was about the size of a beachball, swollen to many times its normal size, presumably with elephantiasis. Even the toes were massive. Did he wear one big shoe and one little shoe, I wondered?

As I continued my journey I searched the ground for his footprints, hoping to find one small dip in the sand next to a giant depression. 'One small step for man, one gigantic impression by Big Foot,' I mumbled to myself with a grin, and looked back. All of the other tourists at the fort stared at the boy but none of them gave him any money. Sympathy, I figured, he doesn't need. Cash, yes; sympathy, no.

When Sanita and I had first arrived in Goa she had instructed me not to give money to beggars, saying that it encouraged them to be lazy and made for more beggars. However, I reckoned that giving money to beggars was good karma – it definitely left me with a good feeling. Ignoring Sanita made me feel pretty good too.

I rickshawed it back to the train station that afternoon, passing the vulture on the way (it hadn't moved an inch since that morning, except that it seemed to be listing slightly more to one side). As we drove past I couldn't resist picking up a pebble from the floor of the cab and throwing it at the bird. I missed, and thought about asking the driver to go around for a second attempt. He carried on, however, and I spent the rest of the ride throwing pebbles out of the window at anything that presented a target: trees, lamp-posts, and especially the mangy old dogs that were laying around all over the place.

The rickshaw was my F16 fighter. I loved the way I could use the momentum of the cornering vehicle to project my bombs. The game came to an end when I ran out of ammo.

FOUR

Back at Umta Vaddo, hawkers were starting to set up their kerosene lamps for the early evening trade. I glanced at my watch, 7.30 p.m., and hurried up the street towards the hotel. Our train south was due to leave at 8.30

p.m. and I still needed to pack my things, unless Sanita had done it for me. Also I was badly in need of a shower. The day's dust from the streets had stuck to my sweat, and the sun had caked it hard. When I grinned I could feel the skin cracking, like a meringue, and huge bogeys had accumulated in my nostrils.

Some of the travellers' cafés along our street were already filling up, and as I neared the hotel I noticed a group of Westerners sitting outside a trinket shop playing chess with a Sikh man. The scene looked pretty cool. All of the guys were very tanned and they all had goatee beards – except the Sikh who had a huge black beard that was entangled with his turban strap. He moved a chess piece and all four travellers rubbed their chins in concentration. Yes, I thought, I too will start a goatee.

Turning the corner at a trot, I pushed through the big wooden entrance doors to the hotel and climbed the narrow staircase, glancing at the keyboard in the reception to make sure Sanita was in. If the key was on the hook it meant that she had gone out. It wasn't, and the little Indian woman behind the counter looked at me and rolled her eyes to the ceiling.

'Thanks,' I said, and taking the stairs two at a time reached the fourth floor and strolled to the end of the corridor. Sanita was sitting on the bed reading her guidebook, surrounded by packed bags.

'Thought you weren't coming back,' she said, looking up as I entered. 'I've packed all your stuff. I didn't touch your surfboard.'

'You're coming then?' I panted.

She looked back at her guidebook, expressionless. 'Doesn't look too bad according to these pictures.'

I walked over to the bed and glanced quickly at the open page. 'Did you put my jeans in this bag?' I said, unzipping my holdall.

She nodded without looking up. 'Some of the hotels down in Kovalom look pretty good,' she said, showing me another picture while I rubbed a hand across my face. I hadn't shaved since arriving in India and my stubble was quite long now. I had toyed with the idea of not shaving for the whole holiday, it would be neat to go home and shock everyone with my dirty appearance, but that was until the herd of goats playing chess had changed my mind earlier. Pushing myself up from the bed, I stretched and then tried to touch my toes.

I continued into the bathroom and studied my reflection in the plastic wall-cabinet mirror. My face was already burnt from the day's harsh sunshine, and the stubble on my face looked the same colour as my skin. I squinted, trying to imagine my face with a goatee beard, and wondered if I would look as cool as the four guys in the street had. Maybe a goatee would help me integrate into the traveller scene and be accepted more quickly. During my brief encounter with the tie-dye traveller at the station the previous morning, a distinct feeling of *Us* and *Them* had come over me.

Feeling like an *Us*, I called out to Sanita, 'Did you pack my razor?'

'I thought you weren't going to shave,' she shouted back.

'Yeah. Did you pack it?' I heard the zip on my bag go and a few seconds later a soft hand was placed on my shoulder, holding the cheap razor. Sanita looked at my reflection briefly, unsmiling, then kissed my shoulder and walked out

After five minutes, my cheeks, jaw, neck and upper lip were perfectly smooth, almost shiny. Closing my eyes and running my wet hand across and then down my cheeks to the top of my lip, and then letting it pass my mouth on to the sudden bushy mound of my chin, I was reminded of a woman's body. 'Cool,' I mumbled, opening my eyes. 'Extremely cool.'

Sanita looked up from her book as I went back into the room, said, 'You've missed a bit,' and went back to reading.

'Yeah, I meant to. It's a beard.' I cupped my chin in one hand and massaged it with thumb and forefinger. 'What do you think?'

She shrugged. 'It's all right I suppose. Not much of it though. Shouldn't you have left the moustache or something? It looks like you've dribbled and the dirt has stuck to it.'

I grinned weakly and stepped forward, throwing the razor into my bag. It was then that I noticed her clothes lying on the floor. 'You haven't packed!'

She closed the guidebook, sighing, and placed it gently in my bag.

Flicking a clump of hair from her face she said simply, 'That's because I'm not going.'

I gagged. 'What?'

'You can go alone. I've had enough of this country, I'm going home.'

I hurriedly slapped my pockets and pulled out the tickets. 'But I've bought train tickets, San! I–'

'I'll give you the money if you want, but don't ask me to go on a two-day train trip to some other shithole. When you were out this morning I went into town and changed my plane ticket. It leaves tomorrow morning.' She looked up. 'Coming?'

I looked down at the train tickets and held them out, pleading. 'But ...'

'Thought not.' She stood up and walked over to the window. 'You like it too much. You and all the other stupid foreigners pretending to be poor. No Indian likes India you know John. It's a toilet. Just one, big, toilet.' She pulled the curtain to one side and looked out, sighing.

'I thought your parents were Indian?'

'So what? I'm not. I'd prefer to go on holiday to Spain like normal people.'

I sat down on the bed with a huff and picked up her guidebook, idly flicking through the pages. 'Why don't you just give it a couple of days more and then decide? It'll be different down south.'

She was silent, and then, apparently ignoring my statement, looked back out of the window and said, 'There was a guy looking for you earlier today.'

I put the book down.

'Said he'd see you later, upstairs. Told me to tell you that he leaves tomorrow for Thailand and wants to have a drink with you before he goes.' She let the curtains fall back. 'Maybe we should have gone to Thailand instead of this dump.'

Suddenly forgetting our differences, I stood up and said, 'English? Upstairs? What did he look like?'

She shrugged. 'Same age as you, I guess. Maybe older. Mid to late twenties, long hair. I dunno,' she crossed the room impatiently. 'Pretty much like all the other foreigners, he—'

'What was he wearing?'

'Huh?'

'Was it a tie-dye shirt with an orange circle on it?' I said urgently.

'Might have been. How the hell should I know? What's so important about it anyway? You've got a train to catch, right?'

If I were going to tell her about the life-saving incident at the train station it would have been right there and then. But I didn't. And, I think, looking back, that it was a measure of how far apart we had grown. As my fiancée I should have been telling her everything, opening my heart. Now, not only wasn't I going to go home on the same flight as her, but I was already trying to think up an excuse not to go on tonight's train. It was as though the shock of the train station incident had somehow helped to focus my life. Like thumping a TV set that has a dodgy reception and suddenly the picture clearing.

'Haven't you?' she prompted, breaking my train of thought.

'Indian train tickets are re-routable,' I lied. 'In any case, I'd rather see you off first, San.'

FIVE

I scanned the quiet moonlit bar and noticed the man who'd saved my life sitting in the far corner at a karom table with two others. He immediately put up his hand when he saw us and we went over.

'Hello again,' I said, pulling out a chair. 'Didn't really get a chance to speak to you before. I'm John, this is Sanita.'

'Rick,' said Rick. 'Nice to meet you, Sanita. This is Zed, and Dudley,' he explained, pointing to the other two.

We sat down and I ordered beer for us all. 'D'you know how to play this?' I asked, picking up one of the karom pieces from the table.

'Haven't got a clue.' He turned a plastic disc in his fingers. 'Basically, I think it's like poor man's pool: you have to flick these discs into these other discs and try to knock them into the pockets.'

We all looked at Sanita for help.

'Don't look at me, I'm as clueless as you.'

'Well,' said Rick, taking a bottle of Kingfisher from the waiter, 'that's what I've been doing anyway.'

Hippies in India all look like down-and-outs. You see them everywhere: unkempt beards, cheap silver jewellery, and reams of beads around their necks. Rick looked different: easy manner, deliberate movements, nothing jerky or nervous; I liked him instantly. His accent was from northern England, and he proved me right by giving the name of a town on the north-east coast that I'd never heard of. With his long hair and big moustache he looked like a long-distance truck driver, or a Dutch rock star from the seventies. When we introduced ourselves, I'd half expected him to say, 'Hi, name's Thor!' and break into an air-guitar solo or something.

Zed and Dudley, on the other hand, were both younger; students from England on a month's holiday from the same university. Zed was tall and slender, with waist-length curly hair, and pretty in a way that probably attracted men as well as women, while Dudley, of a much smaller, slighter build, looked the spitting image of Kurt Cobain. If he hadn't told me he was English, and hadn't spoken, I'd have sworn he was Californian. He wore a woolly hat even though the temperature must have been in the high twenties.

'You haven't been here long then?' I said, pouring out my beer.

'A week. That's enough. Hate the place.' Rick lit up a cigarette and offered one to me.

'No thanks,' I said, flicking my eyes to Sanita. I'd given up smoking for her but the craving was still there. Rick must have noticed because he sniggered slightly before putting the packet back in his pocket. Shit, I thought, how humiliating.

'I thought it was going to be non-stop parties,' he continued. 'You hear so much. But when I got here, well,' he looked around, 'I thought I was in the wrong place.'

'Mmm, know what you mean.' I didn't know what he meant but I didn't want to appear unworldly. Sanita gave me a sideways glance.

'That's why I'm off to Thailand tomorrow; try something new.'

I nodded. 'How long are you away for?'

'Supposed to be four weeks.' He pulled the label from his beer bottle and stuck it to the table top. 'Got a job to go back to unfortunately.' Then added, matter of factly, 'Got three kids and a girlfriend too.'

It was hard to believe. He looked, as Sanita had earlier suggested, in his mid-twenties, but hearing that he had three kids suddenly made him seem much older. I thought it too personal to ask his age and said, 'Me too. A job I mean. I was just saying to San–'

'Right.' Sanita suddenly slammed both hands down on the table and stood. We all reached out and grabbed our beer bottles to stop them from toppling over. 'I'm going back to the room John. Bye everyone.' She turned and walked away.

I was stunned. Speechless.

'Seems nice,' Zed said as she marched across the rooftop.

There was a pause as we watched Sanita disappear into the stairwell.

'So,' Rick said, pulling a little bag of something from his pocket, 'she goes tomorrow and you stay behind. What are you going to do?'

I turned back to the table, taking and lighting a cigarette in defiance. 'Was going south, but I missed the train.'

'Come with me if you want.' He pulled some leaves from the bag and mixed them with cigarette tobacco on a rizla. 'To be honest, it'd be good to have someone to travel with in Thailand.'

Self-consciously I looked over towards the door to see if Sanita had gone, and whispered, 'Whereabouts in Thailand are you going?'

'Dunno really. A couple I met here earlier told me that Ko Pang Gang was a good place. But I'll see when I get there.' He licked the edge of the cigarette paper and stuffed a piece of card into the end. 'Smoke?'

'Not for a long time,' I said, glancing back at the door again. 'OK.'

Ten minutes later the effect of the marijuana was taking hold and I began to giggle out of step with the conversation. Actually, I couldn't really keep up with the conversation at all now, my head was buzzing so much, but I tried to laugh at the right time to make it look good.

'Deformities.' Rick said, smoke easing from his nostrils, 'They're the most interesting sight in India.'

'You too?' I giggled, forgetting to double-check that Sanita had gone. 'I thought it was only me who found them more interesting than bloody temples.'

'Have you seen those guys who go around on the little trolleys?'

I laughed harder, nodding. 'Skateboarders from hell. They're brilliant!'

We ordered another beer and I told him about the boy I'd seen at the fort that morning, with the huge foot.

'The best,' he agreed. 'Number one in the top ten of deformities.'

'You haven't, like, seen Big Balls then?' asked Dudley.

'Yeah, Big Balls is number one,' Zed nodded. 'He's a legend. Though only one confirmed sighting of him and that was by a woman we met on the train coming down here. A Welsh woman.'

'Like, Welsh women don't lie, right?'

Rick leaned forward, placing his forearms on the table, and looked into Zed's eyes. 'You're not seriously telling me that there's a guy walking around carrying two huge testicles?'

He nodded. 'Not carrying though; he wheels them around on a little barrow that the hospital made for him. As big as melons.'

We burst out laughing.

'I swear it. Dud?'

'Like, he's telling the truth. Or that's what she told us, anyway.' Dudley took the joint from Rick. 'Forty-year-old Welsh housewives studying contemporary women's issues in India don't, like, lie.'

'According to her,' Zed continued, 'that's where *Viz* got the idea of Buster Gonad from.'

'That's years old though,' I said, wiping the tears from my eyes.

'That's right. She saw him in Varanasi twenty years ago.' He leaned back on the chair. 'There were loads more deformed people back then, before modern medicine really began to have an impact. Her and her friends were working in the hospital that made Big Balls' barrow and treated all the others. She reckons there are nowhere near as many elephantiasis cases out here as there used to be.'

'Fooking spoil sports.' Rick took out his bag of grass and started to roll another joint. 'Is he still there?'

'Big Balls?' Zed shrugged. 'Probably dead now. But the legend lives on.'

'Why don't we start an expedition to find him?' I said enthusiastically. 'Our task: to find and photograph Big Balls.' I took the joint from Dudley, inhaled, held it down, then let out a thick column of blue smoke into the night air. 'I've already spotted Big Foot, so Big Balls should be a doddle.'

'No can do,' Dudley said. 'We're going north to see the Dalai Lama.'

'Bombay first, though,' Zed corrected.

Dudley shrugged and said, 'Mm-hmm,' through the pursed lips. 'Why don't you two, like, come with us?'

I looked at Rick with a 'why not?' expression, but he said that he'd already bought his ticket for Thailand and couldn't afford to waste it. In any case, he'd seen enough of India to last him a lifetime.

'Don't you need an appointment or something?' I asked. 'The Dalai Lama's a busy man, right?'

A second rush of the drug suddenly swept through my head and I found myself asking the same question over and over again. As far as I can remember Dudley reassured me that chilled-out people like the Lama wouldn't mind other chilled-out people like us knocking on his door at all. Probably invite us in for tea, I kept saying to myself. I think Dudley said that the Welsh woman on the train had met the Tibetan leader before, and she'd had no problems, but I can't be sure; everything was getting a bit woozy in my head.

However, I do remember thinking that a lot of incidents in India seemed to occur on trains, or in railway stations, but I was too stoned to talk about it. It was definitely the last topic that entered my head that night, though, because I always remember my last thoughts before I sleep.

I think I passed out a few minutes later.

SIX

Indian flip-flops are the best in the world; there's no question about that. Flip-flops, as the British call them, are what Australians call thongs. I don't know what they're called in America. A single piece of foam as the sole, held on to the foot by a V-shaped strap that goes between the big and second toes; wherever you go in the world the design is exactly the same, but quality varies. In India the sole is made of rubber, pure rubber, not foam and that's why they're the world's best.

As I walked away from the flip-flop stall in the airport I listened: *flip, flop, flip, flop*. Amazing, even the sound was right. 'Yep,' I muttered, 'the *Lunar* Flip-flop Company of India certainly knows how to make 'em.'

Still watching my feet, I stepped on to the bus that would take me back into town and thought about Sanita again.

We had hardly spoken to each other over breakfast, and hadn't talked at all on the bus journey to the airport. I'd spent the night on the rooftop with Rick, Zed and Dudley, and Sanita, having woken and found the bed empty, had wandered up at six in the morning and found us all sprawled out around the bar. She flared up, and demanded to know why I'd spent our last night together fucking about with them instead of her, and why I hadn't come back to the room, and ... The list of complaints went on. To calm her down, and make her feel a bit better about going home without me, I reminded her that it was only a three-week holiday, and that we'd probably spend the rest of our lives together.

Making love when we'd returned to the room after breakfast hadn't really helped matters either. Her annoyance at my disappearance the night before, at first softened by the closeness of our naked, sweat-slippery bodies, only seemed to return with a vengeance once we put our clothes back on, turning into genuine anger. It was as if she felt taken advantage of. The anger boiled over and she slapped my face.

Sanita had demanded to know what I was going to get up to over the next few weeks without her. That was easy to answer: Zed, Dudley and I would leave the next morning to go to Bombay, the three of us would then go up to Dharamsala where the Dalai Lama supposedly lived, travelling through Delhi and a few other places en route. Simple. It all fitted together quite nicely really, and I'd even managed to change my flight so that it left from Delhi.

When her flight was finally called we both stood up immediately, as though each of us wanted to make the first move. It was an awkward situation, especially as I'd persuaded her to take my surfboard home with her. 'You are coming back aren't you John?' she'd asked. 'You're not going to Thailand with that man Rick?' She narrowed her eyes. 'I've seen how well you two get on together.'

I told her not to be silly. 'He's already left,' I assured her, 'how can I?' The fact that he'd left me with instructions on how to get to the place he'd be staying at had conveniently slipped my mind. Anyway, I *was* only on a short holiday, and all of my time would be taken up getting to the north of India and back.

I watched her struggle out on to the runway with her rucksack over one shoulder, which was now twice its usual weight as she had insisted on taking home anything that I thought I wouldn't need for the rest of my holiday, and my surfboard over the other. She loaded the gear on to a bullock-drawn baggage cart, before turning and giving a last traumatic wave and boarding the plane.

The bus back to town was packed to bursting point by the time it moved off, and the only available seat was next to another traveller. She moved her huge rucksack between her knees and shuffled to one side, smiling at me as I squeezed my way into the seat and sat down.

'On a long trip?' I said, pointing to the pack.

'A month,' she replied, still smiling. Her white teeth were like piano keys against her beautifully tanned skin. 'Only two weeks left though, and then I fly out of Bombay. You?'

'Umm, a few weeks.' I was still holding the leather sandals that Sanita had bought me for the holiday, and they suddenly felt like ten-tonne weights in my hand. 'M-maybe longer,' I stammered, tucking the sandals out of sight.

The bus driver got into the cab and started the engine, while the bus conductor walked up the aisle shooing off the beggars before closing the doors behind them. They ran alongside the bus banging on the window until we picked up speed and they fell away.

When we arrived in town, a new set of beggars poured on to the bus and we had to fight our way out of the doors. As I stepped out I felt something touch my leg. A small boy was tugging at the hem of my shorts and pointing to the leather sandals I was carrying.

'I think he wants your shoes,' the other traveller said, hoisting her rucksack on to her back. 'It's them or money, I'm afraid.'

'What?' I glanced down at the ragged boy. 'Oh, yeah,' I said, and hesitated for a fraction of a second before handing them over.

THIS IS YOUR LIFE

ONE

The next morning we checked out of the hotel and boarded a train to Bombay; Zed and Dudley struggling under the weight of their unfeasibly large rucksacks, me skipping happily alongside, almost floating on air without baggage or girlfriends to slow me down. By the time we boarded the train to Delhi on the fourth day, after a brief, uneventful stop in Bombay, we had our sights firmly fixed on new horizons. However, our new horizons were slightly blurred by the quirks of India's transport system. Getting to the hill stations of northern India, where the Dalai Lama lived, meant going through Delhi, and then from Delhi to Dharamsala by bus: two days worth of sleepless travel at the outside, three or four if we rested halfway.

To avoid Bombay's Monday morning rush-hour madness on the buses we took a taxi to the railway station, making us feel like millionaires. I dreamed of the old days; the Raj, with the spires of Victoria Station above us and our chauffeur-wallah carrying our bags under the huge stone arches.

Ten minutes later, when we settled into our second-class sleeper with five others, the old days were the last thing on my mind. The man sitting next to me had a perpetual cough, and brought up huge amounts of phlegm, which he projected like glistening, wobbly bullets from the open window. One of the blobs landed on the head of a passing beggar who looked up at us. I happened to be gazing out and caught the brunt of his stare, 'Not me!' I mouthed.

Zed and Dudley were no better off in their choice of seat either. Zed, who had sat down and opened a book to read, had inadvertently joined the ranks of Mensa, the Indian chapter. It was a seat I eventually learned to avoid like the plague whenever boarding trains or long distance buses in India. He had sat next to a man in a suit and tie, which automatically meant he would have to answer hundreds of questions of such intricate detail as to drive anyone crazy.

A traveller has a choice upon entering a train compartment, a choice that needs to be weighed up very carefully before sitting down to a twenty-hour journey. Pick your poison with caution because it could be a very slow death. The choices fall into three main groups, all of which have their good and bad sides: Smelly Labourer, Couple with Kid, or Man in Suit.

The Smelly Labourer is, as I've already explained, a spit merchant but other than that he leaves you in peace. Oh yes, another bonus with him is that beggars tend not to bother his end of the compartment. As I was sandwiched between him and the exterior window, the chances were that this would be a relatively beggar-free journey. Most of the limbless tend to stick to the people nearest to the corridor for obvious, logistical reasons. Only if they spotted a suit would they bother to crawl into the depths of a compartment on the off-chance of a rupee. They definitely wouldn't bother for a labourer.

Man in Suit (or Death by a Thousand Questions as he's also known) is a nightmare come true. To the unwary traveller he looks like the best choice: clean when compared to the labourer piled in one corner, and uncluttered when compared to Couple with Kid who're spilling all over the place in the other corner. And when you first sit beside him with an 'Excuse me,' he replies, in the very best English, 'Oh! Please,' and wipes your place clean with his spotless handkerchief. 'Great!' you think, 'I've got the right compartment this time.' Wrong! What starts out as idle chit-chat: 'How long will you be staying in our beautiful country?' and 'Which places have you visited?' soon turns into a non-stop barrage that drives into you like a dentist's drill on low speed. Budget travellers have been known to upgrade to first-class, just to get away from Man in Suit. The effect of twenty hours sitting and answering questions about the price of a car or a washing machine, or the standard of English in India, or how to cook a spot-on tandoori can induce suicide. I once spent four hours under such duress and almost collapsed at the end of it. I was tempted to throw myself out of the window to escape!

Husband and Wife (one child), also known as Couple with Kid, present the third choice. Like all Indian families they seem to be unable to travel without taking the whole of their household contents along with them, including the kitchen sink. Not a terrible prospect in itself, and even the child, seven years old in this case, shouldn't shit herself or cry too much. So what's the down side here? Food. If you choose to sit next to them you'll be force fed until you explode or puke, whichever comes first.

Couple with Kid (and occasionally couple without) always take enough food to feed the entire occupants of all twelve carriages of the train, and still have leftovers for their relatives. They'll offer to share a mind-boggling array of different curries, breads and sweet desserts, all of which, unless you are visibly ill, you'll have to eat. Fat travellers vomit, skinny ones die, and Couple with Kid still scoff merrily in the corner.

So, I had the Labourer, Zed had the Suit, and Dudley chose the food scene from *Caligula*. Within an hour of the train leaving the station the three of us were out of our seats and standing by the open door at the end of the car to escape the torture. Oh, and we wanted to smoke a joint, too.

TWO

Snowflake's in hell. That's how one of the other travellers in our guest house described our chances of getting an audience with the Dalai Lama. He knew someone who'd spent a month up here waiting for a chance to meet the Big D and hadn't even caught a glimpse of the man. 'Flies in and out in a Lear jet,' he'd said, leaning in the doorway to our room. 'Unless you're the leader of a foreign country he's not interested. Dope's pretty good up here though.'

Three rain-soaked days later, Dudley, having not left the room except to eat and shit, was busy testing that last comment. With a truly obsessive zeal, and a kind of 'proof of the pudding' logic, he had lined up three different types of dope on the cabinet beside his bed and was trying each one in turn. Some days he even mixed them together to see just how they affected him. To us the effect was the same, or at least the end result was: he mooched around the room all day in a half-sleep/half-dead, zombie-like shuffle that reminded me of a wind-up toy. If the door was open he'd waddle out and down the corridor to the toilet, but that's all.

To be fair there was little else to do. The rain and sleet hadn't stopped since we had arrived, and it didn't look like it would clear over the coming week. In any case, we knew it would continue because Dudley had said so.

In one of his rare appearances outside the guest house, he had befriended an old Indian man who claimed to be able to forecast the weather by looking at the marijuana leaves on the bushes in the hills. According to him, when they hung down limply it meant that there was no end in sight to the bad weather. That, combined with the taste of this year's harvested and pressed grass, was as good as looking at a barometer. A bit like wine tasting Dudley supposed. Most connoisseurs can tell the year a grape was harvested just by tasting the wine, so why should marijuana be any different?

Dudley believed the old man's prediction, and I believed my own eyes. None of us believed that the weather would let up, and, having grown tired of our wet surroundings, decided to head back south before the week was out.

'Shimla,' I suggested, lying on the damp bed opposite Dudley, trying to think of a possible next destination for us. 'Cliff Richard was born there you know.'

He leaned up on one elbow. 'Cliff Richard is not a good reason to go to Shimla, John.'

We hung around for the rest of the day to watch the hustle and bustle before catching the evening bus south, arriving in Shimla early the next morning. The difference between the two towns was so striking that we might well have taken a bus to another country altogether.

As usual, where the 'right-on' travellers were raving about Dharamsala, and telling us to avoid Shimla like the plague, the opposite was true. In Shimla there were no pretentious backpackers walking around quoting from *The Tibetan Book of the Dead*, and not a 'Free Tibet' T-shirt in sight. The town seemed to have gone in reverse: from being one of India's colonial hill stations, where stiff-upper-lip British officers went during the summer to escape from the heat of the plains, to being the weekend retreat of Delhi's yuppies; Delhi being only half a day's ride away in daddy's car.

· Shimla must be the most Westernised place in India, too. Or, at least, a place where Indians can behave Westernised. School kids in maroon blazers skip along the main street on their way to class, while, in the evening, Indian gents wearing natty tweeds sit around taking in the cool air, puffing away thoughtfully on briar pipes. The town has a town hall, a Scandal Corner, mock Tudor houses, a theatre and a Christ Church. It also has a YMCA that's situated at one end of the main road. Housed in a rambling old colonial house, the Shimla YMCA is like a cross between Colditz and Fawlty Towers. With a fireplace in every room, a billiards hall, table tennis tables, a bed and breakfast-style dining room where one gets 'gonged' for breakfast (tea, toast and marmalade) at eight o'clock sharp, and a ruthless lights-out policy that the governor of Alcatraz would have been proud of, it was, 'Like, far out,' as Dudley put it.

One night, about a week after we'd arrived in Shimla, as the three of us walked through the freezing streets, I started to think about Rick. I hadn't thought about him since we'd left Goa, but I needed to provide myself with a distraction and he proved to be just the thing.

I wondered what he was up to. Was he really still in Thailand? What was he doing there right at this minute, right now? While I was walking down a snowy street in a quaint hilltop town in northern Indian, was he sitting in a beach bar in Thailand sweating freely in the tropical heat? I especially wanted to know whether or not he was having a better time than I was. Maybe he had simply had his fill and gone back to normality, back to his old job and suburban life in England.

Dudley, Zed and I had less than a week left before we were due to fly home and I was beginning to think about my life in England. My regimented, mundane, nine-to-five life. The whole trip so far had been played by ear, and, though it didn't lend itself to any logical order geographically speaking, I was beginning to like the spontaneity of travel without any plans. No airline tickets and no guidebook, just a sense of moving forward as a particular set of events dictated.

Neither of my two companions had actually mentioned our impending departure. On the contrary, the opposite was true. As far as I knew they hadn't even discussed it with each other; a kind of refusal to accept the facts. It's just like going to school for the first time, or Monday morning at work; nobody wants to face it. Human nature I guess. Whenever I thought about going home, really getting on a flight to London, the feeling in my stomach was the same feeling I got as a kid on a trip to the dentist.

Over the past week, the mood between Zed and I had changed from one of complete freedom at having no boundaries, to one of resignation. We were like convicts who had escaped from prison, and, after being on the run, had been caught and told that we were permitted one more week in the free world. Seven days of fun in the knowledge that it would all be over soon.

Dudley, on the other hand, had said nothing, and was generally difficult to read. He'd bought a tabla in the market and was learning to play in the room most evenings. Unlike Zed and I, who were simply dreading going back home and showed our unhappiness, Dudley looked forward and said that he would continue to learn the tabla in London, taking lessons at the local evening institute. He wanted to meet Ravi Shankar. I told him that Ravi Shankar played sitar but he was undeterred, and felt sure that he had what it took to be concert-class, if indeed that's the level that tabla players attained.

Each night Dudley sat cross-legged on the bed, beating out a rhythm: *boing, bing-boing*, that he supposedly copied from the *Tabla in A Day* songbook that came free with the instrument. It had a picture of its author, Mr J. P. Singh, on the cover, sitting cross-legged with his instrument on his lap. Dudley was inspired, and had even been to a local tailor in Shimla and ordered a mundu.

It was easy to imagine Dudley sitting on the floor of his university rooms dressed like an Indian, surrounded by his student friends, about to give a rendition. 'This one's, like, a northern Indian love song, man.' He'd shift his position and begin: *Boing, bing-boing.* His friends would all be so stoned that the music would actually sound good, and they'd all be nodding to the rhythm, saying, 'Like, far out, Dud man.' My imagination went further and I saw him drop out of college to become the world's first white man to be concert-class at tabla. A skinny, blond-haired figure squatting in the first row of the London Philharmonic Orchestra at the Last Night of the Proms. 'Land of hope and glorrr-ry . . . *Boing!'*

Anyway, the point is that Dudley was moving forward and tried not to have any regrets about going home the following week, while I was apprehensive. But then he hadn't split with his girlfriend like Zed and I, so I shouldn't make such simplistic judgements really.

'On the left.' Zed's voice boomed in the quiet street, snapping me out of the dream.

'Upstairs?'

He nodded, and the three of us went through the door and up the narrow wooden steps to the first floor bar. It was the same bar we'd been to on our first night in Shimla but had never managed to locate again. Not surprising considering how drunk we had been.

We ordered some Kingfishers and, even though it was bitterly cold, sat outside on the balcony that overlooked the street. A low, brooding sky full of snow clouds drifted slowly over the rooftops.

'The theatre's just opposite.' Dudley sat down and pointed to the building across from where we sat. 'Like, it was right opposite the theatre after all! Shit, we must have been pissed.'

The Gaiety Theatre was the only theatre in Shimla. A real theatre, I mean, not a cinema, and it stood out like a sore thumb. Its Doric columns and elegant two-storey façade made it look like a high street bank; the only thing missing was a hole-in-the-wall cash dispenser. We had often walked past it in the evening but had never been inside, and had no idea whether or not performances took place there.

Zed silently poured out our beers and pushed the glasses across the table to us. 'Cheers.'

'Cheers.' I shivered as the cold liquid went down my throat, crossing my arms tightly. It's freezing,' I juddered through chattering teeth. 'Must be below zero, easy.'

'Easy.'

'Like, Himalayas,' Dudley agreed, waving a hand through the air. 'Bound to be cold.'

We sat quietly for a moment watching the gentle flurry of people coming and going from the theatre opposite, before Zed broke the silence. 'You're quiet tonight John.'

I shrugged. 'Thinking.'

He nodded. 'About going home, right?'

'Mmm,' I picked up my beer. 'And about that guy, Rick.'

He ran a hand through his long hair. 'Wonder what he's doing now.'

'That's just what I was thinking, Zed.' I hesitated, taking a sip of beer and said, 'I might carry on. You know, go out to Thailand to meet him instead of going home immediately.'

Zed seemed a little surprised and raised an eyebrow. 'He might not even be there. You could have a wasted journey.'

'Well I'll know when I get to Delhi.' Zed frowned so I continued, 'Before he left we agreed that if he wasn't staying in Thailand he'd send me a letter telling me that he'd gone home, or whatever, so that I wouldn't go out there for nothing.'

'How can he send you a letter, you don't have an address?'

'Poste Restante. There's one in every town. We got the address from my girlfriend's guidebook before she left.'

He nodded, deep in thought.

To tell the truth it hadn't occurred to me before not to go home, but on the other hand I didn't want to think about life in dreary old England either. I'd had such a good time over the past few weeks that the thought of going back to a 'normal' life made me feel depressed. If Zed could spot a change in me when I was only *thinking* about going home, then the act of actually going would make me even worse. Sitting on the balcony that night, I think, was the first time since leaving England that I realised how much happier and fulfilled I actually was. I wasn't thinking about work or careers. I wasn't even thinking about my fiancée, which was a bit worrying.

I raised my glass. 'Here's to freedom.'

Zed's mood worsened over the last few days to the point where he seemed to be in a state of perpetual melancholy. Unable to face his flight back to England, he constantly lost his temper with Dudley, and vented his frustration further on the local tailors, haggling needlessly over clothes that were already at rock-bottom prices.

I was still torn between going home to England on my pre-booked flight or continuing my travels. I'd agonised over the decision for days and felt like someone teetering on the edge, just waiting to be pushed one way or the other. I needed an excuse not to go back but the odds seemed to weigh up so evenly that I just couldn't make up my mind which way to turn.

The problem, however, was resolved when I went to check for mail at the Poste Restante and discovered that there was a postcard from Thailand waiting for me. It was compelling:

Dear John,
Beaches, girls, parties and much
much more. It's unbelievable! Fuck
India! Get out here right away!!
P.S. I'll soon be a millionaire!!!

And it was signed, *Sir William George Garthrick Jenner of Thailand.*

Dudley explained that 'Rick' was probably an abbreviation of Garthrick, and when I checked the picture on the front and saw that it showed Hat Rin beach on the island of Koh Pha-Ngan, I agreed that it must have been sent by him.

I double-checked the handwriting with the note he'd left me in Goa and it was confirmed: I would cancel my flight home.

SIR RICK

ONE

Paddy-fields, paddy-fields and more bloody paddy-fields: that's all I could see as I cleared the Bay of Bengal on the way to Bangkok. Flooded land that reflected the early evening sky beautifully; each waterlogged paddy a mirror separated from the next by a thin embankment, so that from the air it looked like one huge stained-glass window.

When I touched down in Bangkok I pondered the difference between air and land travel. Having seen those paddy-fields from the air and expected a city of bamboo houses built along picturesque canals, I thought I'd stepped out of the airport into some kind of time warp. Concrete, concrete and more bloody concrete.

After numerous cups of coffee and a packet of cigarettes in the tiny airport café, I plucked up the courage to venture out into the now dark, humid car park, and stood at the bus stop. I closed my eyes and imagined I was waiting for a canal-boat taxi to ferry me into town.

'You going downtown, man?'

I snapped my eyes open and turned around, for some reason shocked to hear English being spoken. A young man with a backpack and an acoustic guitar strapped on top was standing inches away from me. 'Yeah,' I said, stepping back.

He turned around, gave an ear-splitting whistle, and then cupped both hands around his mouth to shout. 'Hey, Sooze, over here! It's this bus stop, babe!'

A girl came jogging over, finishing in a little two-footed jump to land beside us. The man did one loud clap and turned back to me. 'This here's Suzy-Sue. Hey, you British?'

'English,' I said, wondering why Americans always refer to the nation and not the country, 'yeah.'

'There you go, Sooze, one o' your lot. Told you we'd find someone who knew this place.'

Knew the place! I'd only just stepped off the plane and they thought I was someone they could trust! Before I could explain, he pulled out a packet of cigarettes and offered them to me, along with his hand to shake: cigarettes first, then hand. 'Dave,' he said.

'John,' I took a cigarette. 'Thanks.'

'Hey, John, what's up? You look a leetle glum.'

'Do I?' I was genuinely surprised to hear it at first, but then remembered that I wasn't waiting for a canal taxi. 'Yeah, I suppose I do really. Just came from India and—'

'India? Whoo-ee!' He did a three-sixty degree spin and came to a stop, his cigarette poised in one hand, zippo in the other. He lit up and said, 'India? That's fuckin' Wild West country over there. I had a friend once, went to India,' he moved close to me, shaking his head, 'never returned!' He looked over his shoulder quickly as though about to spill a secret. 'They found him two years later living in a fuckin' cave! Living off snakes and rats and shit. Man, I tell ya,' he lit the zippo and held it above his head like the Statue of Liberty, 'count me outta that crap. Yes siree.' Suzy was standing behind him making a clap-trap movement with her hand, indicating that he talked too much.

The bus pulled up a few minutes later, sparing me from further lectures, and when we boarded it was so crowded that we were unable to sit near each other. Throughout the whole journey, however, I could still hear Dave's American 'whoops' and 'damns' like he was riding a horse in a rodeo. Suzy seemed to have nodded off but he just kept talking all the same, going from one subject to another without any common thread to join them together, or any real point to what he was saying.

'Hey, John!

I flicked my head to him and his hand shot up as if I needed visual help to locate his position on an otherwise silent bus.

'Where you headed?' Suzy an me, we're going to—' he ducked down, apparently checking something, and after a second his head reappeared, 'Khao San Road. How about yourself?'

I checked a piece of paper I'd scribbled an address on and looked up. 'Banglamphu.'

Dave's neck extended above the headrest in surprise before it shot back down to check the name I'd given him. A moment later he raised a hand, giving an OK sign.

The bus journey took hours. What I'd taken to be a thirty-minute ride was turning into an epic, and after an hour and a half of traffic snarl-ups the bus broke down. It seemed like India all over again. For some reason the radiator cap on Bangkok buses is on the inside so when they overheat, as ours did, and the driver unscrewed it, Mount Vesuvius erupted sending a cloud of steam down the aisle. Panic-stricken, the entire occupants of the bus bolted for the door causing a bottleneck of frantic, writhing bodies that eventually spilled out on to the pavement.

'Not a good start, huh?' I said, sitting on my bag at the side of the road.

Suzy put her bag down and sat on the kerb next to me. 'What a night,' she huffed, and offered me a stick of chewing gum. 'What time is it, Dave?'

Dave was dancing around the bus catching raindrops in his upturned palms and rubbing them into his face. He looked at his watch. 'Midnight – BKT. Woo-hoo!'

I frowned at Suzy. 'BKT?'

'Big Kok Time. Calls Bangkok the Big Kok,' and added by way of an explanation, 'He's from New York.'

I paused, unwrapping the gum, and said, 'You two together?'

'Um, not really, just happened to get talking on the plane that's all. You're alone, right?'

'Yep, just me and my bag.'

'Cool.' She fiddled with the strap of her boots before continuing. 'Not going to Khao San Road with the rest of the hoards then? What's the name of that place you said earlier, Bang–?'

'Banglamphu. I don't know anything about it, just a tip-off.'

'Don't you have a guidebook?'

I shook my head and smiled.

After a two-hour wait in which we got drenched to the bone sitting at the roadside discussing our travel plans, Dave catching rain on his tongue, another bus finally pulled up and we boarded. 'Listen John,' Suzy whispered to me as I turned up the aisle towards the only empty seat, 'I'm only staying here a couple of days and then heading south to the islands. We can go together.'

I shrugged. 'All right. We're bound to bump into each other over the next few days, so I'll speak to you then.' I walked away and she went down to join Dave at the front of the bus.

Had I known that Banglamphu was at one end of Khao San Road I wouldn't have said that we would bump into each other. I wanted to see Bangkok and go south alone. So when the driver stopped the bus an hour later and said that we were at Khao San Road *and* Banglamphu, I pretended that I knew where I was and told him to go on. Dave and Suzy got off and I stayed, alighting at the following stop.

The bus pulled away in a cloud of black smoke and I stood, taking in the scene around me for a minute, before slinging the bag over my shoulder and moving off to find a guest house. The rain that had soaked me earlier had turned into a light drizzle, not too much to make me wet through but steady enough to cool the tropical night. Everything was reflected in the puddles and glistening pavements: the shop windows, neon signs, even the car headlights that flashed intermittently in the pot holes like a giant blinking cat's eyes.

After walking the length of two streets and being turned away from at least a dozen guest houses, I began to feel exhausted. A wave of tiredness suddenly hit me along with the fear that I was going to have to spend a night walking the streets, so I decided to sit on a shop window sill to consider my next move. A growling noise caused me to jump up.

The shabby looking dog didn't like me sitting in his spot so I moved wearily on, turned the next corner and stopped.

'Grrr!'

I looked behind. Shit, it was following me. Slowly and calmly I walked on, afraid to look back, but whenever I did I noticed that the dog was still there, about ten paces behind me. Every time I stopped he stopped and bared his teeth menacingly, growling. When I crossed the road he crossed, every street I walked down he followed, and every time I stood still he did exactly the same thing, stopping ten paces behind and sneering. The dog was so fierce-looking that I didn't even have the guts to shoo it away.

I went into numerous guest houses, some of which I'd already tried, and every time I came out the dog was still there, waiting and growling. All of the accommodation was full, so eventually, to get away from the dog, I jumped into a tuk-tuk to the other end of the street; a 500-yard journey that the driver ripped me off fiercely for, but it was worth it just to be out of biting range.

I was so tired by this time that I couldn't be bothered to get my watch out of my bag to check the time, and had to ask a passer-by. The traveller with tattooed arms told me to fuck off. I sank. Any more of this, I thought, and I'll get on the next train south and give Bangkok a miss altogether. What had I done to him? I watched as he walked down the road to see if he had the excuse of being drunk, but he wasn't. Perhaps he'd had a bad night and got ripped off in Patpong.

Having run out of places to stay, and unable to stand any longer, I threw my bag down in a shop doorway and lay down, using my only jumper as a pillow. I think I must have blinked twice before the weight of my eyelids, too great to lift, pulled shut and I drifted off.

I wasn't sure if I had woken up or not. My head rolled from side to side and I jumped a lot – sleep jumps; the ones where you're not quite asleep but you can't wake up and something was tugging at my foot. Again I rolled my head from side to side, my neck sticking to my shoulder with sweat, and opened my heavy, baggy eyes just as a sharp pain shot up my toes and into my foot. I quickly withdrew my leg and blinked the mist from my eyes before screaming. A tie-dye pig! My foot! I pulled both feet up to my buttocks but the pig came nearer, so I quickly stood up, going dizzy with the sudden draining of blood from my head.

The pig snorted around for a second or two before a Westerner, also dressed in tie-dye, grabbed the piece of string that was tied around the animal's neck and led it away like a pet dog.

I crouched and put my head in my hands. 'Oh God, this can't be happening.' My eyes felt like they were burning and I rubbed them hard before looking up to see whether I was dreaming or not. I wasn't. There was a crowd of revellers on the opposite side of the road trying to feed a joint to the painted pig. It sniffed and then bit it in half, causing everyone to laugh and whoop, dancing crazily in a circle like Red Indians.

Coming out of the shop doorway I looked up at the sky, the clouds just about discernible in the early morning light. As I turned to pick up my bag and jumper I noticed the posters in the window: brightly coloured pictures of tropical beaches; blue skies, blue seas, white sand and lush jungle backdrops of the deepest green. *Koh Samui*, read one, *Phi Phi Island*, another. Two bikini-clad models were lying on a gleaming white yacht in one poster, and underneath the operator of the travel agency had written, *KOH PHA-NGAN DAILY BUS / TRAIN*.

My soul lifted like a rocket, my eyes cleared and I took a step back to focus on the door sign. *Opening hours: 9 a.m. to 10 p.m.* it read, and, for the first time since my fiancée had left, I took out my wristwatch to check the time.

TWO

After India, train travel in Thailand was a breeze: the train was clean, each person had a separate coffin-like box to sleep in with a curtain for privacy, the carriage was air conditioned, they served beer and, above all, they ran on time. My train south was due to leave at 6.30 p.m. and it did, to the minute. The only drawback was the price, which was ten times the cost of an equivalent journey in India. In fact I was rapidly learning that everything was ten times more than I'd been paying the day before.

Although I wasn't running out of money yet, the cost of the flight from Calcutta to Bangkok was an unexpected burden on my budget. I had expected to have to fly but, contrary to the advice I'd received from other travellers, there were no cheap flights to be had in Calcutta, and it had cost the same for that one-way, two-hour flight as a cheap return ticket from London to New York. The cost of that ticket alone could have kept me on the road in India, all food and lodging included, for two months at least.

However, I did have a choice when leaving Bangkok to either go by train or bus. The bus was slightly cheaper, but in the end, having weighed up the situation, I chose the train. A wise choice because although the bus left earlier, getting me away from pigs and dogs, I didn't feel up to sitting in a seat for ten hours. At least on the train I could kill two birds with one stone: get there and have a good sleep.

The train pulled out of the station, and at about nine o'clock, after dinner and one beer, I zonked out, fully dressed. The sound of the other travellers around me laughing and discussing their various ports of call faded into infinity along with the sound of the train wheels, and I drifted off, cosy in the knowledge that there would be nothing to disturb me.

The next thing I knew, the guard was walking up and down the train waking everyone up for breakfast. We were transferred on to a clapped-out ferry early in the morning and I lay on deck, soaking up the magical first rays of the sun, content that I was finally, truly out of Bangkok and among blue sea and palm trees.

Little green islands were dotted around the place, coming into view and then, when each person on the boat had discussed whether or not it was their island, passing us by. I had just muttered, 'Ahh, this is the life,' to myself and lain down on the top deck, when I heard a vaguely familiar voice above the whine of the engines shout, 'Hey, Suzy, isn't that John over there, that British guy?'

I opened one eye. There was a pause while Dave fought his way over to me, across the bodies strewn on deck, occasionally giving a one fingered gesture to anyone who complained.

'Well, la-di-da!' he said, standing over me, the sun eclipsed by his head. 'Hey brother, you too huh? Me an Sooze couldn't take it either.' He did his familiar secret agent style glance over his shoulder and crouched down beside me. 'To tell you the truth John, heard there're some, er, babes on this island of ours. Thought I might bag me a couple. Whaddya say?'

I agreed half-heartedly before Suzy came over lugging Dave's guitar and looking thoroughly pissed off. She shoved it at him angrily as he stood up. 'It *is* John,' she said sarcastically. 'Well this calls for a celebration. You hang on to this while I go downstairs and buy us all a beer. How'd that be, *Dave*?'

Dave watched her storm off. 'Whoo-ee, getting touchy aren't we?' he called after her, and, conscious of the guitar that was propped up against him, tried to make light of the incident by kissing it. 'C'mon baby, you an me, don't need three,' and rode astride it.

We drank the beer that Suzy bought, and Dave toasted freedom and 'La-di-da British girls' before dozing off, using his guitar as a pillow. I pretended to sleep to avoid having to talk to Suzy. She seemed nice enough but I had other things on my mind; like how long the rest of my money would last, and what I was going to do if, as I feared, Rick wasn't on the island any more.

I was still thinking about these things when we pulled into the ferry pier on Koh Pha-Ngan and transferred ourselves into one of the waiting Isuzu's that took new arrivals to various parts of the island.

Dave loaded himself and his gear into the back of the pick-up and held out a hand, pulling me up. 'Where're you heading John?'

'Hat Rin,' I said, brushing the dust off the seat before sitting. 'You?'

'Same-same, bro.' He dusted a seat with Shakespearean melodrama, intended for Suzy, but she ignored it, tutting and sitting on the opposite bench to us instead.

Following a bit of negotiation we sped off up the bumpy track into the island, clouds of dust billowing around us and covering everyone except the driver, who sat in an air conditioned cab, in a fine yellow layer.

'You, ahem, know where you're gonna stay?' Suzy asked, opening her guidebook on a map of Hat Rin, leaning across and balancing it on my knees.

I shrugged, twisting my neck to read the map that was upside-down. 'Play it by ear.'

'That's the spirit.' Dave snatched the book and threatened to throw it out the back of the pick-up. We suddenly hit a bump in the road and the book jumped out of his hands and tumbled out on to the track.

'Stop!' Suzy banged on the cab window. 'Make them stop, Dave, John!'

'Shit.' Dave slapped the car roof with the palm of his hand, bringing us to a skidding halt. We reversed, picked up the battered guidebook and drove off again. No one talked for the rest of the journey except Dave, who kept apologising.

We must have passed at least a dozen different sets of beach bungalows as we followed the coastline intermittently across the island, each one stunningly picturesque, but nobody got out. Everyone, it appeared, was heading to Hat Rin beach, and when we finally arrived I could see why: a single crescent of gleaming white sand hemmed in by a turquoise sea. Dave and I dropped our gear on the beach as we ran down and plunged into the warm clear water.

'Woo-hoo!' He belly-flopped like a starfish, turned over and went into a handstand. I dived and swam underwater, and swam and swam, not ever wanting to stop. My eyes opened and the world became a soft blue that was so pleasant I kept swimming until I was in about twenty-five feet of water. A turn on to my back enabled me to see the surface: a gently rippled glass ceiling through which saturated rays of sunshine pierced like a thousand torch beams. Running out of air, I stood on the bottom, did one quick three-sixty to locate the sloping beach and pushed upwards, breaking the surface with a gasp.

'John!' Dave thumbed towards the beach where I could just make out Suzy, standing over his guitar with her arms folded across her chest in anger. 'Gotta go, you coming?'

'You go and find a place,' I shouted. 'I'll catch up with you later.'

He marked the air with a forefinger and attempted a back-flip. It went wrong and he walked off up the beach rubbing his head.

Floating, that's all I wanted to do, face up and face down, forever. Or until the previous two days and two countries' worth of sweat, grime and dust had drifted silently off my body. I felt like a shirt in one of those washing powder adverts, where they have a close-up of the dirt particles lifting off the material. 'Whiter than white,' I mumbled, looking up at the azure sky and marvelling at the single white cloud that looked like it had been stuck on, like a ball of cotton wool on a school kid's collage. 'Bluey-white'.

I floated so long that afternoon that not only did the dirt drift off my body but so did my shorts. The constant use was more than they could stand and the stitching gave way all at once, so that I had to hold them on with both hands when I walked back up the beach. For that reason more than any real sense of bargain-hunting I booked into the first set of beach bungalows that stood on the sand, and, after a filling meal, set about the task of searching out the person I'd come here to find.

I still had the crumpled piece of paper that Rick had scribbled on when we had parted company in India, and after asking a waiter at one of the beach restaurants and being told that the Back Yard Pub was up on a hill overlooking a beach, I went on my way. I was directed down through the main street, and after five minutes was climbing a hill into the trees, with no sign of human activity. 'Shit, this can't be right,' I muttered, and stood, sweating in the evening heat.

'Keep going. You wan' Ba' Yar' Pu'?' A lithe young Thai man pointed further up the hill and walked off into the trees, to do whatever Thai men do in trees, and I continued.

The top of the path levelled off and swung left into a small yard, behind which was a large wooden house. A yard, I reasoned, a pub at the back of that yard. It had to be the right place. I walked up on to a wooden veranda, on to what was obviously a dance floor, and strode over to the far end, facing a jungle hillside. The whole place had a fantastic view overlooking palm trees that ran downhill to another beach. On the blue horizon was another island, lit orange by the evening sun.

'Wha' you wan'?' I spun round, startled. The Thai man who had vanished into the trees climbed over the wooden handrail and jumped on to the veranda.

'Umm, I'm looking for Rick,' I said, slightly unsure. 'Is he here?'

He started to fiddle with the wiring on the sound system, seemingly ignorant of what I'd said.

I cleared my throat. 'Excuse me, is—'

'Li?' he said looking up. 'You wan' Li'? No have Li' here.'

Maybe he was wrong, or maybe he hadn't understood. Pointlessly pulling the scrap of paper from my pocket, I repeated, 'Rick. I am looking for a man called Rick. Do you have any messages for me? My name is . . . '

'No have.'

I sighed and leaned against the handrail, sweat pouring off me from the combined effort of climbing the hill and asking the question. 'Are you sure you don't have any messages?'

He went back to his fiddling. 'Tol' you, man, no have, no have! Why you no listen?'

I deflated. It wasn't possible. I'd come so far. Partly to see other places I had to admit, but mainly to meet up with Rick. Reluctantly I walked out of the house, still wanting to ask him again but knowing that it would lead nowhere. If Rick was, or had ever been to Koh Pha-Ngan he clearly would have left a message. That was the arrangement and I felt sure that he would stick to it. He must have reached the island all those weeks ago and been persuaded, by a girl probably, to go to a different island, or up to Chiang Mai.

No longer wanting to think about where I was going to go next or what plans to make, I went back down to the beach, bought an ounce of Thai grass and crashed in my beach hut. I felt gutted and suddenly very alone.

I rolled a joint and had only smoked half before the room started to spin. I hadn't smoked for a while and the effect seemed to be double what I remembered it to be. Suddenly overcome by a queasy feeling, I lay down in an attempt to keep the room from moving. Phew! Was this strong or was I simply unaccustomed to smoking? I closed my eyes and felt worse, the room whizzed, my stomach felt woozy and I belched before running into the toilets and throwing up a barely digested green curry. 'Fuck!' The sweat ran off my head and fell like rain, cratering the leafy green liquid. I ladled some water on to my head and the dizziness eventually cleared enough for me to go back and sit on the bed.

After half an hour, my body recovered just enough energy for me to stand and fix up my mosquito net, but it felt like such an arduous task to tie a piece of string and attach the loops, that I did it incorrectly. I fell back on to the bed; one end of the net pinged off and it smothered my head like a mist. Too tired and too pissed off to bother, the sleep my body craved enveloped me like the net and I quickly drifted off.

I hadn't even noticed the scribbled message that had been stuck to the inside of my door with a rizla.

THREE

John.
Fucking good to see you!
Contact soon.
Sir William.

I pulled the piece of paper from the door leaving half the gummed edge behind, and stood, pondering the note. The early morning sunlight was streaming through the gaps in the planks of the door making vertical lines like laser beams across my chest. Squinting and moving my eye out of the line of fire, I sat on the edge of the bed. What did it mean?

Of course, I should have been wondering how on earth someone had managed to get into my room the night before to post the message. The door had been locked so whoever it was either had the key or knew someone who had it. The previous night's events went carefully through my mind, stage by stage, in an attempt to sift out a face or a figure that had been hanging around my hut, and who may have been the intruder. I suddenly felt the urge to check my belongings, to make sure that nothing was missing. My passport, video camera and money were all still there, nothing had been touched.

The next question that entered my head was why Rick hadn't spoken to me himself. If he knew I was here why had he only left a message? And what was all this knighthood stuff?

Unsure exactly what to make of these events, I unzipped my holdall, pulled out the postcard he'd sent me and cross-checked the scrawl. The note was indeed in the same handwriting, and not only that but it was written in the same garish purple ink.

Fucking good to see you! I imagined him saying it as he wrote it down, wondering whether or not to spell it *Fooking*. Fook. Fooking fook. The words on the paper went over and over in my head. Written on a rizla, I thought, and sat with my back against the shuttered window, how typical of him. More typical would have been to include a rolled joint as a welcoming present.

I rolled the note into a tiny ball and pushed it out through the window shutter, momentarily blinding myself in the sunlight. Outside, the beach looked almost deserted through my limited strip of vision, and blinking rapidly to stop the bright light from stinging my eyes, first the beach and then the sea came into view.

I pulled away from the window, startled as someone suddenly walked on to the wooden veranda of the hut. 'Goo' mornin', sir,' came a delicate female voice.

My heart beat a little faster, and I pushed one eye up against the shutter again to see who it was. The woman arranged her things on the wooden platform, and soon the sound of fruit being chopped drifted in along with the sweet sticky smells. Peeping through the shutter and manoeuvring my head, I tried to get a look at her face, but my field of vision was restricted so I just eyed her technique. One hand held the machete while the other spun the papaya around in quarter turns, her lurid blue nail varnish like lapis scarabs clinging to the side of the dark green fruit.

Watching the fruit being prepared made me so hungry that I completely forgot to question how she had known I was awake, and after taking a quick bucket shower and dressing, I opened the door and walked outside. She was gone. There was no mess, no peel, just a huge bowl of chopped tropical fruit sitting in the middle of a small red cloth beneath my hammock.

I quickly jumped off the veranda and looked around the rear of the hut. She was nowhere to be seen. I walked around the hut twice, not quite believing the past ten minutes had really happened. I expected to return to the front and find the bowl of fruit gone but it was still there, shining, mouthwatering, like a mirage.

At first I was reluctant to eat it. I wasn't sure whether I was being suckered into some scam whereby I ate the fruit, watched by beady eyes, and got pounced upon and presented with an outrageous bill. So, hesitating for about two seconds, I picked up the bowl, arranged myself in the hammock, hesitated for another second or two while scanning the beach, and started scooping up the fruit whilst swinging to and fro.

A door opened in the next hut along from mine and Dave the American emerged, stretching and yawning. As he came out his hand went down the front of his shorts as though searching for something, his face frowning and confused. Funny how people look different when they don't know they're being watched. I struck the side of my bowl with the spoon. *Bing!*

'Hey,' he said, quickly dropping his hand and walking to the edge of his veranda. 'What's that you've got there John?'

I watched him through my swinging knees, 'Fruit salad,' and struck the spoon against the bowl again.

'Fruit salad?' He looked at his watch – which wasn't there. 'Jesus, are they open already?'

'Don't think they are,' I said happily. 'You could check though.'

He wrinkled his nose. 'So where'd you get that?'

'Some woman's walking around making them.' Another succulent piece of pineapple was slurped into my mouth. 'Jush left.'

'How much?'

'That's the thing,' I said, grinning, 'they're free.'

'Fuckin' what? Don't kid me now John. Don't bullshit me.' He leaned over the handrail, balancing on his stomach. 'You tellin' me you didn't have to pay for that?'

'That's what I said.' Barely able to contain my laughter, I stuffed the rest of the fruit into my mouth and nearly choked. "Ucking tashty, too.'

Dave vaulted over the side on to the sand and stormed off between the huts towards one of the restaurants. A minute later he was back, empty-handed. 'You're shittin' me John, there's no one there yet. Just some old guy picking his nose.' He stomped on to the wooden deck of his hut and leaped heavily into his hammock. The rope snapped and brought him crashing on to his back. 'Fuckin' Jesus!'

I sniggered. 'You OK, Dave?'

'Arrgh!' He rolled over on to his side and rubbed his spine. 'You just eat your free food John, don't worry about me.'

Suzy appeared at the door, looking down at Dave and rubbing the sleep from her eyes, no doubt awoken by the thump. 'Thought you Navy boys were used to hammocks and all that? Morning John,' she said, noticing me.

Dave heaved himself up. 'Modern ships don't have hammocks, Sooze. I was on the USS *Enterprise*, not the fuckin' *Mayflower*.'

She raised her eyebrows towards me, took a towel off her washing-line and went back inside.

I steadied my hammock by placing one foot against my door. 'You were in the Navy, Dave?'

'Bet you didn't guess that one, eh John?' He jumped down off his veranda and limped over towards me, pulling a face at Suzy's back. 'Man, what a start to the day! Wake up, some guy next door gets a free breakfast, an' all I get is freefall!' He sat down with his back against my door and looked out to sea. 'Yep. Never came to places like this though.'

'How long were you in for?'

'Two years basic.' He pulled his knees up to his chest and rubbed his back, wincing in pain. 'Nothing else for black guys to do in the US. No, that's not strictly true, there is something else but that involves breaking the law, so count me outta that shit.'

Dave told me how he'd almost been a boxer first and then a stripper, all before the age of eighteen. Having not been particularly good at either, and not particularly bright at school, he'd had little choice but to go into the forces. Guys like him get steadily pushed further and further towards the back of the classroom until, finally, they are out of the door and are not allowed back in.

'You probably expected me to have a crew cut, right?'

I nodded.

'Well, that was six months ago. Now I'm going for the Hendrix look.' He patted his three-inch afro.

'Why not Bob Marley?' I said provocatively.

'I ain't no Rasta, man. Anyway, my mom wouldn't approve. She thinks Bob Marley was a drug addict.'

'So was Hendrix, wasn't he?'

He nodded. 'Yeah but he didn't have dreads. Even black people are prejudiced John. Take a black guy with dreads an' shit, my mom'll say he's a bad influence, should be in prison. You dress that same guy up in a suit and give him a haircut, no problem – my mom'll ask him round for dinner.'

I considered the image he conjured up and said, 'You don't strike me as the kind of person who's worried about what people might think, Dave.'

'Just fashion, man. All these guys running around with dreads,' his hand swept the air dismissively, 'just fashion. They ain't hippies. Same way I'm not Jimi fuckin' Hendrix.'

I tutted and rubbed my shaved head self-consciously. 'Vanity, is that all it is?'

'That's all. Nothin' more and nothin' less than that.' He paused for a moment. 'Chicks used to go for the Rasta look, now they go for the afro. Same reason you got a shaved melon, right? Chicks dig that on a white guy.'

Dave and I sat outside my hut discussing fashion, or as he called it, 'Chewing the fat,' until there were signs of life in the restaurant, and we went in to eat.

'What about Suzy?' I said as we walked beneath the palm trees at the back of the huts. 'Maybe she's hungry.'

'She knows where it is, don't worry.' He hesitated, stopping mid-step. 'Hey, you hittin' on her?'

I stopped. 'What?' I guessed the meaning but needed time to compose myself. It's a bit of a shock when someone asks that question so boldly. 'Hitting on her?'

He grinned. 'You, man, you an Sooze. Shit, white chicks. Whoo-ee!' He slapped me on the back. 'Listen, if you an' her want to get together that's cool. I know you two are both British la-di-das an' all.'

I shrugged his hand off my shoulder and put both hands up, genuinely surprised. 'Course not! Christ almighty, is that how it looks? Honestly Dave, I've got no interest in your girlfriend, really.'

He closed one eye and looked down his nose at me. 'Hey, it's OK, it means she's marketable. Nothin' worse than havin' a girlfriend that nobody looks at.'

'Dave, I swear!'

'Let's eat.' He put his arm around me again and we went in and sat down in the empty restaurant.

At one end was a counter and bar where a woman of dubious sexual orientation was folding serviettes and placing them in a neat pile. It was difficult to tell whether she was one of the ladymen I'd heard so much about.

D'you think that's a man?' I whispered, and from the cover of my menu flicked my eyes towards the counter.

Dave looked up. 'What, her? No way, man. I tell you, if she's a fella I'd still have sex with her.'

I watched the woman for a moment and said, 'Bet you she is.'

'How much?'

'Breakfast; loser pays the bill.'

'You're on.' We shook hands over the table. 'How're we going to prove it?'

'Ask?'

'Fuck, John, we can't ask!'

I thought for a moment and said, 'You'll just have to sleep with her then.'

'Hey, no problem, it's a girl.'

At that moment the woman looked up from her boring serviette-folding job and winked at us. 'That's it,' I exclaimed, 'she's a he, you lose.'

'I lose cause she winked?' Dave slammed his large hands on the table.

'Course. That's proof enough isn't it? Normal girls don't wink at strangers.'

'Hookers do.' Dave lifted his menu and hid behind. 'Shit, she's coming over.'

The Thai woman was wearing a sarong tied at the waist, and above that a leotard. As beautiful as she was, six-foot tall and incredibly slim, her small hips gave the game away the minute she emerged from behind the counter.

'Looks like I'm picking up the tab,' Dave mumbled nervously. He shook his head. 'Imagine making that mistake. I'm never getting drunk in Thailand.'

With one hand running fingers through her hair and the other placed on our table, the Thai spoke with soft familiarity. 'Wha' you hansoon boy like?'

Dave started. 'Ahem. Um, fruit salad and an American breakfast.'

She leaned forward over the table, pushing her imaginary cleavage together with both arms, and looked at me. I ordered an orange juice and she withdrew to the counter, returning a moment later with some condiments and folded serviettes, which she placed carefully on the table. She took intricate care over the tiniest details, smoothing out the folds in the tablecloth with manicured fingers. It was only then that I noticed her bright blue nail varnish.

I went to speak but she cut me off, stunning me into silence. 'One momen' Lor' John,' she said, walking away with a wiggle.

Dave's eyes nearly popped out of his head and he dropped the menu on the floor. 'Fuckin' what did you get up to last night, man, huh?'

My mouth dropped open but no words came out. I just stared at the sarong as it swayed its way back across the floor. I still couldn't quite register what I'd just heard.

Dave started rocking backwards and forwards on his chair, laughing. 'Man, you *are* a dark horse. Whoo-ee!' I leaned across the table at Dave, ready to protest my innocence. 'Whoa,' he said, 'not so close! No wonder you're not interested in Suzy!'

'Fuck off, Dave. I swear I don't know him . . . er, her. I've never seen her before in my life.'

He eyed me with suspicion. 'Then how come he knows your name, *Lord* John?'

I shook my head, hardly believing it myself.

FOUR

Dave was like a kid, badgering me about the incident all day long. When I asked the ladyman how she'd got my name, and she just laughed, it made Dave worse. Not only did he not believe that I hadn't slept with the Thai but he also thought that I was some kind of royalty, constantly referring to me as 'Your Lordship' or 'Your Highness'. Whenever I asked the ladyman where Rick was, she just said, 'You wai' momen',' and wiggled off to fold some tablecloths or do her hair. I began to think that someone was playing some kind of elaborate trick.

Every morning for the rest of that week a bowl of fruit salad was ready for me outside my hut, and every afternoon she floated along the beach in her sarong to give me the same pointless message: that she would be going off to buy fresh fruit for the next day's breakfast. Everyone had seen us talking and must have assumed that we were together.

'They think you're some kind of fuckin' pervert.' Dave somersaulted off the rock and hit the water squarely on his back. He surfaced a moment later arching in pain. 'Either that or queer. Ow!'

'Let me show you how to do it.' I took two steps back and up. 'It's all in the arms, Dave, watch this.' My crucifix shape hit the water with what I considered beauty and elegance. It hurt the tops of my arms on impact and, although I knew this dive spot pretty well now, I almost head-butted a submerged boulder. 'Fuck,' I gasped as I came up for air, 'where did that come from?'

'Almost hit it didn't ya?' Dave clambered back on to the rock and wiped the water from his face.

'I never saw that before. Christ!'

'That's because it wasn't there yesterday. Take a look up there. See, where that hole is?' He pointed behind him to where the black boulders ended and the jungle began.

'Oh yeah,' I confirmed, looking up and squinting at the sun. 'Jesus, I wonder how that happened?'

'Wonder no more, Lord John. Here.' He held out a hand and pulled me up on to the rock. 'I pushed it down last night. Came out here for a swim alone. Made a helluva splash when it hit the water: *Ker-boom!* Like a fuckin' depth charge.'

'I bet it did.' I wished I'd been there to witness the sight. Imagine, a boulder the size of an armchair rolling down the rocks, bouncing and splintering as it went, until finally impacting like an atom bomb into the water. 'Superb,' I agreed, suitably impressed. 'Any more around?'

'Reckon so. Around the headland there're bound to be more.' He shook the excess water from his afro. 'I swam further out yesterday and it looks like the whole rock face is falling in.'

I shielded my eyes from the sun to look at the headland. 'Fancy a swim?'

'Now?' He looked at his non-waterproof watch that had misted over. 'Shit, I said I'd meet Sooze at one. Ah well, I'll just say my watch was broken.'

We both dived in and began the swim out towards the pile of rocks in the distance.

Because of the shape of Hat Rin beach and the surrounding landscape, it's possible to swim the quarter of a mile or so out to either headland and still see everything else that's contained within the bay: trees, the beach and all the people on it. The other thing about Hat Rin is that despite being a popular place for backpackers, few people, if any, seem to bother with the sea. As beautiful as it is, most people are too busy listening to music or sleeping off hangovers to wade out any further than waist-deep. For that reason more than anything else, once we'd swum halfway out we came across no one else swimming in the other direction.

'Pity there're no waves here,' I said, keeping my chin above the water as I breast-stroked. 'We've got the beach, the sunshine, the parties. Waves would make it perfect.'

'You surf?'

I nodded, unable to speak as a ripple lapped against my mouth. 'Uh-huh.'

'Put it there John.' Dave trod water and held out a hand. 'Man, is it a killer sport or what?'

'The best.' I shook his hand while frantically treading water with my legs to make up for the short-fall in the arm department, and we continued swimming. 'Surf in England.'

'Man, I thought you said you were from London.'

'I am. I sometimes surf on the west coast, though.'

'What, California?'

'The west coast of England, not America.'

Winking at me and smiling, he said, 'You're putting me on, right?'

'Surfed in India once.'

He spat a jet of water at me. 'Fuck, John, now you are going *too* far. Don't start that la-di-da bullshit with me again. First it's that lady– what did you call her?'

'Laddy-bird.'

'Yeah, laddy-bird. Now it's surfing in India.' He chuckled, 'You British. You bloody-fucking-wanker.'

'I'm not kidding.' I rolled over and went into a back-stroke. 'On my life.'

He pushed some water at me. 'Well I got that beat anyway. Friend of mine, used to serve on the *Enterprise*, this sonofabitch took his board out once and, I swear, he surfed the wake of a war ship. How's that for balls?'

'Now that *is* ridiculous.'

Dave dived beneath the surface and came back up again a few feet ahead. 'Bernie Drum's his name, surfin' an' fightin's his game.'

'Next thing you'll be telling me that aliens have landed and the government are trying to cover it all up.'

'Hey!'

We reached the headland, and after a quick recce, Dave climbed up on to a rock that looked like it supported another, thus giving us plenty of opportunity to cause an avalanche.

'Give us a hand,' I called from the water.

He didn't seem to hear me and was staring at something in the distance.

'Dave.'

'Shit!' He suddenly crouched down on to his haunches, hiding behind the rock in front.

He still didn't pay any attention to me so I had to crawl up on to the surface of the boulders, scraping my belly and legs painfully on the barnacles. 'Dave, what the fuck?'

'Stay down!' he hissed. 'Over there, look at those guys.'

There was barely enough room on the rock for two people, so to hide and see meant holding myself at an awkward, uncomfortable angle. 'Where?' I asked, after briefly checking my chest for blood. He pointed around the headland towards the far end of another beach, in totally the opposite direction to where I had been looking.

About half a mile away on a small mound of rocks, two men were holding another man down, one holding his hair and the other his arms. Their captive kicked wildly, his bare legs striking out at them but only hitting the rocks. All three were well tanned so I assumed they were locals, though it was difficult to tell from that distance.

I crouched in closer behind Dave and whispered, 'What are they doing?'

'Looks like a beating to me. Keep down.'

We could clearly hear the attackers shouts as they carried across the water and a muffled scream drifted over as the captive doubled up, bringing his knees to his chest before being kicked into a flat position. One of the men then went knee-deep into the water and pulled a small boat out from between the rocks, and together they picked the man up by his arms and legs and threw him into the boat. The loud *crack* of his skull hitting the wood was sickening, and we both grimaced.

Looking down at my bare legs and chest I suddenly felt very naked wearing only swimming trunks. In contrast, Dave's matt-black skin was perfect camouflage against the black, sun-baked rocks, and I regretted having got out of the water at all. Slowly, I slipped back down the face of the boulder into the water.

Dave did a double-take. 'John, what the fuck are you doing? Ge-get back here.'

'Shh. I'm better off in the water. If they come this way they'll easily see me.'

They didn't come our way. The two men jumped into the boat with their captive, started the engine and zoomed off in the opposite direction, quickly vanishing behind a distant pile of rocks. Soon the water settled and the small beach looked tranquil and picturesque to the max. The backdrop to the white sand, unlike Hat Rin, was dense jungle, with no signs of tourists or accommodation.

Dave was staring down at me from on top of his rock looking thoughtful. 'Whaddya say we take a look at that beach, Johnny-boy?' He clenched his fists. 'Man, I'm fired up now, I can't go back until I've had a look over there.'

'Now wait just a minute, Dave,' I said, 'let's not be hasty, they might come back.'

He looked at his watch. 'Give 'em ten minutes, if they're not back, we go over.'

Although the place where their boat had been moored was further up the beach, I had surmised that the beach itself began just around the curve in the headland from our hiding position. It didn't, and we had to swim in a long arc before we had cleared the rocks and could go ashore.

Dave was lying on his back in the shallows trying to catch his breath when I reached the beach. 'You could have waited,' I gasped, lifting my aching legs and falling beside him. 'I could . . .'

'Notice the trees?' he said enthusiastically, sitting up and pointing towards the jungle.

Still exhausted from the swim, I slowly turned my head to look. Each palm tree seemed to have weird designs painted on its trunk in what looked like fluorescent paint.

'Hippy shit. Let's take a closer look.'

'And they've been having a party or something.' I pointed to the cigarette butts that littered the sand and began to follow him, suddenly forgetting my breathlessness.

'Wow, out here,' he looked at me, 'a party like no other.'

The sweat had started to run down my face and back in tickling rivers, making me feel prickly. Once away from the water's edge there wasn't a breeze, and it began to feel claustrophobic. 'Fuck, it's hot up here,' I said, wiping a hand across my brow. 'Shall we go back into the water?'

'Scared?'

'Course not. What's there to be scared about? It's just a beach.'

'Good. Let's go into the trees then.'

'What for?' I tried to hide the trepidation in my voice, which would undoubtedly betray my sense of foreboding at the dark jungle ahead. 'Dave?' He ignored me and started to walk in. Feeling a little apprehensive about leaving the bright, white light of the beach for the gloomy darkness of the jungle, I loitered, waiting for him to change his mind. 'Come on, Dave, it's a waste of time.'

'This must be where those guys were before they left.' Dave's dusky figure vanished into the shade provided by the tree line before his muffled voice came back. 'Look at these. Ah, Jesus Christ!'

'What is it?' I moved closer, still cautious.

'Ah, man, take a look at this.'

Leaving the blinding sand for the cool shade of the trees, I walked carefully through the undergrowth to where Dave, dappled in golden coins of sunlight, was standing next to a big flat rock. 'Crabs?' I said with barely concealed relief, and wiped a stinging droplet of sweat from the corner of my eye. 'Ha!'

He picked up a stick and flicked one or two of the small crustaceans off to reveal a fresh bloodstain in the middle of the rock. 'Check this out,' he said and, using two twigs as chopsticks, picked up a freshly severed human finger.

FIVE

We made the swim back to Hat Rin at double speed. I wasn't timing us but it was obvious that we were both swimming faster because I was doing freestyle, as opposed to my usual breast-stroke, and Dave struggled to keep up. Every five minutes he shouted for me to slow down but I just kept my head low, pretending not to hear him underwater. At one point, as we cleared the curved headland and Hat Rin came into view he grabbed my foot to slow me down, but I kicked it free and continued, faster still.

If my heart was beating quickly when we made the gruesome discovery, the effort of swimming back had doubled its beat from a march to a drum-roll. My neck pulsed under the weight of blood that had bottlenecked in the veins, trying to find its way to my brain, and the exertion was so tremendous that my whole head was throbbing.

At first Dave had suggested walking back from the secluded beach. By his reckoning there must be a path back to Hat Rin, otherwise how the hell could other people get there? It made some sense because clearly the people who had partied on the beach couldn't have swum; at least, not carrying pots of paint. Packets of cigarettes maybe, but not paint.

Sprawled out on the sand of our own beach with Dave lying next to me, I pulsated, gasping for breath, my feet digging into the sand to push me a little further up, away from the gently lapping water, as though it might drag me back towards the finger.

Ugh, that finger! A perfect finger. For some reason I had never imagined that a severed finger would still look like a finger; all that was missing was the hand, wrist, arm, shoulder ... The finger had obviously been cut from the person we had seen taking a beating, and must have been fresh, almost moving, able to crawl off that rock on its own like a giant maggot.

I closed my eyes, listening to the thump of my heart, and started to imagine the finger rolling off the rock on to the sand on its journey to the sea. As it went, it fought off the crabs that were determined to stop it, and the seagulls that swooped down to pick it off.

'John.' Dave shook my arm. 'What? Are you sleeping?'

I exhaled and wiped the sweat from my face. 'No, just having a nightmare.' Thankful to have been disturbed, I sat up, still sucking in erratic lungfuls of air, and looked out at the headland we had just swum past. 'Amazing.'

Dave followed my gaze. 'What is?'

'You can't see anything from here. Even if you swim right up to those rocks, even from the water, you still can't see that other beach.'

He nodded. 'That's a much further swim than I thought it'd be, I have to admit. Told you we should have walked back.'

I looked at him sceptically.

'What's the problem?'

'Don't like severed fingers, that's the fucking problem, Dave.' I bent forward to catch my breath but couldn't. My heart was still beating too fast to allow my lungs any room for air.

After a few minutes of silence while we watched two girls playing with a frisbee, Dave spoke. 'What did he do to deserve that kinda treatment? Man, I thought I'd seen it all in the Navy but I ain't *never* seen anything like that before.' He punched the sand. 'Man, that's fuckin' freaky. Gotta be drugs related. Got to be. Heard about that kinda thing before but just stories, nothing real.'

'You think we should go to the police?'

His eyes lit up. 'Hell no! What'd we do that for?'

'Just a thought. You're probably right. Anyway, it would be messy.'

'Not to mention dangerous for us two! Shit, if those guys caught wind of what we saw . . .' he pointed to both of us, 'we'd be next. No siree. You may be a British lord but you ain't got no protection out here. Those suckers get a hold of ya. *Wham!* Uh-uh, life's cheap out here, man, you better believe it.' He indicated his point by using one hand as a chopper against an outstretched forefinger.

'Which is precisely why I didn't want to walk back,' I said. 'If they'd seen us we would probably never swim again!'

He made an OK sign. 'Sensible, sensible.'

We both lay back down and gazed up at the cloudless blue sky. I wanted to look at anything other than those rocks; anything that stopped me from thinking about that finger. A pink flying saucer suddenly flew through the blue sky and landed in the sand next to Dave.

'Hey,' he shouted, sitting up again, 'you girls wanna play?'

One of the two topless blondes we'd been watching came jogging over to collect the frisbee. 'If you like.'

'John?'

I tilted my head. 'No, I'm OK at the moment. You go.'

Dave stood up and joined in the game, his slim black body looking funny between the two bare-chested whites, like a sandwich. Every time he threw the frisbee too hard and hit a passer-by a little argument would ensue, not coming to any real shouting, just a 'Watch it man!' Another flick of the frisbee, accidentally-on-purpose in the wrong direction, 'Oops.'

As I watched them play, I began to think about Dave. He was unusual, I thought. Hard to fathom. When we had first met outside the airport in Bangkok, I had taken him for an annoying, clean-cut, middle-class American, like one of the Cosby Kids, only this one had broken away and become a little wayward. Now I had changed my mind. After what he had told me about his background it seemed that I had judged him in reverse, and that he was a poor kid trying to make good. Actually I didn't believe that either, or rather, I believed it but thought there was more to him than that. He was out to have a good time, but unlike many of the other travellers I'd met, he wasn't pretending to be something that he wasn't naturally. He wasn't *trying* to break away, or *trying* to drop out or be a hippy.

Dave knew who he was and didn't avoid the question of upbringing and the financial assistance that had got him out here. In short he wasn't pretending to be poor; whether he was poor or not didn't matter. And he wasn't interested in getting away from the crowd, trying to be the first to discover some far-off deserted beach that only the select few travellers 'in-the-know' were privy to.

If you could bottle his upbringing and sell it like medicine, you'd be a millionaire; the hoards of lost, middle-class, pseudo-hippies would make sure of that.

Dave did a few spectacularly dismal attempts at catching the frisbee between his legs, and when he tried to do it and jump at the same time he came down on his head with a dull thud. 'Gawd,' he proclaimed, trying to mimic my accent, 'landed roight on me noggin!' The two girls lapped it up.

He threw the frisbee to me as an obvious ploy to come over and have a word with me. 'John, these two are real hot, man, c'mon.'

I had regained my composure enough to stand, and joined in, thinking that the girls would help take my mind off the day's events. 'Aren't you supposed to meet Suzy?' I said, brushing the sand off my back.

'John, don't give me that la-di-da crap now,' he thrust the frisbee into my hands, 'throw that mother to Julie.'

I looked up at the two girls who were standing, hands on hips, waiting for the game to continue. They looked like they were discussing which one of us they preferred, occasionally giggling and moving from one hip stance to the other. 'Which one's Julie?'

'The blon– the one with the small bazookas. Your one.'

'That means you get the one with the ... '

'Big bazookas. Right! You catch on fast. Hey,' he said turning back, 'it's my game so I get to choose. And none of that la-di-da British lord stuff. You know I can't compete with that. All I've got is my afro, and once they've seen that a black guy's dick is the same size as any other guy's, it's over.'

We walked towards the two girls and Dave instructed us to fan out. That's exactly what he said, 'OK, now faan-out,' and spread his arms like he was carrying out a military exercise.

'It's not is it?' I enquired before we were all in position.

'Is what not?'

'A black man's ...'

'Why d'you think Suzy lost interest after one night?' He stopped walking backwards and whispered, 'Blonde chicks are the worst. All they want is dick, black dick, and the bigger the better.' He raised his voice. 'Now stop talking and throw that damn thing.'

I was just about to throw the frisbee when I saw the ladyman from the restaurant coming down the beach towards us. Oh no, not me! Why now? Any illusion I may have had that she was possibly looking for someone else was shattered as she drew closer, skipping along with both forearms perpendicular to her body, limp wrists dangling uselessly on the end. 'Lor' John!'

Dave looked at me. 'Oh shit, man, it's that guy-thing from ...'

'I know who it is, Dave!'

Everyone on the beach watched the Thai run down the sand towards me, old hands laughing, while the new arrivals were just open-mouthed at the sight. To take the edge off my embarrassment I exaggerated it, bowing down and holding one hand to my forehead. It brought a few laughs so I went a stage further and behaved like an ostrich, digging a hole in the sand and putting my head in it.

'Lor' John, ha' massage for you.'

I looked up, shaking the sand from my ears, my face burning with embarrassment. 'What?'

'No here,' she panted, coming to a stop beside me and theatrically flicking her hair, 'in you loom.' A roar of laughter went up from the people who'd heard and my face caught fire. The ladyman looked around, angry at the childish behaviour. 'No! Massage in you loom.'

'Oh!' I clarified so that everyone could here. 'There is a *message* for me in my room.' Then she blew the whole thing by calling me 'hansoon' and stroking my head. 'OK, OK, thanks.' She turned and jogged off up the beach towards the restaurant. Unfortunately the restaurant was right behind our huts so I couldn't immediately go back to find out what the message was. If I did everyone would think that I was going off with her.

We threw the frisbee around for five minutes, just long enough for people to get back to their sunbathing, before I made my excuses and left, using a long, tortuous route to get back to my hut.

Looking around the corner to see that no one on the beach was watching, I darted up on to the wooden veranda, key at the ready. Dave was already there, swinging silently in my hammock.

He looked at his watch. 'Ten minutes?'

I stopped, one hand on the padlock. 'What happened to the girls?'

'What do you think happened? They took one look at her ladyship and ran a mile. Anyway, I want to know what you're up to, Lord John.' He swung his legs over and jumped out of the net. 'Can't let you have all the fun around here.'

'I told you, Dave, I'm not a bloody lord.' The padlock snapped open and fell into my upturned palm. 'So don't keep going on about it.'

Dave followed me into the darkened room. 'Hmm, not bad,' he said looking around. 'Cleaner than mine. Wow, man, you got a video camera!'

'Actually, it's now a *broken* video camera. Not much use.' I shut the door and switched on the light.

'Shit, why don't you get it fixed?'

'Where?'

He shrugged. 'Bangkok?'

'I did think about it,' I said, throwing the key on to the bed, 'they've got a service centre there. But what with one thing and another, there just wasn't time.'

'Shame. I could put this to good use out here.' He pretended to film around the room and turned it on me. 'Behind you.'

I spun around. Stuck to the door in exactly the same way that the first note had been was another piece of paper with a message written in purple ink. I pulled it off and read it to myself.

'What's it say John?' I held it out and Dave took it from me. '*Hat Rin beach*,' he read aloud, '*Tonight, 2 a.m. Will pick you up. Sir William.*' He put the camera down and started dancing. 'Sir William! Woo-hoo, way to go Johnny-boy!'

SIX

We spent the rest of the day sitting around: on the beach, in the restaurant, in my hut, discussing what was going to happen at 2 a.m. I should say that Dave discussed it, because although I was curious about the message, I remained cautiously quiet, preferring instead to observe Dave as he ran around, unable to stop rabbiting. I thought he was on drugs or something, and to try to slow him down a little I rolled a joint.

Unable to explain exactly what the note had meant when it said I'd be picked up, I think Dave assumed that, having been knighted by the Queen of England, 'Sir William' would meet us on the beach in a Rolls Royce. 'Listen, man,' he said, 'these Thais are loaded, I'm telling ya. Your friend may have been just another poor backpacker in India but since then he's made it big. *BIG!*'

I wasn't convinced. I suppose it was possible that Rick had made a fortune from smuggling grass, but even that seemed a bit unlikely in such a short space of time. Another thing Dave assumed (though he didn't say, I knew what he was thinking) was that Rick was some kind of elderly gent in a pinstriped suit; a character from a Graham Greene novel that spent his wealth living extravagantly in exotic locations. My video was broken so I was unable to show him that Rick looked more like a character from a Cheech and Chong film. It wouldn't have mattered anyway, if I had shown him a picture he would have said that Rick was an eccentric millionaire.

'Dave,' I said quietly as we left my hut and walked on to the dark beach, 'don't get your hopes up too much.'

A few people who hadn't already gone to bed, too stoned to move probably, had fallen asleep on the sand. Some were still smoking, the red ember from the tips of their cigarettes hovering eerily above the dark sand.

Dave smiled and patted my back. 'Hey, it's cool. Anyways, we're having a good time ain't we?

I ignored the question and said, 'What did you say to Suzy?'

'Told her that I was going out with you. Man, she knows the score. An' if she don't, well, she can't come along anyway. You don't take chicks with you on a night like tonight bro'.' He paused for a moment, walking along the water's edge in silence. 'In any case,' he continued, 'it might be dangerous.'

It hadn't occurred to me. 'Dangerous?'

'Could be a set-up. That freaky chick-a-doodle in that restaurant could be in on it. She definitely scares me.'

'No,' I said confidently, 'this is Rick's handwriting. I told you, it matches the one he wrote in India perfectly.'

He nodded agreement, and we walked in silence along the beach until we had reached about the halfway point. Dave looked at his watch. 'Quarter to. Where d'you think we should wait? 'Bout here should do, I reckon,' he said, putting a hand over his eyes. 'Good clear view in both directions. Not much cover though.'

'Cover?' I exclaimed. 'What do you need cover for? Jesus, Dave, you're not in the Army now.'

'Only kidding. And it was the Navy, not the Army.' He sat down. 'Take a seat John, don't look so obvious. Oh yeah, and get a new shirt.'

I stayed standing. 'What's wrong with this one? It cost me a lot of money back in London. It's the only shirt I have that isn't permanently stained. I save this for taking girls out, they love it.'

'Maybe five years ago they did. You look like a fuckin' beach boy, man.'

'Um, Dave, this is a beach.'

He snorted and shifted his weight. 'Yeah but this ain't the sixties an' you ain't no rock star. Sit down before you do get shot for bad taste.'

'Look at you then,' I said, pointing to his vest, 'you look like Huggy Bear!'

'Don't tell me I don't look cool! Shit, my mom bought this for me.'

I stood for a moment, wondering if my clothes really were out-dated, and stared down the beach. A couple who had come out from one of the huts started towards us and I instantly recognised Suzy. I cleared my throat ready to tell Dave. 'Umm . . . '

'John, sit down, it ain't two yet.'

'Here comes Suzy.'

He spun around on the sand, first the wrong way and then back again, squinting into the darkness. 'That ain— It can't be. Shit, it is! What's she doin' here? I told her . . . '

'She's with someone else, I think.'

The error of Dave's ways suddenly dawned on him as Suzy stopped and started to kiss the man she was with. 'That bitch.' He leaned up on one elbow. 'See, I told you John, once she finds out about the dick size.'

I clucked my tongue dismissively. 'Yeah right, it's got nothing to do with the fact that you haven't taken her out for the last three nights then?'

He didn't answer, and watched in silence as Suzy and the other man kissed then fell on to the sand, one on top of the other, panting passionately. It was obvious what they were going to do next and I couldn't stifle the giggle.

'Oh, man, not that! She's not gonna do it there?' Dave rolled on to his back laughing painfully. 'Man, she never howled like that when we did it.'

'Listen!' I said, sitting up, alert.

Dave waved his hand through the air. 'I've heard enough.'

'Not that, *listen*.' I cupped a hand behind each ear. 'Can you hear it? Like an engine.' Standing up, I turned in a full circle like a radar to locate the sound. 'It's coming from the sea. Definitely, out there.'

Dave stood and we both walked to the edge of the shore and squinted into the blackness. 'Can you hear it?'

He nodded. 'A boat. Small.'

'Where?'

'I can't see it, but it's definitely a small boat.' He looked at the sky. 'No moon, damn!'

'If you can't see it, how d'you know it's a small boat?'

'When you've done a watch every night at sea for two years you get to recognise the sound of an outboard engine.'

I looked at him. 'You're telling me you can tell the difference between the sound of an outboard and an inboard engine? I don't believe you.'

He ignored me and twitched his head from side to side, apparently picking up the sound. 'Two, maybe three people.'

The engine suddenly cut, leaving only the sound of Suzy and her mate panting frantically in the night.

'What time is it, Dave?'

'Two, exactly. It must be Sir William.'

I let out a laboured sigh. 'For God's sake, when you see him don't call him Sir William.'

There was a shallow splash to our left and we both looked in that direction. Out of the darkness a slender long-tail boat appeared just down from where we stood, paddled by two people, while another person sat at the back and steered.

'Three people. What did I say?' Dave slapped my back and jogged off down the beach. 'What're you waiting for?' He shouted, turning his head, 'You've got an invitation!'

Two other people who had been waiting on the beach, and who I had assumed were nothing to do with the rendezvous, waded alongside and jumped into the boat, followed by Dave. I stood knee-deep in water and held on to the prow, debating whether or not to get in.

'John, get in, man,' Dave said excitedly, and held out a hand. 'C'mon!'

There didn't seem any point staying so I dived in head-first, pulled over by the others. It seemed a bit unlikely that any other boat would arrive at exactly two o'clock in the morning so, even though the three Thais in the boat made no mention of Rick, I thought I'd better shut up and get in. The driver fired up the engine, turned us around and sped out to sea.

'John,' Dave whispered as Hat Rin faded away behind us, 'I take it neither one of these guys is your friend.'

'No,' I replied very quietly, and glanced at the other people in the boat, 'not unless he's disguised himself.'

'Are you thinking what I'm thinking?'

'Dangerous, right?'

He didn't answer and sat back on the gunwale, running his hand over the side. After a few minutes Dave looked up. 'Amazing. John, take a look at the wake, astern.'

The narrow prow cut through the water, disturbing the phosphorescence and producing a luminous green line that ran out at an angle either side of the boat. I stood precariously, one hand on Dave's head to steady myself, and checked both sides. It was amazing; the boat producing a green arrow in the water, from its point at the prow, widening until it finally dispersed just behind us. 'Amazing,' I confirmed, still standing.

'You should see it from the conning-tower of a 20,000 tonne Destroyer. Awesome!'

The skipper manoeuvred the boat slightly to the left and I sat down abruptly. He probably thought I was unsteady but he was mistaken. I had just realised where we were heading. 'Dave,' I hissed, 'we're going back to that fucking beach!'

His head pulled back from looking over the side and his mouth dropped open, as the sounds and sights on the beach appeared around the dark rocks like a scene from another world. 'No shit!'

I was about to dive over the side when I noticed that what we were witnessing was a party. Figures danced around beneath the painted palm trees like cannibals around a fire, the only difference being that the light from that fire wasn't red but blue. It was coming from one of those ultra-violet lamps that make everything glow radioactive. The paintings on the trees were now luminous colours of green and pink.

'It's a party! Foreigners! Ha!' I said much too loudly. I almost said, Thank God, we're saved!'

Dave beamed as he looked ahead at the beach. 'Fuckin' God almighty, Sir William!'

Picking up speed, the driver aimed us directly at the middle of the beach and cut the engine. We braced and the boat ploughed smoothly into the soft sand, rising as it went in. Dave was over the side before we'd even stopped swaying, swinging his arms to the beat that was blasting out from somewhere in the trees, while I stepped gingerly out of the boat and surveyed the scene.

The beach looked so different from when we'd been there earlier in the day. Obviously it wasn't sunny, but even though it was night, and you'd expect the place to be more forbidding, it wasn't. The combination of music, people and the cold light that glowed gently pale blue gave it a surreal, almost fairy-tale feel, a bit like a pantomime. No light penetrated past the first row of painted palm trunks into the black jungle behind.

The light also affected the water, and the phosphorescence in the shallows glowed so that the first five metres of sea looked like a luminous green carpet in which I'd been cut off at the ankles. Lifting a foot to make sure that there was more than just a stump on the end of my leg, I walked up on to the beach.

''Llo.' A Thai girl wearing hotpants came jerking down the beach towards me and held my hand. She swished her long black hair and led me to one end of the beach away from the dancing, where a group of people were sitting beneath the trees. 'You li' dri' wa'er or co'nu'?'

Shit, I thought, I'm gonna be raped by a load of Thai girls. Fantastic! 'C-coconut please.'

It wasn't a prerequisite to an orgy, not yet anyway, and it seemed I was being taken across to meet the group and their leader. Lying on the sand beneath three Thai girls was a man wearing a full tie-dye suit. His baggy trousers would have looked too big on a clown, and he had a matching top that looked like it had been made out of the sail of a yacht. One of the girls had her lips clamped over his face like a plunger while the other two, either side of him, giggled in anticipation, stroking his hair and stomach.

Feeling like a spare part, I coughed loudly.

The man pushed the kisser away from him. She tried to move back in but he held her forehead with the flat of his hand and looked up at me, lipstick smeared all around his mouth, making him look even more like a clown. 'You took your fooking time!'

SEVEN

Rick tried to stand but the girl he had been kissing clung on to his arm, forcing him to twist his way free. 'Gerroff.' Adjusting the baggy top, still on his knees, they kissed quickly. 'I told you, Ta,' he said as though lecturing a child, 'don't be so possessive, you know I don't like that,' and shuffled around to the other two girls and kissed their upturned faces. 'Later my dears,' he said, and stood up, brushing the sand out of his clothes before looking at me again. 'Where the fook have you been?'

We shook hands. 'Well it's great to see you too,' I said grinning. 'You don't look like you've had too bad a time.' I glanced down at the girls who were adjusting their skirts. 'It's like a harem. And you look like Coco the Clown in that gear.'

He held his imaginary lapels and pushed his nose up. 'No self-respecting member of the peerage would be seen wearing anything else.'

'I thought you'd been knighted?'

'Same thing.'

'You're not going to ask me to bow are you?' I said. ''Cause if you are you can fuck right off.'

'Oi, you're a Lord, now, John, so mind your fooking language.'

'I'm not a—'

'Shh, not so loud.' He looked back over his shoulder. The three girls on the sand were sipping from fresh coconuts, and one of them, I noticed, was wearing the silver shark's tooth necklace that I'd seen Rick wearing in India. 'Go down the beach a bit further, John, and I'll explain it all to you.' He glanced around. 'Back in a minute, girls.'

As we stepped to one side I said, 'That's your necklace isn't it?'

'Yeah, it means she's the one I'm with at the moment. So no touching! Anyway,' he turned to face me and we moved a step further away from the girls, 'your name's Lord John and I'm Sir William, so don't call me Rick. Least not around here.' He leaned against a tree, lighting a cigarette, and started to laugh.

'What's so funny?' I said, taking one of his cigarettes.

'Your face!'

'I'm the one who should be laughing: a man wearing pyjamas on a beach!'

He stared down at his billowing clothes. 'All my other clothes are full of holes.' Lighting both our cigarettes, he flicked the match into the bushes. 'It's not just your face though. While I've been sitting on this beach with so many pretty girls, I thought about you sweating it out in India. All that shit and stink. It's a funny thought.'

'Hilarious.'

Once he'd stopped giggling at his own joke he continued. 'How'd you get on in India anyway?'

I shrugged and leaned on the tree. 'Not bad. Got pissed off with it in the end, though. All the messing about with trains and that kind of stuff gets on your nerves after a while.'

'Well, I told you to come with me but you wouldn't listen. If you had, you could have been in the same position.' He glanced around the tree. 'See that girl, the one wearing my necklace? Thai royalty.'

I burst out laughing. 'Her? Oh come off it, what d'you take me for?'

'I'm telling you, her father is one of the richest men in Thailand. Don't believe me, ask her.' He started singing: 'Happy days are here again, da da da daa daa.'

'She's a prostitute, Rick.'

'Do you mind? You're talking about the woman I love. Da da da daa daa.'

I couldn't believe what I was hearing. I took a step sideways to get another look at the girl sitting under the trees, just to be sure that we were both referring to the same person. Suddenly I found myself sizing her up, trying to judge if she was blue blood material or not. 'Rick, if she's royalty then I'm a Lord,' I said, immediately wishing I hadn't fallen into the trap.

'Good, I'm glad you accept your new title.'

'Yeah, yeah. Tell me, no disrespect, but if she's the daughter of one of the richest men in Thailand, what's she doing here with you, one of the poorest?'

He held the cigarette daintily between his fingers as though in a holder. 'Because, dear boy, I'm one of the richest men in England.'

'Eh? You've lost me there.'

'Heard of a guy called Jim Thompson?'

I thought for a moment, quickly going over Hollywood stars and famous people. The music on the beach changed from its mechanical beat into a whirring trance that sounded like a thousand police sirens going off at the same time, and I momentarily lost track of what I had been thinking about.

'John?' he prompted.

'Um, no,' I said, snapping out of the rhythm, 'never heard of him.'

'Well Jim Thompson was an American bloke, a millionaire businessman who made his money in Thai silk and shit. Dead now, that was back in the fifties or something. Anyway, it just so happens that I look exactly like him. Everyone says so.'

Eyeing Rick's dress and long, now blond (from the sun) hair, I shook my head doubtfully. 'How the fuck would anyone remember what some fat fifties businessman looked like?'

'Because he's famous. They've still got his house in Bangkok, preserved like a museum. Tourists walk around taking photos, they sell souvenirs and shit with his picture on. That's where I met Ta.' He puffed the cigarette haughtily. 'Ta very much.'

The penny dropped; slowly but surely it all began to fall into place. 'I get it.' I used my cigarette as a pointer. 'She saw you in . . .'

'In the museum, yeah, and said, "You look like Jim Thompson".'

'To which you said?'

'Yes, that's because I'm his son!'

'Fuck me, you didn't?' I doubled over, half laughing and half in shock. 'She thinks you're this millionaire's son then?'

He nodded and puffed elegantly on the cigarette again.

We both laughed and I had to steady myself against the tree. 'I've got to hand it to you, Rick, you certainly know how to get yourself into hot water.'

He was unfazed. 'If all goes well, I'll be taking life very easy in future.' He stubbed his cigarette out on the tree. 'You too if you want to stay. She's got mates down here; those other two girls are her friends from Samui. We're all living in a house up on the hill. I've got no bills to pay, no food to buy, they cook, buy me weed, the works.'

'I can't believe it!' I thought about the last few days and drew in the last of the cigarette. 'How did you know I was here?' I said, looking for a place to deposit the butt. Throwing it on the sand seemed like the wrong thing to do so I held on to it.

'Tom—' Rick kept silent as a coconut was brought across for each of us by one of the girls, and he kissed her cheek. 'Thank you, Toom. Where's Tommy tonight?'

The girl curtsied, said, 'He go Bangko', and ran back with her arms in the air, waving to the sound of the beat.

'Toom?' I asked, scarcely believing what I'd just seen.

'Hmm,' he said, sucking on the straw. 'Toomy, Tommy's sister. Tommy's the guy you met at the Back Yard Pub.'

'He told me he didn't know you.'

'He doesn't know anyone called Rick. When he told me that someone was asking for a man called Rick I knew it must be you.' He paused. 'Fuck, John, where have you been? Every day I've been down to your hut, you're never in.'

I shrugged. 'With Dave mostly. Swimming . . .' Suddenly I remembered the finger. 'Oh shit, Rick, you'll never believe . . .'

Toomy came running back across and grabbed Rick's arm. 'We go now, no more talk. Take drug then dance, 'K?'

Rick turned back to me as he was led away. 'Tell me later, John,' he shouted, 'now it's party time. Come with me, you're gonna love this.'

EIGHT

I was led behind the speakers, behind the first row of tree trunks, to where a ragged-looking Thai girl sat on the exact same flat stone where we'd seen the severed finger. Her body obscured most of the stone's surface but it looked like it had been washed down: streaks of dried sand clung to the side of the rock in little dried up rivulets, some of them a washed-out red colour. Around the base the sand was cratered where the water had dripped off the sides.

The girl sitting on the flat surface had a tiny bottle in one hand and a pipette in the other. One by one the revellers shuffled up in line, went down on one knee and had a single teardrop of clear, glistening liquid dropped into their open eye. It was like being at the altar and accepting the body and blood of Christ.

Rick blinked hard and stood up, letting another believer take his place.

'What is it?' I asked nervously as he came back down the line.

'It ain't eye-drops,' he said, his eye still twitching. 'Acid. LSD.'

'She's not an optician then?'

'You'll definitely see more clearly. Have some.' I winced at the idea of having something dropped into my eye, and Rick said, 'You don't need to put in your eye, mouth's OK, just takes longer to work. It's brilliant.'

I queued up behind the others, presented my upturned face and received the droplet, before turning and going back towards the beach.

Dave was at the back of the queue hopping from foot to foot. 'John, what's going on? Whoo-ee! Way to go, Johnny-boy. Acid, neat, that's cool, whoop!'

'Don't put it in your eye,' I whispered as I went past, still grimacing from the taste.

When Dave got to the front he was bobbing so much that the girl had to put her hand on his head to keep him still. The first drop ran down his chin, which he licked off, before a second one hit the target. He licked his lips with a smack, came running back and leapt on top of me.

'Dave,' I said, 'calm down.'

'JohnnyJohnnyJohnny!' He ran back out through the trees, vaulted someone who was petting a dog, and went mad on the sandy dance floor.

Rick put his arm around my shoulder, his left eye still twitching and blinking. 'D'you know him?'

'Yeah, met him in Bangkok when I first arrived. He's a nice guy.'

'Listen, John,' the coconut girl was still trying to drag him away, 'if we don't talk tonight I'll see you tomorrow and we'll have a chat about everything. Meantime, let's boogie!'

'Rick, what about–' Remembering that he wasn't supposed to be 'Rick', I shut up. It didn't matter anyway; he was gone, swallowed up by the crowd and the music. A trance-like state seemed to be coming over most of the people, and one by one they began writhing to the beat.

At first I just wandered around the beach, walking and gently skipping to the music at the same time, not really intending to dance, the movement in my feet just seemed to come naturally the more I walked. At first a normal step became pronounced, so that when a foot was lifted into the air it took longer than normal to touch the ground again, a bit like when soldiers march in a funeral procession: up, along, down. Like a soldier I marched around, checking out the painted tress, skirting the crowd.

On one of the trees someone had painted a compass in luminous pink. A four-pointed pink star, and at each point of the compass, instead of the usual N, E, S, and W, were the words *Sex, Drugs, Rock, Roll.* And in place of the usual needle was a hand with a pointing finger.

The paint was still wet, and beneath the tree was a can of spray paint so I drew another, this time with the usual north, east, south and west points, but with a penis as a needle. I put the can down and stepped back to observe my handiwork. I couldn't remember who had told me about a compass.

Something moved at my feet, making me jump back with fright. Something bright and hairy, something that didn't make any sense. A dog was pissing against the tree; a dog that had been painted in luminous paint. It sniffed my leg, as though wondering if it had made the correct choice, and trotted off, its pink and green banded tail waving in the air as it went like a poisonous snake.

Fuck, my head felt funny, like it was imploding. Not a headache, just slight pressure; soft hands pushing it from both sides. I put my hands to my temples and closed my eyes in an attempt to clear the confusion, but when I opened them the trees in front of me were swaying in the wind. Close them again. Open again: the trees stopped moving. Close, open: moving again!

My legs, still dancing and making my body bob, were something I'd forgotten about, like they belonged to someone else. I did another circuit of the crowd and walked down to the water's edge, thinking it would be nice to look at the rocks at one end of the beach. A pair of soft hands went up to relieve the pressure on my temples. I started and spun around.

'You wan' ma' lo' to me?'

Without answering the beautiful girl, I turned away to look at the rocks, swallowing hard to rid my throat of the dry coconut-flavoured mucus that had formed. Now the rocks were moving! Not swaying, but gently heaving, like waves lapping the shore. The water was still dead calm when I looked down and blinked hard, but the landscape was moving. First the rocks and then the sand beneath the rocks. The trees around the beach were rigid poles with Rasta haircuts, and the people beneath them were little wind-up toys, but the rocks were soft and flowing, as thick as an oil slick.

'You wan' ma' lo'?'

Dancing now, not marching, my legs carried their alien body back up the sloping beach to the crowd, and the sand, no longer soft, was suddenly as easy to walk on as concrete. I didn't recognise anybody but everyone must have known me, otherwise why were they all smiling in my direction? At first I thought that maybe I'd left my clothes behind, and I consciously looked down to check that I was still dressed. Then I felt my jaw aching because of the smile on my face; a grin so wide it made my cheeks sore.

A girl with hair like flowing gold flung her arms around my neck and at the same time jumped up, putting her legs around my waist. There was a cluck from someone very close behind, like right against my ear, but it was ignored by both of us. Golden hair kissed me and then bit my nose before letting her head loll back and swing its hair wildly from side to side. The muscles on the inside of her groin dug into my waist for support and she let go with her hands, falling upside down. With her legs still around me and her palms flat on the sand, I grabbed her thighs and turned her over and back on to her feet, as though we had meant to do that all along.

'You wan' ma' lo', ni' guy?' came the voice behind me again. An arm tried to encircle my waist, the hand grabbing at my crotch, but I was already moving towards the dark shadow that had surrounded the bright trunk of a tree.

Something was happening beneath one of the palm trees, though nobody except me was apparently paying any attention. The dog I'd seen earlier, or maybe another one, was wildly circling the tree. It reminded me of swingball, 'The game for one or two players', only this tennis ball was capable of going around with no players, and it barked. My head rotated with the barking tennis ball. Around, around, around the dog went.

Gentle fingers went between my legs from behind and came up under my shorts to support my balls. 'I lo' you, man. Wan' ma' lo' to you, man.' The hand couldn't keep its grip and slipped free, unable to find the same rhythm that my legs moved to; a rhythm that was partly dance and partly walking again. I moved near to the dark shadow that was moving up a luminous corkscrew.

A band of black with four uneven corners that moved upwards, first the top two then the bottom two, shimmied up the palm tree. Bright pictures went dark and then reappeared again a moment later as the person climbed until he reached the top. My head was still but however hard I tried to focus on the black object I couldn't. Greenery started to fall around me like heavy rain, leaves and sticks, some fluttering and whirly-birding, others crashing, still attached to their branches. Coconuts started to fall with such impact on the sand that the dog bolted for cover in the trees, and a few people looked up to see where the objects were coming from. 'He's off his fucking head,' someone said. 'Fucking crazy,' another.

My hand was grabbed and I was yanked towards the trees, stumbling through the bushes. I was suddenly standing in darkness, the lights of the party appearing like a stained-glass window that had been shot through with vandals' stones, barely penetrating the leaves of the vines.

'Tha's dangerous, man. Hit you head, can kill!'

My mouth opened but no words came, so I just looked down at the small Thai girl and tried to swallow what remaining spit I had. 'Dry,' I croaked.

'You wan' dri'?' Her arms encircled my neck and I bent forward obligingly as her wet tongue was thrust into my parched mouth.

Pulling out of the kiss, I straightened and tried to move away. 'I just want to get a drink.'

'Tha's dangerous, I tol' you.' Her arms went tighter around my neck. 'No, you stay here wi' me,' she said kissing my lips. 'You safe here.'

NINE

Sand. On my lips, in my mouth, hair, ears, nose, throat, up my arse and down my foreskin; the tiny glassy grains were everywhere. I hadn't opened my eyes to see it but I knew by touch alone, by probing fingers and thumbs. Also my cheek hurt, and every movement or roll of my head was like sandpaper on my face. Slowly I opened one eye to see which direction my body was facing in, to see whether the sight would be blue or green.

It was green. The bright green of the jungle, lush against a blue early morning sky. The slender palm leaves wobbled and waved like individual fingers wagging a warning to me in the almost undetectable breeze that ruffled them awake. Each leaf shining in the sun like a green dagger on a slender spring, angling itself this way and that.

Ugh, my head. My aching head. I tried to open my other eye, the one that was half buried in sand, but couldn't; it was stuck with sleep. Lying parallel to the jungle must mean that my back was facing the sea, so turning over just meant a half roll downhill. The slope of the beach accommodated, and, moving off my dead arm, first the blindingly blue sky faced me and then, with another quarter-turn, the shimmering blue sea. And Dave's totally naked black figure.

Dave was standing knee-deep in the water with his bare buttocks facing the beach, a sparkling jet of golden liquid shooting out between his legs and forming a little hemisphere of foam on top of the water. The word that my mouth tried to form and then shout just came out as a loud groan, and Dave looked over his shoulder, both hands still on their task, and smiled.

'Better out than in, my mom always used to say,' he shouted, the sound of his loud American accent piercing the silent morning air. He started to whistle tunelessly while he pissed, the sound drifting out across the water.

I turned over and my other eye popped open, though it only saw in a pale shade of green for the first minute. Going from one eye to the other, checking their progress vision-wise, I blinked and took in the scene around me. As far as the beach was concerned there were only a few people left on it. Rick was asleep by the trees, using his hands as a pillow, while the young Thai girl he'd been with was just behind him with another girl, cutting holes in coconuts. She looked up and waved a knife at me. 'You wan' co'nu'?' and then continued ramming the pointed blade into the shell, using another coconut as a hammer.

I stood and took a step forwards, tripping over the body that was lying beneath my feet. The Thai girl moaned, turned over in her sarong sheet and went on sleeping.

'Here,' the coconut girl said as I approached, 'jus' for you, Lor' John.'

'Thanks,' I managed to say as the hairy shell was placed into my outstretched hands. I gulped down some milk and nodded at Rick, lying crumpled on the sand beside the girl. 'Is he awake yet?'

She prodded Rick's back with a painted toenail, not bothering to move from her log seat, and pronounced him 'Not. He lazy rich bas'ard.' She suddenly seemed to remember who she was talking to and, looking up wide-eyed and squirming nervously on her seat, she leaned forward and stroked his hair. 'Bu' I lo' him, yeah. Rea' lo' you, man.'

A big splash took my attention away from her and I squinted at the bright sea. Dave was jumping clear of the water, lifting his legs as high as possible and bombing his own shadow. Every time he came up, smiling and wiping the water from his own astonished expression, the sun glinting on his polished skin, he immediately searched the water for his own reflection.

'Do you have another one?' I asked, turning back to the girl.

The other Thai girl who sat behind Ta handed me one and winked. 'For you.'

'No,' I said, 'it's for him,' and nodded at Dave.

'You frien' crazy, he climb tree when I as' him ma' lo',' she said, shaking her head dismissively. 'Loo' at him. Li' a fu'in' kid, playing in the wa'er. Jeez!'

I took the coconut and walked out into the sunshine, trying to remember which girl was which and what their names were.

Where were all the people that had been on the beach the night before? I had estimated there to be at least thirty people dancing, but now there were only us. Not only that but the generator and sound system had gone too. The boat that had ferried us here was gone, and where the tide had flowed and ebbed there were not even any marks where its V-shaped hull had cut a groove into the sand. At the other end, where we had previously seen the long-tail tethered to a ring, only a length of rope hung limp and wet against the rock, like the tail of a buried dog.

Holding a coconut in each hand, I waded knee-deep into the water and scanned the mirror-like surface for any sign of Dave. He was gone. I moved further in up to my midriff before a long dark shadow moved through the water towards me, breast-stroking. Such an obvious attempt to scare me didn't deserve to go unpunished so when he grabbed my ankle and tried to pull me down I didn't move. Instead, I held the coconut just above the water in the place where I thought he was most likely to surface. When he eventually pushed hard off the seabed, his head came up against the waiting shell with such force that it sounded like the *clop* of a one-legged horse.

Dave immediately doubled over, holding his head in both hands. 'Jesus fuckin' Christ,' he spluttered, half in pain and half in shock at the unexpected impact, 'what d'you do that for?'

'Accident,' I giggled. 'Here, thought you might like a split coconut.'

We stood up to our waists in the water for a moment, drinking our milk and admiring our feet through the crystal clear water. Dave said, 'Got to hand it to Sir William. That man really has his shit together here.'

'I thought I told you, he's not . . .'

'Not Sir William, yeah yeah.' He glanced around. 'Anyway where *is* Sir William?'

I clucked my tongue. 'Over there, by the trees. I'll introduce you to him when he wakes up.'

Dave nodded and sucked on the coconut. 'This is beautiful, man: fresh coconuts, clear water, beautiful Asian girls. And that party! *Man*, what a night, whoo-ee!' He gulped the rest of the milk down and lobbed the shell with stunning accuracy on to the only rock that was still visible above the water's surface. The shell splintered, with Dave providing the appropriate sound effect, '*Bwooff!*'

'Good shot.'

'Do better?'

I quickly finished mine and threw it far short of the target, *Plop*.

'Huh! Man, you ain't thrown a grenade before.'

'More used to a cricket ball, I'm afraid,' I said, and did a bowling motion.

'Well la-di-da, Lord John, la-di-fuckin'-da!' He slapped me on the back and dived under the water.

After a short swim to clear away the sleep from my eyes (going underwater and blinking a dozen times always does the trick), we walked back up the beach.

I put my arm around his shoulder. 'Dave, there's something I need to tell you about. These girls think that I'm a Lord and—'

He looked shocked. 'You are, man.'

Suddenly what I was about to tell him seemed a bit pointless. What was the use of explaining to Dave that he should go along with the façade if he believed it anyway? I hesitated and then decided to relieve my conscience anyway.

'Well,' I said, 'as I've already told you, I'm not a Lord, and Rick's name is Rick, not Sir bloody William. But the thing is, Dave, these girls, and everyone else on Koh Pha-Ngan for all I know, think that he is some kind of royalty.' I shrugged. 'He's got something going on here that I'm not really sure about.'

'Listen, man,' Dave turned to face me, 'your friend showed me a good time last night, one of my best and believe me I've had a few. An' if he wants to call himself Friar fuckin' Tuck that's all right with me. I ain't got no complaints. That sucker *knows* how to party.' He slapped my back again and we went over to where Rick was sitting, cigarette in one hand, coconut in the other.

'Morning . . . Sir William,' I said meekly. I felt so silly using the name that it made me blush.

He gestured for us to sit. 'William's fine, as you well know, John.' He looked at Dave.

'Oh,' I said, suddenly remembering that the two hadn't met, 'this is Dave. Dave, William.'

'Hi, Sir William. Pleasure to meet you, heard a lot about you.' Dave reached down and shook Rick's hand, and just as I remembered what else I was supposed to warn Dave about, he continued. 'D'you know, you look just like that American businessman. You know, the one who used to do all that silk shit in the ol' days. Read about it in my guidebook. Jeez, what's that guy's name?' He closed his eyes in thought.

'Thompson,' Rick answered, 'Jim Thompson.'

Dave snapped his fingers. 'Yeah that's him. Man you look just like him!'

Rick looked at me and raised his eyebrows with a 'told you so' look.

Ta perked up. 'Tha's because he his son, man.'

'His *what*?' Dave exclaimed, and eyed Ta as she rubbed Rick's belly with the flat of her hand.

'Willia' his son. My baby son o' rich man.'

'His son?' Dave slapped his thigh. 'Huh! That guy's son would be at least...'

'Not as old as you,' Rick butted in before Dave could say that that made Rick about 150 years old.

Ta frowned but then settled her head back down on to Rick's chest and looked up longingly at his face, kitten-like, and for the first time since arriving I wondered who was hoodwinking who. She didn't look much like royalty, but then what would the daughter of a millionaire Thai man look like? Especially on a beach where the trappings of wealth and city life are stripped away. Take off her crown and put the Queen of England in a supermarket checkout and she'd look just like any other old granny.

I quickly changed the subject. 'What happened to all the other people that were here last night?'

Rick stretched and said, 'They've gone back to Hat Rin probably, the next rave's not until next week. We only have two a week. Too many hassles what with the police and the Mafia. Not only that, but we can't make enough acid for any more parties.'

'You make that stuff?' Dave remarked, clearing away some dead leaves and sitting down on the cool sand.

'Course, up in the jungle where Ta lives.'

I looked up at the trees inquisitively. 'How d'you get it all here then? Where's your boat?'

'Boat?' He laughed. 'We don't use a boat.' He sat up and pointed down the tree line. 'There's a path through there, leads right up and over the hill. If you keep going, eventually you come out at Hat Rin. Fooking long walk though, really hot.'

I was expecting Dave to say smugly, 'Told you they had a land route,' but he was still frowning, pondering Rick's age in relation to his father. Wiping a finger across my brow, a trickle of sweat ran down my palm. 'It's hot here,' I said, and puffed my cheeks.

'Much hotter up there. We spend most of our time down here to escape from the heat. It's OK at night, there's usually a breeze, but during the day,' Rick shook his head, 'forget it.'

I paused to look at Ta and then back at Rick. 'So are you living up there now?'

'Mostly, yeah. I come down to town when I want something different to eat, but that's about it.' He stood up and brushed the sand from his Coco the Clown meets tie-dye hippy outfit. 'I'll explain it all in more detail later.' With his back to Ta he gave her a shifty sideways glance, then leaned forward and whispered, 'Don't want her to hear. Ahem! Anyway, that girl who wouldn't leave you alone last night is Muck. I don't mean she's not worthy, I mean her name's Muck.' He giggled. 'Her and Toomy there are from Samui. Did I tell you this already?'

'Yeah,' I said, 'about six hours ago.'

'Oh. Well anyway, they're all living with us, so you and Muck can share a room, Dave can stick with Toomy if he wants, and we can all sleep at the house. What d'you think?'

'Muck?'

'Yeah I know, funny huh? It gets worse.' He shook his head, grinning. 'D'you remember when we had a top ten of deformities in India? Well, now I've got a top ten of funny Thai names. Some of them you won't believe. There's . . . Oh,' he stopped, having remembered something, 'I almost forgot, did you find Big Balls?'

'No,' I said dejectedly. No sign.'

'Shame, I'd like to have seen some footage. Still got the camcorder?'

Before I could answer, Ta came up and touched Rick's arm. 'We go ba' now. Eat brea'fas'.'

Rick looked at me so I rubbed my stomach and nodded.'OK,' he said, 'wake Muck and we can all go together. Got enough food?'

'I got egg, bacon an' toas' jus' for you an' frien'. Ma' ve' tas'y.' She ran over and shook her friend awake, shouting something in Thai. Muck looked like death warmed up when she woke and didn't seem at all happy with her friend for waking her. A few harsh words were exchanged before she saw me and put on a smile. They gathered what little possessions they all had and walked off in front, talking mostly Thai to each other.

'Dave.' I shook his arm and he snapped out of the trance.'You coming?'

'Uh? Where?'

'To Rick's place. Haven't you been listening to anything?'

'Sir William's place?' he said, looking around in confusion as though he'd just been deposited on the beach.'Oh yeah, course.'

I thought again about how to explain the situation to him, not really wanting to go through the whole thing, and said,'Dave, Rick's not really the son of Jim Thompson, you know?'

He went to pick up his shirt from the beach where he'd left it, staring fixedly at the sand, his brow a ploughed field of deep thought.'John,' he said quizzically as he returned,'if he is the son of Jim Thompson, that makes him fifty years old. At least!'

TEN

The house was stunning, or rather the location was. The house itself was just a two-storey bamboo and wood job with half a dozen largish rooms and a balcony that ran around the outside. It had a small front porch and a sloping pitched roof that came right down almost as low as the balcony handrail, like the brim of a wide hat.

The location of the house was pure tropics. Set high up on the jungle hillside, we had a clear view over the tops of the palms right down to the sea. Standing on the balcony, one could just make out the rocks that separated our cove from Hat Rin, but otherwise our seclusion was complete.

At first Dave wouldn't give up his hut on Hat Rin beach to move into the house. He said that it was too much of a good thing, and that if he did move in with us he'd probably never, ever be able to leave. And although he quite liked Toomy, and had even grown fond of her strange Thai ways, he wanted to retain some sort of link to the outside world; some connection to other travellers who came and went on a weekly basis in Hat Rin.

Rick and I thought this was understandable and attributed it to him being American, and therefore insular, teasing him over it whenever he showed even the slightest fondness for anything Western, or if he expressed a disliking for any local food. Sometimes one of the girls would cook a particularly hot curried fish, or bitter, salty pork, which Dave would say he couldn't eat. 'Go back down to town and get a hamburger,' we'd gibe. In truth, however, Dave was more than equal to the both of us, who struggled through some of the food just because he was watching. Rick told me that before we arrived he often threw a lot of the food out the window when Ta wasn't looking.

After about two weeks of to-ing and fro-ing on a daily basis from Hat Rin through the jungle to the house, Dave gave in. He appeared early one morning standing outside on the path, pack slung over his shoulder and his usual back-to-front US Navy baseball cap on his head, shouting obscenities up at the window. 'You lazy no-good fuckin' hippies, I'll tear ya limb from fuckin' limb! Got me a grenade an' if you don't open this door, so help me I'll blow this house apart along with half this cock-suckin' hillside, God damn it!'

We let him in.

He claimed that he'd become tired of the same old talk at Hat Rin, and that the recent full-moon party had been the last straw. According to him, hundreds of travellers from just about every island in the Gulf of

Thailand had converged on the beach, all waiting for something to happen. Which of course it did: *the moon came out!*

There was no sign of any real partying and, just as Rick had warned, the so-called full-moon party turned the beach into a cross between a flea market and a railway station. Locals made a killing by extending their restaurants so far on to the beach that you couldn't pass by without buying something (at wildly inflated prices), and everyone hung around for the party-train to arrive and carry them on to some unforgettable, once in a blue-moon rave up. The train was delayed. *Forever.*

The real reason that Dave had finally moved up to the house, though, was because Suzy had left Koh Pha-Ngan. It wasn't so much that he wanted to be with her, he spent most of his time with Toomy anyway, but rather that he felt responsible for her well-being. She had almost been raped by a Thai man one night while walking home from the Back Yard Pub along a dimly lit jungle path. Someone had heard her shouts and chased the perpetrator away before any serious damage could be done but the effect on Dave seemed to be worse than on Suzy. He vowed to find the man who had tried it on but, after being told that the Thai had left the island and gone back to his home in Samui, Dave was left feeling guilty. Suzy's leaving to travel north with a girlfriend took the weight off Dave considerably, and he soon had the spring back in his step and the voice in his throat.

Rick and I spent most of our time during those first few weeks without Dave going over the details of what we'd done since being apart, and talking about the people we'd met. I also told him about the beating and the severed finger, to which he gave the same, matter-of-fact reply as Dave had: 'Life is cheap out here, John.'

For his part, he had spent his time after leaving India, first in Bangkok and then had travelled directly south to Koh Pha-Ngan as planned. Whenever I suggested that he might have better spent his time by travelling around the country, he reminded me of the philosophy of staying put when you find something you like. 'When I get bored,' he said, 'that's when I'll move on.'

I agreed.

ELEVEN

Dave was rapidly becoming a convert to our travel philosophy, and although he held a round-the-world ticket that required him to be in certain places at certain times in order to receive maximum benefit, he could see the futility of running quickly from country to country just to satisfy that end. The ticket wasn't refundable or reroutable so, on his first night at the house, we held a ceremonial burning.

The three of us went down to the beach at midnight, alone, and placed the folded ticket on a piece of dry driftwood. Dave squirted lighter fuel that he'd bought for his Zippo on to the ticket and it was lit and sent out to sea, the three of us watching, chest-deep in water, as the dark current took it around the rocks and out of sight. Dave whistled The Last Post.

After smoking a couple of joints we lay down at the water's edge. Rick was lying beside me, snoring evenly, and looked like he had cut himself shaving, a single king-size rizla stuck to the side of his face with sweat. I turned back to look at the night sky, breathing in the air with a deep suck and filling my lungs. I could still smell the grass we had smoked and, reaching out blindly and picking up one of the used roaches from the sand, I sniffed the residue that had stained the cigarette paper jet black, marvelling at its simple narcotic potency. 'There are probably thousands of backpackers on beaches all over the world right this minute, smoking their brains out on grass,' I mumbled to no one in particular.

Resting up on one elbow, Dave flicked a lighted butt into the air, that sailed through the stars like a red satellite. 'Maybe there's someone up there sitting on a beach smoking their brains out too,' he said, his voice soft in the still night air. 'High as a kite on the shores of The Sea of Tranquillity.'

'Millions of them.' Rick woke up and rolled on to one side looking for his lighter, and using his fingers he ploughed through the soft sand, sifting it like a comb. 'What time is it?'

I checked my watch. 'Half past twelve. If you want a paper you don't need to look further than the end of your nose.'

'Uh?' He went cross-eyed and pulled it off, talking to it in an attempt to copy my accent. 'Oh you facking kant, there you are.'

I didn't even realise I had an accent and said, angrily, 'I don't speak like that.'

'You do. You're a cookney incha?'

'Not really.' I looked back up at the zillions of twinkling stars. 'They say to be a cockney you need to have been born within the sound of the Bow Bells in East London. I was born in South London.'

'Well that's London innit?' He finished making the joint and lit it up, the light making his face look scary against the dark backdrop of palm trees and night sky. He lay back down and I watched as he drew on it, producing a red ember bright enough to light his cheeks and nose.

We lay in silence for a few minutes, enjoying the gentle breeze that was carrying his smoke back up the beach and into the bushes, and I said, 'This place is fucking amazing, don't you think, Claude?'

'Hmm.' Rick looked over at me. 'Who's Claude?'

I said nothing for a few seconds.

'John?'

'I just remembered a blue film that I watched once. In it there was this guy called Claude with a cock shaped like a banana.' I turned my head. 'He looked exactly like you; like a Dutch rock star.'

Dave was sniggering. 'Jim Thompson was in nudie movies?'

'I only meant that you look like him,' I laughed, and looked back up at the sky, taking the joint. 'Don't get it out and show us or anything.'

We lay in silence again, listening to the sounds of the beach. The only noise was the breeze when it picked up, just strong enough to rustle the leaves in the trees behind us. Occasionally it stopped, but just as the lull became too long and I began to sweat it would pick up again, cooling me down. Apart from the gentle rustle of the trees the world around us was utterly silent, even the lapping waves had died down and, strangely, so had the jungle insects.

I shrugged to myself at the anomaly and drew on the joint, comforted by the heat that was produced against my nose and face every time a deep enough drag was taken.

As the fuzzy feeling started to hit my brain I noticed a strange light over by the rocks and sat up giddily, trying to focus. 'Rick, Dave, look.'

'Wow, flames!' Rick said, and tried to stand.

As quickly as we could under the influence of the dope (which turned out to be a stumbling, weaving snail's pace), Dave and I walked down the beach towards the rocks for a closer inspection. We couldn't climb over the boulders and decided to swim round to see what it was. When we rounded the curve and saw the enormity of the fire we didn't know what to do.

The piece of wood with the ticket on must have floated into some other driftwood that had been washed up on the rocks, and those few pieces, sun-baked over months, had caught fire, set off by a small block of oily polystyrene that was bubbling away by the water's edge. The washed-up driftwood was in turn entangled with dry, wind-fallen palm branches which ran all the way up the side of the hill, spreading out into the jungle floor. The whole lot was ablaze!

We panicked, climbed up on to the rocks and quickly put some of it out by splashing water over it, but without buckets our meagre handfuls of seawater only went so far. I could only splash about ten feet up the rocks, and Dave could only hold so much in his mouth at one time. We beat it with sticks, threw rocks at it and pissed on it, but all to no avail.

Eventually, having roasted our bare bodies like lobsters on the flames, we gave up and dived back into the cooling sea, the salt stinging my chest and arms so much that it felt like being attacked by a hundred jellyfish at once.

Rick was standing at the water's edge when we got back to the beach, his face lit up by the orange glow above the water. 'Am I hallucinating?' he asked when we approached. 'Please tell me I am.'

From the beach it looked like a scene from one of those old dinosaur films, where the finale inevitably involves the hero escaping from the monsters whilst volcanoes erupt behind him. He simply swims across a small lagoon, towards the cave that leads back to his own time zone, while all hell breaks loose around him in 'The Land that Time Forgot'.

We both told Rick that he wasn't hallucinating and that we didn't think it wise to hang around. At first he couldn't move, and we had to pull him away, but as soon as we cleared the sand and entered the tree line, taking one last look back to make sure that we all weren't hallucinating, the brisk walking pace became a run.

Falling over logs, smacking head first into trees, scraping arms and legs on branches; none of it mattered because we couldn't feel the pain in our panic. Dave was almost castrated when he ran full pelt into a tree root that had worked its way out of the ground and stuck up in the air. '*Ooff!*'

Half walking, half carried, we got him the back to the house, blood gushing down his leg where the root had raked a piece of skin the length of a cigarette out of his inner thigh. In the rush to see how the fire was progressing Dave forgot his pain, and Toomy's attempt at nursing him, and the three of us rushed up the small wooden steps, through the large top floor room and out on to the wooden balcony.

On the way back to the house I'd prayed constantly. Prayed that when we reached the house and looked out from the top floor I would see nothing, just the usual stunning view of the dark palm tops, running like a soft blanket down the hillside to the silvery moonlit sea. Normally the only thing visible in the distance on any given night was the faint, dull shape of the small, rocky outcrop, and beyond that another island.

It was all still there tonight but with one major difference: colour! The view had always been monochrome at night. Dozens of varying shades, but still monochrome, with the possible exception of a blue tinge. Tonight we had glorious technicolour. Or rather, monochrome with more than a tinge of orange in the bottom, right-hand corner of the view.

The flames were now as high as the first palm trees, and, although the fire didn't appear to be broad, two or three palms at most, it was there, glowing as a reminder of how stupid we had been to light a fire in the first place.

Toomy came up and dressed Dave's leg while the three of us sat and watched in silence. And, as if a Masonic signal had passed between us, no one mentioned the fire to any of the girls. If they saw it and smelt the burnt wood on our bodies, they would have made the connection; it seemed safer if we distanced ourselves from the whole episode. If the island did burn down overnight, we didn't want to be held responsible. We were all well aware that each piece of land on the island, each and every bay, in fact every square foot and each individual palm tree, had an owner who was willing to kill in order to protect his investment.

Ta became suspicious every time we went out to check, asking why on earth we didn't stay outside like we always did. 'Too cold,' said Rick unconvincingly, and immediately broke out in perspiration. I said that there were too many mosquitoes out tonight, and Dave said nothing at all, he just stared at me and Rick, nervously trying to read his guidebook.

Unable to sustain our level of anxiety any longer, and eventually too tired from nervous exhaustion, we sloped off to bed, each of us using the excuse of relieving ourselves to check the blaze one last time.

'I'm just going outside for a piss,' Rick explained woodenly to Ta, and left.

'Why you tell me, man?' she asked. He went out and came back a moment later shaking his head. He looked at me, very worried.

'Umm, I'm just going outside for a piss,' I said to Muck.

She frowned. 'Why you don' use toile'?'

'Me too,' Dave said, running in behind me, 'I, err, need to pee,' We went out and came back in without even going through the motions.'Jeez,'he said through clenched teeth, and we all went to bed

I lay and stared at the ceiling; a ceiling that I was sure looked much more orange than normal, though whenever I looked out of the window to see if it was the glow from the fire, all I could see was a moonlit sky, the blackness of the jungle, and the same orange glow near the rocks. With a sigh in my throat and an empty butterfly feeling in my stomach, I lay on the bed and tried not to think of fire.

When I was about eight years old, almost exactly the same thing had happened to my brother and me. Adjacent to the council estate where we grew up was a piece of land that all the local kids referred to as 'the dump'. No one had used the acre or so of land for years and, although ear-marked for development of public housing, the council had fenced it off and let the footings of the previously demolished brick houses become a weed-infested playground for the kids from the nearby tower blocks. (Who says the government doesn't provide adequate recreational facilities for youngsters?)

My brother and I, along with our friends, spent most of our childhood on this stretch of wasteland, smashing up old TVs, playing war and climbing the few remaining trees in order to place a sofa at the top-most branches as a comfortable lookout spot. We always used the dump to burn our plastic Air-Fix models too, and it was on one such occasion that, what started as the ceremonial melt-down of the *Bismarck* almost turned into the Great Fire of London II.

We beat the burgeoning flames with sticks and branches that night as best we could but couldn't contain them as they quickly spread among the dry summer grass and bags of fly-tipped household rubbish. After five minutes of trying it was called off, and the half-dozen of us ran out through a hole in the corrugated iron fencing and back to our respective homes.

All night I lay awake in bed, listening to the sound of fire engine sirens as they were summoned from all the nearby stations in a joint effort to put out the fire. My brother and I lay there trying to pick up the gist of the earnest conversation my mum and dad were having in the next room. 'I don't know, Rose,' I heard my dad say with mounting concern, 'there're a lot of fire engines, it must be something big.'

We were shitting ourselves!

The next day, eager to see what had happened, but at the same time afraid that the police would make a house-to-house inspection using sniffer-dogs that were trained to smell burnt wood on little boys' clothes, my brother and I went down the road to school. The devastation was considerable. What had once been a greenish piece of land amongst the concrete of the estate, was now a single black square on an otherwise grey chessboard. There were no remaining trees, apart from one Hiroshima-style charcoaled stump, and all of the perimeter corrugated metal fencing had melted and twisted, buckled beyond repair.

The others who had been party to the sinking of the *Bismarck* were also standing on the roadside that morning, uneasily watching the few remaining firemen as they rolled up their hoses and prepared to leave. We stood around, occasionally stepping aside at the request of the council operatives who now had the grim task of cleaning up the black, sooty water that ran like rivers of carbon in every direction.

None of us went to school that day, afraid that the police, alsatians walking obediently alongside, would be scouring the place and asking all sorts of difficult questions. My brother, with his usual imagination, said he'd seen a meat wagon pull into the schoolyard and that we would probably be hung for the crime. He said it would be safer if we all went home and complained to our mums of stomach pains to get the day off. I already did have pains in the stomach! And, as a silent signal passed between us, we all went home and agreed never to speak or boast about the incident to anyone, ever. A vow of silence that I have maintained until now.

When I did manage to doze off, I was only asleep for about an hour before a cockerel started crowing and woke me up. Rick and Dave were already standing over me. 'C'mon, John, let's go,' they said in unison.

Without needing an explanation, I looked around at Muck, rubbed the sleep from my eyes, and quietly slipped off the bamboo mat on to the creaky wooden floor. The three of us tiptoed out into the morning sunlight and made our way down the long jungle path towards the beach. Dave led the way, commando-like in his blue, Navy-issue vest and cap, his wild afro sticking out of the sides like a bald man.

'D'you keep your money under that hat, Dave?' Rick said as we rushed downhill.

He didn't turn around to answer the question. 'Think I'd tell you if I did? Helps me to think.' He hurdled the tree root that had injured him the night before like an Olympian.

'Think about what?' I asked.

He shrugged. 'Stuff.'

'Stuff? What stuff?'

'I dunno, stuff,' he said irritably. 'Don't ask, man, we're in enough trouble as it is.' He pushed through the last bush and trotted out on to the sand followed by Rick and I. All eyes swung right towards the rocks.

'It's all right,' Rick said happily, almost overcome with joy, 'the trees are still here.' And without another word, the three of us stripped and ran into the water, in a mad rush to swim to the rocks and be the first to proclaim it 'OK'.

Dave was the first up. He swam hardest and seemed most anxious about what damage we might have caused, probably because it was his ticket and his idea to set fire to it.

'How is it?' I shouted, and climbed up out of the water. Dave was a good twenty feet ahead, climbing hand-over-fist up boulders towards the trees. 'Dave?'

'Fuckin' brilliant!' he called back, standing on the highest rock, hands on hips. 'Huh!'

For the first twenty feet or so the rocks were completely blackened. Where the rocks stopped and the foliage began, the grasses and bushes had been completely wiped out, flattened into a carpet of fine grey ash with delicate little grilled twigs standing up like charred hairs, ready to fall at the slightest breeze.

Barefoot, we walked into the jungle, trying not to brush up against the tree trunks. Although the bases of the palm trees were black up to about head height, they were still healthy and as sturdy as ever.

'No problem,' I proclaimed, with both hands against a trunk. 'Go in further, Dave, let's see how far it went.'

'That's it! It stops right here.' We stood side by side, toes touching the line where the black ash stopped and living grass began: a perfect, crisp line that ran in a semi-circle. 'It just stopped,' Dave said, incredulous.

'Looks like it. Unless someone put it out.' I turned to Rick. 'Does anyone else ever come around here?'

He shook his head, still staring at the ground. 'I didn't think so, but, looking at this, now I'm not sure.'

Dave took his cap off and wiped his forehead. 'This has been put out, look.' He bent down and picked up a clean cigarette butt from the ashes. 'New.'

'Rick, what about Toomy's brother?'

'Tommy? I haven't seen him since you guys first got here.'

I turned to Dave and inspected the used cigarette. 'That guy we saw being beaten up,' I said slowly, 'the one who had his finger chopped off. They didn't call him Tommy did they?'

TWELVE

Whether someone had put out that fire or not, and whether or not the guys doing the beating up had called the beatee Tommy didn't matter to Rick. As far as he was concerned the fire was out, we had been saved from a fate worse than death, and Tommy, as his sister had stated, was in Bangkok visiting relatives. After all, Tommy was a popular name in Thailand; Hat Rin beach even had a 'Tommy's Bungalows'.

Rick also pointed out to me that he'd been here quite a while and hadn't seen anything untoward happen yet, not to him or anyone else, and reminded us how easy we had it. I had to admit that he was right. When he went through the good points: the beach, the parties, the drugs, the house, virtually free living, and beautiful Thai girls to boot, I quickly forgot about any of the possible dangers involved, if indeed there were any, and went about the business of having a good time.

The one and only important thing Rick and I still had to do was phone England and tell our families that we weren't coming back: something I'd been dreading and avoiding like the plague ever since the three of us had agreed not to go home.

'How long d'you reckon you'll stay away for?' I said as we walked along the jungle path towards Hat Rin, trying to size up my companion's situation. I needed a long-term commitment.

'As long as it takes, John,' Rick replied without looking up from the uneven track. 'Or until I run out of money.'

Good reply, I thought, and nodded my approval.

Rick held a branch aside for me to pass. 'What d'you think they'll say when you tell them?'

'Dunno really,' I said, ducking under. 'My ol' man'll probably go on about my career, my house and all that shit.'

He let the branch spring back. 'You got a house?'

'Yeah, well, a mortgage anyway.' I'd already thought about this once or twice over the past week. At first it had worried me, but as the days went on it seemed a lot of fuss over nothing. Why the fuck should I worry about a pile bricks and mortar? 'What about you,' I said walking on, 'what'll happen with your missus?'

'Hmm,' he shrugged, 'just tell her. Cross that bridge when I come to it. I dunno, I haven't thought about her really. Strange when you think that we've been together for seven years.'

We wended our way through the steamy jungle and came out on to Hat Rin beach, and by the time we got to the telephone office we were both prickly with sweat. The company that ran the international phone service was obviously reasonably well off, installing air conditioning that was much too powerful for the size of the room. It was like walking into a fridge. We both flopped on to the leather couch by the service counter, and the receptionist looked at Rick before glancing outside to see if it was raining.

'Yes, sir,' she said looking back, after seeing that it was still sunny, 'where you like telephone?'

'I would like to telephone England,' I said and stood up, 'London to be precise. And he would also like to phone England.' I thumbed at Rick, slouching behind me.

'Thank you, sir, booth number two please.'

I turned to Rick. 'Who's going first, you or me?'

He pointed at me and said nothing.

'Coward.' I walked into booth number two and stared at the telephone. Someone at the other end is going to get a shock. Who should it be first: parents, fiancée or work? Hardest first: parents.

I dialled work. 'Hello, Norman Jarvis please,' I said into the mouthpiece with an affected air of authority. The secretary put me through without realising it was me, and not wanting to get bogged down in nervous chit-chat, I didn't let on. My heart beat a little faster. I'd been working there for five years.

'Jarvis,' said my boss.

'Hello Norman, it's John, John Harris.'

Delay. 'Dear boy, hello! How was your holiday? Inja wasn't it?'

Shit, I thought, how *was* my holiday? 'Err, yeah, it's great. I wa—'

'Back on Monday, I believe, tell us ...' delay, 'tell us all about it, what?'

'Yeah, well, that's the thing Norman, I, err, I'm not coming back.' I inhaled and closed my eyes, waiting for the explosion at the other end.

It came. 'W-what? You've found another job you mean?'

'No, nothing like that,' I exhaled, 'I'm not coming back to England. It's pretty good out here, you see. I'm going to travel around a bit, see what happens, you know.'

'Not coming back?' he choked on his words. 'You've got to come back. What about all those projects you're working on, you can't just leave them, who's going to run them?'

Not saying anything seemed like the best thing to do, he'd probably answer his own questions.

'Good heavens, man, have you taken leave of your senses? Inja!' I said nothing for thirty seconds as he ranted on. 'John . . . John . . . you there?'

'Can't speak much longer, Norman, I've got to go, there's a time limit on international phone calls from here,' I lied, faking static. 'My mum will come in with my written notice next week. If there's any problem just tell her and she'll get in touch with me, OK? I'll see you Norman.'

'Fine, good luck, but I thi–'

More fake static. 'Bye, Norman . . . ' I put the phone down and flew into a minor rage. 'Projects!' I screamed at the phone, 'Who gives a fuck about your stupid projects?' It was hard to believe that while my life was about to change in every way possible, my boss was only concerned with some crappy building project. A project that made him rich and me miserable.

When finally feeling composed again, I telephoned my parents and then Sanita. The conversation with my parents was similar to the one with my boss, just substitute 'house' for 'project'. Strangely enough my mum was more understanding than my dad, she seemed to know how I was feeling. I helped the situation along by telling them that it was just a fad, that I'd be home in two or three months; all that was needed was for me to see a bit of Asia.

Before even dropping the bomb-shell on Sanita the tears started. Why else would I be phoning? Again my reasoning was straightforward: three months maximum and then back home to normality, that's all I needed.

Taking a deep breath and walking out of the booth, I felt like I had been through ten rounds with Mike Tyson. Rick looked up at me. 'How'd it go?'

Shaking my head and puffing my cheeks, I clenched my eyes in a tight blink for two seconds. 'Fucking nightmare,' I said, holding open the door to the booth and gesturing inside. 'Your turn in the dentist's chair.'

THIRTEEN

Work! is a four letter word. It conjures up the same image the world over: getting up in the morning to do something you don't want to do, day in day out. After a few months of *work!*, or years depending upon the person's primeval yearning for freedom, you feel like a robot: alarm clock, get up, wash, catch the train, *work!*, go home, watch TV, go to bed. In that one sentence I've probably just described the daily routine of ninety-five percent of the working population of England. It's the same in every other developed country in the world. Routine is the cause of most marriage break-ups and social discontent.

That's my theory anyway.

It came as a surprise to me, therefore, that I accepted my new routine with open arms. There's no question about it, life on Koh Pha-Ngan was routine, but there were two fundamental differences between my new routine and the old one.

Firstly, although daily actions remained constant, the people around me changed. New backpackers would arrive and leave Hat Rin every week, and either said they were staying long-term and did, or said they were only staying for a few days but ended up not being able to leave. The latter was usually the case.

The second, more obvious difference between now and then was the nature of my daily routine. For the first time in my life it felt like my reason for waking up in the morning was just that: to wake up. If I didn't want to, nobody was saying I had to. If I wanted to go to the beach I'd wake up and go to the beach. If I wanted to mess about with Rick and Dave all day long in the jungle, that's what I'd do. That's not to say that I didn't get bored, but when boredom did set in I just did something else. When you *work!* you don't have that option.

Waking at around eight every morning, my first job was to actually get out of bed. How drunk or stoned everybody got the previous night usually dictated my ability to roll off the floor mat. Sometimes rolling over and off was quick and efficient, while other times the roll sideways ended at the edge, leaving me teetering on my side for a few seconds, before rolling back. Sometimes this rolling around went on for hours.

The one effective cure for a hangover in the tropics is the sea. Before we had breakfast, without even washing, we often just got up, put on some shorts and ran down into the cool morning ocean, keeping on running until we were submerged in the water.

Some mornings I wandered off down the jungle path to the beach while the others slept off their hangovers. Lying on the sand on my stomach, my chin resting on the palms of my hands, I would watch in intrigued silence as the crabs, unable to break free of their routine, went to *work!* around me. They seemed to live a pointless existence on the beach, coming out of their little holes and going back in again. They would come out and make minuscule little balls with the sand, first eating it then sucking out the nutrients and spitting out the grains, mashed together with crab spit. Flicking a jellyfish tentacle into their midst gave them something else to eat and provided my morning's entertainment.

Learning to tell the time without looking at my watch gave me something to concentrate on every day too. The best way was obviously by looking at the sun and checking the position of shadows that were cast by its position in the sky, but I soon found that the body has its own clock, and that it's possible to guess the time of day without even looking at the sky. Sometimes I got it wrong but usually it was possible to be accurate to within an hour.

So, in what we considered the true spirit of freedom and the timeless nature of our travel plans, a few months after the sacrifice of Dave's airline ticket, the three of us ceremoniously burnt our watches too.

FOURTEEN

The months rolled by and we spent Dave's and my birthday in true, drug-crazed party style. Rick and I also celebrated our one year's anniversary since leaving England on that beach by having one of the usual parties, only this time everything was free.

We should have realised beforehand just how crazy people get when something is being given away. It was like a buffet dinner where everyone goes up to get food even though they can't eat any more. The queue for the acid never stopped, and it wasn't until five in the morning on the third consecutive day of the non-stop rave that the drug finally ran out. The beach was strewn with bodies, all in various states of sun-baked, drugged-out madness for three more days after that, and even when they left, some people lived in the jungle for a few more weeks, hoping, no doubt, to cadge a few more freebies.

For Rick, Dave and I the ease of our life and the need to keep up the charade with Ta and co were made all the more evident by our financial situation. I never did like the idea of living off someone else, especially by deceit, and would never have done it if Rick hadn't already been set up with Ta. But the fact was that we would have run out of money after about six months if we hadn't had free accommodation. As it was, the money I had left when arriving in Thailand was still in my pocket, and that meant that the inevitable four letter word could remain lodged in the back of my throat, unspoken, as long as I stayed put.

Far from my finances dwindling they had actually grown slightly. The acid that was sold on the beach paid for food and drink, with enough left over for us all to share and do what we wanted. It wasn't a lot by Western standards, pennies really, but when you're living cheaply in a Third World country those pennies go a long way. 'It's all relative, boys,' as Dave was so fond of saying.

The acid, despite what Rick had originally said, wasn't produced entirely by using plants from the jungle, but was brought over from

Holland by some contact of a Thai girl called Ning. Ning was the female, Koh Pha-Ngan version of Timothy Leary, and could supply Rick with copious amounts of anything. The arrangement was simple: she paid the man from Amsterdam, Rick paid her, the party-goers paid him, and we all lived happily ever after.

Ning scared the shit out of me though. Her wild eyes, and even wilder look, made me think that she could flip at a moment's notice, and I avoided her whenever possible, even avoiding eye contact with her if I could help it.

Empress Ning, as we called her — partly because of the name (Ning the Merciless) but also because she dressed like some absurd woodland nymph — was a forty-year-old Thai drug addict. Unlike most people, especially Thais who live on beaches or in jungles, she wore very long flowing dresses that had been torn to shreds by years of clambering through trees and over rocks. Someone forgot to tell her that she was dressed for the urban jungle, not the real one. But above all she was just plain weird.

Dave also thought she was nuts, and, like me, avoided her at all costs. He said he'd seen a similar look once when he was stationed in the Gulf and had been asked to guard a condemned man. The person in question was an Iraqi who had defected and entered Kuwait, raping and torturing his way through the town, out of control, until he was finally stopped by a US patrol. They had intervened during his lynching and didn't know what to do with him. Dave said that the man had possessed the most horrible look in his eyes; a look, he said, not dissimilar to the Empress Ning.

Rick of course, with characteristically dark humour, thought this was hilarious, and went out of his way to make sure we bumped into each other on the gloomy jungle path that led up from the beach. He always found a new trick up his sleeve to get our paths to cross, and I fell for it every time. 'John,' he'd say as we sat on the beach at night having a smoke, 'I'm just going into the bushes for a crap.' As soon as he disappeared, so Ning would appear, staring and grinning like a psychopath. I hated that.

Apart from being terrified of Ning, Dave settled in really well at the house, and with some of the money he'd saved he set about building a small extension to the top floor balcony. Not really an extension, more of a tree-house that leaned half on the building and half on an adjacent tree, it could accommodate only two or three people. It was open to the elements on all sides, but it was a nice place to keep cool in the evenings, and it kept him busy.

Dave was like that; if he wasn't doing something with his hands he was talking, and nobody wanted to listen to him all day long. Building the tree-house kept him constantly busy because pieces were always falling off in the wind. 'Where're you going, Dave?' we'd ask as he left the beach. 'Too hot down here,' he'd reply, and disappear up the path. Twenty minutes later we'd hear the sound of hammering over the treetops like a giant pterodactyl-sized woodpecker: *clock clock clock.*

As for me? Well, apart from learning to tell the time and watching the crabs I just mooched about having a laugh. I wasn't into drugs really, apart from the odd smoke, and didn't think Dave needed any help in reconstructing the island, I didn't even keep a diary, so my hands were pretty well idle. I did like to keep in with the crowd on the main beach though and often went down to meet new people.

So, there we were, the three of us enjoying life with our three Thai girlfriends, with not a care in the world. We'd even forgotten about the conspicuous absence of Toomy's brother, Tommy, and the severed finger incident that had given me nightmares for the first two months. Toomy went to seemingly unnecessary lengths to explain that Tommy was no longer in Bangkok, and had now gone north to visit other relatives in Chiang Mai and probably wouldn't be back.

It all sounded very probable, and if I hadn't become sick we would have believed it to be the truth. But I did get sick; I caught dengue fever, and the truth behind the severed finger was finally revealed.

THE GREAT ESCAPE

ONE

The jungle at night can be a mosquito-infested scene from a horror film: mozzies come out at dusk, fly around with a high-pitched buzzing sound that's more like a squeak, suck the blood of humans and then go back into hiding before the sun rises at dawn. It's a nightmare; we all know that. What I didn't know, however, was that there's another kind of mosquito, one with stripy legs, that's not like a vampire. It does suck blood but isn't afraid of daylight, and hangs around jungle paths like ours during the daytime waiting for people like me to pass by. The reason I'm explaining all this, and my ignorance of the species, will become clear in a moment.

It was about six o'clock at night, just a few days after Dave's birthday, and the three of us, as usual, were getting ready to defend against the evening's onslaught of blood suckers. We were sitting atop Dave's platform, enjoying the sounds and smells of the vegetation around us and discussing our plans for the future. The mosquitoes were a pain in the neck but it was far too hot to sit inside, the fans we had were next to useless and only moved the same sweat-laden warm air around the room. Dave was telling us how he'd like to live in a huge jungle mansion, somewhere not dissimilar to this. We had a nice place but he wanted a bigger house, preferably one built with his own hands.

'How 'bout you, John?' he said, stretching out and pulling a leaf from the top of the nearest tree.

'Hmm, dunno,' I said. 'Don't like to make plans really, they always seem to fall through. The best things always happen by accident, I reckon.' I looked out at the trees. 'Take this place for instance. When I went to India for a holiday I never imagined I'd be here a year later. OK I have to put up with you ...'

He wagged a palm leaf at me. 'Careful, Lord John, this is my throne you're sitting on now.'

I asked them if they wanted a beer and brought up the remaining cans of Singha that hadn't already been consumed, heaving myself back on to the platform with great effort and much groaning.

'Getting old, John,' Rick said, taking a can from me. 'I'd better drink it for you.'

I sat back down and tried to cross my legs, once again letting out a long sigh. 'Strange, I feel really tired. I think it's this bloody platform. Couldn't you have made some steps up on to it, Dave?'

'Hey, that's a regulation entrance gantry.' He took a beer and opened it, spraying his face with froth. 'Shit.'

'See,' I said with some satisfaction, 'if that step had been lower the beer wouldn't have been shaken up. And if you had remembered to keep it in the cooler, instead of leaving it on the floor since yesterday morning, the bubbles wouldn't have expanded and exploded in your face now would they Dave?'

'Fuck,' he swigged and belched. 'Who do you think I am, Einstein?' He drained the can before continuing. 'Rick?'

'What?'

'Plans?' he added, lighting a candle and dripping some wax on to the bamboo floor to set it in place.

Rick drew his knees up to his chest and looked up at the overhanging trees. 'Think I might marry Ta.'

I put down my beer and stared at him.

'I mean, if it all works out with the millions from her father, why not?'

'Because she might not have millions from her father, that's why not.' Dave let go of the candle and it fell over. 'Because her father's probably poorer than us guys, that's why not.'

Rick wasn't going to be drawn, and just grinned, pulling his cigarettes from his pocket and lighting up before offering them out. He'd been through this argument a thousand times before with us and had grown used to it.

'Man, you don't still believe that shit about her being royalty?' Dave took a cigarette. 'Shit.'

'You believed that he was knighted by the Queen of England,' I said, 'that's pretty unbelievable.'

'Yeah, well, that's before I found out that they don't knight North Sea fishermen.' He leaned forward and took a light off the candle that Rick had managed to stand upright. 'How the hell was I supposed to know what you British get up to in that weird country of yours. Fuckin' bunch o' goddamn homosexuals the lot o' ya. Beats me how you ever won two world wars. What is it you call those guys who wear skirts into battle? Scottish? Jeesus!'

A sudden heavy weight of fatigue seemed to push down on me and I found I was too tired to support my own weight, so I got up and staggered off the wooden deck.

'You all right, John?'

'Just a bit tired, I think.' I blinked heavily, the strain hurting my eyelids. I massaged my temple and sighed. 'Think I might have flu coming on. Anyway, I'm going to bed.'

'Bed?' Dave checked his wrist where the watch used to be. 'It can only be seven-thirty.'

'Yeah I know but I feel wasted. My arms and legs ache. Are there any candles left?'

'There's one in my room,' Rick answered. 'The girls have gone into town, I told them to get some more. They'll be back in an hour or so.'

I said I couldn't wait that long and left them opening another can of beer each. As I walked into Rick's room I could hear Dave in the background still arguing with Rick about how unlikely it was that Ta was the daughter of a millionaire. I picked up the stubby remains of the candle and lumbered down the hallway, closing my bedroom door behind me and falling on to the bamboo floor mat that served as a bed. The candle remained unlit and I fell asleep with it in one hand.

I awoke in a pool of sweat, my face stuck to the pillow, little rivulets of water tickling the back of my neck like ants. The candle was still clutched in my hand and had deformed under the combined heat and pressure. I sighed and rolled over on to my back to try to see if there was any light coming through the window. It was still night but there were no longer any voices outside so it must have been quite late. My ears picked up the sound of cicadas in the trees outside but definitely no voices.

I reached across in the darkness to put the candle down and blindly elbowed a face. Muck twitched and groaned but remained asleep. Although the bed was at the same level as the floor I still thought of the edges of the mat as a bed. Years of sleeping on raised, Western-style mattresses had conditioned me into thinking that a bed must always have defined borders, and I went to unnecessary pains to place the candle on the floorboard side of the line, before collapsing on to my back again.

Directly above my face, on the pitched roof joists, an insect of some kind had made a little mud home the size of a golf ball. Through a gap in the roof's palm frond weather-proofing, a slither of dusty moonlight struck the nest, bathing its uneven sides in cool blue light. The flying insect that had built it popped in and out of a hole in the bottom every few minutes to tidy its home. Even when it didn't come out I could just see it as it walked across the hole, occasionally letting a careless, silvery wing drop and catch the light. I pondered on the possibility that if I snored the whole thing: mother, father, eggs, house and all could drop silently into my upturned mouth. With a snake-like slither I moved my body an inch to the left, just out of range.

I watched that mini beehive of activity most of the night. That and the mouse that came under the inch-wide gap at the foot of the door. 'Ledged and braced,' I muttered, remembering the correct technical term. The ping-pong ball with fur and a tail stopped, turned ninety degrees and followed the gap to the door jamb. To test the mouse's reflexes, and make sure that it had decent hearing, I drummed my fingers on the floorboards. It froze as though caught in headlights. I tapped again and it moved on.

I blinked the sweat out of my eyes and buried my face into the hot pillow to wipe away the moisture. A noise outside the door made me stop and listen. Voices and then the shadows of some people walking past the gap. Thai noises, Thai voices and a high-pitched Thai laugh. I tried to sit up but couldn't move, except for a simple sideways roll. Jesus, what was wrong with me?

An hour or so later, unable to stay awake alone any longer, I began to make exaggerated movements to wake Muck. She stirred a little and sniffed the air like a rat, opening one eye. I immediately pretended to be asleep, waking up only because she had. 'Hmm?'

'Why you wa' up so early?' She stretched and opened both eyes. 'Shi', wha' wrong wi' you, man?'

'Don't know, I feel terrible.'

Her warm hand landed on my forehead. 'Jeez, you burn up, man. Loo' at you face!' She quickly left the room and came back a minute later with Ta and a wet towel. They both felt my head again and pronounced something morbid in Thai, one agreeing with the other's diagnosis. 'You no ha' p'o'lem, we take good care,' Ta said unconvincingly, and led her friend out of the room for a discussion in their own language.

Well that's really perked me up – reverting to their own language. Any moment now they'll start sliding food under the gap in the door.

The whole of that day was spent indoors alternating from bed to chair, with an occasional visit to the balcony to piss into the trees. The girls brought me all kinds of food and medicine, all local concoctions: mostly foul-smelling and even worse tasting. Rick and Dave agreed that it was just flu, and everyone said that after a full day and another night indoors I'd be as right as rain.

When I woke up the following morning I could no longer walk.

TWO

Not only couldn't I walk but I could barely move, and even while lying down, trying to turn over took most of the little strength left in my muscles. It wasn't the muscles that hurt so much as the joints between the bones, especially elbows and knees, which meant that just straightening a leg or an arm brought me close to tears. It was like flu but twenty times as bad.

My bodily functions had also started to cause problems. I was no longer able to hold my shit and it came out in foul-smelling jets of hot, brown liquid. No lumps, just dark water, which meant getting to the toilet on time was impossible, so I gave up eating to stem the flow. I didn't like relying on others to take me to the toilet, even though they kept a vigil over me like true friends.

Food was brought in on an hourly basis and rejected; left in a pile around me like offerings to a Buddha. Each and every time they came in to give me something or to test my temperature, they always asked me if there was anything I would like. I always gave the same reply: 'my mum', and received a gentle cuddle as a substitute. The surrogacy of the gesture always made me feel slightly worse, and seemed to extend the pain in my arms and legs to an unknown joint in my heart.

The visits by any two or more people were always followed by hushed murmurings in the hallway outside my door. I wished they'd go further away and talk, at least then I wouldn't have to guess what they were talking about. The girls were the worst, just standing right outside the door, sometimes absent-mindedly holding it open and whispering and pointing at me, usually shaking their heads morbidly. At least Rick and Dave kept it to a minimum: 'Shit. Looks bad,' Dave would say, and they'd both walk creakily down the hall discussing their own experiences of influenza, their common seafaring background usually providing the backdrop to the story.

I was still the only person among us who thought that the illness was something other than flu, and when I suggested that it might be malaria they were shocked into silence. 'Fuck, man, can't you die from that?' asked Dave, taking a cautious step back. I told him that it wasn't contagious and not to worry; I had no intention of dying and letting him and Rick enjoy Ta's millions without me.

I thought it best if I was taken to see a doctor, and we all agreed that if my condition hadn't improved by the third day, two volunteers should take me over to Koh Samui where, according to Dave's guidebook, the best hospital in southern Thailand was situated. I felt sure they would know how to treat tropical diseases. The girls seemed to think otherwise.

Ta was furious when she found out about the plan, saying that Thai doctors were useless and would probably make me worse; she'd had a grandmother who once went into hospital and ... Rick pointed out that I was in a bad way and that the treatment I'd received from her and Toomy hadn't exactly achieved much. Her response was simple: 'He well tomo'ow, you see!' and stormed out of the room adding, 'You no ta' him anywhere, man.'

I sweated it out through the rest of that day and night with delirium, unable to sleep. My mouse companion came in through the door as usual, blissfully unaware of my predicament, and I flicked little morsels to him until I passed out from the effort. Dreams came and went, and usually involved obscure references to family and old school friends; nothing profound or earth shattering, just dreams. It was the first time though that I realised how much dreaming we all do. I had always equated one night's sleep with one dream, but that's not the case. For every time my brain drifted in and out of sleep, a dream went with it, like a neat package. I tried to predict the next dream, even direct it, but they never followed on from where the previous one left off.

By the next morning my condition hadn't improved at all, and to add to my repertoire of misfiring body functions I had started to vomit. There was no food to bring up so I gave up drinking water to stem the flow of acid in the back of my throat. The early hours were spent heaving little spoonfuls of clear, sour water on to the floor that seeped slowly through the cracks in the floorboards.

The debris was appalling, looking back I can see that, though at the time it wasn't obvious to me because I'd lain in my own fetid juices for three days and had become accustomed to the smell. If I'd been more alert, however, I would have noticed how each person entering the room pulled a face, stopping just short of holding their noses, before turning on their heels.

Rick, Dave and I sat in the room discussing our next move, and when Ta and the girls went into town to shop, we packed my gear and left, using a jungle path to get to the pier. Having to stop every few yards to rest, it took us nearly two hours to cross the small hill, skirt Hat Rin and make it to where the Koh Pha-Ngan to Koh Samui ferry left from.

'You go back Dave, leave the guidebook with me.' Rick lowered me gently on to a bench on the jetty. 'I'll take it from here.'

'What d'you want me to tell Ta?'

Rick thought for a moment and said, 'Just tell her the truth. I'll be back by eight o'clock tonight, with or without him.' He glanced at me laid out on the bench. 'Without probably.'

'She ain't gonna like it.' Dave marked the relevant page of the guidebook showing the location of the hospital, and slipped it into my bag. 'Good luck John,' he said, squeezing my limp hand, and he left.

The ferry was full when it pulled in and almost empty when it left. Fresh faces and clean backpacks coming one way, bedraggled, tired bodies going the other. We boarded and made the short crossing between islands without a word passing between us. Rick chain-smoked as usual, talking to one or two travellers he knew, most of whom had seen enough of Thailand to last them a lifetime. Rick propped me up against one of the red plastic buoys, and I spent the entire journey with my head lolling over the side of the boat, silently staring at the blue sea. I didn't feel up to talking to anyone; all I could think about was how long it was going to take to get to this hospital.

At the port in Koh Samui we didn't bother to haggle for a jeep, instead jumping into one of the air-con taxis that plied between the port and the various resorts on the island. Like a sack of potatoes I was heaved in and slid across the back seat of the car, the driver pushing my feet in to avoid them being trapped in the door. My knee-joints almost exploded and I let out a painful cry.

'Wha' p'ob'em you f'ien'?' the driver asked with alarm, quickly dropping my feet.

'Sick,' Rick replied. 'You take us to hospital, quick-quick.'

The driver took the instruction to heart and seemed to think that his car was now an ambulance. He leapt over the bonnet, got behind the wheel and we sped off in a cloud of dust. 'You f'ien' no p'ob'em now, I ta' you fas',' he said, cornering at ninety like a rally driver and almost killing half a dozen tourists in the process.

Lying on the back seat, my head rammed against one door panel and my feet on the other to stop me from being thrown on to the floor, I was unable to see outside. Rick leaned over and locked the doors in case I slid out. 'Don't worry John, be there in no time.' I wanted to say, 'Alive please!' but couldn't muster the will-power to form the words.

From wood and jungle to concrete and jungle, after what seemed like an age watching treetops and blue sky flash past, we came to a screeching halt outside a brand new three-storey hospital. Nurses in starched white uniforms (still drop-dead sexy and unable to disguise that beautiful Asian look) busily came out of one door and went into the next, while doctors with stethoscopes around their necks watched them wiggle.

Rick went inside and came out with a wheelchair.

'You're fucking kidding?' I exclaimed as he wheeled it up to the car. 'I'm not getting in that.' The journey to get there had almost killed me but there was no way I was going to get into a wheelchair. The driver helped me out of the car, I took one faltering step before my legs buckled and I hung on to him for support. 'Shit!'

Rick pushed the chair towards me. 'You should see the nurses inside, John, I wish I was sick. Just imagine how much more sympathy you'll get from them if you sit in this. Thai nurses . . . ' he sighed.

I sat in the wheelchair.

Rick wheeled me through the main entrance to the reception to register and said that he'd wait outside while I went through the form-filling.

'Koh Pha-Ngan?' the nurse behind the counter read from my form. 'Why you no go ho'pi'al there?'

'I didn't know there was one,' I groaned.

'Bes' in sou' Thailan'!'

'Dave and his fucking guidebook,' I muttered, 'I'll kill him.'

'You no kill anyone, mis'er Ha'is, ha-ha, too si'.'

I spent the next hour inside a small disinfected room being probed with stainless steel. I had to provide a stool sample, which involved having a shit and scooping a piece up into a bottle using a little plastic spoon. Blood was taken too, and, unable to find a vein, the nurse decided to prick my finger with a scalpel. She squeezed the end and sliced, blood exploded on to her white smock, sweat poured down my face, voices became loud and I fainted very embarrassingly.

The doctor said that they wouldn't be able to read the results of the tests until the next morning and, given my condition, suggested that I stay in one of the wards overnight for observation.

'What do you want me to do?' Rick asked when I told him the news.

'Go. There's no point in you hanging around here.' He was suddenly distracted as a particularly beautiful nurse passed by. 'Give it a rest,' I said wearily. 'There's plenty of time for that.'

'You're only saying that because you're staying.'

'I'd swap positions with you right now if I could.' We both stared as she bent over to retrieve a thermometer from a small boy's mouth, revealing the tops of her smooth thighs. 'No, you go,' I said, tearing my eyes from the vision, 'I'll stay and suffer the consequences.'

Rick left, having chatted up most of the nurses, and I was checked into a spotlessly clean ward with ten beds in it, only two of which were occupied. One had an elegant looking Thai man in maroon silk pyjamas lying on top of it, reading a copy of *National Geographic* and smoking a cigar, coughing occasionally. 'Like one?' he asked, taking a packet off the side table and offering them to me as I was wheeled in.

'No, I'm OK thank you.'

'You can't be OK, you wouldn't be in here if you were.'

I didn't quite know what to say. Not because of his abruptness but because of his perfect English. The nurse guided me to the opposite side of the room from Thai man, next to the only other occupied bed. No one was in the bed, but judging from the paraphernalia that spilled out of the drawers in the side cabinet: books, airmail letters etc., and from the pair of tie-dye trousers that were laid out on the bed, he was either a foreigner or a Westernised Thai.

I glanced at the clipboard hooked on to the bottom rail of the bed as I was wheeled past. Name: *Phinopan, Tommy R.* it read. I passed out again.

THREE

Since seeing the clipboard at the end of his bed earlier that afternoon, I had spent the whole day walking, or rather wheeling, around the hospital. Not because I was interested in three-storey white buildings, but because I wanted to think about what I was going to say to Toomy's brother, if indeed it was him. I didn't think that I had any real reason to be nervous or scared, after all, Tommy, as I've already said, is a popular name in Thailand, and it was even conceivable that there was another Tommy on the island with the same surname. But if it was the same Tommy, and he wasn't in the north of the country, then why were the girls lying to us?

At first, to be doubly sure of not being seen, I'd asked the nurse if it would be possible to be relocated to another ward, saying that the sun coming through the windows hurt my eyes; a pretty feeble excuse but all I could think of on the spur of the moment. Predictably she dismissed it, and to change my mind showed me that the only alternative was a ward full of screaming Thai kids and their distraught mothers.

I wheeled around aimlessly trying to think what it all meant, occasionally passing by our room to see if the mysterious 'Phinopan. Tommy R.' was back in bed yet. I even thought about discharging myself immediately and heading back to Koh Pha-Ngan to warn Rick, but that seemed a bit over the top considering that I hadn't ever clapped eyes on him yet.

I explored all three floors of the building before, on my ninth circuit, just as I came out of the door from *Surgery/Radiography*, I saw a man going into our room. He was on crutches and had splints on both legs, one arm was in a sling and, despite his badly scarred face and missing ear (just a hole), I recognised him instantly as the same man who had told me to get lost at the Back Yard Pub a whole year before.

I quickly wheeled backwards around the corner so that he wouldn't see me, and watched him enter, my gaze immediately falling on his crutch-holding hand. If it was Tommy who Dave and I saw taking the beating, he would have a missing finger. 'One, two, three, four . . . five,' I counted, they were all there. So much for the left hand. Now the right.

Wheeling noiselessly down the corridor to our ward, I stopped by the door and watched as the nurse helped Tommy on to the bed. She said something in Thai and pointed at my bed, and I guessed that she was telling him that another guest from Koh Pha-Ngan was staying here.

'Mis'er Ha'is,' Tommy's nurse said looking up, and pulled back the covers on my bed, 'wha' you doin'?' With my head bowed, I let her come over and push me to the bed. 'Get in bed an' I bring you dinner. Wha' you wan'?'

I patted my stomach and pulled a face, indicating that I still had the shits. If Tommy hadn't recognised my face I didn't want to tempt fate by letting him hear my voice. Empress Ning had once told me that all Westerners look the same to Thais, it's only their voice and actions that tell them apart.

The nurse got the message and helped me into bed, informing us that the lights would be switched off soon, and that if I wanted to read or eat then I was to use the cord switch that operated the reading lamp above my head. 'Mis'er Ha'is, why you no tal' frien' Koh Pha-Ngan?' she asked, tucking in my sheets.

'Tired,' I croaked, rolling on to my side to face away from Tommy and praying that she would go away.

The nurse went out, and a moment later the lights went out. As silently as possible, I turned and watched in the darkness as Tommy, still holding the magazine in his left hand, leaned across and pulled on the lamp cord with the other. The lamp came on, bathing his stitch-scarred face and what was left of his right hand in light. He pulled the cord between thumb and palm, and my heart skipped a beat. *All* of his fingers were missing!

FOUR

The next morning I ambled, bleary-eyed from a sleepless night, into the doctor's room and sat down next to his plastic skeleton.

'Well Mister Harris,' the doctor said, dropping his implements noisily into a kidney tray, 'you were wrong and I was right.' He turned and said something to the nurse, who rummaged through a box-file on his desk. The previous day I had argued with the doctor, saying that my symptoms were the exact same ones as malaria, and that he should look for those signs when examining me. He had disagreed, his counter-argument being that no malaria existed in Thailand, a suggestion I found a bit hard to swallow considering the number of travellers taking malaria tablets on the recommendation of their own doctors.

'Ah-ha, here we are.' He took the file from the nurse and laid it out on his desk, pinching his nose in thought. Behind him, in the frosted glass that separated his surgery from the corridor, a kid was standing on a chair with his face pressed against the glass. The nurse saw him and went outside, pulling the chair from under his feet so that the image dropped like a stone. There was the sound of a motherly slap followed by crying, before the nurse returned and stood obediently beside the doctor.

'Yes, it looks like dengue fever, Mr Harris,' the doctor continued. 'It's certainly not malaria; all of the tests show no signs of that and they show no signs of anything else.' He went on to explain how dengue fever, being some kind of virus, didn't show up on the kind of blood and stool tests that he'd carried out, and that because it was a virus there was nothing I could do but sweat it out. He also informed me that the disease's common name was break-bone fever, because of the amount of pain suffered by each victim in the joints.

'As I explained yesterday,' he went on, 'there has been an outbreak of the disease in southern Thailand, especially among the islands of Koh Samui, Koh Tao and, of course, Koh Pha-Ngan.' He sat back. 'There's very little we can do about it, I'm afraid. Even the usual precautions of covering up at night and sleeping under a net are useless because this little fellow bites during the daytime.'

I rubbed my aching temples. 'Is there nothing you can give me?'

'Painkillers?' He closed the file, indicating the end of the consultation. 'You can expect the symptoms to last about a week before your body fights the virus off. A week, ten days, not more.'

Defeated, I took a prescription and followed the nurse out into the corridor, and was directed towards a hole in the wall where drugs were administered. I should have been over the moon at the news but instead felt curiously let down, as though my suffering had been for nothing. All this pain and just for a virus, not even a real disease.

A bottle of painkillers was duly issued. I turned to go back to the ward and was stopped in my tracks by an eerily familiar smell. I shivered and the hairs on the back of my neck stood up.

Smells, like music, remind one of places and people in a way that photos or video footage never can. I don't know the psychology or physiology, or whatever, behind the phenomenon, but a smell can provide instant recognition of a place and a point in time, as well as a person. Especially when she's sprayed half a bottle of Chanel No. 5 (Khao San Road variety) all over her body.

Toomy! it said to me, as the sweet perfume hit my nostrils and stopped me from going any further, like I'd walked into a wall. For a moment I wasn't sure what to do, it was as though the smell of perfume was choking me. Only Toomy used so much of it, sometimes getting through a bottle a week, spraying on so much that even on the jungle path, wind and all, it was possible to tell if she had walked to or from the house in the previous ten minutes.

Cautiously I walked down the corridor to our ward and, with my back and both palms flat against the cold painted wall, shuffled sideways towards the door, allowing one eye to peep around the door frame. Toomy was sitting on the edge of the bed, while Tommy cowered against the wall under a stream of what appeared, from Ta's expressions anyway, to be Thai expletives. She wagged her finger again and again. Poor Tommy didn't have a chance. Every time Ta bollocked him and waited for a reply, he just sank further into the pillow trying to get away from her.

'*Da, Da!*' she screamed, pointing at my bed, picking up my clipboard and stabbing it with her finger before throwing it back down and continuing the abuse. Even Toomy seemed a little alarmed at Ta's noise level and looked about the room nervously, holding up an apologetic hand to the old man in the bed opposite.

Sliding my cheek back across the door frame, I closed my eyes and sighed. The painkiller I'd taken outside the pharmacy was beginning to work but it did nothing to make me feel better now. I was distracted for a second or two as a cockroach came scurrying along, then stopped outside the room. Its body-length antennae waved in the air before it shot off into a ventilation shaft, probably to escape the nauseating perfume. Just where I want to go, I thought and peeped into the room again.

Toomy was now standing, and Ta had picked up her handbag and was wagging what looked like a final warning to Tommy. In her hand she held a British passport! I blinked and looked into the corridor, unable at first to believe what I'd seen, before looking back into the room.

Ta put the passport into her bag and they turned to leave the room. I panicked, first turning one way then the other, before turning back again and walking quickly away. Stupidly I went in the direction of the exit, which meant that I had to do a full circuit of the floor to avoid being spotted before coming back to the room. When I got back to the ward, Tommy was sitting alone, looking pensively at my bed as though staring into the tomb of an ancient king and trying to visualise a lost civilisation.

At first he didn't see me walk in, and it wasn't until the old man said, 'Ah, Harris, you appear to have countless enemies and few friends!' that he looked up. He would have started the verbal abuse immediately but delayed it when he saw what I was looking for.

'No you pa'por',' he screamed.

I looked at him. 'What?' It was the first time that I'd looked Tommy square in the eye and the experience wasn't a pleasant one. He'd lost one eye, which had been replaced with glass, and it stared out of his skull like a window that had been vandalised and boarded over. I looked away.

'You, you fuck! You frien', Li', he no ha' money, he lie eve'yone. Say got lo' o' money from daddy bu' no tell tru'. He lie Ta, tell got lo' o' money. He fuckin' dead. An' you, man, you bo' fuckin' dead! Same people do this to me, do you, man.' He pointed to various parts of his body and I obediently followed his finger.

He could hardly get out of bed to give me a beating so I said, 'Don't know what you're talking about,' and started to put the few things I'd unpacked the night before back into my bag.

'Where you go, man?' he demanded, leaning over. 'You go, we fin' you, man. We go' Li' pa'por', you ain't going nowhere!' He suddenly lunged sideways and grabbed the back of my T-shirt with his good hand, and I pulled away so hard that he fell out of the bed. 'You fuckin' no chan', man!' he screamed, pushing himself off the floor. 'No chan'!'

With grim determination I rapidly packed all of my things, ignoring the torrent of abuse and occasional attempt to grab me. All the money I had was in my pockets already so, checking that my own passport was intact, I zipped the bag shut and hoisted it on to my shoulder with surprising vigour. The painkiller was charging around my body now and, though not as good as new, I felt capable of making the journey back to Koh Pha-Ngan to find Rick. Without a word of return abuse, I took a deep breath and walked out of the ward, Tommy still shouting behind me, 'We fin' you, man, no p'o'lem!'

As I walked through the swing doors and out into the car park, the sun warmed my face and made me feel better than I had felt for almost a week. On the way towards the taxi stand I bought a coke and popped another pill just to keep me going. Realising that I needed to keep well out of sight, I skirted the edge of the car park, keeping beneath the palm trees. It was possible that the girls, or someone working with them, were on the lookout for me, so I wasn't taking any chances. Not only that but since leaving the hospital I had the distinct feeling that I was being watched.

Putting it down to healthy paranoia, I gulped down the remaining coke and continued towards the main road where the taxis stood, crunching my way through the jungle foliage.

There was a noise among the bushes ten yards to my left. I froze; my heart started to beat faster. 'Shit, get moving,' I whispered to myself, and taking a look in the direction of the rustling leaves, I quickly walked on.

It came again, only this time closer, so I picked up the pace, ignoring the twigs that scratched against my legs. I cursed myself for having been so stupid as to walk in the jungle where anyone could clobber me over the head without being seen.

The noise came again and I started to jog. The taxis were only fifty yards away and I could see their bright paintwork through the tree trunks. Two drivers stood against one of the cars chatting idly, eating melon seeds.

A crash of branches. Fuck! I ran faster and now heard the sound of someone else's feet running, pounding on the dead foliage, each crunching footstep as clear as a bell over the silent jungle floor. Clearing a group of trees, I allowed myself a quick glance back to make sure that I wasn't hearing things. No one there, the noise of footsteps wasn't behind me! 'Keep going, John,' I mumbled, '*keep going*.'

'John!'

'Keep running, don't stop now, you're almost there.'

'John!'

I fixed my eyes on the taxi driver ahead when a figure jumped out from behind a tree and I did a sort of sliding tackle to stop myself running into him. The soil and leaves churned up against the soles of my feet into a soft black pile and I came to a rest on my back, looking up at the tree tops, patches of blue sky filtering through, and Rick's worried face looking down at me.

FIVE

'You scared the shit out of me!' I gasped. 'What the fuck are you doing creeping around out here?' Rick held his hand out and I grabbed it, pulling myself up. The decomposed leaves had gone up my shorts and become lodged in my waistband so that even the smallest movement pricked me. I stood rummaging around inside my fly to retrieve the pieces of twig and earth, waiting for Rick to reply.

He sighed heavily. 'Ta's a confidence trickster, John, we're in deep shit.' The rigidity in Rick's muscles suddenly left him and he relaxed, leaning against a tree for support. It was as though having told me this had lifted a huge weight from his shoulders.

I stopped rummaging and looked up. 'You're telling me? I've just spent the morning watching her scream and shout in there.' I thumbed over my shoulder. 'All of them are in on it.'

He seemed surprised at the news. 'Ta, in there? What did she say to you?'

'Nothing, I hid.'

He thought for a moment, his mouth gaping. 'Why did she come to see you?'

'Me? She came to see Tommy, for Christ's sake, not me!'

His chin nearly hit the floor. 'Tommy! What's he doing in there? I thought he was in Bangkok.'

Rick's ignorance of the whole chain of events was slowly dawning on me. Of course he didn't know any different, how could he know about Tommy? I shook my head slowly from side to side and put my hands on to my knees to catch my breath. 'Tommy's not in Bangkok, Rick, he's in there, crippled for life. He's got busted legs, only one eye and no fucking fingers.' I stood straight. 'So when you say we're in deep shit, you're not fucking kidding!'

With his mouth open, and still staring at the hospital, he slid slowly down a tree trunk on to the leafy ground and put a hand to his forehead. 'That guy you saw on the beach that day you first arrived. Remember?'

I started to nod deliberately.

'The one who took a beating from those Thai's?'

I nodded harder. 'Yes?'

'The finger.' He closed his eyes as though hoping to shut out the reality. 'Oh fooking hell, that was Tommy!'

'Well done.'

Then Rick came out with the most blindingly stupid comment I'd ever heard: 'But that's Thai Mafia business, what's it got to do with us?'

'Fucking hell, Rick, use your brain!' I slumped down on the ground opposite him. 'If Tommy's involved then so are the girls. They must have been banking on you as their meal ticket.' I pointed at the hospital. 'Whoever did that to Tommy has been promised a pay-off from Ta.'

He looked up and shrugged. 'That's her problem.'

'It's your problem now, you've got the payroll. Or so they think. Jesus!' I slapped my forehead with my palm. 'All this time we've been living for 'free'! They're going to want their money back; with interest!'

'Yeah, well that's why I moved out last night when I found out about Ta.'

Rick proceeded to tell me how, on the way back to Koh Pha-Ngan on the ferry the previous day, he had met an old Thai hand who'd been travelling in and out of the islands for years. Rick had asked him about his travels and had discovered that, among other things, he had also been mixed up with a girl called Ta the previous year on Koh Pha-Ngan. The man knew Tommy and the girls and had told Rick how they'd cleaned him out of every penny he had, even stealing his camera. At first Rick hadn't believed it was the same girl, but when the man went into detail about her pretending to be Thai royalty he knew there could be no mistake. When they had alighted from the ferry, Rick went straight up to the house and packed his gear.

'What about Dave?' I asked.

Rick shook his head forlornly. 'He wasn't there. I looked everywhere for him: on the beach, on Hat Rin beach, I even swam around to those rocks we used to dive off, but he wasn't there. I reckon he must have been fooking about in the jungle, you know what he's like. Anyway, it started to get dark so I took my gear down to Hat Rin and booked into a really obscure set of bungalows, way off the beaten track.' He pulled out a cigarette. 'They'll never find us there.'

'Too late.'

'Mm?'

I took a deep breath. 'Did you check your gear when you left last night?'

He drew on the cigarette and exhaled. 'Course. What d'you take me for?'

'Was your passport there when you left?'

'Yeah.'

'Then they know where you live, because Ta's got your passport now. She was here with it not ten minutes ago, I saw her waving it about. And Tommy told me they had it.'

'No way. They're just trying to scare you. It could've been anyone's passport. Did you look at it?'

'Only the cover. From a distance.'

'Then they're bullshitting.'

I raised an eyebrow and reached over for one of his cigarettes. 'I hope you're right, because we're not going to get very far without it.'

We smoked a cigarette each and I quickly ran out to the car park drinks vendor and fetched two cokes. At first I shouted the order from the cover of the trees but the man would only open them, refusing to bring them over to us. Unusual, I thought, for a country that operates on those old-time, shoe-shine values, and began to suspect that he too was working for Ta.

Handing one bottle over to Rick, I squatted and said, 'You know, you should have brought your gear over with you. Now we've got to hike back to Hat Rin.'

'I only came over to tell you what I knew, I didn't expect to see those two on the bloody ferry.' He wiped the rust off the top of the bottle and took a sip. 'I thought i'd come here, pick you up and go back to pick up my gear. Head off in the morning.'

'You were on the same ferry as Ta?'

He nodded seriously. 'I had to hide all the way over, not easy on a boat that size. I saw her get into a taxi at the port and I caught the bus. I had no idea she was coming here.'

There was something about Rick's story that didn't quite fit. One small piece missing from the jigsaw that nagged me. 'If you knew about Ta,' I queried, 'but she didn't know about you, why the hell did you run and hide last night? You'd have been better off staying put until we left the island for the mainland.'

'Good job I did, huh? Otherwise you would have had to come and get me up at the house.'

'So? We could have sneaked away from the house when they were out and caught the first ferry over to the mainland.'

'Don't be silly, she saw you here with Tommy, in the same room. She'd know that you knew, and would've beaten you back.'

I frowned. His logic made little sense to me. Rick couldn't have known last night that Ta was going to see me with Tommy today, so why had he left the house last night? My head spun with one of those verbal conundrums, like the ones you get in cartoons, or Laurel and Hardy films: 'How did he know last night that she would know today that I knew he knew ...' I rubbed my temple to relieve the headache that was steadily building. There didn't seem to be any point in pursuing that line of questioning so I moved on to the present as opposed to previous events. 'So what now?'

'So now we go back and get the gear.' He picked up a twig and began to drive it into the soil like a drill-bit. 'Then we fook off.'

'What about Dave?'

He shrugged, concentrating on the drilling. I knew that Rick was right, and that his shrugged answer to my question meant that we couldn't go back to the house for Dave. If we saw him in Hat Rin then all well and good, but otherwise we would have to part company without saying goodbye.

Anger started to boil up inside me as Rick lit another cigarette and continued twisting the twig into the ground. I wanted to blame him, to tell him how it was all his fault for lying in the first place, but the words only formed in my mind and got stuck in the back of my throat, unable to work their way out into audible sounds. A gasp was emitted instead, which probably more adequately summed up my feeling of resignation.

How could I blame Rick when I had gone along with the scam for so long?

A rustle in the bushes broke my concentration and I watched as a monkey, as small as a cat, ran along the ground, snatched something in its paw and climbed another tree. 'Where are we going to go?' I sighed, still watching the animal. 'I don't fancy going back to Bangkok. What about Chiang Mai?'

Rick noticed the monkey and looked up, as it leapt from a high branch into thin air and glided for twenty feet before sticking to another tree trunk.

'Rick?'

The monkey did the same again, only this time over a much greater distance to a lower treetop where its mate was waiting. When the male came crashing down on the palm leaves, the female immediately lifted her rear into the air and they started mating.

'Malaysia,' Rick said looking back. 'I've always wanted to go there.'

'Malaysia? I was thinking more along the lines of Phuket.'

'My dad always said that the prettiest girls in the world are Malays.'

I stood up, brushing the earth from the seat of my shorts. 'Rick, you've got no passport,' I reminded him, 'it'll have to be Bangkok or Chiang Mai. Shall we go?'

'When it gets dark,' he said, flicking the twig into the bushes. 'I don't want anyone to spot us. There's a ferry at eight, we'll get that one.'

SIX

'The Fugitives,' Rick whispered, grinning furtively, and held his hand up to keep me back. 'Wait till they start to raise the gangplank and then we'll run on.'

Standing behind him, I watched the scene through the crook of his arm. The fat Thai dock-hand was leaning against an oil drum, the rope that was attached to the draw-bridge in one hand, cigarette in the other. 'Boom!' I said quietly.

'What?'

'That guy, he's smoking a cigarette and practically sitting on an oil drum. Boom!'

'Fat bastard, serves him right.' Reaching into his trouser pocket, he pulled out his cigarettes. 'Want one? Go on, it'll calm your nerves.'

'Who's nervous?' I said, taking one.

'You are, I can feel it.' He took one himself and we both sank back around the corner to light up, out of sight.

We had spent most of the day outside the hospital, hiding in the trees watching monkeys shag. We didn't really expect Ta to come back to the hospital that day, but if she did we thought we could scare her into emptying the contents of her handbag for our inspection. We were kidding ourselves of course, it was just brave talk; neither of us had the inclination to approach her ever again after seeing what had happened to Tommy.

However, neither Ta nor any of her cronies did come back to the hospital, and at sunset, having smoked our way through two packets of cigarettes and drunk the vendor out of coke, we set about our long, arduous route to the ferry pier, deciding to play it extra safe and catching a local bus instead of a taxi. The logic behind our choice of transport stemmed from the fact that all members of the Thai Mafia have their sticky fingers in every business on every island from Koh Samui to Bangkok, so a bus should be a safer bet. We felt it unlikely that the driver of a government run service was the employee of a crime boss, and promptly boarded a bus that took us in completely the wrong direction, deliberately, to confuse whoever might be following us.

First catching a bus one way, and then taking two more around the island, plus a taxi to get us to where we wanted to be, we finally hitched the last mile or so to the ferry on the back of a lorry full of copra. It was probably over-elaborate, but neither of us wanted to be knee-capped so we suffered the journey in silence. It never occurred to us how pointless it all was considering that we were about to catch a ferry right back into the lion's den.

The light from the match lit a circle on the wall behind Rick's head like a saint's halo, the shadow in the centre wobbling gently with the flicker of the flame. I leaned in to light my cigarette and accidentally extinguished it. 'Oops.'

Rick sighed. 'Some fugitive you turned out to be, you can't even light a fooking cigarette!'

'I don't think lighting cigarettes is a requirement, do you?'

He lit another match. 'Course it is, everyone knows that.' With his hand still out-stretched I lit up and followed his gaze around the corner. A last lone backpacker flip-flopped on to the boat deck, handing over his ticket to an inspector as he went, and the fat gangplank operator flicked his cigarette away, both hands now holding the rope. 'What a shit job,' I remarked, 'pulling that rope up and down all day.'

'Some— Ouch!' Rick shook his hand and blew on his burnt fingers.

'What were you saying about fugitives?'

He replied with a look and turned back to the dock. 'Right, you ready?'

The fat man took one heave on the rope and the pair of us darted out from around the corner of the building. I slipped on a mini oil-slick but recovered quickly, catching up with Rick. Fatty saw us running out on to the floodlit dock and stopped pulling, his hands high on the rope. We waved our tickets in the air and, realising that we were going to jump straight on, the man put his hands slightly further down the rope, allowing it to slip through his chafed palms. The broad entry ramp dropped three feet, and we leapt at the same time, clearing the ramp edge and the three or four feet beyond, and came down, still running, on the deck of the ferry. We didn't stop jogging and laughing until we were standing at the prow of the boat.

Rick looked down at the burnt match that was still pinched between thumb and forefinger and flicked it over the side before looking at the horizon. 'Here we go again.'

The engines roared into life and churned up all the small-fry too young to know what a propeller was, the world turned and the dock of Koh Samui edged away from us. Both of us turned on cue, the stiffening breeze giving the signal, and squinted at Koh Pha-Ngan in the distance. Its few twinkling lights looked ominous, beckoning, not beautiful as they once had been, and not 'home' any more.

Twenty minutes later we were pulling into the pier on Koh Pha-Ngan.

'Now comes the hard bit.' Rick jumped down off the gunwale and moved forward towards the few people who were lined up to disembark. 'I think it's best if we stick to the crowd. What there is of it.'

I jumped down and immediately went into a squat in pain.

'You OK, John?'

'Need another pill, that's all. Let's go.' I straightened and we followed the rest of the passengers off the boat. I popped another painkiller but didn't have enough spit to swallow and had to cough it up. One of the backpackers on the boat asked me if I was OK and gave me a drink of her mineral water. 'I've always laughed at backpackers for carrying their little plastic bottles of water wherever they go,' I said, and swallowed another pill, gulping down half the bottle with it. 'Thanks.'

She turned out to be just the cover we needed and we continued talking until we reached the path that split two ways: right to Hat Rin and left to one of the more remote beaches. 'OK,' I said, raising a hand, 'Hat Rin's just over that hill, ten minutes walk.' Rick and I pretended to take the left-hand fork and, when the crowd had gone, went in behind them and disappeared into the jungle to avoid the more obvious route to the main beach.

The hill rose up from one bay, where the ferry port was situated, crossed the top and then descended into the next where the main beach was, and where Rick had booked into a hut.

Although we didn't follow the path up the hillside, there were numerous small animal tracks that wound their way through the dense foliage, making the climb easier for Rick than we'd expected. For me the effort of staggering upwards was exhausting, and I had to stop every few paces for breath, sweating like crazy in the evening's humidity.

'What about the Back Yard Pub?' I gasped as Rick forged ahead.

'We'll just have to go around it and hope that no one sees us. It's way over there anyway.'

When I got to the top of the hill he was already descending the other side towards the town, and with a quick, apprehensive look down at the lights of the restaurants along the beach, I took a deep breath and jumped, sliding in the loose earth and dead leaves.

The hair-raising slide to the bottom was like skiing on a dry ski slope: fast and fun, but unbearably painful on the hands and arse. At one point there was a dip ahead of me and the top of Rick's head went up and then vanished as he slid out of sight. I followed, first hitting a rock that sent me sprawling forwards, scraping my palms painfully, before correcting my balance and sliding on. The slope ended in a gentle levelling out where Rick was standing, casually smoking a cigarette. In a blizzard of airborne particles I slid to a halt right at his feet and went into a coughing fit.

He held out his hand and slapped my back. 'What a ride, eh?'

'The, ahem, best.' I stood, blinking the dust from my eyes. 'Fucking fantastic.'

At the bottom of the hill where we stood, a group of tourist huts began almost immediately, the harsh jungle floor turning abruptly into smooth cultivated earth. The hut nearest to us had a couple sitting on the veranda, and I was just about to comment when I noticed the expression of utter horror on Rick's face.

'They know where I live!' he hissed through clenched teeth.

Cleaning off the dirt from my shorts and picking out the leaves, I was so preoccupied with my grooming that I had hardly noticed the acrid smell in the air. With one finger still in my ear to clear out the dust, I said, 'How do you know?'

Rick stared into the clearing and slowly pulled the cigarette from his lips. 'Because when I left my hut this morning it wasn't on fooking fire.'

SEVEN

At first I couldn't quite grasp what Rick was talking about and had to ask him to repeat what he'd said. He raised an arm and pointed. All I could see was a neat row of white-washed little buildings with their wooden verandas jutting out like bottom lips on a dozen, bodiless square heads. 'There!' he repeated impatiently, 'between the second and third row.'

And I saw it; the charred, smouldering wreckage of blackened wood, lying like a slaughtered, barbecued elephant between two huts. I cautiously moved forward a step, sticking my neck out as though still not able to believe my eyes, having already not trusted my ears. 'You're not telling me that that ...' I pointed and looked at Rick, ' ... that pile of burnt wood is, *was*, your hut?'

He nodded heavily and buried his head in his hands.

Up until that point in time, that very moment when he nodded, the whole of the previous day's events had seemed like a game; just another adventure to add to my list of things I'd done while travelling. Even seeing Tommy all bandaged up in that hospital, I told myself, didn't concern me; it wasn't my body lying there broken and useless, he wasn't my brother.

Now that I was looking at the remains of Rick's accommodation, burnt to a cinder along with our belongings, the seriousness of our predicament loomed over me like the palm trees. I had prudently taken my indispensables with me from the house to the hospital: passport, money etc., but I knew that Rick hadn't, and that, along with a few of my tatty clothes, he had lost all of his gear.

He looked at me and smiled lopsidedly. 'Doesn't matter about the passport now does it?'

I closed my gaping mouth. 'Are you sure that's your hut?'

He pulled the key from his pocket and held it up. 'Go and try the door if you want.'

'Arrgh, I don't believe they did that!' I turned away from him and sat down on a log. 'Why? Why would they burn your hut down? Now you've lost everything.'

He was silent for a minute, staring at the wreckage, before turning and standing over me. 'There's something I didn't tell you, John. I haven't quite lost everything.' I looked up, wondering what the fuck he was talking about, and frowned. Rick put his hand into his pocket and pulled out a huge wad of Thai baht, waving it in the air. 'She may have taken my passport but I took that bitch's money. All of it!'

'You did what?' I exclaimed, standing up and hitting my head on an over-hanging branch.

'Heh heh. If she thinks she's got one over on me wait till she looks under the floorboards.' He ran his thumb over the end of the notes and they purred like a pack of cards. 'That'll teach her to steal my fooking passport!'

I stopped rubbing my head. 'That's *why* she burnt your fucking hut down and stole your passport, you moron! That's what she's after, not me, not you, that fucking money! Jesus, no wonder you left the house last night, it all makes perfect sense now!'

'What's got into you?'

'What's got into me? What's got into you, you idiot? You're the one who's stealing money from a Thai Mafia bird, not me.' I leant against a tree trunk to steady myself. 'Fuck me, Rick, if someone told me you had done this I'd never have believed it possible, not in a million years.'

'Don't get so ratty.'

'Ratty! Ra—?'

'I've got money.'

'A lot of fucking good money'll be to a dead man.'

'Who's a dead man?' He looked about. 'I'm not, you're not. I told you before, if she wants to fook about with the Mafia that's her problem. If

Tommy fooked about with some hard men, that's his problem, it's between Thais, it's got nothing to do with us. You and me just leave this island on the next boat out tomorrow morning and go to the mainland. Simple.'

'Huh.' I picked up my bag and slung it over my shoulder, nearly knocking Rick's head off in the process, and put one foot on the slope that we had just slid down. 'You can wait until tomorrow if you want, I'm going now.'

'Where?'

'Koh Samui. I can't see any point in waiting around here to be found and beaten. Let's go back to the ferry and leave now. We can stay there overnight and leave in the morning.' I started to climb the muddy bank.

Rick coughed sheepishly. 'That was the last ferry that we came in on John, it'll have gone by now.'

Suddenly, as if I'd been shot with a tranquilliser dart, all of my energy seemed to leave me.

'Sorry Olly!'

I don't know where it came from but I laughed. I had to; otherwise I think I might have cried. I sat down on the edge of the clearing and buried my face in my hands, unable to even look at Rick for fear that I might blow up at him. One thing I have to say about Rick, though, is that he knows when to shut up and leave someone to their thoughts. And the thoughts I had in my head were things that he wouldn't have wanted to hear anyway, because mostly they involved insulting him.

We sat there for about an hour while I tried to figure out what to do. I say 'I' tried to figure it out because, judging by the way Rick sat around idly flicking twigs on to a nearby veranda, his mind wasn't on the problem at all. Eventually I got fed up with the silence and the sound of my own thoughts inside my head. 'Rick.'

He looked up mid-flick. 'Hmm?'

'Don't keep playing with those sticks, it's really annoying. What are we going to do?'

He released the twig and sighed. 'The first ferry leaves Thong Sala for

Surat Thani at seven in the morning, I think. Otherwise we go back tomorrow morning on the one to Koh Samui and leave from there to the mainland.'

'Thong Sala? That's on the other side of the island!'

'Yeah, we'd have to get one of the trucks from here: a bit risky. We could walk.'

'Don't be silly, I came in that way when I arrived. It's ten miles, at least.'

'Well then the only alternative is to go back the way we came, through Samui. At least we won't have to walk far.'

'Mmm,' I considered the options, stretching out my aching legs and digging my feet into the soil. 'The only problem there is that they'll probably be expecting it. Remember, as far as they're concerned I'm still in the hospital. Tommy can't tell them otherwise because there's no phone at the house.'

He nodded. 'Thong Sala will definitely be safer, especially if they know about the money. They could be all over that ferry tomorrow morning.'

'You seem to forget, Rick, it's not us against the mob. We've only got the girls to contend with.' I sat back down on the log and thought. I could see that he was hiding something else about Ta and co but didn't bother to ask, there didn't seem to be any point in going over old ground. We needed a way out and I was determined to find one, however daunting the odds.

In the end, after hour upon hour of discussion, we agreed that the best thing to do was to stay on Koh Pha-Ngan and go out on one of the pick-ups early the next morning, catching the first ferry over to the mainland. The first part was very risky, but we both agreed that it was better than the Samui option; at least we should be in the clear once we were on the ferry. To lessen the risk, we needn't catch the pick-up in town but could jump in at one of the resorts further along the coast. Rick seemed to think that there was a small group of tourist huts on a fairly remote beach about two miles along from Hat Rin. He and Ta had gone there once, before I had arrived, on a day trip to some unspoilt corals, and, though his memory was vague, he thought that it wasn't far from the main Hat Rin ferry port road.

The escape plan seemed sound enough and, unless one of the girls just happened to be in the pick-up truck, appeared to be foolproof. The main drawback for me was going to be the walk to get to that beach. If we were going to get the first ferry out in the morning it would mean walking through the night; a prospect that filled me with dread.

We had two choices of route: either along the dusty main road or up the coastline. The coast route would involve clambering over rocks and swimming across dark bays, while the road, even if we tried to follow the tree line, left us dangerously exposed to all passing traffic. We couldn't decide one way or the other and, as ridiculous as it seems, ended up flipping a coin.

'One more time,' I said, the coin having come up heads for the coast route. 'Best of three, how about that?'

'You can't make a decision, that's your problem.'

'OK then, you decide which route to take.'

'I've already told you, I think we should go along the coast. You only want to flip again because it didn't come up tails, admit it.'

We needn't have bothered flipping the coin; after only half an hour into the journey we came up against a series of rocky outcrops so ragged that we were unable to cross. At first we stood and stared, trying to gauge the amount of effort required to swim around the headland, but even in the dark I could see that the rocks jutted out at least twice as far as the ones between Hat Rin and our party beach.

'What do you think, John?' Rick leaned against a rock, pulling his cigarettes from his pocket.

I looked up at the escarpment, its outline black and jagged against the night sky, the base strewn with huge boulders that had tumbled down, finally smoothing out into the shimmering moonlit sea. 'Not with this bag,' I said, patting my holdall, 'I can't swim with this. To be honest, even if I didn't have this I don't know if we could make that swim. Who knows how much further around before we hit a beach on the other side?'

Rick rolled the foil from his cigarette packet into a ball and flicked it away. 'You're a better swimmer than me, I suppose. If you can't do it then neither can I. We can't go over the top, it'll take forever. We'll have to turn back.'

'Shit.'

'There's nothing else we can do.' He sighed heavily. 'What time d'you reckon it is?'

I looked up at the sky and said, 'Two, three latest.'

'We'll have a ciggie and then move off. We should be able to cut through the fields at the back of town.'

We smoked a cigarette each and walked back the way we'd come, and, as Rick had suggested, turned off into what looked like a cultivated piece of land behind Hat Rin. Besides the odd shout in the distance, carried by the gentle breeze across the relatively flat land, and the occasional boom of a loud speaker, we heard nothing. There was something quietly soothing about finally being out in the open field, away from the choking jungle, and with the aid of another painkiller I felt my spirits lift, as the land sloped upwards very gently to meet the dusty main Hat Rin–Thong Sala road.

'Which way d'you want to go?' Rick asked as I stood beside him, the dirt track cutting through the palms left and right of us like a perfectly routed channel. 'Don't answer that,' he said, and put his arm around my shoulder. 'Go north young man, and avoid being cut up into little pieces and fed to the sharks.'

We walked through the night along that dusty track as it wound its way through the trees like the course of a river, changing direction when the engineers came, like we had, up against rock faces too large to cross. Up and down we went, a rollercoaster with two people side by side, rising and falling with the track and puffing away on cigarettes, the puffs of blue smoke hanging breathlessly behind us.

The width of the track was exactly the same as the height of the palm trees and dense jungle that lined it, and I felt like I was walking down a tunnel, square on cross-section and open at the top. The moon was only a slither, a toenail clipping, but provided the tunnel with just enough light: silver on the tree tops when we reached a brow in the road, orange on the sandy clay soil of the track.

By the time we reached a small lane that turned off the main road the moon was only just visible, lying on its curved back on a bed of palm tops, comfortable and snug.

'This looks like it,' Rick said, stepping off the track on to the grass verge.

'Two miles my foot. More like five.' I leaned against a signpost, exhausted.

The sign was obscured by sun-dried mud that had splashed off the road during the rainy season. Rick nudged me to one side and chipped off the two-inch thick mud cake. '*Cosy Resort and Bungalows*,' he read. A small arrow pointed down the narrow jungle path. 'This is it. Now we just wait until it gets light and get into the first pick-up that comes by.'

I immediately threw my bag on to the ground and blinked hard, squeezing the sting out of my tired eyes. 'Fuck, I'm knackered.' Trampling down the grass by the roadside, I made a small sitting area. 'How long d'you think before the first truck comes along?'

'Before the first ferry. Around six, I think.'

'Think?'

'Definitely before seven anyway. Someone's got to come by before seven if it takes half an hour to get there. What time now?'

'Five,' I said, yawning, 'not later.'

'Course, there may be other transport before then. I think we should stay alert and get anything that comes along. If–'

I squatted and then laid down, using my bag as a pillow.

'What the fook are you doing?'

'Going to bed, what does it look like?'

'Bed? Someone's got to keep an eye out.'

'You can,' I rolled on to my side, smacking my lips. 'Wake me when a truck comes along.'

'But why me?'

'Because you fucked up,' I said closing my eyes. 'Goodnight.'

EIGHT

'How the fuck are we going to know if they're friendly or not?' I shouted, still blinking rapidly against the bright, early morning sky and trying to locate the shoulder strap of my bag. 'It could be one of Ta's cronies.'

Rick was standing in the middle of the track waving his hands wildly above his head as though directing a helicopter in to land. 'Try,' he replied, 'see what happens.'

Amidst a cloud of orange dust and the sound of tyres grinding on hard earth, I clambered up the incline to the road where Rick had been. It was like the scene from a magician's stage show where a puff of smoke heralds the disappearance of the beautiful assistant. Rick wasn't beautiful but the effect was similar. In the time I had taken my eyes off him to pick up my bag he was gone, replaced by the cloud of dust.

He reappeared to my right leaning into the window of a pick-up. My heart was in my mouth: either they didn't know Ta and would drive us to the ferry, or Rick was about to get his brains blown out.

The driver thumbed behind him and Rick put a thumb up to me. 'We're in!'

'Brilliant,' I shouted back, and ran to the vehicle and jumped in the back with him. 'So far so good.' For one heart-stopping moment the driver started a three-point turn, but then, after looking out of his side window to ensure that he had cleared a pot-hole, we drove on.

Rick was regaining some lost ground in my estimation, after messing up so badly: he had been right about the field that took us around the back of Hat Rin, and now about the first pick-up of the morning. Things were definitely looking up on his part. We reached Thong Sala ferry pier and went to the ticket office of the ferry company.

A tight-lipped, weasel-looking Thai man opened the shutter for the first business of the day, arranging the cushion on his seat before sitting on it and looking up at us. 'Ngh?' he grunted, still not fully awake.

'Two tickets to Surat Thani, please.' He punched them out and slid them across the counter, writing the price (different to what it said on the ticket) on a scrap of paper. We didn't argue and paid. 'What time does it leave?' I asked.

He stabbed the ticket with his finger and huffed.

'Eleven! Isn't there one before that?'

His stabbing finger came up and tapped on the window, where a timetable had been stuck with tape. It confirmed what was written on the ticket: KPG VIA K. TAO AND K. SAM. – ARR. KPG 11.00

I deflated. 'Now what?'

'Wait. What else is there to do?' Rick scanned the dock-side. 'There're a few cafés around here, they're not open yet but we can get something to eat when they do, and hide in them until the ferry comes.'

As we walked away in search of some breakfast, I glanced back at the ticket office and saw the weasel pick up the phone. 'D'you know anyone who's got a phone on Koh Pha-Ngan, Rick?' I said.

He shook his head. 'I don't know anyone who has, but plenty of people have got phones. Most of the bungalow owners and restaurants have a phone, why?'

'Nothing,' I said, turning back and walking on. 'Just paranoia.'

Having not seen anyone that we recognised while hanging around the cafés, we assumed that we were in the clear, and when the boat eventually arrived and the passengers started to board, Rick and I waited on the top floor balcony of a restaurant that overlooked the jetty just to be sure.

'See anyone?'

'Nope,' he replied, 'not a sausage. We've been here for three hours and I haven't recognised a single person from Hat Rin, or anywhere else for that matter.'

'Good.' I stood up. 'Let's get on that boat and get the fuck out of here.'

The ferry wasn't the same as the one I'd arrived on when first coming to the island. Unlike the previous, smaller two-deck passenger ferry that usually plied these waters, the one that came in now was a huge steel car ferry with five decks, snack bars and air conditioned TV lounge. When it came alongside, it nearly took the jetty from its moorings under the impact, sending most of the queuing passengers to their knees.

As with the previous night's ferry from Koh Samui, we waited until the last minute before running out from our cover and boarding the boat, not even bothering to show our tickets for inspection and running straight on deck. Whether my earlier paranoia was justified or not, when we got to the front of the upper deck and looked over at the passengers below, we got the shock of our lives to see Toomy sitting up front.

Rick pushed me back against the steel wall. 'She must have already been on the ferry when it arrived!' He peeped back over the edge. 'Shit!'

'Impossible,' I said, 'this boat came from Koh Tao.'

'Yes, but before that it must have come from Surat Thani.'

I made a quick mental adjustment. 'Are you thinking what I'm thinking?'

He nodded. 'They're waiting for us in Surat Thani,' we both said. 'Fuck!'

Because of the number of decks and the size of the boat it would be easy enough for us to keep out of sight during the four-hour crossing. The decks fore and aft were tiered, like most large vessels, so that the lower decks were wider and longer than the next one up, a bit like a wedding cake. All we had to do was stay seated on the deck above Toomy and look down occasionally to see if and when she moved. The difficulty would be getting off the boat in Surat Thani without being seen. I suggested getting off at Koh Samui, but as Rick said, we still had to get from there to Surat Thani, so the problem wouldn't be solved.

'Then there's nothing we can do,' I sighed, peeping over the edge of our deck beside Rick, 'just stay here and sit tight. Maybe she'll get off in Samui.'

'Maybe.'

The boat blew its horn and we parted company with the island. The brown, churned up water cleared and we picked up speed, first running near to the shore and then clearing the headland at Hat Rin, where the water turned a familiar blue. If Toomy hadn't been on that boat I would have felt my spirits lift as high as the sea birds flying above us. Rising and dipping as they scooped up the fish that had been chopped to pieces in our wake, their white bodies flashing brilliantly against the tropical blue sky.

We pulled into Koh Samui briefly to let on a handful of passengers before moving away into open water again, but Toomy didn't get off, and, apart from once going into the snack bar and bringing back a pot noodle for herself, she didn't move for the next two hours.

Eventually the boat gave another loud blast of its horn and we pulled in at Surat Thani. Toomy got up and did a full circuit of the bottom deck before checking out the upper ones, obviously looking for us, and when she came up to our end of the boat we hid in the toilets and watched through a gap in the door. Thinking that we were not onboard, she shuffled dejectedly back to her deck and waited by the side, staring vacantly into the water.

The boat drew up alongside the dock and slammed into the shore piles once or twice, sending the passengers sprawling again, before going into reverse and lining up to drop the gang plank.

'She's not getting off!' I hissed as I watched Toomy below us. Other passengers were disembarking but Toomy just stood there. A moment later she started waving at someone in amongst the crowd on the dock. It was Empress Ning!

'They're all in on it!'

Toomy shouted something down at Ning and shook her head, as if to say that we weren't onboard. Ning's shoulders dropped and she pushed her way back through the crowd and out into the car park where we saw her board a local bus.

'Wait until the last minute,' Rick instructed, 'when Toom' sits back down, then we'll get off.' Toomy immediately went back to her seat and Rick and I quickly descended the stairs of the boat and jumped in behind the rear of the crowd, crouching down as low as we could. 'Keep low,' he whispered, 'and keep on going until we get to the car park.'

We shuffled down the ramp and mingled in as far as we could, before the crowd dispersed and we were left exposed, conveniently next to a row of taxis. The driver must have been asleep because when we dived in through the rear door his head shot up from the passenger seat, his eyes blinking incessantly as though he'd been halfway through a dream.

'Wha'-wha'-wha'?'

'Train station,' Rick barked. 'Move it!'

'Hold it! I said, putting one hand on his shoulder and staring out the window. The bus that Ning had boarded started up and left the car park in a huge cloud of black diesel smoke. 'OK, follow that bus.'

NINE

By the time we arrived at the train station in Surat Thani I had fallen asleep in the back of the taxi. Our driver had told us that it was the shuttle bus between ferry and train station so we followed it just in case Ning got off halfway. Wishful thinking. Rick nudged me awake and we watched as she got off the bus and headed straight for the north-bound platform of the station.

We paid the driver and crept over to the opposite side of the track, hiding behind the stinking toilet block. 'Now we are done for,' I said, pinching my nose against the pungent, sour odour of ammonia that was being let off in waves from the urinals. 'They're not stupid, they know you've got no passport.' Rick looked at me, puzzled, and I added, 'They've got your passport, d'you see? They don't need to cover the south-bound platform cause it only goes to the border with Malaysia, they know you can't cross. They're expecting us to go north to Bangkok.'

He thought for a moment, hoisting up his baggy Coco the Clown tie-dye trousers. 'So we go south. Screw 'em.'

'You've got no passport, how are you going to cross the border? We can get a bus to Bangkok.'

He shook his head. 'Toomy's half-brother works in the ticket office at the bus depot, he'd tell her straight away.'

I fell back against the wall. 'Are they so well-connected these people?'

'Believe it, John. Everyone knows everyone else down here. Nothing happens without somebody else knowing about it, or without someone's permission. Even us, living at that house, you can bet that half of the Thais on Koh Samui knew about it.'

I sighed. 'Christ. It's a pity you didn't tell me all this a year ago, I wouldn't have fucking stayed there. Jesus, it's like a bad dream!'

'Well there's no use crying about it now,' he said, pulling his damp, sweaty shirt from his body. 'Anyway, dreams never come true. Let's get out of here, this place stinks.'

We cruised up and down the back streets until we found a suitably inconspicuous café and went in. We were both shocked at the difference in temperature between the islands and the mainland where the sea breezes were blocked out by buildings. Having spent months living right by the sea, the extra five degrees, plus added humidity, made it seem like we had left Thailand already and gone somewhere further south.

Wafting the air under his shirt to dry the sweat, Rick suddenly looked very odd amongst the tablecloths and plate glass windows. The trappings of civilisation were a stark contrast to the soft surroundings of the bamboo, jungle and beaches that we had become accustomed to. Rick's clothing and bleached hair made him stand out a mile.

'You've got to get some new clothes, Rick.'

He stopped wafting to inspect himself. 'What's wrong with these?'

'Too conspicuous, you look like a clown.'

'Well it's all I've got for now. Anyhow, that's the least of our worries.'

We ordered two coffees from the waitress, who smiled politely and asked if we'd just come from Koh Pha-Ngan. She was probably only being friendly but my paranoia was getting the better of me, so I said we hadn't but were thinking of going there, and immediately left the restaurant and went into another that looked like a karaoke lounge.

The new waiter took our order without asking any questions, and Rick continued where he'd left off. 'Forget the clothes, what are we going to do to get out of here?'

I'd been racking my brains and I thought I had the solution. 'The only way is to get a later train south, a night-train if there is one. We can get onboard without being seen, no problem. Then we change further down the line, during the night, and get the first train back up to Bangkok. Even if Empress Ning is still awake by then, I doubt that she's going to board the train and search every bloody compartment.' I took a sip of my drink. 'In any case, when we get back to this station we can always hide in the train toilet. What d'you think, good idea or not?'

'Shit idea. But it's all we've got.'

'Well thanks for your contribution.'

'Don't mention it.'

While Rick stayed seated in the lounge, I went back out to the station to check the timetable for trains towards the border. Ning was smoking a joint and chatting to a street vendor when I reached the station, so I quickly ran on to the opposite platform and darted into the waiting room where the ticket office was located. The timetable was indecipherable so I went to the window and woke up the clerk who was dozing behind the counter, his head resting on a dog-eared copy of a Thai girlie magazine.

'Ahem!'

His head came up as slowly as treacle, opening one lazy eye, and he pushed himself over to the window on his wheeled office chair. The concrete floor between his desk and the window was dark and smooth where years of five-wheeled vehicles had passed across it. 'Mm?' His head peered over the top of the ticket counter.

'Next train tonight, what time?' I prayed for him to understand.

'Bangko'?'

'No, Malaysia. But no go to Malaysia. Next station from here.'

Still seated, he pushed off with his feet and whizzed backwards across the floor to the window that faced the platform, coming to a stop exactly where he needed to be. His accuracy on that chair was astounding, and after issuing a ticket to a woman who I hadn't even noticed waiting, he pushed off again and came back to me, his chair never bumping into anything en route. He said something in Thai, I frowned, and he wrote *22.45* on a piece of paper. The five was written backwards so I double-checked the timetable and it corresponded.

'Two,' I said, making a V sign, quickly handing over the cash and running out with the tickets.

When I got back to the karaoke lounge, Rick was talking to a Thai girl, or, rather, he was speaking to her breasts. She was sitting on his knee, her legs swinging to and fro in a split skirt, her high heel shoes balancing seductively on the end of her toes.

He looked up as I walked over. 'Did you get them?'

'Yep, two tickets s–' I glanced at the girl as she twirled the hairs on his chest around her finger, and then back at him, frowning.

'Now you just go and do your work and let me talk to my friend for five minutes,' Rick said to the girl. 'I'll see you in a moment.' She reluctantly stood up and went off behind a velvet curtain.

'Who's she?' I asked, looking back at Rick.

'She works here.' He pulled me into a seat. 'You'll never guess what, John, this is a brothel! Honest to God, it's a fooking brothel. Ahem, now what were you saying about the tickets?'

I hesitated, dumbstruck for a moment, and blinked the vision away.

'Yeah, um, oh yeah, two tickets south, the train leaves tonight at a quarter to eleven.'

'Fantastic.' He clapped once. 'Fan-fooking-tastic.'

'Yeah that's what I–'

'Quarter to eleven, you say? That leaves us . . . ' he looked at a clock above the bar, 'five hours, great! I think we should stay in here, keep well out of sight, it's safer that way.'

By eleven o'clock that night I was so drunk I could hardly stand.

At first I had protested to Rick (somewhat feebly I must admit) that we should spend the time somewhere else because neither of us could afford to throw our money down the drain buying over-priced cans of beer in a knocking shop. He wouldn't budge, however, insisting that we should celebrate our departure from the island, and eventually I caved in and got pissed with him.

From what I could gather, very few foreigners ever visited the bar; no one ever stayed in Surat Thani for longer than it took to change from train to ferry, or vice versa. Consequently, the girls were all over us, and, like the idiots they took us for, we went along for the ride, throwing our money about like there was no tomorrow. It was only the appearance of the ticket clerk in the bar at half-ten, searching out a young girl after a hard day's chair riding, which reminded us of the train. I wouldn't have recognised him with legs if he hadn't tapped me on the shoulder. 'Here! Now!' he said, stabbing his watch with a finger and pointing at the door. I swayed drunkenly and looked down at his newly acquired bottom half before jumping up.

'Rick! The train, Rick, quick!' I grabbed my bag and we shot out of the door without settling the bill, only to be called back by the owner. A wad of baht went from us to him, and we ran through the town and on to the platform, boarding the train just as it was pulling out of the station. Both of us immediately ran to the opposite window and blew raspberries at

Ning, who was lying asleep on a bench and had a rat chewing at the ragged hem of her dress.

'That's it, we've done it!' I said, and promptly threw up out of the window on to the track.

After an argument with the ticket inspector, in which he insisted that we only had third-class tickets and therefore had to sit with the sacks of rice, we bribed the guard and settled into a comfortable, reclining aircraft seat in first-class. The previous two days had drained me of any energy I might have had left, and that, combined with the tranquillising effect of the drink and painkillers, had left me almost senseless.

So senseless in fact, so obliterated and almost unconscious, that I was asleep before my bum even landed on the seat. I didn't hear Rick's snoring and I didn't hear the mobile snack bar wheeled past.

I think I heard the train driver's announcement that we had arrived at our station, but that was just a dream, and dreams never come true.

TEN

'John ... John ... '

'Mmm ... '

'John ... '

'Mmm?'

'John?' (A gentle nudge), 'John!' (A shake, harder this time so that my head was made to roll against the headrest.)

'Mmm ... '

'*JOHN!*

I woke with a start; the sunlight streaming through the train window and forcing me to keep one eye tightly shut.

'We're at the wrong station!'

The voice gave me the correct direction in which to swivel my head. I turned towards the aisle and looked up at Rick, still blinking through slits. 'What?'

'We missed the station, John. We're at the wrong station.'

The words went around in my fogged up mind as it made its journey from slumberland to the world of the awake. 'We,' I mused, 'have missed the station?'

'We've *missed* it,' Rick growled.

My mind cleared a little. 'Missed it?'

'Missed it. We've stopped. We're at the fooking border.'

'Missed it? At the fuck–?' I quickly turned to look out the window and almost head-butted the bearded man who occupied the seat next to me. 'Yes,' he said in a voice much deeper than Rick's, 'you are now at the border with our beautiful country, yes.' A mass of facial hair almost hid the man's features, and when I nodded at him the hair nodded back. 'Yes.'

The train had indeed stopped, and everyone had either got off or was in the process of getting off. From my window I could only see tracks and sidings, but when I leaned forward to look past Rick's legs I could see a queue of people gathering along the platform. 'What, Malaysia?' I enquired

'Yes, our beautiful country, yes. Now, if you will excuse me I would like to pass. I think it is time, yes.' One of my legs had gone to sleep and I had to pick it up with both hands to clear a path for the bearded man to pass by. 'Yes,' he said again, waddled out past Rick and went down the aisle.

Rick frowned. 'C'mon, John, get your bag and let's get off, before they take the train somewhere else.'

The people outside queued single file beside the train, along the length of the platform, yawning and wiping their puffy faces down while trying to shelter from the sunshine. They stood with their backs pressed up against a wall, petrified, the shade edging towards their toes menacingly as it was forced back by sunlight.

Rick and I stopped at the foot of the train steps and looked down the line to its end, where a group of officials in uniforms were busy stamping passports and checking through the odd backpack. Most of the people in the line were Asian and carried a suitcase, lined up as though ready for the firing squad. It reminded me of pictures I'd seen in history books at school, where a Nazi concentration camp officer had captured the scene with his Box Brownie.

'What d'you think?' I said to Rick, stepping off the train and blinking against the light.

He sighed angrily. 'We'll have to get the next train back, I suppose.'

'We could tell them that you lost your passport, or had it stolen on the train. They might let us through.'

'Come off it, John. Look at us.' He presented himself, using his hands as the guide, and pinching a fold in each trouser leg, held them out like First World War flying leathers. 'Malaysia's got the strictest customs in the world and we've just come from Thailand. Think about it.'

I yawned and looked down the line again, wondering if there was another way through a customs check-point without a passport, and said, 'Let's have a look down there and see what the score is before we decide.'

What we saw at the head of the queue was a surprise to both of us. The line of passengers went into a small concrete shelter, where it passed by one officer who stamped passports, before moving on to the bag-check. Two uniformed women stood behind a knee-high concrete bench, like a fishmonger's gutting slab, and occasionally searched a bag. After that there was nothing.

The main surprise to us, though, was the poor design of the whole checking station. The fishmonger's bench ran down the middle of the hall and was only open at one end, where the passengers, already checked and cleared, did a U-turn and came back down the other side to where the exit door was situated. Not only that but a huge concrete column that held up the roof had its foundation right on top of the slab, so that only the passport stamper could see the exit, and he was much too busy stamping.

I barged through the queue with Rick and stood against the slab, within touching distance of the people exiting on the other side. 'Tightest customs in the world huh?' I said airily.

'It's a joke.' Rick was stunned too, and said that he wished he'd brought some dope with him from Thailand. 'Are you thinking what I'm thinking?' I said after a pause.

He looked at me. 'I don't know, what are you thinking?'

I smiled and waved my passport in his face.

'Fooking hell, if we get caught!'

I looked over the top of the queue to the passport stamper, then back at Rick. 'All you've got to do is jump over that bench and go out the door.' Just at that moment an officer came in through the exit door and asked us to move back, away from the slab.

'Shit.'

'That's the end of that idea.'

We talked as we walked along the platform to the back of the queue, and I said, 'No it's not. They never check the photo in a passport, right? Hardly ever anyway. All I've got to do is somehow get in the queue a few people ahead of you, clear customs, tear out the page that they've stamped and then give my passport to you. You then go through with my passport.'

'Suppose they do look at the photo?'

'Well for a start off, by the time we get to the front that guy may be gone again and you can just hop over the counter and walk out. If he is there, and we have to resort to Plan B and they do look at my photo, they most probably won't even notice.'

Rick burst out laughing. 'But I don't look anything like you!'

'To them you do, there's no difference.'

'But I've got long hair and you haven't got any, how's that for a fooking difference?' He sighed. 'Do you know what the penalty is for forgery out here?'

'No.'

'Neither do I, but I know they hang you for possession of an ounce of marijuana.'

'Well we don't possess any so there's no worry there.'

We stood in silence for a moment looking up and down the queue and smoking a cigarette each, occasionally taking a step forward as another person was checked and deemed worthy of treading on Malaysian soil. 'Why don't we just go back up to Bangkok then,' I said, 'if you think we're taking too much risk?'

'Run over it again for me,' he flicked his cigarette butt beneath the train and exhaled, 'just to make sure I've got it right. You're going to go in first.'

'I go in first, six or seven people ahead of you, with your shirt in my bag. By the time you get to the front I'll be cleared. They're bound to ask you to put on a shirt, you know what these stamp-happy officials are like with hippies and—'

'I ain't a hippy.'

'Well, doesn't matter. Anyway, they ask you to put on a shirt, and you say?'

'Ahem. Oh dear! My, friend, has, it.'

I sighed. 'Right, but with more feeling, that was a bit wooden. I'll then come over, unzip my bag and give you my passport.'

'Wrapped neatly inside my shirt,' he completed. 'It's a crap plan.'

'No it's not. Anyway, if it looks too risky when we get to the front, just go to Plan C.'

'Plan C? You didn't tell me about Plan-fooking-C.'

'That's because I just made it up. Plan C is when you have a fit on the floor and start foaming at the mouth. They'll take you to hospital and you can get in that way.' He didn't reply. 'Right,' I checked our progress, 'we're almost there, give me your shirt.'

'Don't make it dirty.' He handed me a moth-eaten tie-dye shirt.

'Phew, it stinks!' I held it up to the light. 'And I can see daylight through it!' Quickly unzipping my bag I stuffed it inside. 'OK.'

'How are you going to get into the queue?'

I stood on tiptoe and looked over the heads of the line of people.

'Those three *Austrian* girls.' Two of the girls turned their heads and smiled at me, recognising the familiar word.

Rick leaned out, looked at the girls and smiled, then leaned back in and said, 'How d'you know they're Austrian?'

'They've all got blonde hair,' I said, still smiling back at them, 'and the national flag sewn on to their backpacks. Here goes . . .'

'Wait!' he held my arm. 'What happens if it all goes wrong and I get arrested?'

'We stick together whatever, Rick, you know that. Tell them you're with me. They'll have my passport so I can't go anywhere anyway. I told you, if it's too risky we back out, OK?'

We shook hands and parted.

Getting into the queue further down was the easy part, all I had to do was launch into a familiar chat-up routine with the three girls and I was in. At first we spoke about why they had sewn their national flag on to their packs for all to see; a good starting point as all Europeans are obsessed with national boundaries, especially northern Europeans. All I had to do was appear indifferent to their patriotism.

'But you're just born on a piece of land that happens to have been named by someone,' I pleaded with the girls, 'it's just lines on a map.'

'Oh surely not,' one countered, 'surely it is more. Is it not culture and . . . oh, so many other things that make us all different?'

I put my bag down, thus staking my claim in the line. 'You're just another person born on this planet of ours,' I said with contrived free spirit. 'Imagine, if you had been born five miles to the left you would be wearing a German flag. Isn't that a bit silly?'

'German!' she gasped. 'Oh I think not. We can *never* be *German.*'

The queue moved along and I pushed the bag up with my feet. 'Personally,' I said, entering the shade offered by the hall roof, 'I'm from earth.'

The girl started to argue her point again while her two mute friends listened, expressionless. I didn't catch what she was saying because I was too busy calculating: summing up the distance between Rick and I versus the time it took for a person to clear the customs and go out through the door. Assuming I got searched, which was pretty likely considering my dress, I seemed to have judged it just right. Nine people were between the two of us, which left enough bodies in the line not only to allow me clearance in time, but also to keep Rick on the column-side of the queue when I handed over his shirt.

The queue shuffled forwards and the first Austrian girl crossed the yellow line to get stamped. My hands were beginning to shake and the sweat was pouring in rivers down my back, but when I checked behind me Rick seemed as cool as can be. He stood smoking a cigarette at the edge of the hall, huge puffs of sunlit smoke rising up into the roof space like escaped gas. I looked back, more nervous than ever.

The second girl went up and plonked her passport on the desk while the one who had just been cleared opened her pack for the two women to search. They gave only a cursory look inside before waving her on and beckoning the next one to step up, allowing the chain to move forward one more person.

The officer who had been standing by the exit door suddenly went out again. 'Great,' I whispered to myself, and Rick and I nodded at each other, gently acknowledging the perfect timing. I'll never forget his calmness at that point. Far from being nervous he appeared to be enjoying the whole thing. I knew from my activities as a schoolboy that breaking the law provided an adrenalin rush, but this was way beyond that. I was almost fainting from the exertion.

'Hey!'

I spun around and pointed to myself. Me?

The rubber stamper stared, too tired and too bored with his job to do anything else. He had those customs officer eyes – the ones that look right into your soul and say, 'You're guilty, just admit it and save us all the trouble of checking.' I stepped forward and presented my sodden passport, wet from the sweat that ran from my palms, and the customs officer held it by the corners to avoid touching its glossy surface. The edges were crinkled like corrugated cardboard.

'First time Malaysia?' he enquired with monotone efficiency.

'Y-yes.'

Flick-flick. Dhoom. Stamped.

The two bag-checking women called me over with their eyes but I was stuck to the spot. '*Go!*' I said to myself, and looked down at my passport lying on the table, its pages slowly closing by themselves, the corrugation softly falling back into place seated crest-to-groove. There was a loud sigh in my right ear as the stamper lost his patience at the hold up.

'I think you are clear,' someone behind me said, and peeped around my arm. 'You can move along now.'

'Um, oh yeah, thanks.' I snapped out of the stare, snatched the passport and moved on. I was given only a token bag search before moving along to the end of the slab, doing a U-turn and walking back towards the column and the exit door. The officer had finished his cigarette and was now back inside the hall, standing, hands behind his back, looking bored.

The next part went like a dream. As I approached the column, the officer snapped his fingers at someone in the queue and held the lapel of his jacket. Quickening my pace and at the same time pretending to unzip my bag, I said, 'Oh, I've got it!' and took out Rick's shirt. The officer looked me in the eye and held out his hand, but so that he wouldn't get a chance to handle it, I immediately slid the shirt over the counter to Rick, trying to clear up any confusion by saying, 'It's his shirt. Him.'

'OK, you go now,' the officer barked as Rick snatched the shirt, and pointed at the exit.

Counting down the nine people before Rick was awful; like waiting for a long-lost relative who never arrives. When the tenth person came out into the car park and it wasn't him I sank, staring vacantly down at my wrists and imaging the hand-cuffs on them. I looked back up and there he was, walking through the doorway, smiling like a Cheshire cat.

'Your passport, sir,' he said, walking out into the Malaysian sunshine and holding out the little maroon book.

I stood up. 'My God, what happened?'

'Got chatting to that bird who checks the bags. Shall we go and have a cup of coffee? There's a tea stall over there.'

'Coffee?' I snatched the passport from him. 'Never mind fucking coffee! Let's get out of here.' I pointed across the car park. 'Those buses go to Kuala Lumpur, I think.'

'Think?'

Picking up my bag, I started to stride towards the buses, trying desperately to control my temper. 'I don't care where they fucking go. I've been looking over my shoulder for a week now and I'm developing a stiff neck. As long as they go south we can end up in Timbuc-fucking-tu for all I care.'

The buses did go to Kuala Lumpur, and by early evening we were standing outside the main city bus terminus in the middle of a rush-hour river; a river of people going home from work. We were lost but happy; the anonymity afforded by the crowd swarming around us filling me with warmth.

Of all the lasting, snapshot images I have, I think the one of Rick and I standing in that busy main street is probably the most vivid. It seems strange to me that something as mundane as that can take precedence over much more significant events. How can one compare standing outside a bus station watching the pedestrian traffic to seeing a freshly severed human finger? Or allow it to take precedence in the mind over the sight of a beautiful Thai stripper in a Patpong bar?

The brain, however, is a funny thing, and I still have this image: Rick, dressed in tie-dye shirt and trousers and wearing sandals, with shoulder-length blond hair, standing next to me. I'm wearing shorts and a T-shirt, and my bag, containing what few valuables I have, is at my feet. Our skin is darker than any of the Malaysians who are walking past. Yuppies in suits, beautiful secretaries, grannies and school kids, all turn to stare at us.

Looking back at that crowd and nodding to each and every one of them was a tonic. The memories of recent events in Thailand seemed to float out of my head, as though washed in the river of people, and carried downstream. The longer we stood and stared, the less I remembered.

'A change is as good as a rest' are words I now live by ever since that time we first arrived from Thailand. Life on Koh Pha-Ngan had become the norm and city life was something that we'd forgotten even existed. A change *is* as good as a rest providing it's a real change of lifestyle and not just location. There's no point going from Hat Rin to Phuket, because they're both beaches, and, likewise, it isn't a change if one spends six months in Phuket and then goes to a beach in Goa. I actually looked forward to breathing in the diesel fumes from the clapped-out buses and taxis that only city life has to offer. I wanted to be lost in the crowd and get pushed and shoved by people who were too busy to show any manners.

I remember feeling like Tarzan when he was brought out of the jungle and taken to the developed world. All the sounds and smells were different but vaguely familiar, having their origin somewhere in the natural world, and somehow refreshingly new. The people that walked past me looked refreshingly new too, like apes wearing clothes, as though it had taken a stark change of our lifestyle to become receptive enough to see it. It was like a short-sighted person being given a pair of specs for the first time in their life and suddenly everything coming into focus.

TALES FROM TWO CITIES

ONE

Although not expensive by Western standards, Malaysia was still a shock after Thailand and India, so we limited ourselves to a cheap guest house and only the essentials, such as beer drinking and the occasional disco. Our main task while in KL was twofold: to get Rick's stolen passport replaced and to get my camcorder repaired. I'd missed a lot of photo opportunities since it had packed in and didn't want to let any more once-in-a-lifetime experiences pass by my lens unrecorded.

Obtaining a passport turned out to be easy: Rick filled out a form, paid some money and a week later it was issued. Getting a camcorder repaired, on the other hand, was like asking them to build the space shuttle. Eventually, I resigned myself to missing out on any film-making opportunities that Malaysia had to offer, and convinced myself that memories of a cerebral kind were more meaningful and longer lasting then celluloid anyway.

A week into our stay in the Malaysian capital we came across a young traveller who'd also just left Thailand. He checked into our guest house one rainy afternoon and took the bunk-bed next to me, settling in without saying a word to anyone. His traveller clothing of khaki army shorts and baggy shirt gave him an air of experience that belied his youthful features, and upon first glance I took him to be in his early twenties. However, when I had a chance to study him closer I could see that he wasn't any older than twenty. He later revealed his age to be seventeen.

Tom, a gay Englishman who was also staying in the dorm, started the ball rolling. Jumping off the top bunk and holding out his hand, he introduced himself.

The boy looked up as the body went past. At first he didn't seem to realise he was being spoken to and immediately looked back down at his hands.

'Where are you from?' Tom asked.

'Holland,' the boy replied sheepishly.

Everyone in the room continued with what they had been doing but listened with pricked ears at the two soft voices.

'Been here long? Malaysia I mean.'

'Just arrived, from Thailand.' The boy lowered his eyes when he said the 'land' of the word 'Thailand'.

Tom, picking up on the body language, pretended to busy himself with something before continuing. 'Been there myself. Didn't like it much, though, I had really expensive pair of designer jeans stolen from my washing-line on Koh Samui.' He paused, waiting for a reply, and said, 'How about you?'

'Terrible.' His reply was barely audible but was said with such heart-rending sadness that the other half-dozen of us in the room immediately stopped what we had been doing and turned to face him. He blinked hard as a tear formed in his eyes and nervously picked up a pen that had been lying on his bed. 'Just terrible,' he repeated, fiddling with the cartridge. 'I've lost all my money.'

'What d'you mean, stolen?'

He nodded, looking down at the floor. 'In Bangkok.'

Tom looked at each of us and tensed the veins in his neck.

I put down the dice I'd been playing backgammon with. 'What happened?'

'It was at the Palace in Bangkok, on my first day, last week.' He took a deep breath, fighting back the tears. 'I was just taking a look around, and this man came up to me and asked if I needed a guide. I said . . . '

'What, a Thai?'

'Yes, he was Thai. And I said no, but he follows me.' He twiddled the pen between his fingers as though lost in the bad memory.

'Go on.'

'So I allow him to show me around. He did not want money, and I say to him, "Look, I will not pay you for this," and he agrees: no money, just friend. So, around one o'clock he asks me to go for lunch. He says that he knows Thai restaurants, and if I go with him he can get a good price for the food. So I think, OK, I am hungry, why not?'

Everyone in the room was now facing the boy, listening to the story.

'Then we go to a cheap restaurant and have some nice food.' He looked at the floor and shook his head. 'I don't know why I did it, I ask myself many times, "Joseph, why do you do this stupid thing?"'

'Fooking hell, you only had something to eat.'

He looked up. 'No, he put something in my food. I do not know what, but something bad. One hour later we are in my room and he tells me, "Get your passport and your traveller's cheques and come with me." So I do what he says and go to the bank with him and cash all of the cheques. I sign each one because he tells me to, I give him the cash because he tells me to, and I go back to the room because he tells me, "Go back to your room and say nothing."'

We were dumb-struck; eyes like saucers, mouths agape.

'He even give me back the passport,' the boy continued. 'The next day I wake up and remember everything. I go to the police but they can do nothing. I go to the bank but they tell me, "You come here yesterday and sign the cheques, so we issue cash."'

'Shit, you remember doing all of these things?' I said, and leaned closer. 'Everything.'

I turned to look at Rick who was watching the distant lightning through the window. 'What kind of drug can do that Rick?'

He shrugged. 'Nothing I've heard of. Except maybe that date-ra–' Rick caught himself saying rape and corrected the sentence, aware that the boy may have left out some less choice details of the tale, 'that stuff they've got in America. I've heard that can be pretty weird.'

The boy looked embarrassed and took the pen apart with trembling hands. Tom tried to step in. 'So,' he said breezily, 'how long are you travelling for?'

'Supposed to be three months. But now, after losing my money, I will be lucky if I can have three weeks.'

There was a deafening clap of thunder and the room was lit up by lightening. Tom walked over to the open door that led out to the roof and shut it, looking up at the brooding sky, his hands in his trouser pockets. 'I was thinking of going out tonight as well. Does anyone want . . . ' He turned to face the room but stopped speaking when he saw the boy, tears rolling down his cheeks.

TWO

'He's been raped.' Tom undid another button on his shirt as the three of us left the guest house and walked out into the wet humid night air. 'No question about it. Either that or he's a good actor.'

We had decided to take up Tom's offer of a night on the town. The weather had improved, but more than that we wanted to be free of the atmosphere that had descended upon the guest house since the Dutch boy's arrival. Everyone in the room had done their best to cheer him up but it was a lost cause; he'd probably be better off if he went back to his family in Holland and forgot all about Asia.

'He should write if off as a bad dream,' I said, stepping over a black bin-liner full of rubbish that floated past in the street. A minibus went down the road, the spray from its wheels fanning out in four shimmering arcs of gold under the glow of the yellow street lights. 'Jesus, what happened to the road?'

The street outside the guest house was now a river that ran shopfront to shopfront, a foot deep, the wave created by each passing vehicle lapping against the doors and window panes before being sent back like an echo. There were black bin-bags floating everywhere like mines, menacing, ready to go off when struck by an unwary moped.

I rolled up my jeans and took off my trainers. 'It's now or never.'

'Never,' said Rick, and did the same. 'You coming or not, Tom?'

Tom looked out from the safety of the entrance step, left-right, left-right. 'Can't let you boys have all the fun now can I? Besides,' he said, taking off his Gucci shoes, 'I'm the only one who knows where the Bongo disco is.'

Earlier in the day, and in fact twice previously, Tom had invited us to go out on the town with him and we had refused each time, concocting poor excuses why we had to stay in, only to go out the minute he had left the guest house. The reason was simple: he was gay.

When Tom had first arrived at the guest house two days after us, I had been out eating some noodles, and on the way back passed a Danish guy who'd been sharing our dorm. He was carrying his backpack. 'Where are you going?' I'd asked, knowing that he'd only arrived the day before us and had said that he intended to stay in KL for a week.

'To find another place, then I can sleep at night,' he replied gruffly. 'You will see. Goodbye to you, John.' He shook my hand hurriedly and walked off. Mmm, strange behaviour.

Back at the guest house, however, everything became clear the moment I entered the dorm. All of the men, Rick included, were huddled in one corner, while the new arrival, Tom, stood in the other, unpacking his silk travellers' bed sheet.

Typically, the girls fell in love with him instantly, buzzing around him and checking out his designer bits and pieces as though they were antiques, holding them with kid gloves and cooing longingly. Tom went through his essentials for their benefit, on a sort of guided tour of the stuff that he considered absolutely necessary for a successful world tour. He laid out immaculately folded silk socks and underwear, all monogrammed, crocodile skin diary with his name embossed on the front in gold leaf, gold fountain pen, lap-top and palm-top computers, and a baffling array of personal products, from anti-wrinkle eye cream to gold-plated shaving brush and matching traveller's toothbrush. He even carried a solid silver knife and fork. 'Don't want to get caught eating with my fingers,' he proclaimed, holding them up for us to see.

Rick, who'd been occupying the bottom bunk beneath Tom, immediately moved his gear to the other side of the room under the pretext of wanting to be closer to the window for fresh air; I think if he could have put a bed on the roof he would have slept outside. Tom brushed the snub aside with congeniality born out of familiarity. He unpacked his gear, and after a brief conversation with us, got ready to sample the best of the nightlife that KL had to offer, using the gay man's equivalent of *Lonely Planet* as his guide. 'Anyone like to join me?' he'd asked as he slipped into a pair of Versace jeans. His reply was four vigorously shaking heads from people who looked like they'd been asked to witness an autopsy.

Two sisters who were also staying in the dorm went along with Tom that night, and rolled up drunk in the early hours of the next morning while the rest of us were just waking. 'Fantastic,' they both said, 'the best party I've ever been to.' They also said that the places they had been to were not excessively gay, though there were gay people in them, the same as in any straight place. Twice more the following week they went out together, and both times came back with the same glowing reports. 'John,' said my backgammon partner, 'the women in these places are stunning, just stunning. Go with him. You'll love it.'

The three of us tiptoed down the street, ankle-deep in warm brown water, and turned alongside an embankment of the so-called river that runs through the city. I say 'so-called' because it's really just a concrete storm drain no more than thirty feet across.

'It's shown as a river on the maps to make KL look more impressive,' Tom said in answer to my query. 'Nobody's going to write *KL storm drain* on a tourist map are they?' Rick and I walked on in silence and Tom continued. 'I mean, here they are trying to bring KL into what they think is the twenty-first century by cutting down all the trees and pouring concrete over everything, while the developed world is moving forward by doing exactly the opposite! Building roads through jungles, and concreting over the banks of a river isn't going to convince anyone outside of Malaysia that they're forward-thinking is it?' He swept a hand through the air. 'Look at it; one rainstorm and the place comes to a standstill. It's just politicians and their developer friends playing their little games, that's all.'

We stopped at a roadside stall to put our shoes and socks back on and, much to the proprietor's disappointment, left without eating, only using his toilet paper to dry our feet.

'Food here's terrible anyway,' Rick said as we walked on. 'Wait till we get to Singapore; none of that fish-head curry crap down there, you'll see, John.'

'Are we going to Singapore?' I said. 'That's the first I've heard.'

Rick shoved his hands into the pockets of his new marbled jeans and shrugged. 'Might as well keep going south.'

While we walked through the shiny, wet, concrete streets to the disco, past shopfront after bland shopfront, Rick told us how his father, an engineer in the RAF, had taken him to a Singapore nightclub at the tender age of eleven and shown him what real men get up to at night. According to Rick's memory there were more strip joints in Singapore than there were people to fill them, and you literally had to fight the girls off. We reminded him that the memory of an eleven-year-old, combined with the dramatic changes that had swept through Asia over the past decade might mean that Singapore wasn't the place it used to be.

'Bollocks,' he retorted, 'nothing changes out here. Least not deep down anyway.'

We crossed a busy main road, got lost, crossed the same road twice more, perspiring heavily as we walked down the humid streets, and eventually entered the Bongo disco. The club was a pretty standard affair, typical of all KL's discos; serving as a pub for the business clientele at lunchtime and early evening, before the city's young and trendy, either from work or home, descended and got the place moving at night.

'You two ought to go to Australia if you're running out of money,' Tom shouted over the bass-line, putting the drinks on the table. 'At least then you can earn enough to move on.'

'Have you been there?' I asked, taking my beer.

'Loads of times, I love it.' He offered a small cigar and I took it. 'Sydney anyway,' he continued. 'The rest of the country's OK; Gold Coast, Byron and what have you, but Sydney's the only city.'

Rick took a cigar. 'What about the other cities, what are they like?'

'There are no other cities in Australia. Not as you'd imagine a city anyway. You're from London, right, John?'

I nodded.

'Then all the other places Melbourne, Adelaide, Brisbane, they'd be like villages to you. Christ, Adelaide isn't even a village!' He leaned over the table and lit us all up. 'No, your best bet, if you're low on dough, is to get to Sydney and find a job. At least you won't have to go home. All you've got to do is make it as far east in Indo as you can and then hop over.

'Where?' I said moving closer, unsure of the last part of his sentence.

'Indonesia,' Rick clarified. 'From where?'

'I usually go from Bali, but then I'm not short of cash. If you haven't got enough money just keep going east.' He took a sip of his martini. 'Remember, the further east you go the nearer you'll be to Australia, and the cheaper the fare'll be. Don't let anyone tell you it's cheaper to fly from Bali because it's not.'

I looked at Rick again. We hadn't really discussed any plans other than saying, 'when the money stops, we'll stop'. He shrugged back at me, indicating that he had about as much idea of where to go as I had. I looked back at Tom and said, 'What about boats? Can't we get from Indo to Oz by boat and save on the airfare?'

'Dunno. There's a rumour, but I haven't done it, and I don't know anyone who has. Timor's within spitting distance of Australia's northern coast, and Indo's a sea-faring nation, so it seems likely.' He waited and watched our expressions. 'Surely you two have got the money for the airfare, it's only a couple of hundred bucks.'

I gulped down the beer he'd bought. 'Buy us another.'

'Christ, are you really that strapped for cash?'

'I reckon we've got enough to get through Indo,' I said, 'but that's about it. We couldn't afford a flight, no way. Remember, we've been on the road for over a year.'

He seemed taken aback. 'Haven't you worked in all that time?'

'Nope.' Rick and I grinned proudly and puffed on our cigars.

Tom hadn't been the first person to suggest Australia as a possible goal. The two sisters at the dorm had also just come from there and, like many of the people we'd met in Thailand who were going in the opposite direction to us, said that they'd had a great time. Nobody had a bad word to say about the country; Travellers from Britain to Israel gave it ten out of ten on all counts.

In fact the only people I'd heard giving Australia a bad press were the Australians themselves, who were either indifferent about the place or said that it was boring. One Aussie we'd met in Hat Rin had remarked that the country was OK but, 'Mate, the women are dogs.' When I queried his statement, suggesting that the ones I'd seen so far didn't seem too bad, he just nodded wisely and said, 'You haven't been to Australia!'

I was going to ask Tom about the female situation but thought better of it, instead raising my glass and saying, 'Cheers!'

THREE

Rick was half a dozen people ahead of me in the queue at the Australian embassy, and had already reached the counter by the time I'd finished filling out the form. His head bowed down to speak into the perforated glass screen that separated the interrogators from the interrogated and he disappeared from view, obscured by the queue.

The rest of the people in the queue were Malaysians, either businessmen or women with two or three kids in tow. Each time a person went up to be refused a visa, kowtowing their way to the front of the queue, the person who had just been turned away walked back down the line, head bowed, gazing down at their rejected pink application form as though they were holding a still-born child.

The fat, pallid Australian woman who sat behind the screen looked at the people queuing as though they were insects. She was looking through the glass viewing screen as though staring at a giant experimental ant colony, the look of thinly concealed distaste on her face said, 'I hate insects!' When another person had been turned away she would either go off for five minutes, pretending to do something in an adjoining office, or use the millisecond between customers as an excuse to make tea on the cabinet behind her.

There were four queues for visas, and locals staffed all but one. Partly for reasons of language, and party because we knew that age-old prejudices were still alive and well in Asia, we chose the queue with the Australian woman behind the counter.

'I'm sorry,' I heard her say, and Rick came walking down the line screwing the pink form into a ball.

'Who want's to go to that fooking country anyway?' He stopped beside me, reading the look on my face. '"No, I'm sorry, sir, you can't have a visa because you haven't got enough money." Silly bitch.'

I stared at him. 'Haven't got enough money? But you wrote on the form that you had two thousand pounds; the requirement.'

'They asked me how much money I had, so I said, "What, on me now you mean?" So I emptied my pockets and showed them twenty dollars.'

I held my head in my hands. 'What the fuck did you say that for? Jesus Christ, Rick, they mean how much money have you got in your bank account, not in your pocket!'

He lobbed the ball of paper into a nearby bin. 'Well they didn't say that.'

'Well maybe you should have realised,' I said, holding up the form and pointing to the *Independent Means* clause. 'Fucking hell, that's like a spelling mistake on your CV. Unforgivable.'

Rick walked off and sat down without another word. The queue moved forward and I presented my form.

'How much money do you have to support yourself during your stay in Australia?' the woman behind the counter asked, unwrapping a chocolate biscuit.

'Three thousand pounds,' I lied.

'Do you have proof of your means?'

I took out my Visa card and slipped it over the counter. The account that it pertained to had nothing in it. She glanced at the front and then the back of the card, as though my bank balance was written on it, before sliding it back across the stainless steel counter. 'Everything seems to be in order, Mr Harris. Come back tomorrow before twelve to collect your visa. Next!'

'Got it,' I said when I'd returned to Rick, who was busy using his lighter to burn the leaves off a rubber plant, 'no problem. Just showed them this old credit card and Bob's your uncle.'

'What about me?'

'Don't worry, I'll send you a postcard.'

He stopped burning the indoor landscaping and paused before saying, 'Let's go to Singapore, John. The bus goes at six-thirty, I've already checked the times.'

'Aren't you going to get a visa?'

'There's no point in trying here again is there?'

'Mmm.' I flexed my useless credit card between thumb and forefinger. 'Anyway, I doubt there's much likelihood of us getting as far as Australia. I haven't got much money left, and your baht is about as useful as Monopoly money outside Thailand.'

He put his lighter in his pocket and stood up. 'Let's just get out of here, I'm sick of this place.'

While we had been inside the embassy it had rained again, and the wet streets were rapidly being dried by a crisp new sun. The moisture was slowly evaporating, pulsating from the ground in waves of heat and hanging in the air like a hot, wet blanket, pushing back the sweat that was trying to escape from our perspiring bodies. My hands were freezing cold from the air con but were running with sweat; a really strange sensation that made me feel a bit like a piece of meat, recently removed from a deep-freeze.

We walked around the centre of the city for a while, one minute gazing up at skyscrapers and the next down at the beautiful women, and bought tickets for the next day's bus to Singapore before going into a bar to cool off. Also I'd purchased a pocket atlas and wanted to check exactly where we were and where we were heading. I still turned my nose up at guidebooks but thought that an atlas was an acceptable compromise: falling somewhere between educational and awe-inspiring, without being of assistance.

The atlas I bought was called the *Collins Gem World Atlas*. It's a great little reference book containing not only maps of the world, both physical and political, but also time zones. The world environment, including sea currents of the world's oceans is shown in glorious colour, along with the different shipping lanes, and journey times between New York, London and Singapore by every type of modern boat and aircraft. It has a hundred pages of maps and another hundred for the index, all in a book the size of a cigarette packet.

'D'you realise how far we've come?' I asked as Rick came back with the beers. Using thumb and forefinger as dividers, I measured Goa to Kuala Lumpur on the page and held them up. 'That far.'

'Yeah, what scale's that map?'

'Hang on,' I measured again and held my fingers an inch apart, 'that's five thousand kilometres.'

'Has it got populations in there?' he asked, taking a seat.

'Think so. Yep, here it is, "Major Cities by Continent". Which one do you want to know about?'

'Jakarta.'

'What, Indonesia?'

'Of course Indonesia, unless you know another place called Jakarta.'

I quickly ran a finger over the page. 'Umm, here we go, nine and a half million people.'

He nodded. 'And what about Singapore?'

I flicked though the pages. 'One and a half million. About fifteen hundred kilometres by land. Why?'

He leaned back in his chair, picking up his bottle of Beck's and grinning. 'D'you know that women out-number men in Singapore by three to one?'

FOUR

My Australian visa was issued the next morning and, as expected, was given a stingy three-month limit. We bussed it down to Singapore that evening, arriving around midnight in some obscure part of the city. The underground railway system had all but shut down for the night so we decided to stop at a roadside food court to sample some of the famous cuisine that Rick had been going on about, before heading into town to find a place to stay.

'What you like?' The Chinese waitress asked. I looked at Rick.

'Um, we'll have what those people are having.' We both swung round to see where Rick was pointing. 'Whatever you've got,' he added, putting the menu back on to the plastic table. 'A general selection. And two Tiger beers please.'

She nodded.

'I used to live here. Up at Changi.' Rick said airily.

She mouthed, 'Oh?' And went back to the kitchen.

'Well that really impressed her,' I said.

'Fook off.'

We sat in silence for a moment, taking in the deserted shopping arcade, and I said, 'This stuff had better be good, I'm starving. Bus journeys always make me hungry.' I leaned back on the plastic garden chair and patted my stomach. 'First impressions?'

He looked around and smiled weakly. 'I hope it's not all like this concrete. When I was here as a kid it was all bamboo housing. All I've seen so far is concrete tower blocks. It's like a giant fooking council estate.'

'Mmm, well, it's dark, it'll probably look better tomorrow. And I'm hungry, that always makes everything look crap.'

Two cans of beer were eventually brought over, and after another five minutes the food arrived. It was horrible. Rick tried to put a brave face on it, swallowing large amounts so that he didn't have to chew, trying to let it slip down without touching the sides, but I could see that he was struggling. One bowl contained what looked like eyeballs in green stew. The waitress was summoned and asked to identify the spherical objects bobbing about in the bowl, but all we got was a Chinese name.

'They're mushrooms I think.' I was laughing so much at the eyeballs that I almost gagged on the noodles that were lodged in my throat. 'Try one.'

He tried to pick one up with his chop-sticks but it rolled on to the floor. 'Fook it, you can have them,' he said in disgust, and pushed the bowl towards me. 'It's shite.'

We stayed for another beer and watched the Asian version of MTV as it blurted out an endless supply of the latest pop videos accompanied by a running commentary from a slick local teenager. For all his trendy clothing and state-of-the-art grooming, he sounded like he had about as much of a clue about the music he was playing as my granny does.

We paid the bill and hailed a cab, handing over a piece of paper with the address of a cheap guest house written on it in Chinese by the food-stall owner.

The driver cowered against his door, holding his hands out, palms forward, as though fending off a punch.

'What's up with him?' I asked, looking at Rick.

Rick shrugged and leaned into the passenger window. 'Can you take us here, please?'

The driver peeped between his fingers and slowly reached out to pluck the note from Rick, his hands trembling with fear.

'OK?'

He read it and flicked his eyes up and down from the paper to us, his bald head running with little glassy beads of sweat even though the cab was air con.

'OK?' I repeated, trying the back door. Rick was already in the front seat. The driver nodded until I thought his head would fall off, and pushed a button. The back door swung open. 'Did you see that Rick?'

He peered around the headrest. 'No, what?'

I shut the door and stood outside, rapping on the window for the driver to give a repeat performance. *Push, click, swing.*

'Fooking hell, they only had rickshaws when I was last here, and they didn't have doors. They didn't even have a roof come to think of it.'

During the twenty-minute journey downtown we became friendly with the driver and he told us why he'd been so scared. Rick broke the ice with his standard 'I used to live in Singapore' routine, and the driver gradually started to talk. As it turned out his English was quite good, and he told us that he thought we were football hooligans who were going to beat him up and steal his cash. His hands were gripping the steering wheel so hard, and shaking so much that it gave the car premature speed-wobble.

To calm him down, for our benefit as much as his, I told him our story, with particular emphasis on the world-wise love and peace stuff, chucking in a touch of poverty for good measure. I probably over-played our hand a bit, because by the time we'd arrived at the guest house he was feeling sorry for us.

'Hippy is good,' he proclaimed, 'you no pay fare,' and gave a wrong way round V sign with his fingers. I was going to say that I was no fucking hippy but didn't want to look a gift horse in the mouth, and thanked him instead, superficially agreeing to meet him in his favourite bar one night over the coming week. He drove off waving his two fingers out of the window and honking his horn.

The woman at the food-stall had understood us perfectly: the guest house was two illegally converted flats in a government tower block, right in the centre of the city. I knew it was a government block because the clanking metal lift that took us to the fourth floor guest house stank of stale piss and there were prostitutes hanging around on the walkways.

We were shown quietly into a dorm of a dozen or so occupied beds, each one with a backpack stowed underneath, and allocated a space.

'Breakfast is at nine,' the Indian man said gruffly as he turned to leave.

'Till when?'

'Nine-fifteen.' He disappeared down the darkened hallway.

Neither of us were expecting breakfast to be included so that was a bonus. After smoking a cigarette each in the toilet and having a quick, silent game of backgammon in the hallway, we turned in, undressing in the dark before creaking our way into the bunks. As I climbed into bed I had the distinct feeling that ten pairs of eyes were watching me, and began to wonder what the other people in the room were thinking. Another fucking hippy from Thailand? A football hooligan who's going to come back drunk every night and wake us all up, then beat us up for looking at him?

I lay awake for hours that first night, sweat tickling me as it ran down the nape of my neck before being soaked up by the damp pillow. Moonlight came in through the window and lit the face of the girl sleeping beneath it, making her face a blue mask, frozen in a smiling, sleep-filled expression of awe. Actually it was probably street lights reflected off the ceiling that caused the effect. Anyway, light came through and lit the girl's face, and as I watched her she turned on to her side and opened her eyes slightly.

I quickly shut mine, counted to five and then opened them, hoping to turn the tables, but when I did she had turned back. Shit, now I'd be awake even longer wondering if she'd noticed me watching her. I turned over in the damp bed and, in an attempt to take my mind off being awake, started to think about what we were going to do over the next few days.

There were two things that were high on our list of 'things to do' while we were in Singapore: to have a Singapore Sling in Raffles Hotel and to visit Changi Yacht Club. In fact they were our only things to do; neither Rick nor I were particularly interested in sightseeing.

My mother still has the postcard of Raffles that her brother sent her from Singapore in the forties, after the allied forces had liberated it from the Japanese. I'd always looked at it as a kid, wide-eyed, wondering what Raffles meant, and who the funny-looking people were standing outside beneath funny looking trees. I grew up with the impression that her brother was the owner of some kind of gambling house or bingo hall, where the main source of activity came from selling raffle tickets.

Coincidentally, Rick had an almost identical story to tell. A member of his family had been there in Singapore in the forties, and had had a photo taken in the Long Bar: Sling in one hand, Asian beauty in the other. It was our aim to re-enact these memories.

As far as Changi Yacht Club was concerned, Rick's dad had been posted in Singapore while in the RAF in the seventies, and he used to go there as a kid on his dad's boat for day-sailing. He wanted to see his old stomping-ground, roll back the years and try to relive old memories.

Rolling over on to my side for the twentieth time, the bed sheet stuck to my back with sweat, I turned to face the wall and accidentally head-butted it, squashing my nose. When I opened my eyes and looked closely I could see that everyone who had previously occupied the bed, had written minute graffiti all over the plaster, like lines left by tiny spiders.

Names, dates, places, even the odd traveller joke was there. That'll give me something to do, I thought, and began to read them.

I discovered something mildly important about myself that night: reading books in bed doesn't help me sleep; reading graffiti does.

FIVE

Changi Yacht Club (or Sailing Centre as it's now called) turned out to be a huge disappointment, mainly for Rick but also for me because I'd heard him talk about it so much over the past week or so. He'd spoken of his childhood memories: how he used to dive off the pier and hold his breath underwater, swimming along in the crystal clear sea. How, once, while swimming alone by his dad's boat, a bunch of schooling fish had started to leap and dance all around him, jumping over his head and darting about in circles, glimmering in the sun like silver discs. He'd splashed about with joy trying to catch them, before looking up at the beach and noticing the horrified look on the faces of his father and friends. 'Don't move, son,' his father had shouted, and came running down the pier to his rescue. After being pulled from the water, the infant Rick had turned and looked back down as the stealthy grey shadow of a fifteen-foot tiger shark glided past.

'Moral of the story?' Rick bent down and picked up some sand from the beach, watching it sift through his fingers. 'When schooling fish start to behave erratically, get the fook out the water.' He released the sand with a huff.

I looked out at the collection of boats moored offshore. Sleek white yachts stood next to decrepit old wooden schooners that looked like they had already sunk and been brought back up. 'Disappointed?' I asked, shoving my hands into my shorts pockets.

'Look,' he bent down and scooped up another handful of sand and we both watched as it ran through his fingers, 'even the beach is man-made now.'

'How d'you know that?'

'Because it was always a black sand beach, not golden.'

I cupped a hand and caught some grains as they fell. 'Maybe it was golden, you just don't remember it that way.'

He looked at me as though I'd accused him of insanity, and gestured towards the clubhouse. 'Let's go up there and see if they've got any old records of my dad's boat.'

Walking through Changi Village when we'd arrived from downtown hadn't been any less of a let-down for Rick either. The wooden house he'd lived in for three years as a kid was no longer there, and the whole main street was now a row of sharp, three-storey concrete blocks with shopfronts at ground floor level and flats above. He had conjured up an image of bamboo houses on stilts, each one different from the next, but all that stood in their place now was a bland concrete terrace, a mile long and as straight as the cross hairs on a surveyor's theodolite.

To top it all off, when we tried to get to the yacht club along what Rick said used to be a winding jungle path, we found that our way was blocked by a newly built golf course. Fat businessmen pulled up in their Mercedes to spend the afternoon whacking balls around on the land that Rick said used to be his jungle playground. He pointed out to me where, on the exact spot now taken up by the first tee, an old Chinaman's house used to be, where Rick and his sister spent endless lazy afternoons watching the old man repair boats.

'D'you know what I'd love to do, John?' Rick stopped on the steps leading up to the clubhouse and looked out at the yachts rocking in the harbour. 'Have one of these boats. Then we wouldn't need money; we could just take off around the world, stopping when we wanted, moving on when we felt like it. Imagine,' he turned to face me, both hands held up, 'all the islands in Indonesia. How many?'

'About fourteen thousand,' I said, remembering the appropriate sentence from my atlas.

'Fourteen thousand. Fourteen-fooking-thousand islands to choose from. Imagine the birds!' He whistled. 'And if we ever got bored with those we'd just move on to the Philippines, there're another seven thousand islands there!'

I nodded in agreement, squinting against the bright sunlight reflecting off the shimmering sea. 'D'you think you could sail one of those things?'

He snorted. 'Are you kidding? See that one on the end? The one with the red tarpaulin over the boom.'

'Over the what?'

'Can you see the red tarpaulin?'

I scanned the bay, wishing I had a pair of sunglasses. 'Umm, yep, got it.'

'That boat's forty-two feet long and it's made in England. I know because my dad had exactly the same one. I learned to sail it when I was twelve, and by the time I left here I could sail it single-handed around Singapore. I know that boat like you know your car.'

I was impressed.

'You've probably forgotten how to sail it by now,' I said after a pause. 'That was years ago.'

'Have you forgotten how to drive?'

Good point. I sighed. 'Well there's nothing we can do about it, we'll never have the money to buy something like that, not unless we steal it.'

I remember what he said next as though it was yesterday. I remember the look in his eyes as though it was today. 'We can dream,' he said, going misty-eyed. 'Let's make a deal John. That'll be our dream: to dream the impossible dream. If we get to Australia and make enough money, we'll buy that yacht.'

I waited for what I thought would be the negative of the sentence but it didn't come. 'And if we don't get the money?' I prompted.

He didn't reply and continued up the steps towards the clubhouse. No answer was all the answer I needed. No answer was as good as saying, 'Then we'll just have to steal that beautiful little boat some day.'

I knew that Rick often said things that had no real link to possible actions in real life, but there was something in his eyes this time that told me he meant what he said. Just as he had once said in India that we would meet up on Koh Pha-Ngan, and I'd thought: how fucking ridiculous; so this time I thought: how very fucking likely that we'll one day have a yacht and sail around all fourteen thousand islands of Indonesia.

I followed him up to the clubhouse reception with the silence of his answer still ringing in my ears like a bell. The woman who staffed the counter in the well-appointed lounge looked so far down her nose at us that I'm surprised she didn't tip over, her head was tilted so far back. We persuaded her to get the old log books out, but there was no record of Rick's dad or his boat. It turned out that servicemen were never official members of the club and therefore didn't need to register.

'If you want to trace an old friend from days gawn by,' she said with a plum in her mouth, 'you should speak to Mr Chan, the boatman. He's just dine thar in the chandlery.'

Chan-the-boatman? I thought, and suppressed a giggle. The pressure forced a fleck of mucous out of my nose, making her look down her nose at us as though we were vagrants. She probably already thought we were tramps but the snot didn't make us look any better, and I quickly wiped it on to my sleeve.

'Oh, Lord!' she said, handing me a tissue. I thanked her, and we started to walk out when she called after us, 'I say, are you members?' We feigned deafness and went back out into the hot midday sun.

'Have you noticed, Rick, that people keep staring at us?' I said as we went back on to the sand. 'Like that woman.'

'Silly old cow.'

'Yeah, but it's not just her.' I studied my battered old shorts swinging to and fro as we went down to the water's edge. 'Maybe we should smarten ourselves up a bit.'

'You should, not me. I've only just bought new gear.'

He slapped the thigh of his new jeans and I burst out laughing. 'Marbled jeans went out with the Ark. Why didn't you buy normal ones?'

'I thought these looked pretty cool. Plus they were half price. Anyway, who cares?'

I pointed down the beach. 'Not Chan-the-boatman, that's for sure.' Just a short distance down the beach a wizened old Chinese man was sitting on the ski of a Hobi Cat smoking a cigarette. When he saw us approaching he immediately stood up, extinguished his cigarette and tried to look busy. 'I bet they treat him like shit,' I commented as we walked up to the old man.

'We used to.' Rick held out his hand. 'Chan my man, good to see you again.'

The old man didn't know what to do. At first he ignored us, but then, realising we were talking to him, he did a little bow and nervously shook Rick's hand, 'Hello sir.' Rick told the old man that he didn't need to call him 'sir' but I could see that he was quaking in his boots. Or he would have been if he was wearing any. Rick launched into his familiar 'I used to live here' stuff, this time adding a 'do you remember me?' and Chan nodded vigorously, his tired old eyes darting about as though he was looking for an exit. The old man said that he remembered everything, but I could see that it was just out of a sense of duty, or politeness, and nothing else. He was probably too scared to say no.

'Who does that belong to?' I asked, referring to the boat Rick and I had discussed.

'Japan man,' Chan replied, and swept his hand through the air. 'All Japan man now. Own everything,' he snorted dismissively. How sour it must have tasted for a man like that: someone Chinese who'd probably been in Singapore under the occupation and witnessed all of the aggression and brutality, only to have to serve the same people years later. 'They never come here,' he continued, 'never use boat, only for tax dodge.' He broke off abruptly and turned to leave. 'OK, sir, I go now, thank you.' He did another little bow and was gone, disappearing up the beach into a little wooden shack.

'Shall we go?' I said, turning back to Rick. He was still staring fixedly at the boat. 'Rick, shall we? Or d'you want to stay here?'

Silence.

'Rick?'

SIX

Our first encounter with the Raffles Hotel wasn't a very good one either; Rick and I were turned away at the entrance.

'Well what's fooking wrong?'

'Rick, hold on hold on!' I put a calming hand on his shoulder to stop him punching the doorman's lights out. 'This poor guy's only following rules, it's not his fault.' The turbaned India man looked relieved and instantly broke into a sweat. People were pulling up the driveway in Rolls Royces, dressed for dinner, and the last thing the doorman wanted to deal with was us. He anxiously left our side to open the door of another car and greeted the occupants, 'Welcome madam, sir,' before coming back to us.

'So,' I said calmly, completing Rick's sentence without the expletives, 'what's wrong with our clothes?' I must have sounded resigned, as though I'd been turned away a thousand times before.

He looked sheepish. 'Please, sir, no shorts allowed, thank you, sir.' Rick began to speak but the man cut him off. 'And no sandals also, sir, thank you.'

Rick looked down past his marbled legs at his tatty old leather footwear, and swore.

'OK,' I counted out the conditions of the dress-code on my fingers, 'so it's no shorts, no sandals. Anything else? Can I wear a T-shirt?'

'That is OK, sir, thank you.'

'Then that's it,' I said, turning to Rick. 'We toddle off back to the guest house, get changed, come back here and blow this joint apart. What d'you say?'

Rick agreed.

FAST FORWARD

Twenty minutes later we were back, dressed in our dirtiest clothes but meeting the requirements laid down by the management. We sauntered through the swing doors and asked for the Writers' Bar.

'Over there, sir,' a worried looking waiter replied, 'but—'

Through another set of teak and glass doors, silently across the carpeted main hall with its three-inch thick pile, beneath the huge chandelier and over to the small bar where a dozen bloated, red-faced businessmen and their wives, dressed in DJs and gowns, sipped martinis before eating in the adjacent dining room.

'This looks all right,' I said, taking in the opulence. 'You make yourself comfortable on that sofa and I'll get the drinks. What d'you want?'

'Sling,' Rick replied without hesitation.

'That's easy.' I turned to go to the bar and ran straight into the manager, who'd obviously been alerted by the doorman.

'Umm, wouldn't you rather go to the famous Long Bar, sir?' he said nervously. He was Singaporean but his English was perfect.

'Two Singapore Slings,' I said over his shoulder to the barman, completely ignoring the manager's presence. The barman started to panic, unsure whether to wait for an instruction from his boss or not. Unfortunately for him there were no other people waiting to be served so he started to polish some glasses instead.

'Sir?'

I faced the manager.

'Wouldn't you much rather go to the famous Long Bar, sir?'

This business of wearing the wrong clothes was beginning to get on my nerves; clothes that were de rigueur on the beaches we'd stayed on were about as welcome in the real world as a tuxedo on Hat Rin. I was beginning to feel like I was being firmly but politely put in my place; it seemed as though everyone was saying, 'Yes, well, you may have been a big-shot back then with the other wasters and party animals, but here you're nothing. Get a life!' I could feel the anger boiling up inside me.

'Wouldn't you, sir?' he repeated, his nose almost touching mine. There was complete silence all around us as everyone stopped chatting to watch the stand-off. It was me against him, *us* against *them*, fat businessmen against travellers, down-trodden workers like him versus the pricks that push him around.

'You're taking the wrong side,' I said evenly, staring into his eyes.

He blinked once, the tension beginning to show. 'sir?'

I didn't repeat it, instead letting the air escape from my lungs. My head was pounding with built-up pressure. I turned to walk away, catching my own reflection in the mirror behind the bar, and got the shock of my life. The person staring back at me was tanned, young and full of life, while the people around me were dead, like over-stuffed, over-cosmeticised corpses. The contrast between us couldn't have been greater if I'd walked into the bar stark naked. My reflected image and I patted both Ricks on the shoulder and said, 'The Long Bar it is, then.'

The Long Bar, as you might expect, is little more than a theme pub; a modern replica of the one where my uncle and Rick's relative had once sat all those years ago sipping cocktails. Nowadays the Singapore Slings are ready-mixed in a large plastic barrel, so that the barman doesn't need to strain himself with a cocktail shaker, and cost more than double what we were paying per night for a bed at the guest house.

'One Singapore Sling or two extra nights' kip?' Rick asked himself sarcastically after ordering them. 'So we choose the drink. How sensible.'

'That's a dollar a gulp,' I said, taking mine from the bar top. 'Sips only, it's got to last.'

We sat at the bar for a while listening to the band; Rick took a couple of photos to send home to his mum and dad as a keepsake.

'Find a girl,' I said, before he could take another picture. 'Any Asian girl. You said that your mum's photograph was of a man with an Asian girl on his lap.' I scanned the bar, settling on two girls sitting in a corner. They must be tourists, I reasoned, they're drinking Slings. 'Those two look OK.' Without waiting for a reply I walked over to them. 'Excuse me, do you speak English?'

They both giggled into their hands and hunched their shoulders. 'A 'ittle,' said one, holding her thumb and forefinger an inch apart.

I mimed taking a picture. 'Can *you* (point at them) take a *picture* (close one eye, wink and cluck tongue) for *me* (point at myself) and friend (point at grinning Rick).'

'Yes yes.' She stood up and bowed twice, one for each 'yes'.

At first she stood ten feet away, expecting to be the one holding the camera, but I explained that I wanted her in the picture, on Rick's lap, and she moved forward timidly and leaned against him. Rick immediately grabbed her around the waist and deposited her soft bottom squarely on his groin. 'Weh-hey!' Before she could protest I took the picture.

I've never seen that photograph, but to this day Rick's mum is probably looking at a lovely shot of her son cuddling with a cute Asian girl in Raffles hotel, Singapore, blissfully unaware that two seconds later he was wincing from a slapped face.

'You won't do that again in a hurry will you?' a voice behind us said as the girl walked smartly back to her friend. Rick stopped rubbing his cheek, surprised to have suddenly heard an Irish accent, and we both spun around to locate the voice. The woman was sitting alone at the bar, Sling in one hand, camera in the other. 'How long you been here?' she asked, turning her attention to me in an obvious attempt to alleviate Rick's embarrassment.

'Two days. You?'

'Same. Just came down from bloody Thailand.'

I picked up my drink. 'Didn't you like it?'

'You could say that.' She took a deep breath. 'I spent one night in Bangkok, hated it, so I went down to the islands.'

'Just left home then?' Rick added.

'Yeah. I've only been away,' she looked at her watch, 'one week tomorrow.'

'One week!' I put my glass down. 'How'd you get this far in one week?'

'Got a round-the-world ticket. Flew Bangkok to Samui, spent one night on,' she paused to remind herself, 'no, two nights on Koh Pha-Ngan, hated it there, went back to Samui and flew here via KL. Kuala Lumpur was all right,' she sipped her cocktail, 'spent two nights there.'

'Hated Koh Pha-Ngan?' Rick said, incredulous, and glanced quickly at me. 'We loved it.'

She raised her eyebrows as if doubting Rick's sanity, and said, 'It's all right if you like being in a war-zone, I suppose, but personally I want to relax, that's why I left Northern Ireland.'

By 'war-zone' I took it that she wasn't into the party and drugs scene on the island. 'Yeah I suppose the nightlife can be a bit of a shock for someone who's expecting a deserted island,' I said, and popped the glacé cherry from my cocktail into my mouth.

'Nightlife? I'm talking about all that other stuff that's going on there; all that Mafia bullshit.' She shifted on her stool. 'I don't mind parties day and night but I draw the line at gang warfare.'

I swallowed the cherry whole. 'What?'

'When were you last there?'

I looked at Rick and he answered. 'About three weeks ago; something like that.'

'Well,' she continued, taking a peanut from a bowl on the bar, 'maybe it was different then. I don't know what it was like when you were there, but the Thais are shooting each other on Hat Rin beach now.'

Rick's mouth gaped open, I could see his fillings and I'm sure he could see mine too as we looked at each other in silence, forgetting the woman beside us. Images suddenly flashed past my eyes like the dramatic headlines in a newspaper, the same way they do in the movies when a blank screen is filled from infinity with a spinning tabloid: *Dhoom!* "Koh Pha-Ngan in Mafia Bloodbath!" Or, *Dhoom!* "Massacre At Blood Beach!"

'Shit,' I finally managed to say, and bowed my head. 'What about poor Dave?'

The woman's mood seemed to brighten. 'Oh, they weren't touching the tourists, the Thais were only killing each other.' She gulped down the last of her drink and ordered another. 'Dave?' she said, frowning and cracking a peanut shell between her teeth.

I looked up at her.

'You said Dave. There's a guy at my youth hostel here called Dave.'

'So?' I didn't mean to sound rude but it came out sounding like a rebuff, and she frowned to remind me of my curtness. I couldn't quite make the connection between what she was saying and what I was thinking.

'Well, he's just been on Koh Pha-Ngan. Black guy.'

My heart stopped. 'With an afro?' I said, leaning forward and inadvertently placing a hand on her thigh.

'And about seven-foot tall?' Rick chipped in excitedly, also leaning forward and putting a hand on her leg. 'Including the hair I mean.'

She moved back instinctively, surprised at the intimacy of the gesture. 'Yeah, used to be in the Marines I think.'

McPLAN

ONE

Dave was sitting outside McDonald's when we saw him, on the open-air kiddie seating area. He was stuffing a Big Mac into his mouth and had another two lined up alongside, ready, like a conveyor-belt eating machine. Even from where we stood on the other side of the road I could see the relish all over his mouth. It made him look like a half-starved, rabid animal with white foam running down his chin, the other half of the kill clenched tightly in his hands.

The meeting place had been Dave's idea. Not that I don't like McDonald's, I do, I just didn't think it was a very grown up place to meet, that's all; I'm used to meeting people in pubs. After the Irish woman had told us about Dave we had left Raffles immediately and went to the youth hostel she was staying at for a positive ID. She showed us to his bed space, it was empty of human life but piled high with stuff: clothes, books, guitar strings (no guitar), all of which I recognised as Dave's belongings. 'When d'you think he'll be back?' I'd asked the Irish woman.

'Usually doesn't come back until quite late, when the rest of us are asleep. Keeps some pretty weird hours this mate of yours.'

I'd nodded in agreement. Dave, like Rick, often stayed awake all night, whether he had something to occupy his time or not, and I could easily picture him walking around the streets of Singapore, chatting to anyone and everyone he came across. Also like Rick, he loved video games, and I knew that at a push I could find him in the main arcade in the biggest shopping mall on Orchard Road.

The Irish woman had said she was staying in for the rest of the night and would pass on our message to Dave, that we were alive and well and in Singapore, so we wrote down the address of our guest house for him to get in touch and left. On the way out, to confirm that it was indeed the same Dave, I'd checked the register at the reception and found his name: '*Lord David Norton - NYC*'

The next day we missed each other again. This time he'd come to our place and left a typically militaristic message saying that we should meet him at the big open-air McDonald's on Orchard Road at 20.00 hrs.

'D'you think he's going to be pissed off?' I asked Rick as we crossed the road towards the McDonald's. I'd been thinking a lot about this question over the past forty-eight hours. In fact, since we were first told that Dave was here I hadn't thought about much else. The way I saw it we had left him for dead on Koh Pha-Ngan, and however I tried to justify it in my mind I came to the same conclusion; that we should never have left him behind.

'About what?' Rick replied, looking left and right to check the traffic.

'You know. Koh Pha-Ngan.'

'Careful!' Rick put his arm in front of me as a truck rumbled past, the question going unanswered until we had sprinted across the last lane of traffic, on to the steps of the restaurant. 'Guess we'll find out now.'

Dave was so busy on his second burger that he didn't notice us until we were standing beside him. Some kids were jumping on the playground toys around him so he probably wasn't paying any attention anyway. Every time a kid strayed too close to him a watchful mother would panic and come to the rescue, looking at Dave as though he was some kind of alien, or pervert. I don't think Singaporeans have seen many black people before.

I cleared my throat. 'Ahem! Sir David Norton I presume.'

His head shot up; eyes like saucers and cheeks puffed out with food. 'You . . . ' He hurriedly chewed the food that was stored in his mouth to leave room for talking, and then launched into a five-minute verbal attack, spraying us with hamburger chunks.

I didn't bother to argue with him because most of what he said was true: how we could have come back for him, or at least warned him in some way of what was happening. At first I attempted to give my apology but he wouldn't accept it, saying that I could 'shove it where the sun don't shine'; my strategy after that was to just say nothing until he calmed down a bit. I knew he didn't mean what he said and would soon be swapping stories with us, and asking questions about how we'd escaped from the island. Dave's youthful sense of adventure didn't allow his memory room to store grudges.

'I couldn't Dave,' Rick spoke softly after the five minutes of abuse we'd received. 'Be realistic, you weren't there, how could I?'

Dave had settled down enough to start eating again. 'You could have left a message. Shit!'

Rick tried to placate him and explained how he'd spent most of the night, after going to Hat Rin, looking for Dave in and around town but hadn't been able to find him. Dave wasn't convinced. 'Did you look in at the house? Did you think,' he put a finger to his temple, '"I wonder if Dave's at the house?" huh?'

Rick didn't repeat that looking up at the house wasn't an option, and accepted responsibility. We both did, and we both apologised. This turned the tables slightly and Dave blushed.

'So what happened to you after we left?' I asked, finally sitting down. Dave avoided eye contact with me. 'Dave?'

'Well actually,' he paused to open his third Big Mac box, obviously trying to hide a grin, 'I left pretty soon after you guys.' He pulled out the burger and took a bite, more to hide the spreading smile than out of hunger.

'Yeah, just how soon?'

'Look, you guys should have told me.'

'How soon?' I raised my voice and he lowered his eyes like a scolded child. 'You fucker. I bet you left the same night, right?'

He spread his arms. 'Well I wasn't gonna hang around to see what happened. Man, those girls were going ape-shit when they found out we'd taken you to the hospital.'

'You wanker, Dave. Here we are feeling guilty, and you left before us! We're supposed to have come back for you and you'd already gone?' I reached over and grabbed his coke, taking a gulp.

'Hey, get your own, Lord John,' he said, snatching the cup back possessively. 'Remember, I ain't forgiven you two yet.'

I paused. 'How did you know something was wrong anyway?'

He tapped a nostril with one finger.

'What's that supposed to mean?'

'Highly-tuned senses, John. Trained to sniff out these kinda things, know what I mean?'

Rick snorted. 'Funny you didn't sniff it out beforehand, Mr Highly-Tuned Marine.'

Dave just grinned behind the up-ended coke cup.

We sat and talked through the past few weeks, each person giving his own account of events and analysing each other's. Upon Rick's disappearance from the house, Dave had spent one night in Hat Rin and had then boarded the first ferry out the next morning, via Samui to the mainland, catching the next train south to Malaysia. He told us how he'd come back from the jungle and found the house empty, most of his money gone, and thought that Rick and I may have double-crossed him; that we were both in on the game with Ta and her friends. He had actually left Thailand before us, taking the train only as far as Butterworth. His original intention had been to spend only a night or two in Pinang to obtain a new visa, and then to cross back into Thailand and head north into the mountains. However, after meeting a Japanese girl who, according to Dave, was loaded, he had decided to stay on that island. A week later they split and he had changed his mind about Thailand, choosing instead to continue south to Singapore, missing out KL altogether.

'So, what have you boys got planned?' Dave said, after we'd shaken hands and agreed that Thailand was water under the bridge. 'I know you British, always got something up your sleeve.' He crushed the paper cup. 'Or perhaps you need a new leader?'

'I'll ignore that last comment.' I glanced at Rick. 'How about a drink to celebrate?'

Rick rubbed his hands. 'Don't mind.'

'Dave?'

'Sounds good to me. Hey listen,' he leaned over the table as though ready to tell us a secret, 'I know this great little bar just down here, got the most gorgeous Singaporean girls inside.'

'What's the name of it?'

'Umm, don't remember, exactly. But who cares? I know where it is.'

I thought for a moment and said, 'Ever been to Raffles, Dave?'

TWO

'It's simple,' Dave shouted over the music, 'just lie. You know, just like that Lord John and Sir Rick stuff. I'm telling you, man, it works every time.'

I nodded at him, indicating that I'd heard what was said. The noise from the band in the corner was far too loud for the size of the bar, and every time the drummer hit his snare drum it made me blink.

'I didn't know they were making a James Bond film out here.' Rick was cupping his ears to shield them from the music. 'Where?'

'Maybe not here in Singapore,' Dave replied, 'but somewhere around this part of the world. I saw it on the TV yesterday, at the hostel.' He looked back at the four Japanese women sitting at one of the tables and winked. They giggled into their hands.

Dave had a new way of chatting up girls that involved him pretending to be a film star. Apparently inspired by Rick's audacity in Thailand with the Sir Rick/Jim Thompson façade, he had taken the idea and developed it into his own American style. It had worked for him in Pinang so he saw no reason why it shouldn't be just as successful in the city. The fact that a 007 movie was being shot somewhere in the region would add credibility to his act.

'007 is a white man though,' Rick said incredulously. 'Even Japanese people must know that. Christ, Dave, that drink's gone to your head.'

Dave rolled his shoulders. 'I don't need to be James Bond. Fuck, Rick, you can be him if you want. I'll be Cubby Broccoli.'

'What?' I exclaimed, and burst out laughing.

Dave looked surprised. 'Why not? They won't know what the fucking director looks like.'

Rick shook his head in disbelief. 'Dave, Cubby Broccoli's a white man as well, and about seventy years old!'

'Not to mention dead,' I added.

'Well, fuck him then, I'll be the black dude in the James Bond movie, they always have a black guy.'

'How d'you know there's a black actor in this James Bond film?'

He pushed his fingers into his curly hair. 'They always have at least one black and one Chinese. Gives the movie wider appeal.'

I took a sip of beer and thought, before saying, 'Come to mention it, Dave, you look a bit like that guy in the old Bruce Lee Films.'

Dave's eyes widened. 'I'll be him then. What's his name?'

'Couldn't tell you. Tell them you're Samuel Jackson.'

He pointed at me. 'I fuckin' love you John. That's me, Samuel L. Jackson. Right, John, you're the cinematographer, and Rick, you can be umm ...'

'Stunt co-ordinator!' Rick suggested, pushing out his chest. 'It's a Bond film, there'll be loads of stunts.'

'Right on, Rick. You can be the hard man. Let's move it.'

Dave got up to leave and I caught his arm. 'Dave, you can't just go bowling over there and say, "Hi, I'm a movie star. Want a shag?"'

'Yeah? I don't wanna dance!'

We looked at each other, puzzled. 'What?' I said.

'What?'

'Dance?'

'Shag, you said, right? That's a dance. I don't want no fuckin' dancing. Not unless it's in the ol' boudoir.'

'Dave, shag means ... Oh never mind.' I pushed him into his seat. 'We'll go over and sit at that table next to theirs.' He looked over and then back at me. 'And casually, as though we've just got into town, we'll start talking about location shots.'

'Location shots and shit, yeah.' Dave repeated my words, nodding, and the three of us leaned in, almost touching heads. 'Then what?'

'That's it. They'll overhear us talking about the movie we're making and fall right into our laps.'

Rick looked over at the four women. 'I'm not having that fat one.'

'You don't have to,' said Dave, looking over, 'there're three others to choose from.'

Dave was wrong; there were not three others to choose from. At best there were two to choose from and even one of those was a bit iffy. I was beginning to wish that we had followed Dave's earlier advice and gone down to one of the discos in town, rather than come to Raffles. It had been my idea, suggesting that a night of passion with a rich tourist would make a welcome change from the usual energetic young backpacker girls.

Raffles, as usual, was full of married women in their thirties, sitting around sipping cocktails after a hard day's shopping in the expensive malls. Most of them were either Japanese or Taiwanese, dressed up to the nines in Gucci and Versace gear that made them look ten years older than they were. Their sole purpose for being in Singapore was to have a weekend shopping spree on their husbands' credit cards, and, we hoped, to have a good time.

Rick said they wouldn't have known a good time if it jumped up and hit them over the head. 'Too blinded by money to know what a good time is,' he said. Of the three of us he was the most reluctant to go along with the game, but Dave and I buttered him up with tales of the possible rewards involved.

'Passion,' I said, as Dave and I went through the list of pleasures that awaited us. 'Passion and good living.'

'Five-star accommodation,' Dave added, 'in the Ruffles Hotel, don't you know!'

'*Raffles*,' I corrected. 'Caviar.'

'You'll be a toy boy,' he said to Rick, tilting his head to one side and grinning.

'Never have to work again,' I added.

'Just think, as much champagne as you can drink!'

'OK, OK.' Rick picked up his glass. 'Let's go over.'

Dave slapped his back, 'Thataboy,' and we went over to the table next to the four women and listened for clues as to their origin. As soon as they saw us walk over their language changed from Japanese to English, as though they were expecting us to talk to them. We all nodded a gentle bow towards them and sat down. Dave immediately flew into the act.

'Sir William?' he said far too loudly, gesturing to a chair.

'Thanks, Dave.'

'Now,' Dave said sitting down, 'about those stunts, Sir William. Where do you think we should shoot those city scenes from the new *Bond* movie?'

'You can call him William, Samuel,' I said, 'no matter.'

'Yes. William it is then. Where do you think, William? And please, call me Samuel.'

Rick and I had our backs to the women but it didn't matter, I could see their interest reflected in Dave's face.

'Well, I thought we could shoot the city scenes here in Singapore. Make a nice contrast, what?'

'Uh-huh.' Dave looked at me. 'And what do you think, John? A nice contrast?'

Contrast to what? I wondered. Dave was looking right through me at the women, his head constantly bobbing about, eyes blinking incessantly. His manner was so obviously faked that I had trouble keeping a straight face. 'Yes,' was all I could manage before picking up my glass and releasing the laugh, echoing inside.

Dave clapped once. 'So, that's the location sorted. But what about Bond girls? We need lots of girls for this movie. James Bond needs *women, women, women*! Am I right, John?'

'Yes,' I said, trying to take the glass away. 'What we need . . .'

'Mm?'

'Are . . .'

'Yes?'

'Some, um, local girls.'

'Japanese girls you mean? That's a great idea.'

'Yes,' chimed Rick, and said, '*Japanese girls!*' so loudly it nearly burst my ear drum.

'Hi ladies.' Dave had made eye contact. Rick and I moved apart slightly, allowing Dave to shoot down the centre like a bowling ball, pushing our table to one side.

We all shook hands (a bit formal I thought, though obviously a requirement in Japanese greetings because it was their idea) and introduced ourselves exactly as we had rehearsed. I was a famous cinematographer who, along with Rick, had worked on all of the Bond films in recent years, in addition to half a dozen epics that Dave reeled off in quick succession. Thankfully they hadn't heard of any cinematographers.

Dave had supposedly met us on the set of a film he was shooting with Tarantino, and although two of the women had seen the film, neither of them knew the names of the black actors. As we suspected they couldn't tell one black face from another, and soon Dave was signing autographs. He could have said he was Al Jolson and they would have asked for his signature.

Also as suspected, they were bored housewives of Japanese businessmen on a weekend's spending spree. Every drink, like everything else they bought, was charged to their gold cards, which were paid for, of course, by their husbands in Japan. It occurred to me later, while I was in bed with one of them, that their husbands were probably doing exactly the same thing at home at exactly the same time plus two hours, according to my *Collins Gem World Atlas*, with their mistresses.

Once the barriers were down between us the rest was easy. We ordered drink after drink and their husbands paid for them, and every time I pretended to put my hand in my pocket the women would protest, saying that they'd been to Singapore many times before and it was their privilege to pay for us. After all, it was our first time in Asia!

After an hour or so the fat one stood up drunkenly and said that she was tired, and was given the job of taking all of the day's shopping back to her room.

'Oh,' I said, trying to look surprised, 'are you staying here, in Raffles?'

'Yes, but the rooms are awful, so small. We have one each you know.'

Rick, Dave and I looked at each other and tried to hide our astonishment. It must have looked odd because all three of us suddenly felt the urge to scratch our faces. I turned to the one I'd been talking to and whispered, 'I tried to book a room here but they were full.'

'Would you like to share mine?' she whispered back, slurring every word. 'There's plenty of space.'

I spent a night in heaven, that night in Raffles hotel. After living in crappy backpacker guest houses and sleeping on shitty old trains and buses, the crisp white sheets and marbled bathroom alone were enough to give me an orgasm. We ordered champagne and caviar, polishing off two bottles at God knows how many dollars a throw, before clearing out the mini bar and making love for the umpteenth time.

Their rooms were on the second floor of a courtyard that overlooked a lawn, and every so often I'd go outside for a spot of fresh air, only to find that Rick and Dave had had the same idea. It was like telepathy: three doors swung open and three figures in underpants came outside smoking a cigarette. We always ended up having the same three-way conversation, and always started by Rick.

'Any luck on finding that Bond girl, Samuel?' he'd ask.

'Not yet, Sir William.'

'John?'

'Nope. Still looking, I'm afraid.'

'Me too,' he'd reply, and the three of us would go back inside.

THREE

We'd been in Singapore about ten days, and were planning on catching the boat to the Indonesian island of Batam before our limit of stay expired, when something happened that changed the course of our plans completely. All the talk of Australia had gone out of the window for the time being, and none of us could see beyond the Indonesian island that was visible from the top floor of a CBD skyscraper on a clear day.

None of us were bored with Singapore, in fact quite the opposite. Despite all other backpackers' advice to the contrary, we were having a good time, spending the nights in Raffles, playing our James Bond game, and spending the days in one of the open air public swimming pools in town. We had discovered that for one Singapore dollar a day it was possible to stay out of mischief and spend very little money lounging around a spotlessly clean, almost empty pool, which also kept us cool in the tropical humidity that constantly hung over the city.

Our tenth day in the city started out no different to the rest, and after managing to wake at nine for a breakfast of one boiled egg and two slices of bread with butter *or* (not *and*) jam, we grabbed our shorts and headed to the pool in the park near Raffles Place. As usual I took my pocket radio along to listen to the day's pop on Singapore FM, while Rick went off to the bank to change some money, saying that he'd meet us at the pool later.

'Don't know why you bother with that thing, John,' Dave said, standing over me as he emerged from the pool.

'Dave, d'you mind?' I picked up the radio quickly to stop it from getting wet. 'You're dripping on my trannie!'

He slumped on the sunbed next to me. 'Fuckin' trannie. Jesus! We're putting men on Mars and you British are still listening to the wireless.'

I put the radio down on the opposite side to Dave's spreading puddle of water and squinted at the swimming pool. A woman was breast-stroking up and down, and I watched as the ripples from her wake caught the light of the morning sun before they spread out, hit the sheer tiled sides and made their way back into the middle.

Most of the other travellers staying at our guest house had declined this morning's offer to go to the pool – they always did, 'Go to a swimming pool?' they'd baulk. 'You should go to Thailand or Malaysia, to the beautiful beaches. Why do you want to spend more than one day in this city?' They all said the same thing, day after day as one left and another one came. As soon as they put their backpack down and sat on the bunk bed, out would come the guidebook with the possible routes in and out of the city. 'How long have you been here?' they'd ask me. The look on their faces when I told them two weeks was one of utter shock and disbelief. Of course, they would only be staying one day, two at most. They had only just arrived and had never been here before 'but the guidebook said . . .' Sometimes I wanted to shove their book down their throat.

Guidebooks have got a lot to answer for – guidebooks and the bush telegraph. Word of mouth can often be worse than a book for spreading misleading information. Backpackers gossip like old women, and all it takes is a word from one traveller to another, overheard in the reception of a guest house, to guarantee continent-wide broadcast. And that's exactly the way it was for Singapore. One person went there and told somebody else that it was only worth a day, 'just to say you've been there', the word spread and eventually became written in stone.

I looked from the glimmering water up to the geometric patch of hazy blue sky. It was like lying beside a rectangular pond in the valley of a canyon, the buildings appearing to lean inwards, allowing only a piece of sky the width of a football pitch to shine through the top of the canyon.

The only gap in the canyon wall was where side streets separated one row of buildings from another, producing V shaped ravines in the crisp line between rooftops and sky.

'John!' I snapped out of the daydream. 'Listen!' Dave shouted, picking up my radio. At the end of all the hourly news bulletins, Singapore FM always has a couple of items of local news; nothing earth-shattering, usually a cat stuck up a tree, or local boy saved in storm drain drama, but today's local item was different. 'It's about us!'

'Shh,' I said, leaning closer.

The over-concerned radio presenter was explaining to the listeners that some men, pretending to be involved in the latest James Bond movie, were conning locals out of money. He said that the 'gang' was potentially dangerous.

'No way! Dangerous? That's bullshit, man.' Dave stood up and waved my radio in the air. 'All we did was talk to girls and have some fun, that's all. We didn't take any fuckin' money!'

'Dave, do me a favour and give me the radio will you.'

'Sorry.' He handed it over. 'But, hey, that's bullshit, John. We didn't hurt anyone. I've never broken the law in my life.'

'What, never?' I asked doubtfully.

He hesitated. 'Well, at school I maybe stole some candies from other kids, but that's it.'

'Yeah, same as me really.' I held the radio to my ear, expecting it to crackle out an apology. 'It must have been the staff at Raffles who reported us. Why d'you think they're making such a big deal about it? Propaganda?'

'How's that?'

'Well, you know how over-protected the Singaporeans are. Maybe the government just blows everything out of proportion to keep everyone in check. Scare them into thinking that the government's watching.'

'Conspiracy theorist huh?' He nodded, turned and dived into the pool, swimming a full length underwater before surfacing. 'They're probably watching us right this minute,' he shouted back from the other end.

I looked up again at the buildings around us and nodded. 'A few thousand office workers are that's for sure.'

Another good thing about the one-dollar swimming pool was that it allowed us to catch up on the sleep we weren't getting at night, and to the sound of Dave's splashes mixed with the hum of the traffic I closed my eyes and started to drift off. Like pink shutters my eyelid membranes went down and warmed, heated by the mid-morning sun. The smell of chlorine mixed with the odour of freshly cut grass from the nearby park reminded me of the lido where I used to live in London, and the warmth, smells and sounds all came together at once, so perfectly, and in such harmony that I would have slept and dreamt if I hadn't heard a voice.

The next thing I knew I was being shaken. 'Sir. Excuse me sir, your friend is outside. Sir?'

Wiping away a slither of dribble from the corner of my mouth, I turned over and looked up, squinting hard at the bright face.

'Sir, your friend is outside,' the pool attendant repeated.

'Well tell him to come inside,' I said sleepily.

'He has no money. Cannot come in.'

I crawled wearily off the sunbed and stood up, going dizzy from lack of blood to the brain. Dave was still doing lengths underwater, his brown figure wobbling with each thrust of his arms, and I cursed him, following the attendant to the turnstile where Rick was waiting.

'Didn't you hear me shouting?' he said as I arrived.

'I was asleep, sorry.'

'Where's Dave?' he puffed, wiping the sweat from his face.

'Underwater.' I rubbed my eyes. 'Haven't you got any change?' I said, handing him the dollar coin I'd brought, correctly assuming that he didn't have any.

'Worse than that,' he said, pushing through the turnstile, 'I haven't got any dollars. You know all that baht that I knocked off from Ta? It's forged.'

'You're kidding?' I said, suddenly waking up. '*Forged?*'

'Yeah, I'm kidding, and I just stood out here for the past five minutes for the fun of it. *Of course I'm not fooking kidding!*'

At first I didn't know what to say so I didn't say anything, and we walked over to the sunbeds in silence, Dave following alongside in the water.

'Dave,' I said as we reached the other end, 'you'd better get out and come over here. We've got some serious thinking to do.'

FOUR

We were still thinking about the forged baht that night when we walked along the well-lit streets towards Little India. I hadn't yet told Rick where we were going because I knew that if I did he'd flip. He had never liked India, and the idea of wasting a night on the town in what would probably be the dirtiest part of Singapore wouldn't make him happy. I was mildly interested to see if it would live up to its name, and we could hardly go back to Raffles. In any case, I needed a change from five-star luxury and rich women; their perfume always made me sneeze.

At first none of us spoke, we just trudged along the streets wondering what came next. The whole episode with the forged money had really put the dampers on everything, including Rick's birthday, which we should have been celebrating that night. Rick told Dave and I what had actually happened at the bank that morning, and it was amazing that he had returned to the pool at all; he could easily have been behind bars.

Thinking that we were soon going to Indonesia, Rick had decided, after some deliberation, that he would be better off with a fistful of dollars and not Thai baht. He stood to lose some money, changing from one currency to another and then back into rupiah later on, but we all agreed that it made sense in the long run. None of us had ever been to Indonesia before and therefore had no idea how easy it would be to change Thai currency there. Singaporean banks were happy to take it, so better to be safe than sorry.

Rick told us that he'd walked into the bank, first customer of the morning, and plonked the wad of cash on to the teller's counter. They agreed the exchange rate, and were about to start counting out the US dollars when the woman who was serving him noticed something odd about the pictures on the notes. She put one under an ultra-violet lamp, frowned, and then tried another. And another, and another. 'What's wrong?' Rick had asked. The woman ignored him and whispered something to a colleague who then went out the back, presumably to fetch the manager.

By now, Rick said, it was obvious that the money was forged. He sweated, his heart pounding as he looked nervously around for his escape. There was no point in waiting about to find out what would happen next so he just said goodbye to the clerk and walked very casually out of the bank. When he hit the street he ran, and didn't stop running until he got to the swimming pool.

Dave naively suggested that Rick should go back to the bank and explain that he had received the money from a licensed money changer in Malaysia. Pretty ridiculous considering that our passport stamps would show that we were heading south and not north. Why the hell would he be changing money into Thai baht?

'You're a businessman doing deals in–'

'Shut up, Dave!'

He shut up.

Rick looked up as we went to cross the road and then looked back down as we walked. 'Where're we going, John?'

'Just have a walk around,' I said, momentarily looking up to check that the road was clear. Dave looked up at me but didn't speak.

We walked half a mile or so before Rick noticed a change in his surroundings, and then only because a rat ran across his feet. He looked up with a start, left, then right and finally doing a three-sixty spin and sniffing the air. 'Fook, it stinks around here. Where are we?'

I didn't answer.

'And there's loads of rubbish!'

'There's a little bar over there,' I said quickly, pointing down an alleyway. 'There're lots of them. Shall we have a drink?'

He eyed me cautiously before turning into a bustling side street, crammed full of tables and chairs. People, mostly Indians and a few Chinese, were sitting outside shops eating noodles or curries and swigging bottles of beer.

'Fooking hell,' Rick said, stopping in his tracks, 'now that's what I call a birthday present.'

Dave and I followed his gaze past the tables, and noticed to our astonishment that the whole street was wall-to-wall brothels. Little doorways with a tatty curtain across them were cheek-by-jowl, the glow of a red light warming the first few feet of the pavement outside each one.

'Happy Birthday,' I said, surprised at the discovery. 'Now let's sit down and have a drink.'

'Thanks, lads, I knew I could rely on you two to cheer me up.' Rick patted our backs. 'Nice one.'

Dave looked at me, raising his eyebrows as if to say, 'What the fuck's he on about?' and sat down at the nearest table.

I ordered three beers and they were on the table being opened before I'd even sat down. 'So,' I said, pouring mine into a glass, 'what are we going to do?' The cold beer hit the humid air and foamed. 'I've got some money, not a lot, but enough to get me into Indo. What about you Dave?'

He looked up mid-pour. 'I've got to get a job if I don't want to be on the next plane back to the States. Let's face it, we've all got to get jobs, otherwise, boom!'

Rick suddenly stood up, looking down the street. A beautiful Indian girl, five feet ten and dressed in a full length, red evening dress was walking towards us. Her full, round breasts were almost falling out of a V-shaped slit in the gown that ran from her collar bone down to a point just above her navel. She looked like she was wearing it back-to-front.

'Look at that!' Rick gasped, putting his glass on the table and nearly missing.

Dave looked, proclaimed himself in love, and went to stand up but Rick pushed him back down.

The woman in red approached our table, her red high-heel shoes clip-clopping along until she reached Rick. She was even more beautiful close up, no pimples or pock-marked skin, just the perfect woman. She stopped, put one hand on Rick's crotch and kissed his lips.

'Jesus,' I said, staring and trying to form another word.

Dave's month was hanging open, and the beer in his hand was spilling on to the table so I nudged it upright. 'Thanks,' he managed to say, still spellbound. 'My God, have you ever seen anything like her before?'

We watched Rick float down the street behind the woman, led like a balloon on her string, and disappear into one of the doorways. A moment later he was back, asking for money, his face smeared with lipstick.

'Only if I can share her,' Dave replied as he put his hand into his pocket to cover half the cost.

Rick placed a reassuring hand on his shoulder. 'I'd do the same on your birthday, Dave, you know that.'

'I had my birthday on Koh Pha-Ngan, remember? Fuck, you only rolled me a joint!'

'Yeah I remember that,' he said, laughing nostalgically. 'Toomy made you a seashell necklace, how romantic. Cough up.'

Dave begrudgingly put his money on the table. 'Whose idea was it to come to Little India anyway, man?'

Rick looked down his nose. 'So, that's where we are. No wonder you wouldn't tell me. Well, serves you two right then.' He scooped up the cash and turned to walk off. 'Back in an hour.'

Dave and I sat and drank, and waited. Occasionally we talked about what we were going to do next, but mainly we just got drunk and speculated as to what was going on in that room down the street. The more drunk we got the more jealous he became. 'D'you think she's a he?' he slurred, pouring out yet another beer that neither of us could really afford. 'I think so. I think Rick's got more than he bargained for.'

After nearly two hours Rick came back down the street with a look of awe on his face. That's the only way I can describe it. He wasn't smiling, which was strange, but he looked totally at peace with the world, and totally in awe, as though he'd seen an apparition.

'Well?' Dave said as Rick sat back down at our table. 'Spill the beans, man.'

I nodded and leaned forward, eager to know the ins and outs. 'C'mon, what happened?'

Slowly Rick took hold of his warm beer and poured out a full glass, as though in a dream. He seemed to be staring right through the table. 'We're leaving. Tomorrow night.'

Dave and I were gagging, leaning way over the table, willing him to give us more information. I swallowed hard. 'Yeah?'

Rick glanced at both of us. 'She read my palm.'

Dave burst out laughing. 'Read your fuckin' palm, man? Ha! Is that it? Didn't you fu–?'

'Yeah of course I did, but *then* she read my palm.' He took another drink and looked starry-eyed at his hand. 'We're leaving tomorrow night. On a boat.'

Dave looked at me, and then at Rick, his white eyes swivelling like ping-pong balls against his face. 'Says who?'

'Her.' He pulled a business card from his pocket. '*Lady Mysta Geng.*'

'Gimme that.' Dave snatched the card.

'We haven't got a boat though,' I said dismissively. 'She's not a very good palmist.'

There was a moment's silence as Rick smiled to himself before saying.

'We will have tomorrow. Remember that boat we saw in Changi Yacht Club John. The same as the one I said my dad used to own?'

Dave frowned at me in confusion, unable to follow the sudden change in the course of the conversation. 'The one owned by the Japanese businessman who's never here,' I said, 'yeah?'

Rick leaned back in his chair and placed his hands behind his head. A broad grin spread across his face. 'Well I'm going to steal it.'

FIVE

There was no way Dave or I would entertain the idea of stealing a boat, it was just too ridiculous to be true. After Rick had first told us his scheme we were in tears of laughter, rolling around outside the bar, slapping him on the back. The more we laughed, however, the more serious became the look on Rick's face, as though he was being insulted, and the more serious his look, the more I realised that he wasn't joking.

As we walked back to the dorm that night he told Dave and I that if we didn't want to come along it would mean the end of his travelling, that he'd have to get a job, because although he felt he could sail a boat he didn't want to do it alone. 'Come on,' he goaded, 'what have we got to lose?' Dave and I pointed out that we had many things to lose, including our lives, and told Rick to drop the idea once and for all. We were not going to do it and that was final.

We all went to bed thinking about boats and the images that Rick had conjured up; of sailing off into the sunset and drifting around the fourteen thousand islands of Indonesia. The next morning when I awoke Dave was already staring at me from his bunk on the opposite side of the room. He wasn't saying anything, just lying on his side in his boxers, with his hands under his head, staring. He wasn't smiling, but there was the hint of a smirk on his lips, the glint of mischief.

As if to confirm what was on Dave's mind, I rolled on to one side and hung my head over the side of the bed frame to check on Rick who had the bottom bunk. He too was staring up at me with the same look, only a wider smirk. 'Oh no,' I mumbled, and rolled on to my back.

'Listen, John.' Dave swung his legs over the side of his bed and sat up. The person on the bottom bunk groaned and Dave checked his watch. 'Oops,' he mouthed, and pointed upstairs, 'only eight-thirty. Breakfast?'

I wasn't hungry but it seemed too important not to join in the discussion, so I dressed quickly (shorts and flip-flops never take long) and we went up the stairs.

The breakfast-room had just opened and the grumpy old Chinese guy who served the meals was just boiling the eggs when we arrived.

'Wha' you wan'?' he growled, his eyes peering through puffy slits. 'No foo'.' He tapped his watch so hard that the impact made the fat under his arm wobble. 'No foo', only eigh' thir'y.'

'Fuck him.' Dave turned on his heels. 'Let's go to McDonald's.'

Mornings in the tropics are almost as good in cities as they are in the jungles and on the beaches. The air is warm, but not uncomfortably hot, and always seems to carry more smells with it than it does in temperate climates. I don't know if it's got something to do with the humidity, or perhaps simply that tropical places are smellier, but the air is tangible, almost alive. There's only one thing that beats tropical mornings, and that's tropical mornings when you've got all the time in the world and a plan to work out. Add to that a McMuffin and hash brown and you're in dreamland. An English breakfast would have been better but what can you expect from the tropics?

We sat down at the open seated area, and to my surprise Dave threw my pocket atlas on the table. 'Just borrowed it.'

'Thief.'

Dave sat down. 'It's your turn to buy the breakfast, John.'

I got up again and sauntered to the counter, bought three breakfasts and took them back to our table.

'OK,' Rick started, sliding his tray of food over to his side, 'let's talk about what we're going to do. Dave and I reckon that if we can get a boat, between us we can sail it to Bali.'

Rick concentrated on the atlas momentarily, looking for the appropriate map. 'It's really no distance at all, look.' We leaned closer to see where he was pointing on the map. It certainly didn't look far. 'And,' he continued, 'if we stick to the northern side of Sumatra and Java, in the Java Sea, we'll be avoiding the Indian Ocean. It'll be like sailing on a lake.'

Dave nodded, so I nodded. He may have been young but he'd spent enough time at sea during his service to know danger when he saw it. The serene expression on his face and ready agreement with what Rick was saying was comforting.

'We'll have to watch the Makassar Straits,' Rick went on, 'between Borneo and Sulawesi, but other than that . . . '

'Why,' I said, 'what happens in the Mak–?'

'Makassar Straits? North-east equatorial current comes through there. So long as we've got wind we should be all right though.'

Dave nodded seriously again. 'I've been through there twice before, it's a breeze.'

'What, literally?' I asked sarcastically.

'No, I mean it's easy. But there usually is a breeze.' He hesitated. 'That was on a 20,000-tonne warship, though.'

I leaned back in the chair and rolled my head. 'This is too ridiculous. Here we are, looking at a ten-dollar pocket atlas, and you two are using it to navigate around the globe! Be serious for Christ's sake, we'll get ourselves killed.'

Rick pushed the south-east Asia page towards me. 'See this?' he said, pointing at a patch of blue, 'I've sailed all along there before with my dad. It's so easy.'

I looked up from the map. 'Have you sailed to Bali before?'

He slid the book back to his side of the table. 'No, but it's the same. So long as we don't cross over into open ocean swells, that forty-two footer is more than equal to these seas. Christ, I could do it in a boat half that size.'

'What about charts?' Dave rested his chin in one hand. 'Where can we get charts for these waters?'

'No problem. We can go to the admiralty office in town, or, better still, buy them at the yacht club. Anyway, chances are they're already on that boat.' He closed the book and looked at me. 'Oh come on, John, it'll be brilliant.'

I shook my head. 'And what if we get caught?'

'All we've got to do is get it out of Singapore waters and we're free. The border with Indo is only about ten miles away, that's an hour's sailing! We'll do it at night, under steam.'

I looked at Dave with a question mark in my eyes.

'Engine, he means. What about fuel?' he said, turning back to Rick.

'Easy, we take a can of two-stroke with us.'

'Fresh water?'

'Get it in Batam. Come on, Dave, these are minor obstacles, you know that. All we've got to do is have the balls to jump on the boat, start her up and go. Simple.' Rick folded his arms. 'That yacht club's empty during the daytime so there'll definitely be no one there at night. You heard what Chan-the-boatman said John, no one ever uses those boats, they're just a tax dodge.' Rick sat back and then leaned forward again. 'The owner's Japanese for Christ's sake, he lives in Japan! He probably comes here twice a year. He won't even know the boat's missing until next year!'

I looked at Dave. 'What d'you think?'

'Me? I'm in! Sailing is no problem. Like Rick said, that's virtually an inland sea. You'd get bigger waves on the great lakes in Canada than you would on that.' He stabbed the book with his finger. 'I think we should go tonight if we can get the charts. Rick?'

He shrugged. 'Why not?'

'You two are serious aren't you?' I shook my head and stared at the table. 'This is crazy.'

'Does that mean you're in then?'

'No, it doesn't. If we've run out of money then we'll have to get jobs.' They both moved back as though threatened, a look of shock on their faces. 'Yeah, I don't want to go back to work either,' I said. 'This past year has been the best of my life and I want to go on travelling. But without money . . . '

There was a moment's silence as we all stared at the floor, before Rick spoke. 'How can we get work here, we don't even have a work visa?'

'Bar work?' I suggested half-heartedly. 'Any kind of work that's temporary. There're bound to be places where they need English speakers.'

They both looked unimpressed, shaking their heads at one another as though I was the one who was suggesting something extraordinary. 'I'll tell you what,' Rick leaned over the table again, 'we'll go around all the bars today and see if there's any work. If there is, we give it a go and try to earn enough cash to move on.'

'And if there isn't?' I prompted, knowing what the reply would be.

'Bon voyage!' Dave put his hands into the middle of the table. 'That's the McPlan. Agreed?'

'Agreed,' said Rick, and put his hands on top of Dave's. They both looked at me.

I quickly ran over the likelihood of getting work in Singapore but drew a blank. It was an unknown factor. I didn't know anyone who had recently acquired a job in Singapore, or anywhere else in Asia for that matter.

'John?'

Surely it must be possible to find a bar job in a modern city like this. I'd seen foreigners working in some of the pubs and restaurants, and . . .

'Agreed?' they asked together.

I sighed. 'OK, agreed,' I said reluctantly, and put my hand on top of theirs.

SIX

That whole day was spent searching the bars all along Orchard Road, frantically looking for jobs. Bars, restaurants, nightclubs, we perspired through them all in an attempt to avoid the inevitable. I should correct that sentence, *I* went through them all, Dave and Rick were not interested.

At first the pair of them trudged into a few places out of a sense of duty. After the first two refusals they both started to hang around in the doorways, letting me go in alone, and by lunchtime they were giggling every time I emerged, rejected. I soldiered on, unwilling to admit defeat without at least having given it a shot.

My token spell of childhood delinquency had never been anything more serious than a bout of mild kleptomania and an interest in lighting fires. Joyriding in stolen cars was something that I admired from afar and left to those who were determined to make a career out of crime. Stealing a boat was way out of my league. Stealing penny chews from the newsagent's, yes, but stealing boats?

By the time evening came I was shattered. Covering miles of concrete paving in flip-flops had left my calf muscles shaking uncontrollably. Add to that a nice open wound where I'd stubbed my big toe on a curb, and you get some idea of what kind of mood I was in.

I went to bed that night less than happy, and resigned to stealing a forty-two-foot yacht.

The whole of the following day we spent apart, each with our own task, and each with a clearly defined set of objectives.

Rick's job was to go to the yacht club, suss out the lie of the land and buy the correct nautical charts that covered the area we intended to sail through. Failing that he was to go to the Singapore marine department and get them, and if that failed the whole plan was off. If he didn't appear back at the guest house rendezvous at the agreed time of six o'clock in the evening, we were to assume that he had been successful, and meet him in Changi Village at midnight.

Dave's task was shopping. As someone who knew less about sailing than Rick, but a million times more about it than me, he was to go around town and buy 'essentials'. Every time I asked exactly what he meant by 'essentials', he patted my shoulder and said, 'John, just you leave it to the men of this outfit.' Dave was to meet me at the guest house at six, and we would go together to meet Rick.

My job was twofold: I had to settle the bill at the guest house (our attempt at running off without paying had already failed) and pack everyone's gear, ready for the off. All of which took no more than an hour so I drifted around the streets for the rest of the day feeling like I was hopping off school: playing video games in the arcade, eating Big Macs and hanging around the shopping malls. I don't know if I'm alone in this, but whenever I kill time in shopping centres I feel guilty. It doesn't matter what the circumstances are, I always feel guilty as hell.

At six o'clock on the dot, Dave turned up at the guest house with a holdall full of 'essentials' that ranged from torches to fishing lines and hooks to a pocket pin-ball machine. 'Neat huh?' he said, holding up a telescopic fishing rod. He flicked his wrist and it shot out, nearly hitting a traveller who was waiting in the reception area.

'Oh! You will go fishing, no?' the boy said, leaning to one side to avoid having his eye poked out.

'Something like that, yeah,' Dave said, and collapsed the rod.

Rick didn't return, so we hung around the dorm until nightfall and caught the night bus out to Changi Village.

It hadn't occurred to either of us how on earth we were going to get so much gear out to the boat, and I think we assumed somehow that there'd be a rowing boat waiting to ferry us over to the mooring. Dave and I had even had trouble getting it all on to the bus. I was carrying mine and Rick's gear, while Dave carried his plus the essentials.

'Rick'll have a boat waiting,' Dave said confidently in answer to my query.

'Hope so.' I lifted the two bags as the bus cleared the brow of the hill towards the village. It was hard to recognise at night, there were hardly any street lights on and all of the houses along the way seemed to be unoccupied. Either that or the occupants were all asleep. Everyone else had already alighted from the bus so I asked the driver to drop us as close as possible to the yacht club.

The driver checked the bus in his little overhead convex mirror to see if there were any other passengers onboard and said, 'Take you right inside if you want?'

'No!' I shouted, slightly panicky. 'Um, just by the junction, next to the sign post, that'll be OK.'

He drove over the hill and put his lights on full beam. 'Where that man is standing you mean?'

'Yeah,' I said, squinting at the road ahead, 'that's exactly where I mean.'

SEVEN

Once I started laughing I couldn't stop. Rick put his hand over my mouth and ordered me to 'Shh!' but it just made me worse. It was the sight of Dave trying to be stealthy, swimming out to the boat, that was doing it to me, that and the sight of us two crouching low behind the bushes. In the end I had to turn away and look at the darkened hillside behind me to take my mind off the scene.

After meeting Rick at the bus stop we had walked through the village to the golf course, climbed the fence and run across the greens, using the tree line as cover to the beach. Dave thought he was on special ops, and when Rick took his shirt off to make the swim out to the boat, Dave put his hand out firmly and said, 'No! This is my job.' He said it so seriously that I burst out laughing and hadn't been able to stop since. I think if he'd had a tin of green paint he would have camouflaged his face.

The swim was about a hundred metres, and when I stopped giggling enough to look back again Dave was almost there. I wiped the tears from my eyes and tapped Rick on the shoulder. 'Got any–'

'Shh!'

'Got any cigarettes?' I whispered, trying not to start laughing again.

'He's almost there,' he said, offering the packet to me. 'Looks like that old geezer's asleep.'

I leaned forward, parting a bush to look along the beach, and stood on a twig. It cracked like a banger going off.

Rick sighed heavily. 'It's like being with fooking Laurel and Hardy.'

'Sorry.' I bit my lip and leaned forward again, scanning the dark bay.

Chan-the-boatman's shack was just along the beach from where we were, and I could see his silhouette, back-lit by the light coming out through his window. Either he was asleep in a chair or dead, because he hadn't moved for the past half an hour. An opaque column of blue smoke drifted up from a small chimney on the shack's roof into the night sky, before being caught by the breeze above the palm trees and dispersing seaward.

To our right was the clubhouse, but from where we were it was almost entirely obscured by trees as the beach curved out of sight. There were no lights on in the building, as expected for a weekday, and apart from the old man we hadn't seen another person anywhere, even in the village.

'Mmm,' I mumbled thoughtfully, and leaned back into the bushes to light the cigarette. 'What's he doing now? I can't see him.' Dave had vanished from sight, leaving only ripples in the inky water where he had been a second before. A moment later his head came back up through the surface, like a buoy.

'Checking the anchorage,' Rick replied quizzically. 'What's he doing that for, it's tied to a mooring isn't it?' He leaned forward, thinking aloud. 'Come on, Dave, get the tender. Get the fooking tender.'

Dave appeared to hesitate, treading water, as if thinking, then disappeared around the other side of the yacht, and a moment later came up on deck. Unless you were specifically looking at that boat among the many moored up, you would never know he was there. Occasionally there'd be the glint of moonlight against his shiny wet skin but that was all. He made the perfect secret agent.

'He's like James Bond,' I whispered.

'Shaft.'

At that moment there was an enormous splash, and we both sank back into the bushes, waiting to see what had happened, unsure exactly where it had come from. A dog barked in the distance and we held our breath, praying that no one had heard, until a set of ripples echoed out from the yacht, indicating that it must have been Dave. The sound of a squeaky pulley wheel drifted over. I couldn't stand the tension.

'Must be the tender,' Rick said firmly, 'got to be.'

There was another, quieter splash more like a wet 'slap' before a white square edged its way around the front, rowed by Dave. He ducked under the bow of the yacht and paddled towards us, constantly keeping an eye on the sleeping Chan.

'He's done it!' we both whispered, and crept down to the water's edge.

Dave beached the little fibreglass dinghy and we quickly threw in the gear. 'It's not anchored,' he whispered enthusiastically, 'just tied to a buoy.'

'Told you it wouldn't be.' Rick chucked his rucksack in and pushed us off the sand before jumping in behind. 'I think he must be stoned,' he said, looking back at Chan's house. 'If that splash didn't wake him, nothing will.'

We rowed silently out to the yacht, Dave painstakingly dipping the oars so as not to make a sound, and climbed up a small ladder, hauling the dinghy in behind us.

'Smaller than I thought,' I said as I climbed on deck, grinning and giggling as my apprehension turned to excitement and I forgot to whisper.

Dave clamped his hand over my mouth. 'Shh! Sound carries over water. Wait until you see inside, it's deceptive.'

I had a million questions to ask about what we were going to do next. How do we get the engine started? Which direction do we go in? Can we sail at night? But I thought it best just to say nothing for the time being and let those two sort it out. I'd never been on a yacht before and I didn't want to go around asking stupid questions if the answers were staring me in the face. Even though I knew precious little about boats, I was determined not to show it. Look natural, act chilled, I told myself, and leaned against the mast.

'Great, it's unlocked! No need to break it open.' Rick pulled open the double doors that led down into the living quarters and went inside. I went to follow but a second later Rick came back up, blocking the entrance. 'Dave, you're not going to believe this,' he said, beaming.

Dave was tying up the dinghy and turned his head. 'What?'

'The keys are in the ignition!'

Dave mouthed, 'No way!' and quickly knotted a loose end before jumping across the deck and darting into the hole behind Rick.

'Fucking dark in here,' I said, following in behind. They both tutted at my ignorance.

'Did you get that booster-pack, Rick?' Dave asked, lifting a small hatch in the floor. 'The battery's gotta be flat.'

'Yeah.' Rick turned to me. 'John, up on deck, get that holdall with all the shit from the yacht club in it.'

'Yes, Captain.' I saluted and went out to fetch the bag, wondering if I had inadvertently assumed the position of onboard skivvy.

When I came back down, all the doors were open inside and Rick was reeling off names of things that I'd never heard of, while Dave rummaged around to see if the items were onboard. Every reply was, 'Yep', and sometimes, 'Yep, got two o' them suckers'. I dropped the holdall at Rick's feet and went for a look around.

Dave was right, the size of the boat upon first glance was deceptive. From the outside the yacht looked tiny, about as long as a stretch limo and only a little wider. I'd have believed that its depth was only four feet, and couldn't accommodate a grown man. However, when I walked through from one room to another, only slightly stooped over, I was agog at its size. Not only at how big it was but also at its level of comfort: almost luxurious.

From where Rick was standing, messing about with something called GPS, there was a small step and sliding doors that led into a kitchen/dining area, before terminating in two small doors that separated living from sleeping quarters. 'There're only two beds,' I called out from the bedroom doorway.

'The dining table pulls down,' came a bored response from the darkness.

I did a walk-through in both bedrooms, opening up drawers and cupboards to see what had been left onboard. There were plastic oilskins on hangers and some bedding, but otherwise it was empty. Catching my reflection in a cabinet mirror made me jump and then smile at myself. 'Guilty,' I mumbled before turning and somersaulting on to the bed, landing squarely on my back. 'Guilty of finding the easy way out.'

I lay on the bed looking up at the white formica ceiling, hands behind my head, and began to wonder.

I wondered what the owner did for a living. I hoped it was some rich businessman who'd forgotten he even owned a yacht in Singapore. I hoped he'd got so many houses and toys in different parts of the world that he wouldn't care less if one went missing. Anyway, I reasoned, he'd only claim on the insurance when it was reported stolen.

On the other hand, it could've belonged to someone who'd worked their whole life, toiling day-in day-out, scrimping and saving in the pursuit of a childhood dream. A little unlikely, I told myself, all the odds were pointing to it being owned by a wealthy businessman; Chan-the-boatman had said as much. And if it did belong to a local who'd spent his life nurturing his dream there would have been signs of use onboard: cups in the sink, sheets on the beds, shoes and socks in the cupboards.

A gift, I thought to myself, a gift from someone who's too busy to have a good time to three young men who can't get enough of it. Maybe the owner would be happy to know that all his hard work was being put to good use. Maybe.

I've thought about these things quite a lot since that night we first took the yacht, and however much I try to feel ashamed of stealing it I can't. I once stole a kid's dinner money at school, but an hour later gave it back to him because I knew he'd have no lunch and would go hungry. If that same kid had been throwing his money around all day, leaving cash here, there and everywhere, I would have had no qualms about keeping it.

The bed shook slightly and I sat up, leaning on my elbows. There was the cough and splutter of an engine before it roared into life and settled into a steady chugging sound. I looked out through the doorway and Dave appeared.

'We have ignition. Woo-hoo! C'mon, John, I need you up on deck.' He disappeared again.

When I got outside, the tree line was already moving past us and I could no longer see Chan's shack or the clubhouse. The wind was rushing into my face. 'We're moving!' I gasped, scarcely believing we were. I was grinning so much that it was hard to see.

'John!' I spun around and looked to the rear of the boat. Rick was turning a huge chrome wheel in his hands and he had a cigarette gripped between his teeth. 'Is this living or what?'

I stretched and almost touched the sky, shaking my head in disbelief. 'I can't believe we're doing this! What's the penalty for TDA in Singapore?'

He pulled the cigarette out of his mouth, sparks flying in the wind. 'TSA you mean. This is taking and *sailing* away.' He turned the wheel slightly. 'Aren't you glad you didn't get a job now?'

'This is fucking brilliant,' I shouted at no one in particular and jumped up on to the mast. 'Dave, this is the best moment of my life.'

'Thought you'd like it,' he shouted back, and pointed over Rick's head. 'Look.' Behind us in the distance we could see the city lights, glowing against the black sky above the landscape, shrouding the heavens in a warm glow. 'Impressive, huh?'

'Absolutely,' I shouted at the sky. 'Abso-fucking-lutely.'

THE WET DREAM

ONE

None of us went to sleep that first night. Dave was like a cat on hot bricks, flying about from the mast to the deck: first running up to the bow, to lean over and watch the waves as we chugged through the inky water, and then skipping along the sides, whooping and hooting his way to the stern.

Every time he reached the rear, Rick would say something to him to check this, or look over that and he'd bolt off down the hatch like a rabbit, only to come up a minute later, beaming, both thumbs held up. He handled the motion of the boat beautifully, much the same as Rick, while I held on to everything and anything within arm's reach to steady myself.

I could barely contain my level of excitement, and because I was restricted physically (I didn't want to pull the wrong ropes) the energy and enthusiasm eventually worked its way out of my system verbally. All of the things that I'd told myself not to voice through fear of appearing idiotic came out in a torrent. I may not yet have had the sea legs to sprint about like Dave, but I matched him word-for-step.

'Why don't we put up the sail, Rick?' I'd shout, while hanging on to the rigging.

'We don't want—'

'What's this stuff do?' I'd ask impatiently, cutting him off in mid-reply.

'That's for when we—'

'Which direction are we heading in; north, east, south or west?'

'Well at the moment we should be—'

'Can I have a go at steering?'

'Fooking hell!'

I don't think I kept quiet for more than a minute that first night. Looking back now, I wish I'd taken some more time to quietly reflect on what was going on around me. In fact my whole time aboard that boat now seems more like a snapshot than an adventure lived. It's like it happened to me, but because it was so new and exciting, and because I didn't allow my eyes or brain time to take it in and store it properly, the memory of it isn't as clear as it should be.

In contrast, Rick, characteristically, took it all in without a word. I do remember standing on the boom that first night, clinging to the mast and looking back at Rick holding the wheel, and thinking: so young and yet so wise.

After a few hours, I don't remember how many but it was before sunrise, we cleared Singaporean waters and Dave let out the main sail to a cheer from all of us. He then went down below again and cut the engine. The silence was deafening. The flapping sound of the canvas turned into a loud *crack* in the swift breeze as the wind filled the sails and we picked up speed.

Abruptly, Rick spun the wheel through his hands and we changed direction. Dave shouted something from below, and Rick adjusted the wheel accordingly. 'South-south-east, right?' he called to Dave. There was another brief exchange which made little sense to me, and the two of them quickly changed positions. Two minutes later they changed back again, obviously a check to make sure there were no mistakes on Dave's part. Pretty shrewd, I thought.

I jumped down off the mast and went to Rick's side. 'What's going on? Where are we?'

He leaned forward and shone the Mag-Lite at the compass, pushing his billowing hair out of his face. 'Heading south-south-east. We're more or less in the South China Sea.' He thumbed over his shoulder. 'That was the Singapore Strait, and over that way's Borneo. Ahead of us is . . . ' he leaned over to one side and looked down at the chart I was standing on. I moved back slightly. 'Nothing really.'

I glanced around and noticed a huge land mass to our right. 'Isn't that Singapore over there?'

He shook his head. 'Bintan. Part of Indonesia. The way I see it we'll keep going until ... Pass me that chart, John. Thanks. Until ... Kep' Lingga, and stop off for some decent supplies. If there's fook-all there we'll just keep going until we get to a place called ... Dang ... something, on the island of Bangka. There.' He pointed at the map with his torch beam. 'We've got fishing gear and a big bag of rice, so we won't go hungry.'

'I've got thirty tins of sardines in my bag,' I said enthusiastically.

'Ugh, I hate sardines. You should have bought tuna.'

So much for my contribution to the ship's rations. There was a pause, and I said, 'Not much about. Ships I mean.' It seemed odd, apart from the occasional tanker that we spotted as a black rectangle on the horizon, we hadn't passed a single vessel.

He switched off the torch. 'Busiest shipping lane in the world, this. Lots of pirates around.'

'Pirates?' I exclaimed. 'Come off it, not in this day and age.'

'South China Sea is the most notorious stretch of water in the world for piracy.' Rick took his hands off the wheel to light a cigarette, speaking with it hanging from his lips. 'Forget cutlasses and all that shit, this is modern stuff. These guys go around in power boats.'

'Doing what?'

'Ripping off expensive yachts like this one.'

'Great! You never told me that before.'

'Didn't want to scare you.' He cupped his hand over the match to light the cigarette.

'Well you just have. Cheers.'

'Heh heh, don't worry, we'll only take a week or so to get to Bali at this rate. These trade winds are pretty constant.'

'I thought we were going to sail around the fourteen thousand islands of Indo for ever and a day?'

'Yeah, I've been thinking about that,' He flicked the match into the air directly above his head and the wind carried it away.

'And?'

'And I think we should get to Bali before we do anything else. At least then we'll have a proper base, and we can decide which islands we want to visit: Indo, Philippines, whatever takes our fancy.'

A spark from his cigarette flew into my face so I went around to the other side. 'Why don't we just do that now? Stop in that place we just looked at on the map, and start from there.'

'Too close to Singapore John. We can't afford to hang around here. Even if the owner of this boat doesn't use it, chances are Chan-the-boatman's going to notice something's afoot.' He drew on the cigarette and released the smoke, giggling. 'Can you imagine his face when he wakes up tomorrow and thinks, "Eh? I'm sure there was a yacht there yesterday!"?'

'I doubt if he even cares. The way he spoke the other day I reckon he'd be pleased if someone took it. Get his own back on the owners.'

As we sat there looking up at the stars, there was a noise down below and Dave climbed out of the hatch, bounding down the deck towards us.

'Hey, you two,' he said, 'we're bang on target, the wind's force four, according to the radio, and we are mooo-ving. Yee-hah!'

'You're more excited than I am Dave,' I said. 'You should be used to this sort of thing by now.'

'John,' his arm went around my neck, 'once it's in your blood, you never get tired of it. Am I right Sir William?'

Rick nodded.

'This is *living*,' he grinned, sitting down beside me. 'We've got everything we need to sail this mother around the world if we wanted to.'

'Mm, what we need now is a nice cup of tea,' I said. 'Get us nice and relaxed just before sunrise.'

Rick narrowed his eyes in delight. 'Good idea, John. Did you bring the tea bags?'

'Don't look at me, Dave's the essentials man. Dave?'

Silence.

'Dave?'

He pinched his nose. 'Oops.'

TWO

Sunrise was beautiful, and unlike many of the days we'd spent in Singapore, the sky had cleared of haze, leaving the sun to add or take away different colours as it moved through the sky. A slither of orange lined the horizon first, while the sky and the sea remained a dark blue-black. Then, when the top curve of the orange disc peeped over the horizon, the sky went purple and the sea, as though in competition, started to change to a deep, dark green.

The sun was like the conductor to an orchestra of light, dictating to the elements which colour at what time. The earth turned and presented yet more of herself to the fire in the sky, like a stripper slowly revealing herself through her fancy plumage. Five more minutes went by and the horizon was a cord, slicing through the sun. At these times the sun is never a sphere but a disc, and it's impossible, even while watching, to imagine a ball of fire.

Purples went to blues, while, not to be out-done by the sky, the sea followed suit as the sun made that last bit of effort and pulled its bottom out of the sea. Borneo, too far away to actually see, was enjoying every second of the show a few minutes before us, and, west of that, a few other Indonesian islands had watched the same show an hour earlier.

The boat dipped into the water, momentarily breaking the spell, and I looked at the two faces beside me, glowing orange against the sunlight. Their eyes squinted, making the bags underneath vanish temporarily, their neck muscles standing out through their skin where their heads were turned to face east. Their faces were as beautiful as the sunrise, picked out against the dark backdrop of the sea that raced away behind us.

Rick gulped down the last dregs of coffee, a puff of steam emitting from each side of the rim as he drank and breathed at the same time. He noticed me and smiled before looking back at the sun. Typical, Rick would never speak during such moments, preferring instead to reflect on the momentous events that were going on around us. He swept the hair from his face and looked down at the compass, before poking Dave in the ribs and tapping his wrist.

Dave jumped, looked at Rick, and without a word passing between them, he hurriedly drank his coffee and went down below. The question, 'What's going on?' came into my mind, but got no further; my voicebox had orders from my heart to keep quiet, and I wasn't about to disobey them just because my brain was impatient.

Rick shot a look towards the hatch and I followed. Dave's dismembered top half popped up like a jack-in-the-box, gave the thumbs up, and went down again. His heavy footsteps thudded through the hull towards the bedrooms and I followed his progress in my mind's eye, counting the paces and minutes.

Exactly two and a half minutes later the footsteps went back the other way and his whole body came up through the hatch. As soon as his head emerged, the wind caught his afro and the whole thing moved en masse, as though it would lift off his head. 'Almost missed it,' he gasped, climbing out. He walked over and sat beside Rick. 'We're on it now.'

I looked at Rick inquisitively. 'On what?'

Rick cupped the compass with a hand to shield it from the angled sunlight, then leaned back and nodded. 'The Equator,' he said, and turned to Dave. 'Did you check the GPS?'

'Yep. Zero degrees.'

'Long?'

'Hundred and seven.' Dave held up his clenched fist revealing the twiddled tops of three joints. 'This,' he said, holding out his arm like the statue of liberty, 'is a moment we ain't never gonna forget, boys.'

'Three joints rolled in two and a half minutes.' I raised my eyebrows, 'Impressive.'

'On a rolling boat too. Not bad huh?'

I grinned so broadly it hurt my cheeks.

We took one each and I counted us down before we lit. 'Three, two, one, ignition!' All three of us put our heads up my shirt to shield the flame from the wind, there was a moment's puffing in silence, just the sound of the rizla buckling as we drew on the flame, and we each sat back with a sigh of satisfaction.

During the five minutes of silence that followed (or it could have been an hour, it's hard to tell with dope) we each retreated into our own private worlds. Personally I remember frowning a lot. Frowning and blinking, partly because of the wind and sea spray, but also because of my chosen subject of reflection: I started to think about our tiny little boat on the earth.

Now I'm not going to start waffling on about how surreal the moment was, or how insignificant I felt on a planet that's two-thirds ocean, but I did start thinking about 'the compass' again. I kept getting images of a papier maché globe I had once made at primary school.

It was the usual thing that everyone does in a school art class: blow up a balloon, smother it with wet paper and let it set, come back a week later, cut the ball in half and paint a face on it. Yipee. Only I had decided that I would make a globe instead, and with the teacher's encouragement I set about painting it: green powder paint for land, blue for the sea. I had no idea what the countries looked like, or even which continent was America and which was Africa, I just copied it from a library atlas.

When I'd finished the globe I decided the sea needed a boat on it for added realism, so I stole the relevant playing piece from my sister's Monopoly set, sticking it in mid-Atlantic. The finishing touch was a compass with sixteen points that I drew on the Pacific with a felt-tipped pen. The lines were a bit wonky because of the undulating surface but that didn't matter.

With the teacher's permission I hung it from a piece of string above the blackboard in the classroom and everyone admired it. I can still remember the headmaster's words when he did his weekly rounds: 'Well,' he said as the teacher introduced the perpetrator to him, 'looks like we have a future globetrotter among us.' He said some other crap as well, the usual sarcasm something about drifting continents on my globe, ha ha, but I choose to forget that.

Anyway, the point is that the more I thought about what Rick kept saying about compasses, the more sense it all made. I felt not only that my dick was a needle, directing me to go here or there, depending on the availability of loose females, but that on a larger scale my body was a needle. And so on: the boat on the sea, the earth around the sun.

I tried to focus on my toes, looking for answers to the questions swirling around in my head, wondering if my reasons for travelling were the right ones, whether I shouldn't be at home doing a job like everyone else I knew. But the more I thought about it, the more ridiculous all the money-chasing seemed. I had very little cash, none of us had, but we were the three happiest people alive; we hadn't stopped grinning since we'd met. Every day was different, often spent with different people from every conceivable background, and usually in a new place, which I loved.

You get that same buzz when you're introduced to someone you fancy for the first time. It's addictive, I couldn't get enough, it's like the best Friday night you've had, when everything clicks; people and chemistry, mood, drink – except suddenly it's every day. Freedom, in its absolutely purest form, freedom from any ties whatsoever.

It's the compass; not just little head ruling the big head, though that's part of it. It's the natural instinct of following your heart, your eyes, to move from place to place, country to country, and do what you feel inside, to *find out* what you feel inside. How can you find yourself if you stay in your country of birth? It's important, vital, to stand aside and take a look from a different angle, to look with a fresh pair of eyes. As a friend of mine said from the safety of his office in Greenwich, when I'd called him from Hat Rin, 'Go for it, John. You only live once, and when you're dead, you're dead for a very very long time.'

Whoosh. A sudden wave of the drug hit and I couldn't concentrate properly, couldn't fix squarely on those toes at the end of someone's feet. Were they mine?

Paranoia. Beads of perspiration and sweaty palms. Did I lack a certain direction in life? Do people like us turn into people like them; washed up down-and-outs, street people with no one to love them and no one to love. Shit, did anyone love me? I knew that my philosophy was right, that we should live each day as though it's the last, that every day should be burned, lit at both ends, shouted at, but I couldn't keep the negative thoughts out, however hard I tried. I began to feel like a boat without a rudder.

I shook my head, unable, or unwilling, to carry the theme too far. Trying to focus on something solid was suddenly a big problem. I'd never been stoned on a boat before, and as soon as I brought my eyes back from the thousand-yard stare and looked at Dave, I felt sick.

Dave was lying down, looking up at me, his hair set in a lopsided wedge from the wind's buffeting. 'John, man, you've stopped smiling.'

'Nggh!' was all I could say before jumping up and throwing my head over the side of the boat to vomit. There was a chuckle from Rick, and Dave said, 'John, don't pollute the ocean.' Not very funny or original, and I told him so in between retches. Luckily the wind wasn't from the side so we were spared a shower of cold coffee and amino acid.

When I'd recovered, having washed my face in sea water because we couldn't waste the bottles of mineral water, I started to feel tired. The adrenalin that had kept me going through the night was beginning to desert me; Rick and Dave seemed fine, but that was probably because they had responsibilities.

'Are we going to pull over anywhere?' I asked, unsure of the correct terminology.

'Pull over?' Rick looked at the map and shook his head. 'You tired, Dave?'

Dave rolled his head to one side. 'Not really.'

'Neither am I. I think we should press on. Kep' Lingga's over there; we've already passed it so we may as well keep going to that other place. At this rate we'll be there by nightfall, easy.'

'Easy,' Dave agreed, stretching and yawning. 'You can get some sleep if you want, John, Rick and me'll take it in turns.'

Gingerly letting go of the steel handrail that ran around the boat, I said, 'What bed d'you want?' before quickly grabbing it again.

'Cabin, John. Doesn't matter, we won't all be sleeping at the same time so take your pick.'

I nodded wearily, turned and staggered below deck, still holding on to rails and walls as I went. The boat seemed to be pitching and rolling a lot more than it had been during the night and some of the steps I took, just as the boat dipped, left me in mid-air for a second before landing heavily.

After a quick check in both bedrooms to see which one was the best, I settled for the right-hand side because less light came in through the porthole window. A self-righteous glance out at the sea to make sure we were still heading in the right direction was all I could manage before collapsing on to the bed and falling into a dream.

I dreamt about fairground rides, and in particular the Jolly Roger: a huge swinging boat that holds fifty puking people at one time.

I was at the front.

THREE

It was the sound of silence that woke me, that and the fact that the boat wasn't moving about any more. With my eyes still closed I put both arms out and laid my palms flat on the mattress to check if I was dreaming or not. No, we'd definitely stopped. I opened my eyes. I closed them and opened them again to the same blackness as before, and quickly sat up, blinking rapidly. My ears tried to pick up any sound they could and I turned my head one way and then the other, even tilting it to one side and squinting, but still there was only silence.

Not enough light to be daytime but too much for night. Surely I hadn't slept until night, that would be over ten hours! With one jump I stood beside the window and drew back the curtain. It *was* early evening. Outside, the lights along the quay of a small town twinkled seductively.

Within seconds, having quickly checked the other bedroom and found Rick sleeping, I ran up the ladder and out on to the deck to find it empty. We were anchored about fifty metres offshore in a small harbour full of fishing boats. The stone quayside ran along the harbour-front in either direction until it ran into the hilly sides of the bay, and in the middle of the quay a small stone jetty jutted out into the sea, terminating in steps that led down into the water where Dave was just stepping into our dinghy.

As he rowed back towards me I studied the hillside above the quay. 'More than a village,' I mumbled to myself and nodded, resting one hand against the mast and yawning. It was at least a town, with two and three-storey concrete buildings stretching into the distance and then petering out gradually as the hillside steepened, finally terminating in dense jungle. A few lights flickered two or three miles away at the top of the hill, and some smoke from what looked like logging fires drifted into the air, but other than that there didn't appear to be too much activity. To one side of the bay all of the trees were gone, leaving a huge brown scar on the side of the hill where erosion had washed away the soil.

'John!'

I looked down with a start.

'It's excellent, man. *Oof!*' Dave crashed into the side of the boat and threw a rope up to me. 'Tie us up will you?'

I tied the dinghy and he climbed up, throwing his holdall on to the deck. 'Man, this place has got everything,' he said, bending down and unzipping the bag, 'and so fuckin' cheap. Check this out.'

'More fishing gear?' I sighed, seeing the things he'd bought.

'Yeah, Rick says that other stuff I bought was too shitty. "Wouldn't catch a herring," don't you know? Anyways, it's so cheap here I thought I might as well.' He started to place the things on deck. 'Here we go: pots, frying pan, knife for gutting fish – if we catch anything that is – instant noodles, more fresh water down there, fuckin' tea bags for you two la-di-das – no more complaints on that score – sugar, tins of tuna, more rice, gaff in case we catch anything big. And, the crème de la crème . . . ' He held up what looked like a mini torpedo. 'Da-daa!' Pulling the sheath off, he revealed a bottle of Johnny Walker Scotch whisky.

'They got a bar in town?' I exclaimed, touching the bottle.

'They've got more than that, Johnny-boy. They've got a bar *and* a disco.'

'No way!'

'Way!'

I looked around and shook my head. 'Where are we?'

Dave started to put the supplies back into the holdall. 'Island's called Bangka, don't know what this town's called. We weren't aiming for it, but when we saw the boats in the harbour we thought it'd be a good place to restock.' He puffed his cheeks and stood up. 'Shit, John, we've covered some ground over the past twenty hours. Whoo-ee! Can that boy sail a boat. Man, I gotta tell ya, truthfully, I didn't think we could get this far in one day.' He looked around. 'Where is my man?'

'Sleeping,' I said, glancing over the side at the porthole. 'He must be shattered. You too.'

'Haven't had time to think about it really. Too excited.' He paused to rub the tiredness from his face. 'Need a shower though. Let's get this gear stowed and get something to eat, then we can decide what we're going to do later.'

'Shower? I didn't know we had one.'

'Follow my lead.'

'Sorry?'

'I'll show you, come this way.'

Because we hadn't filled the tank with fresh water, the shower was salt. A bit pointless really, considering that we were floating in it and could just as easily have jumped over the side with a bar of soap. The soap wouldn't lather, which meant using almost the whole bottle of shower gel between the two of us. Nevertheless I felt a lot cleaner than I had before, and it was in a happy mood that I agreed to be the cook onboard.

Rice, noodles, tuna and fried patty of corned beef, all washed down with coke. The battery was charged from running the engine the previous night so we even had ice from the fridge. Rick still wasn't awake by the time we'd finished so we left a huge plate of food in the kitchen and went back on deck.

Dave checked the radio's digital clock. 'Ten o'clock,' he said, coming up on deck and crouching down at the wheel. Idly flicking through the charts that had been weighed down by a large pebble, he slid the stone off and used it to crush a cockroach. 'Fuckers. How do they get on here so quick, man?' The insect waved its antennae about in its death throes.

'Fly, don't they?' I suggested, looking over the side at the dark water. 'Or swim.'

He stood up again and stretched. 'Reckon we ought to hit the town, see what's up.'

'What about Rick, should we wake him?'

'Naw, he's only been down a few hours.' Dave walked over to where the dinghy was tied. 'Someone's gotta stay onboard, he knows the drill,' he said, stepping into the dinghy. 'Security's important.'

I jumped in behind, nearly capsizing us, and he rowed us over to the jetty, stopping only occasionally to drown a cockroach with his oar.

The whole place was like some kind of frontier town, and as we walked off the quayside into the main street I was surprised at the amount of activity. Every shop and street corner was bustling with people either buying supplies or getting drunk, and cars and motorbikes were zooming about everywhere with such reckless abandon that we frequently had to step into doorways to avoid being run down. There wasn't a pavement to speak of, and when we did find pedestrian areas there were either bikes whizzing along them or they were cluttered with hawker's stalls.

'This is crazy, Dave.'

'Told you it's a mad place.' He jumped behind a food-stall, dragging me with him, as a moped carrying two women screeched to a halt beside us. 'Gotta watch your step around here.'

The two women blew us a kiss. 'You want good time, handsome boys?' one said, running a hand seductively up her leg. They both wore long sequinned dresses with huge splits up to the top of each thigh. With her feet high on the footrests of the moped the split was fully open, revealing stockings and suspenders. I couldn't stop staring at the sight, and one of the women lunged forward with one hand, trying to grab my crotch. 'C'mon!'

'No!' I screamed, so stunned that I almost stumbled. 'I-I'm going for a drink first.' I put both hands over my fly and backed away.

'Where you stay?' she pouted.

'Out there on—'

'Up there,' Dave interrupted, 'on the hill.'

The woman winked at him. 'I think you on that boat. I see you before.'

'Not me,' Dave said, shaking his head.

The driver leaned forward. 'You no want play with me? OK. See you later.' She turned to her friend and said something in Indonesian, before winking and roaring off. The high-pitched noise of the clapped-out engine was so loud that I had to cover my ears.

'What a place!'

'Mad ain't it, John? Whoo-ee! Have you ever seen so many girls? So many hookers?' He shook his head. 'I ain't.'

It was just like the Wild West, and to complete the scene a plastic bag blew down the street, rolling over and over like a tumbleweed. Every car that went past stopped to ask if we wanted a ride anywhere, before bombing off, and every bike either did the same or carried two prostitutes. One bike went past with three women on it, all wearing bikinis!

'I thought Indonesians were Muslims,' I said, watching as the three ladies waved at me and nearly totalled themselves on an oncoming car. When I turned back to Dave he was gone, disappearing into a doorway up the street, only his afro and one arm sticking out as he beckoned me to hurry up. I walked up towards him, checking out the houses along the way.

Most of the buildings in the town seemed to have several businesses going on in them at one time. Restaurants with bowls of fried snakes in the window shared floor-space with people mending ropes or repairing outboard engines. Shipping clerks and agents ran an office that was being used partly as a garage and partly as a barber shop, while another place that looked like it was tailoring suits shared its cluttered floor space with a furniture manufacturer and a guy selling pots and pans. All of the buildings had brothels on upper floors with rooms for rent by the hour.

In just that short five-minute walk from the quayside, up the street to the *Star Trek* bar and disco, a hundred girls called out to me. Sometimes it was hard to pinpoint the direction of a voice, and I stood looking around gormlessly before noticing the waving hand on a third-floor balcony. I always waved back, and by the time I walked into the bar my arm felt like it was hanging off.

The ache disappeared the moment I walked through the door.

Dave was sitting on a purple velvet sofa, his arms stretched out either side along the top of the cushions, grinning at me. Surrounding him were dozens of beautiful young girls in bikinis, all posing as through I had a camera aimed at them. A girl by the doorway with a number pinned to her bikini strap slotted her arm through mine and led me over to the table.

The darkness of the room was punctured by strategically placed spotlights that lit the bar, a small stage, and each table. It seemed fairly small for a disco but that could have been because of the amount of girls standing around. They were everywhere. So many in fact that they lined the walls like wallpaper, their light-coloured skin and luminous bikinis brightening an otherwise gloomy atmosphere.

'There're dozens of them,' I finally managed to say, sitting down beside Dave as two ice cold beers arrived, delivered by a girl who must have been no more than fourteen. The spotlight caught her features as she grinned, outlining her button nose and shiny, jet black hair.

'Seventy-five to be precise,' Dave replied. He took his beer and toasted the girl before adding, 'Each one has a number, look: twenty-two, thirteen, nineteen ...'

I peeled my eyes off the girl and looked around at the smiling faces. 'They're so young.' I wanted to tell Dave that we shouldn't be in here, that it was wrong to take advantage of these girls, all of whom had probably been dragged away from their home towns all over Indonesia to earn a living by sleeping with men. I wanted to say that we should forget the beer and go now, before we got sucked in by their beauty, but I couldn't. They were forcing me to stay just as surely as if they'd held a gun to my head. The least I could do was to have a drink and talk to a few of them.

One drink, as usual, led to another, then another, and soon we were ordering shorts, along with bar snacks for the girls, with money that neither of us had.

Like Dave and Rick, I'd almost run out of money after Singapore, but I still had what I called my 'crash fund'. The other two didn't know it, but I had kept a small amount of money hidden in my wallet, in case of emergencies. It wasn't through deceit that I kept the knowledge of it from them, just common sense. If they knew that there was still some cash floating about it would eventually get spent on something useless. I was determined that the money should only come out in a life or death situation, such as medical care or transport, and not on getting pissed.

So when, an hour later, Dave came back from the toilet and told me how he had just fallen in love with the prettiest of Indonesian girls, and that he only needed a few dollars to spend an hour with her, I tried to look helpless. The more innocent I behaved the more obvious it was that I had some money stashed away. I felt myself blush.

'Look, they won't take Amex,' he said holding up his card.

I put my glass on the table. 'Where did you get that from?'

'Still got a few dollars back in the good ol' US. Well, a credit limit as least. Shit!' He tapped the card on his palm, 'if I could only use this now.' He looked at me like a wounded puppy and I looked away. 'John?'

'I told you, Dave, I haven't got any money left, it all went in Singapore.' Once I'd started the sentence I couldn't stop, I just didn't want to lie. 'All I've got is a few quid for an emergency. *Any* emergency for *any* of us. We've got to have a little cash in case we have a problem.' Fuck, I immediately thought, why did I tell him?

'John, this *is* an emergency. And anyway, there's a bank in town, I saw it. Tomorrow I'll go in and draw up to my credit limit. What's the big prob' man?'

I drank some beer, trying to ignore the figure standing over me. He was asking for about half of what I had in my crash fund, so if I was going to give that away, I figured the best I could do was hang on to the rest. Whatever I did, he knew I had the money so it was going to get spent sooner or later, and definitely not on an emergency. I would keep the other half for myself, to buy myself a gift or something.

'John?'

I sighed. 'All right, Dave.'

'John, I love you, man.' He leaned over and kissed my head, much to the delight of the girls standing around. 'I promise, soon as the bank opens tomorrow morning . . .'

'Don't matter, we're all in the same boat, Dave.' I slid the neatly folded notes out of my wallet. They hadn't been uncovered since I'd left England, apart from the occasional inspection during the Ta episode to make sure they were still there, and were still crisp and new.'

'Pounds?' he exclaimed as I handed them over.

'Yeah, pounds.'

'Man, these are ancient. Don't you carry dollars like everyone else on the planet?' He inspected the note, holding it up to the light. 'Wow, the Queen of England!'

'They'll take them, don't worry. Money's money, they're not stupid.

You'll get a lot of rupiah for that.' I put the other note back into my wallet. 'That's worth a bit more than they're asking for, so don't let them tell you it's not enough.'

He smiled. 'How about you, John? Not in the mood or what? Be the first time I've seen you turn your nose up at a beautiful girl.'

I downed the last of my beer and stood up. 'I'll have a walk around town.'

'Early night huh?' He put the note into his shorts pocket. 'I've only got an hour, so wait on deck and I'll shout over for the tender.'

'Tell you what, Dave, I'll wait on deck and you shout over,' I said sarcastically, and turned to leave.

'Sure you won't join me?'

'No, you go. I'll see you later.'

I left the bar and, after a ten-minute walk that led nowhere, decided to head back towards the harbour.

One of the streets I turned down led straight from the quayside inland, so I walked back via the base of the hills, where the suburbs rose gently towards the jungle, and had a clear view out over the bay. The town presented a series of concrete terraces, like hillside rice paddies, each building's flat roof a step down towards the sea, and I could just make out our boat among the many in the harbour. I stood and marvelled at its smallness against the huge, dark ocean backdrop beyond. What had been our world now looked just like that Monopoly piece on my papier mâché globe; a tiny toy on a huge, deep sea.

The town was also deceptive. In the same way that I'd stood on the boat earlier looking in and thought that the streets were deserted, so now, having walked out of town and looked down, I had the feeling that it was the centre of Indonesia.

For a bit of fun and the thrill of a near-death experience I paid a few rupiah to a motorcycle taxi and got driven down to the quayside where I waited for Dave. I thought I could easily pass a quiet hour watching the boats bob about.

However, the quiet hour turned out to be non-stop hassle as wave after wave of Girl's Angels pulled up in clouds of two-stroke exhaust fumes to offer their services. It became such a bind that I ended up walking to the end of the jetty and sat in our dinghy until Dave arrived, passing the time by crushing cockroaches and feeding them to the fish that darted about around the stone wall.

'So,' I said quietly, pulling on the oars and looking over my shoulder to check our progress, 'what was she like?' Dave had been almost silent since arriving back at the quay, and hadn't spoken at all about the prostitute, his head resting in the palm of one hand, deep in thought. The only sound, now that we'd left the town, was the plop and drip of each blade as I dipped the oars beneath the calm surface.

'Mmm?' He looked up with his eyes only, the sound of his voice gentle and soft in the warm night air.

'The girl. What was she like?'

He sighed heavily. 'Like a young girl who shouldn't be doin' that kinda thing. I wanted to bring her with me, John, I really wanted to.'

'You mean you wanted to save her.'

He shrugged. 'Yeah, maybe.'

We reached our boat and climbed up, hauling the dinghy up on to the deck. Just as I bent down to retrieve my flip-flops, there was a woman's laugh from down below, not loud, but startling in the silent night, like talk in a library. We froze.

The laugh came again.

'Don't look at me,' I said in a hushed voice, 'it's coming from down below.'

We tiptoed across the deck and went down the stairs. The smell of sweat was overpowering inside the confined space, and I saw Dave wince. 'It's coming from Rick's room,' I whispered, inadvertently allocating quarters.

Rick's laugh came booming out just as Dave and I peeped around the door. He looked up and smiled, the girl lying next to him pulling the yellow oilskin over her bare body like a sheet. 'Come in, have a drink. Found this bottle of scotch in the galley cabinet,' Rick said, pouring out another cupful, 'the owner must have left it there.'

'The owner didn't buy that, I did!' Dave said, straightening up.

'Oh, really? Well have a drink anyway.' Rick poured one out for the girl. 'This is Titty,' he giggled, looking at her. 'It's true, isn't your name Titty?' I immediately recognised the girl as the passenger of the motorcycle who'd first spoken to us in town. Her silver sequinned dress was draped over a chair.

'Hello again,' she sang from behind the anorak, 'it's me.'

Rick looked at the girl and then at me. 'You know each other?'

'Yes,' I said, turning to get two more cups from the kitchen, 'we saw her in town earlier. D'you want water in yours, Dave?'

Dave was still standing in the doorway of the bedroom, either surprised to see the girl or shocked that his whisky had been opened. I was still a bit shocked myself at the speed with which the girl had managed to find her way onboard.

The last of the ice chinked into the mugs, and I turned to go back to the bedroom but jumped back at the sight of Rick, standing right behind me.

'John. I haven't got the money to pay her,' he whispered, glancing back at the bedroom. 'What am I going to do?'

I sighed, looking over his shoulder at the pair of naked legs on the bed.

'So much for the crash fund . . .'

FOUR

Dave's credit card was accepted at the local bank, and that, along with the remainder of my crash fund, fuelled a week long stay in Bangka.

Dave went into the local bank that first morning, bright and breezy from his first proper night's sleep since leaving Singapore, and came back out a millionaire. A rupiah millionaire, that is. Hardly the same thing, but none of us had ever been one before, or were ever likely to be in the future, so we celebrated accordingly, getting well and truly wasted for the next five days.

The boat turned into Indonesia's (and possibly the world's) first floating brothel, to add to the hundreds already scattered about the town. With Dave having drawn the maximum amount possible on his credit card, we began to live life accordingly. Women were ferried backwards and forwards from the quayside at all hours of the day and night, crates of beer were brought over, food if we couldn't be bothered to go to town and, on one occasion, a freshly roasted goat was delivered to us by the brothel owner.

During the course of the week, Rick had a brain-wave and suggested that we change the name of our boat. None of us felt that its current, single word name was really appropriate any more, so, along with the help of some local girls, we racked our brains for a new title.

Dave suggested typically militaristic words with a sexual twist, like USS Torpedo Lover, or sci-fi names of a similar ilk, such as Starship Lover and Meteor Power. All a bit childish we thought, and told him that if he couldn't come up with something a little more mature, and a little less comic book, he shouldn't bother at all.

It seemed to be very telling of his character and I've since used the same 'name-the-boat' game to see if it's a good indicator of other people's personality, to amazingly accurate results. Even sitting in a pub somewhere, nowhere near the ocean, I still ask people what name they would give a yacht if they had one, sometimes just to test the theory and sometimes as a chat-up line. It yields startling rewards.

My suggestions tended to combine being at sea with the essence of travel, and were usually names like Free Spirit, The Compass or Joyrider. I suggested calling it Big Balls as a tribute to the infamous Indian deformity but the others thought it was too obscure. The girls who were onboard at the time thought that we should name the boat after themselves, but we all agreed that sailing around in a yacht with the word *Titty* splashed across the side would make us all look like idiots. Rick pointed out that that's exactly what we were, but generally agreed that something else would better fit the bill.

That something else was Rick's suggestion, and it won the name-the-boat competition hands down. Dave and I went into town, accompanied by his young 'girlfriend', Watti, to secure the services of the local sign-writer or, failing that, to purchase paint and brushes to do the job ourselves.

Watti came in very useful in town when it came to buying anything, not only because she spoke the local language but also because we found that, even though Bangka was far from any tourist destination, we were still being ruthlessly ripped off. Everything we'd bought, from tomatoes to ropes, cost us double what anyone else in town paid for the same item. All we did now was point to something in a shop, out of view of the shop owner, and ask Watti to buy it with our money.

Within an hour of asking around town we rowed back to the boat accompanied by an eighty-year-old man who said he'd once had the job of repainting the name on the side of the *QE II* when it had docked in Jakarta once for refuelling. Credentials aside, he had the right equipment: pots of paint, brushes and a two-foot long stick with a rubber ball on the end so we assumed that he knew what to do and let him get on with it. He also had his own floating platform that we towed out, consisting of planks of wood strapped on to three oil drums, which he stood on to do the work, only occasionally falling into the water.

Every so often, while we lay around on deck drinking beer and sunbathing, the old boy's head would pop up over the prow of the boat, 'Beer, beer,' he'd say through his gummy, one-toothed grin, and one of the girls would top him up. I checked his progress to make sure that he wasn't too drunk to write, and to make sure he had the piece of paper with the name on the right way round. The last thing we wanted was an upside-down name on the side of the boat.

When he'd completed the task, we made the mistake of telling him how great it was, each of us thanking him profusely for a job well done. He asked for another beer as a bonus, which we thought fair considering how little we were paying him, and said he'd like to come aboard to drink it. One beer, as ever, led to another, and before long the old man was falling about, apparently pissed out of his brains. He even started to fawn the girls, grabbing their bottoms as they walked past and falling on to the deck with a dull thud as they brushed him off.

The girls hated it. To them, I suppose, he represented everything they were trying to get away from: poverty, filth and poorly paid manual work, among other things, and they eyed him with barely concealed contempt. The more they pushed him off and tried to appear above his level, the more ironic it seemed. There they were, lounging around in bikinis, trying to convince themselves that they were high-class women who had rich boyfriends, while all along they did a job that was far less noble than the old pervert's.

Whenever they shoved him away, one hand clawing feebly at their breasts, he would turn his nose up and say something in Indonesian before moving back in and getting his wizened old hand slapped. I asked the girls what he was saying but they wouldn't let on, the old man just pointed to the town, tapped the glass face of his wristwatch and laughed. It was pretty obvious that he was reminding them where they worked and that he could go into the bar and buy their affections any time he wanted to. He just laughed at their haughty behaviour, his one tooth going up and down like a baby without a dummy, and they hated him for it.

Half a dozen bottles of Bintang later we found him crashed out on one of the beds (my bed) and decided, rather than have to carry him off, that we'd let him sleep and leave under his own steam. He slept for six hours, and when he did wake up, all previous payment of his services was a mystery to him, and we had to go through a long, drawn-out argument over the amount of money he'd been paid. Or, rather, Titty did.

The whole thing ended rather badly, with the two of them nearly coming to blows and the old guy slipping and falling into the water. Dave rescued him and we paid him again, much to the anger of the girls, who thought we should have let him drown.

Over the course of that week, we had all but forgotten about travel, and the boat became nothing more than a floating hotel. However, the money began to run low and our thoughts eventually turned back to moving on, and our possible next destination before Bali. Considering our penchant for spending money at the most inappropriate times we all thought it best to keep moving, and Rick reminded us that we hadn't really moved very far from Singapore. 'This boat may be carrying our name but it belongs to someone else,' he said, wagging a cautious finger.

We were fully stocked up with food and water, and, given the constant wind conditions that were forecast, Rick reckoned on making the journey to Bali in just over a week. I had no idea about boat speed and nautical miles, but said that it just looked like a long way. Dave countered by saying that because we were three-handed (well, two and a half), and because he and Rick could both sail, we would effectively be on the move around the clock, only one person sleeping at any one time.

None of us knew exactly what we were going to do when we got to Bali, but Rick suggested that if we grew bored of the ocean (which was very likely according to him) we could sell the boat. I thought that was a little unlikely seeing as how we didn't hold any of the necessary proof-of-ownership documents. It was possible that the legitimacy of three foreigners wouldn't be questioned, especially if the boat was at a rock-bottom price, but Dave and I dismissed the idea, saying that we wanted to sail around the world for ever and a day, and not just a week.

There was, however, one more pressing problem to consider, and that was the relationship between Dave and Watti.

FIVE

During the course of the week we spent in Bangka, Dave and Watti had been in each other's company twenty-four hours a day. At first he'd paid the owner of the brothel, but after two days Watti had all but left the place and moved on to the boat. She did all our washing and cooking, among other things, and was generally a pleasure to have around. But more importantly for Dave, on top of all the domestic chores she was so good at, she was very young and very beautiful.

If Rick or I had to go to town for anything Dave would immediately suggest that Watti came with us, reeling off her attributes as though without her the world, or our boat at least, would fall apart. Similarly, when we had our bedtime smoke and started to talk about places we wanted to travel to, each suggesting our dream location, Dave, one arm around Watti, would always say 'We' would like to go to such and such a place, or 'We' think so and so would be nice.

Dave hadn't brought up the subject, but I knew sooner or later he was going to suggest that Watti would make an invaluable addition to the crew, someone we couldn't possibly do without while travelling through Indonesia. Either that or we would weigh the anchor and sail off, and two days into the voyage find her stowed down below deck. 'What's she doing here?' I'd say, discovering her beneath the life jackets. Dave would look blankly back and say, matter-of-factly, 'It's *Watti*, my *girlfriend*, John.'

So, when, on the night before we planned to leave, Dave asked us if we minded taking a new passenger onboard, Rick and I were unhappy but not altogether surprised.

Watti had already gone to bed, the other girls had been sent ashore without any hassles and the three of us were smoking on deck beneath a brilliant starry sky. The only sound around us was the 'ping' of the rigging against the steel mast, caught by the strengthening wind.

'No,' Rick replied firmly. He leaned to one side and flicked his ash over the gunwale. 'Dave, you're forgetting yourself. We're going to Bali, remember?'

'Yeah, and she can come along. I–' He hesitated, tapping his cigarette even though it wasn't lit. 'Look, I really like her, man.'

'Then stay here with her. Or go with her to her home in Java. But we're not going to fook about sailing all the way down to some obscure port in Java, just so she can tell her mum and dad where she is!'

'It's on the way, guys.'

Rick slapped his thigh. 'It's not on the way, Dave, it's miles *out* of the fooking way.' He exhaled heavily. 'What's going to happen, Dave, ask yourself that question. We'll sail all the way down to wherever it is, you'll be sick of her by then and we'll be fooked because we haven't got the money to move on.'

'We would be fucked,' I added, and nodded sagely. 'He's right, Dave, see sense. You've only known her, what, less than a week?'

Rick quickly chimed in. 'And you want to throw everything away? Fook it up for yourself if you want but don't ask us to come with you.' Rick got up and went down below to fetch another beer, bringing the conversation to a close. I just shrugged.

The next hour was filled with heavy silences as Dave avoided eye contact with us, picking at the stitching on his shorts. I felt sorry for him. I knew that he was really torn between being with his friends and being with someone he had fallen in love with. He never mentioned the word love, but it was pretty obvious that he had strong feelings for her, ever since their encounter in the bar on our first night in town.

I didn't sleep at all well that night, probably because I was used to the double bed and had decided to sleep up on deck instead with Rick. I told him I fancied a night under the stars, but the real reason was to be as far away from Dave's love-making as possible. I couldn't bear to listen to what I suspected would be their last night in each other's arms and Dave's pathetic attempt to lie about the following day. I knew he wouldn't have the guts to tell her the truth and would make up some excuse why she had to go into town without him.

I lay awake, watching the stars move across the sky, accompanied by the sound of gently lapping waves whipped up by the wind, and the sound of the rigging. All of which was very nearly drowned out by Rick's snoring.

I must have fallen asleep eventually, because when I awoke at sunrise the dinghy was gone and I hadn't heard a sound. Rick was still snoring evenly so I made coffee and, after checking the bedroom and finding it empty, waited on deck for something to happen.

'Did you make me one?' Rick opened an eye, having apparently sucked in the aroma while snoring.

I pointed to the steaming mug beside his blanket and kept my eyes on the figure that walked along the quayside towards the dinghy. Dave stood on the jetty and looked back up towards the main street for a moment's reflection, before turning and walking down the steps to the boat, his skin glowing brown-orange in the early morning sun. The T-shirt he was wearing was taken off angrily and thrown into the bottom of the boat as a cushion and he stepped in.

'D'you think we should have let her come?' I asked, unable to keep my thoughts to myself.

Rick leaned up on one elbow and followed my gaze over the prow to where the small, white plastic square edged through the water. 'No. If he really wants to be with her he can stay here, or take her to Singapore, or back home to America. He doesn't need us to do that.' He sipped his coffee noisily. 'Bringing her on this boat with two other single men is the last thing he needs.'

I nodded unhappily. Rick was right. He could easily have gone overland with her to Java, or anywhere else for that matter, and they could have lived together. As it was he must have had the same doubts as us.

I watched as Dave drew alongside us, but averted my gaze when he climbed up. 'OK then,' he said with contrived enthusiasm, 'let's get the sails up before I change my mind.'

Neither of us replied. I tied up the dinghy that Dave had left free, and Rick started to unfurl the sails. Dave went down below and started to play around with the radio and navigation equipment and, apart from the odd instruction given without emotion, none of us spoke.

Slowly at first, with just part of the sail up, we drifted out of the harbour past the fishing boats. Women were washing pots and pans in the water, while men took their early morning bath, occasionally waving to us, as we went by.

We cleared the headland and let out the rest of the sail; the wind filled the flapping canvas and our newly named yacht picked up speed, leaving the town and so many girls as nothing more than a memory.

Within an hour we were out of sight of land, and out of mind of everything other than the sea and the sky, and the re-named vessel beneath our feet: *Wet Dream.*

MARINE

ONE

FAST FORWARD. Two weeks later. Dave and Rick took it in turns to steer the boat, as planned, usually doing a whole day or night on and half a day off. One slept while the other steered, and when they were both awake (usually half a day) one of them operated the radio and navigating equipment. As well as doing most of the cooking, I sort of floated about, helping here and there where possible; rolling joints, that sort of thing.

The weather for the whole time was perfect for sailing; that is to say a constant force five blowing from the north and a clear sky to navigate by. We had GPS but it was nice to be reassured; none of us felt entirely at home relying upon electronics in an all-natural environment. Horses for courses, you might say.

One drawback to the clear weather, though, was the constant exposure of our skin to the harsh tropical sun. Despite all of our time spent on beaches, it didn't prepare our soft, northern bodies for the battering they received, as the salt sea-spray wet us and the sun baked us to a crisp. Every time I looked at Dave he was grinning as though trying to crack his face, his gleaming white teeth and eyes peering ghoulishly out of a black skull. He looked funny because his hair had lightened while his skin had gone to the other end of the spectrum, turning as black as shoe polish and making him look like a yellow-haired old granny.

Rick's hair and moustache had turned almost white too, in contrast to his deep tan. Even his eyebrows had changed colour, making him look like a hippy version of Santa Claus. The constant lashing of salt water, wind and sun, along with no shampooing, had left his hair ridged. Sometimes, when he passed me on his way to the bedroom having just spent ten hours on deck, his hair stood up two feet into the air, as though he'd shoved his fingers into an electric socket. I once woke from a dream to find him roaming through the closet in my room, after a night at the helm, and thought that the boat had been over-run by aliens. He was like an apparition standing there; his sticking-up hair, back-lit by a ceiling-mounted tilly lamp, looking like a golden halo.

Apart from lowering the sail and drifting around an island called Bawean in the Java Sea one afternoon, we didn't anchor until reaching a place called Changu. It was two weeks since we had left Bangka; we were burnt to a crisp and almost out of water but too exhausted to continue that night. We were no more than a day's sail from Bali by Rick's reckoning, and as we still had a north wind it should be a cruise.

A small bay appeared in the distance, and after a minute's observation we aimed for it, anchoring a mile offshore above a beautiful coral reef. If we could have seen Bali we would have pressed on, but because it was so nice to spot land after the boredom of open sea, we all agreed to stop there for the night, and possibly the next day. We could fish on the reef and generally relax in calm waters before moving on.

It turned out to be the worst decision of our lives.

TWO

The exhaustion of the past weeks, just as Rick had suggested would happen, had given us all the feeling that a life spent sailing around the world in search of paradise wasn't all it was cracked up to be, and that maybe it wasn't what we were looking for after all. Rick was the first to voice a sea change by continually speculating on the selling prices of second-hand yachts, and, as the days wore on, Dave and I found ourselves joining in the discussion with increased fervour. Dave was still missing Watti, and going ashore anywhere, he thought, would help take his mind off her.

'How much do you think, Rick?' I called, searching around in the clutter of fishing gear that Dave had so neatly dumped on the deck. The two of them sat at the rear of the boat, feet dangling over the end, fishing on the reef.

'Enough to keep us three travelling for a few years, that's how much.' Rick lifted the rod behind his head and cast it a short way out into the shimmering blue sea. He had woken up early that morning and had taken the only rod capable of handling a fish of any real size. Dave had his flimsy little telescopic that he'd bought in Singapore (the gear he'd bought in Bangka broke the first time it was used).

To one side of us was nothing but shades of blue that changed colour the further away from the boat I looked. Beneath us the highs and lows in the reef created a patchwork of different shades, until the angle of my vision was at about forty-five degrees and the colours became more uniform.

Over the prow, a far away island that looked like a policeman's helmet protruded from the water, a single, almost circular white cloud hanging above it like a Red Indian's smoke signal. Probably a volcano, I thought, vaguely remembering something called the 'ring of fire', and turned around.

On the other side of the boat was the nearest island. A single peak tapered each side into what looked like smaller islands that had once been separate, but were now glued on to its sides, a bit like a half submerged head and a pair of ears. There didn't appear to be any beach, but because we'd arrived late the previous night and anchored against the first dark shape we'd come to, it didn't necessarily mean it wasn't approachable.

I went over to that side of the boat and looked at the sheer face of rock that ran down into the sea, letting my head tilt down slowly until I was looking directly at the side of the boat. With nothing else to occupy my mind, I took off my shorts, stood up on the side rail and dived off into the cool water.

The first thing that struck me when I opened my eyes and looked down was the depth. I blew out a little air to maintain equilibrium and studied my dangling feet, and the amount of space beneath them, before looking horizontally at the boat's keel to gauge the depth. About fifty feet I reckoned.

I love to look at the underneath of a boat, to see the parts that are not normally visible. Seeing it in dry dock is no good, it has to be in the water, surrounded by blue sea, its shadow cast on to the seabed, giving it scale and definition. A boat in dry dock is like a fish on a fishmonger's slab, it's out of context and has no place in a dry world, no meaning among its surroundings like a fish out of water.

Time for a game, I thought, looking to the stern and seeing two pairs of feet: grab the two fishing lines and give them a yank, then surface in time to watch Rick and Dave fight over nothing and later tell me about the one that got away. If they had only been fishing at different ends of the boat I could have tied their lines together.

Coming up and taking another gulp of air out of sight, I dived back under the boat and swam to the rear in search of the lines. I had just reached their ankles when a dark shadow passed beneath me. Automatically I flinched and froze, blinking rapidly as though it would clear the water from my eyes. Without the movement provided by my arms, my body drifted upwards and my back bumped against someone's feet, making me jump. The dark shape cruised along the seabed then doubled back on itself, apparently heading towards me.

Surfacing with a gasp of air, I looked up to find the other two no longer sitting on the low platform at the back of the boat, but looking down at me from the deck, astonished looks on their faces. 'Jesus fuckin' Christ, John, you scared the living shit out of me!' Dave slumped, as though releasing built-up tension. 'We thought you were a shark, man.'

I giggled and hauled myself on to the platform. 'Reel yours in, Dave.'
'How's that?'

'Your line, reel it in. There's a fucking big fish down there.' I stood up, wiping the water from my eyes with both hands. 'I don't know what it is, but it's about this big.' I held my arms as far apart as I could. 'It'll snap your rod like a twig.'

At that moment Rick's rod arced violently downwards and he almost let go under the force. 'Fooking hell!'

I immediately looked from him to the water. 'That's it, I think you've got it!'

Rick ordered Dave to reel his in, and then told me to put some clothes on, which I did. The three of us stood on the edge of the deck and watched the water, as Rick fought against whatever was on the other end. 'Fooking hell!' he kept saying, and the only other thing he said over the next thirty minutes was, 'light me a fooking fag'.

'There she blows!' Dave shouted, as the line, the rod, Rick, Dave and I all turned and went to one side of the boat as the fish shot off towards deeper water. Wherever the fish went, us three followed, like a tightly packed herd of sheep, all bunched together. Rick would strain and gasp, sucking in air through the corner of his mouth, as he let the rod drop almost horizontal and then heaved it up again, emitting his usual expletive. He talked and breathed through a tiny slit in the corner of his mouth, the other side being occupied by the limp, saturated cigarette.

I plucked it from his mouth and he gasped as though breathing for the first time. 'Another.' I lit him another one and poked it in. 'Here we go,' the cigarette said, bobbing to the words.

We all turned on the spot, watching as the shiny, taut line, like a precisely aimed laser-beam from the tip of the rod to the surface of the sea, slowly swung through ninety degrees.

'The front,' Dave said excitedly, and the three of us all moved as one, up to the prow.

Rick suddenly had a look of concern on his face, the cigarette hanging down, almost resting on his chin. He began to wind slowly, and we watched as the laser beam began to shorten, coming nearer to the boat. He reeled harder and faster, trying to take up the slack, before the rod arced once again and the fish darted off, this time towards the island. 'Fooking hell!'

We all shuffled over to the other side of the boat and stared at the water, the fishing line almost pointing downwards. There was a screech of the ratchet, the reel letting out line under too much pressure, and once again the fish swam out into the distance. We waited, tensed. Dave and I jumped down to the lower platform while Rick stood on the upper deck sweating and holding the rod up in the air.

'Is it moving? The fish?'

'No. Hasn't done anything for five minutes. Can you see it?'

'No, but I can feel it,' I shouted, 'in the line.'

There was a puff of smoke and he put both hands back on to the rod. The cigarette was immediately doused by dripping sweat and I could see him sucking frantically to re-light it. 'Stick your head under and have a look,' he shouted.

It wasn't easy to see something that wasn't moving because of the changes in shade presented by the holes and dips in the reef, but then, just as I was about to surface for air, something down to my left moved three feet and I saw it. From where I was it appeared as just another dark shape, but it had moved, revealing its location. Looking back up out of the water I quickly checked the angle of the fishing line and followed its probable direction under water, before going under again. It was exactly where the shape was, and I raised my arm, making an OK sign while still looking down.

Dave tapped me on the shoulder and I came up, wiping the water from my face. 'See it?' he asked, wide-eyed.

'Nggh,' I gagged, clearing my nose. 'Down there. Huge fucker.'

'Shark?'

I shook my head. 'Don't think so.' Rick called over and asked the same question and I gave the same response. 'It's just lying there, Rick. It looks fucked.'

He nodded wisely. 'Yeah, they always do that when they're exhausted. He's probably had enough. I know I have!' He gripped the rod suddenly. 'Ooh, fook!' and the fishing line came cutting through the water towards us. The angle between the line and the sea surface became more and more acute until, about twenty feet from us, the fish broke the surface with a huge splash and a flip of its tail fin.

'Garoupa!' Rick shouted. 'It's a fooking garoupa!'

The fish had started its final run, swinging around to the rear of the boat, the line slicing through the air. Dave and I ducked, almost too late, and nearly got scalped, much to Rick's amusement; Dave patted his afro to make sure it was still there. The fish surfaced again, this time rolling over languidly, its huge pink belly like a giant shiny blancmange in the sunlight. It was bigger than our dinghy!

'How the fuck are we going to land that?' The fish was more or less finished and was lolling around on the surface, only occasionally righting itself for a token dive before it came back up. 'I've never seen a fish that big before,' I said shaking my head at the sight.

'It's fuckin' huge, man. And ugly too.'

'To tell you the truth,' Rick said, sweating from the exertion, 'I haven't seen a fish that big either.'

I don't think any of us really thought we'd be at the point of actually catching it, and none of us were sure what to do next.

'What are we going to do with it?'

Dave looked at me. 'Eat it?'

'It's six-foot long, Dave! And about six-foot wide. How can we eat that between three of us? Be serious, that'd feed a family of four for a month!'

'It'll taste like shit, anyway,' Rick said knowledgeably, and we both looked up at him. 'It's too old.'

'How d'you know it's old?' I said.

'Look at him! No fish gets to be that big without being very, very old.'

We all stared for a moment, and I said, 'What then?'

'Let him go.' Rick sat down on the edge of the deck. 'Dave, there's a pair of pliers in that tool kit down below, go and get them.'

Dave went off and came back with the whole toolbox, opening it up on deck. 'These?'

Rick looked up. 'Yep.' I reached up and grabbed them. 'Right,' Rick said, easing himself down on to the low platform next to me, 'I'll reel him in to the back of the boat. John, you take out the hook.'

'Me?' I exclaimed, slightly taken aback at the idea.

He nodded.

I held the pliers out to him. 'You take the fucking hook out.'

'Oh don't be such a pussy.'

'Yeah, John,' Dave said from the safety of the deck, 'don't be a pussy.'

'I'm not doing it,' I said, shaking my head vigorously.

'Go on!'

'Nope.' I pushed the pliers into his chest.

'Why not?'

'Cause I don't want to get my hand bitten off, that's why not.'

Rick laughed. 'They haven't got teeth. Anyway, that thing's so old it's probably lost all his by now.' The fish, as if insulted, tried a final run, but gave up almost as soon as it had started. Rick reeled it in like a piece of flotsam until it was floating right beneath our feet.

I still held the pliers out to Rick. He sighed. 'Oh, OK, you hold the rod and I'll take the hook out.' We exchanged implements. 'Now pull him round, John. Bring the mouth towards me.' He knelt down and I pulled the rod to one side with all of my strength. I couldn't believe how much effort it took just to get the fish to rotate in the water. I wondered how on earth Rick had managed to play it for over thirty minutes.

Rick tilted his head and looked at me. 'If he runs, for Christ's sake don't let go of that rod.' He reached out and grabbed hold of the line, pulling the fish through ninety degrees so that they were head to head. 'Great, just lipped him. Slacken off a bit, John.'

I dropped the rod down a foot and Rick grasped the hook with the pliers and twisted it free, taking a two-inch chunk of lip with it. The fish was full of battle scars so I don't think a split lip bothered it.

'Look at the size of that mouth, boy. Whoo-ee!' Dave jumped down between us. 'And those lips, like fuckin' liver sausage.'

I couldn't have put it better myself. Its mouth was two feet in diameter and rimmed by a pair of lips as full and round as a salami. 'Is it dead?' I asked, gingerly leaning closer, the fish's big inky eye staring blankly back.

'No, but it will be if it doesn't get oxygen. It needs to move through the sea so that the water passes over its gills.' Rick held one of its dinner plate-sized gill flaps open, revealing thousands of soft, feathery red ridges, all in rows. He looked around and swore. 'We'll have to use the dinghy. Dave, get the dinghy untied.'

Dave went over to the dinghy and stopped halfway. 'What for?'

'We're going to row out. I'll hold the fish and you row. We can't use the boat, it'll take too long.'

So, five minutes later, with Rick hanging over the back of the dinghy holding on to the fish and Dave pulling on the oars for all he was worth, they edged away at a pathetic speed. 'Can't you row faster, Dave?' Rick said, looking under his arm.

Dave put his back into it and one of the oars snapped, sending him sprawling and cracking his head on the hard plastic shell of the dinghy. He cursed, rubbing his head. 'Now what?'

I don't know if the fish just needed the rest or whether it had been given enough oxygen, but it turned over from its side on to its front, and with one flick of its tail, drenched the two of them and swam off.

I looked into the distance to catch another glimpse but it was gone. It was only then that I noticed just how dark the sky had become.

THREE

Being at sea is a bit like being in the desert; when the weather changes you get warned in advance because of the amount of unobstructed space. Nothing creeps up on you at sea, unless of course you're too preoccupied with a big fish to notice. If we'd have taken time to look up at the sky that morning we would have seen the clouds boiling up in the distance. As it was we didn't even realise that the sun had been blocked out; it was the first time we'd been in shade in two weeks and that there was no longer enough light to see the corals.

Rick looked at me from the dinghy and then looked skywards, the smile he'd been wearing as we watched the fish swim away instantly disappearing. All of the muscles that were used to hold the grin suddenly relaxed and his whole expression dropped an inch. I didn't need to be a meteorologist to know that the sudden appearance of cloud, plus the alarmed look on Rick's face equalled bad weather.

Dave looked up too and frowned, making an O-shape with his mouth. 'This looks bad . . . ' I heard him say, before a roll of thunder in the distance obliterated the rest of the sentence. He pulled the remaining oar out of its holder and started to paddle them back in, canoe-style.

Within minutes the wind began to pick up and it started to rain.

'We've got three choices,' Rick said as we crammed into the small radio room-cum- galley. I think he must have been talking to Dave more than me because he started to use technical terms that I'd never heard before. Dave was nodding, so I assumed that he recognised the vocabulary and I just nodded anyway. 'We can stay anchored here and hope that we don't get torn off the anchorage. If we do break free we're going to get battered on the rocks, guaranteed. Or we can look around the island for a beach and moor offshore. That way we can take the dinghy and paddle in if the boat breaks loose. At least we won't be on it.' He took a deep breath. 'The problem with that is we don't even know if the island's inhabited.'

'Why do we need to do anything?' I asked. 'Maybe it's not a bad storm.'

Rick leaned across me and flicked a switch on the radio. It buzzed and crackled with static, nothing else. He switched it off as though my question had been answered. 'There's nothing coming through, John. Either all of the radios on all the boats in the vicinity have broken down, which is very unlikely, or that's a typhoon and it's buggered all reception. I've tried every channel and there's nothing.'

Dave looked sceptical and leaned back against the stainless steel sink. 'Typhoon?'

'Either that or a very bad tropical storm.' He reflected for a moment and added, 'It's not strictly typhoon season, but weather patterns around here can be pretty weird. I've seen it before.'

I leaned against the ladder that led up to the deck as the boat rolled gently. 'Number three?'

Rick looked blankly at me.

'You said we had three choices. What's the third one?'

He puffed out his cheeks and exhaled. 'We put up the sail and head off to Bali; try to ride it out, get in front of it. It looks like it's coming from the north-east so that should suit us, seeing as how we want to go south.'

I sat down on a rung. 'I don't know, you two are the experts, I'm only here for the ride. You decide.'

'Dave?'

Dave shook his head, thought for a moment and said, 'I think we should go for it. At least then we'd be moving along. You know what it's like in a boat without forward motion.'

I didn't know, but I guessed from his expression that it wasn't a pleasant experience. I pictured a person riding a bike, and the ease with which it's done providing one has forward motion. As soon as you stop peddling the bike tips over. I supposed that a boat in a storm was a bit like a push-bike.

'What time is it?'

Dave checked the clock. 'Twelve.'

Rick put his hands flat against the ceiling. 'OK. We'll try to make it to Bali. John, you get the life jackets out; they're in the bedroom beneath the bed. Dave, how's the GPS working?'

'Seems OK.' He turned on the stool and started to fiddle with some knobs.

'I hope so. With so much cloud cover we won't see the sun or the stars.'

There was a flurry of activity and noise as each of us went in different directions. Dave went to the controls while Rick ran out on deck to untie us. I heard him curse as he went up, and then the sound of his footsteps thumping above my head. Rummaging around beneath the bed I pulled out a crate full of life jackets and put one on. It stank of mildew so I took if off again, intending to wash it in the sea, when I heard Dave say something that left me cold.

'Oh no . . .'

It wasn't a loud 'Oh no', but it was the way he said it that was so ominous. Not full of alarm, but the sort of 'Oh no' you express when you hand in an exam paper to an invigilator, realising too late that you've added up a sum incorrectly.

I sat on the bed waiting for Dave to say, 'Oh! That's OK then,' but all I heard was the sound of the anchor chain dragging against the side of the boat. *Drrrrr*. I willed him to say something more, and he did. This time he just said, 'No . . .' only softer than before, as though he'd been winded and didn't have the breath to say the other word.

When I staggered out of the bedroom, holding on to the walls to stop me from falling over as the boat rolled, Dave was sitting on the stool with his back to the equipment. His legs were slightly apart and he was looking at the floor, his hands on his lap, one on the other's palm as though holding a dead bird.

'What's up, Dave?' I asked, putting one palm flat against the low ceiling. 'Has the GPS gone wrong or something?'

He sighed, looked up at me with sad eyes, shook his head, then looked back at his dead hands. 'Worse.'

'What then?'

He looked up again. 'You'd better get Rick down here.'

When I got outside I was shocked to see how quickly the weather had deteriorated: the day had turned to night and the sea was a mass of white foam, whipped up by the howling wind. The nearest island was no longer visible through the torrent of rain that hammered down horizontally in sheets, and I couldn't even see the top of the mast. The sail wasn't up but we were already moving quickly through the water, just under the force of the wind on the side of the boat.

I slipped my way along the deck towards Rick, who was by the wheel, blinking the rain out of my eyes and taking slow steps so as not to fall overboard. We were already leaning over so far that I could have touched the surface of the sea just by crouching and putting my hand through the rail. 'Where are the life jackets?' he bellowed, still concentrating on the compass.

'Forget that,' I shouted, 'Dave's got a problem. He wants you to come downstairs.'

He looked up. 'What problem?'

I wiped the rain from my face. 'Don't know, just come down.'

He threw the anchor back over the side and followed me back along the deck. When we reached the hatchway the anchor must have got a hold in the reef because we were thrown to one side and I had to hang on to the doorframe to stop me from falling.

Dave was fiddling with the buttons again when we got back inside, but it was immediately obvious to me that he was just trying to look busy.

'What is it, Dave?'

He picked up a chart, shook his head and put it down again. 'I don't know. We're . . . not where I thought we were.' He buried his head in his hands. 'I don't fuckin' know.'

'What d'you mean?' Rick leaned closer, standing behind him.

Dave picked up a pen, went to point at the chart but put it down again. 'The reading I'm getting, the co-ordinates. Man, they're not what they were last night! I don't get it . . . ' He picked up the pen again, pointing at the chart that was laid out on the desk top in front of him. 'Last night, the fuckin' same as I've been doing every night for the past two weeks, I checked our position. We were here,' he dotted the location, 'Kangean island.'

'So?'

'So now when I turn on this piece of shit, it gives the co-ordinates as here.'

Rick looked closely at the second dot. 'Damar? But that's twice as far! It can't be right.'

'Watch.' Dave pushed buttons while Rick observed, occasionally saying 'OK' or 'Yep'. The co-ordinates came up the same as Dave had suggested so they did it once more. Again the satellite told us that we were about twice as far east as we thought we were.

'It's wrong,' Rick finally asserted, standing up straight. 'Has to be.'

Dave shrugged. 'I suppose it's possible. If it hasn't been used for years.'

I tutted. 'How can it be wrong?' They both looked at me as though someone new had walked into the room. 'You tested it in Singapore and it gave the right co-ordinates. And what about the first place we went to, Bangka?' I felt my voice rising in anger.

'Could have been anywhere, John,' Dave said evenly. 'No one ever told us that that was Bangka, we just assumed it was.'

'But Rick, I thought you said that you'd been using traditional methods as back-up?'

'Yeah, John, I did for the first day, but this stuff seemed so accurate that I gave up. There didn't seem any point.'

'We could be anywhere then.' Dave and I both looked at Rick.

'No, not anywhere.' He leaned down and pointed at the chart. 'I've been sailing east, I know that because we've sailed into the sun every morning and away from it at night. So we're not anywhere, we're somewhere along this line, from Sumatra to . . . well . . . '

'New Guinea?' I exclaimed, drawing a mental line on the map. 'For Christ's sake!'

'No, course not. We can't have sailed that far in two weeks. Christ, the wind's been good, but not that good.'

'Why not?' Dave presented the chart to Rick, 'We've been sailing twenty hours a day.'

Rick shook his head. 'No way, it's not possible, not in this thing. I say we're exactly where we think we are and we keep heading south. Within the next ten to fifteen hours we'll be in Bali.'

The boat suddenly lurched to one side, sending us all against the far wall. Cups fell off hooks and smashed on the floor, and the charts and pens were all thrown through the air, landing on top of us. 'Shit, the anchorage has come loose.' Rick pulled himself off the floor and clung to the ladder. 'Look, we can't drift about out here, we'll be smashed against the rocks. Wherever we are we've got to move. Everyone on deck.'

Without another word we took out the life jackets, followed Rick's instructions and went up on deck to get the sail up. One by one we emerged on to the deck and stood, open-mouthed at the sight that loomed up above us. For a moment we were paralysed, like three rabbits caught in the beam of a car's headlights. Rick shouted at me, 'Move it!' but I just stood, blinking the rain out of my eyes, transfixed as the cliff face came into focus through the mist.

FOUR

The next ten minutes were mayhem. Everyone shouted at the tops of their voices, either giving instructions or replying to them. Rick was still shouting for me to get a move on and stop staring at the wall of rock that was moving closer and closer, and if the bottom of the boat hadn't hit the rocky seabed I think I would have stared forever.

There was a deep, grinding *boom*, and I was thrown headlong into the steel handrail that ran around the edge of the boat, my feet lifting off the deck. I put my hands out in front of me to lessen the impact but they missed the bars and went through the gaps. Tilting my head to one side, I landed on my shoulder. It was a bit like a rugby tackle, and if I hadn't been wearing the life jacket, with its built-in polystyrene shoulder pads, I'd have probably broken a shoulder blade.

My arm went elbow-deep into the sea as the boat listed over, pivoting on its keel which had come into contact with the sea-bed, acting like a fulcrum. I gagged on seawater, spluttering and blinking, but I just couldn't get up. Holding out a hand desperately, hoping that someone would grab hold of it, I shouted for help, writhing on my back, supported only by the handrail.

Dave was holding on to the other rail directly opposite me, hanging, his feet flailing wildly in the air, trying desperately not to let go. The bar that he was holding was bending under the weight, designed for aesthetics and not as a swing. His feet scuffed against the deck but couldn't get a grip. He looked like a mouse on a treadmill, running but getting nowhere. Bizarrely, I laughed at the sight.

Rick was clinging to the mast, his stomach and face flat against the cold steel so that, from where I lay, only his two disembodied arms were visible. He shouted something but it was lost in the sound of the boat scraping against the bottom. Both of his arms were wrapped around the pole in a morbid sort of hug, one hand still holding his coffee mug, as though it was the most precious thing on the boat.

Just when I thought the boat couldn't lean over any further without us all drowning it juddered violently, sending vibrations through my body, did a sort of kangaroo hop in which I was pressed further down, and then swung back upright, rocking from side to side. Rick immediately unravelled the sail so quickly that he looked like a film in fast motion. 'Dave! Quick, get the anchor up!' he shouted over his shoulder. 'Now!'

Dave pushed himself off the deck and started to run around in circles like a headless chicken.

'Dave!' Rick screamed, jabbing the air with his finger. 'The fooking anchor!'

First going one way and then the other, Dave ran to the end of the boat, did a double-take, realising he'd gone the wrong way in all the confusion, and came back to get to the anchor.

As I picked myself up off the deck, one hand still on the rail, I looked up at the rock face towering above us. I remember this clearly because we were so close that I could see every nook and cranny, and I could actually see a bird nesting in one of the rock fissures. All I could see was the bird's head sticking out, the rest of its body hidden in the rock-face, but I remember feeling mocked by it. I felt as though we were being laughed at, and I really wanted to throw a stone at the bloody thing and knock its head off. My attention, however, was drawn away by Dave, who was shouting something to Rick. I steadied myself and looked round.

Dave was holding on to the rail with one hand and holding up a length of chain in the other. 'It's gone, Rick!' he shouted, as a wave struck the side of the boat and he momentarily disappeared from view.

Rick ran past him and fixed the sail, and Dave jumped behind the wheel to stop it spinning as the wind caught us. Within minutes I looked back to see the bird but it had gone, along with the cliff face, hidden once again behind the sheets of rain. Rick and Dave swapped positions again, Rick continually nodding as he glanced down at the compass, then up at the rain ahead, while at the same time spinning the wheel around in his hands, before giving it back to Dave and coming across to me.

'You OK, John?' he gasped.

I shook my head but said yes. 'Jesus, Rick, what's happening? I thought we were going to die or something.' We both grabbed hold of the mast, bodies going up and down, side to side in perfect unison as the boat rose and fell. 'What was that noise, did we hit the bottom?'

He took one hand off the mast and pulled it across his face to wipe away the rain. 'Yeah, I think so. Shit, we could be in trouble here, John.' He shot a quick look, first aft, at Dave, and then forward, as if checking on our course. 'I'm gonna go down and check if there's any damage,' he said, 'but really we need to dive over the side to see how bad the keel is. There's only so much you can check from inside, but at least I can see if she's taking on water.'

I loved the way he spoke when we were on the boat. Those little terms like, 'taking on water', and referring to the boat as 'she'. So comforting, I thought. My mouth opened to ask a question, but suddenly there didn't seem to be anything worth asking, so I closed it.

'You're bleeding,' he said, looking at the bottom half of my face.

As soon as he said it my lip started to sting, and I ran the back of my hand across it and found it smeared with blood. Shocked at the sight, I ran my tongue over every tooth to check that I hadn't lost any. It wasn't a bad cut, just a split lip, caused, I think, by the rough material of the life jacket as it rode up when I fell. I nodded and pressed on the cut with my thumb. 'Is there anything you want me to do?'

'Just hang on. And keep your life jacket on,' he said as an afterthought, before staggering off.

I watched as he unfurled the rest of the sail. The wind caught the canvas and we shot forward so fast that it felt like we were engine-driven. As he came back down the boat to go below, he came back to the mast. 'John, sort out your valuables and put them in a plastic bag: passport, any money. It's just a precaution, but if we do lose our shit at least we'll have something to get by on. I'll do the same now, and I'll tell Dave to do it as well. Just wrap them tightly in a bin bag or something, so that they're waterproof.' He turned to go.

'And do what with them?' I asked.

'I'm going to keep mine in my shorts, I suggest you and Dave do the same. If this thing rolls and we get thrown out, at least we'll be carrying some ID.'

I was astonished at the change in the tone of his voice. Not half an hour before he was saying how easy it would be to sail to Bali, and now we were discussing what we should do if the boat sank! I opened my mouth to speak and he read my mind.

'Look, we're not going to sink or anything, don't worry. By tomorrow morning we'll be propping up a bar in Kuta, laughing about all of this. Don't worry.' He slapped me on the arm and went down through the hatch, leaving me to worry.

When anyone says 'don't worry' twice in the same sentence, alarm bells start ringing in my head. It's like in the films, when a soldier has been shot twenty times and is lying on the battlefield, in a pool of blood.

His buddy is pouring water into the wounded man's mouth from a canteen, saying, 'Don't worry, bud, you're OK, you're gonna make it. Don't worry.' We all know he's going to die, not because he's full of holes but because his mate told him not to worry.

Rick's head disappeared through the hatchway and I took one last look around me before following him. Dave was squinting ahead, nervously snatching quick glances down at the compass. The sea was in turmoil around us: waves were breaking in every direction at once, some we rode, the boat clearing the water to at least half its length before crashing down, a fan of water arcing out from each side, while some hit us side on and exploded into the air, blown by the wind, to cover the whole deck in heavy spray.

I put a thumb up to Dave but the space between us became a wall of whitewater as a wave broke against the side of the boat, obscuring the view for a few seconds. I noticed that Dave had attached a piece of rope, about five feet long, as a safety line, directly from the steel handrail of the boat to his waist. I considered doing one for myself. The only problem was that I didn't really have a job, so where was I going to stand and tie myself on to? I felt a bit useless so I decided to go below to sort out my valuables. Apart from anything else I didn't even know how to tie a knot!

When I got down below I wished I hadn't bothered. Rick was standing in the middle of the galley, ankle-deep in water. I stopped on the bottom rung of the steps, as though afraid to get my feet wet, and stared at the sight. 'Fuck!'

There was a long pause as we both hung on to the sides and watched the water swill around. Every roll of the boat sent the water over to one side, splashing against one wall where it peaked before going back along the floor and slapping against the cabinet doors on the other side. Some of the doors were hanging off their hinges, the rusted old screws having broken free after years without maintenance, and everything that hadn't been fixed down, including all of those things that had but were too old to withstand the beating, were rolling and floating around on the floor.

Maps, books, charts, pens, pots and pans, fishing gear; the whole lot rolled or floated to and fro with the boat's movement, rattling and clanking as it went.

'It could be water from the deck that came down the hatchway,' Rick said, causing me to look up. I shook my head. I knew Rick was lying, just by the way he stared at his feet while speaking. 'The hatchway was loose, we forgot—'

'Rick, we're sinking aren't we?' He looked up as though noticing me for the first time, then went into the bedroom and started to look for something under the bed. I followed. 'Rick. We're sink—'

'These boats can't sink, John, they've got buoyancy built into the hull.' He heaved something out from under the bed and came back into the galley. 'They can roll over but they can't sink, don't worry.'

'Stop telling me not to fucking worry!'

He seemed slightly taken aback at the anger in my voice. 'All right, sorry. But the last thing we need to do is panic.' He threw something on to the floor. 'I've had a quick look around and I can't find any damage to the hull. The only way to find out if it's cracked is to pump out the water and see if it comes back in again. Do you know how to use a pump?'

'Course I fucking don't.' I looked down at the equipment and then back at him. 'I thought we just threw a switch and it pumped out automatically.'

'Yeah, but the battery's fucked. Everything's soaked, you'll have to do it by hand.' He took his hands off the ceiling and walked over to the radio.

'Me? What are you going to do?'

He sat down on the stool and put on the headphones. 'I'm going to send out a mayday.'

FIVE

If, reading this, you're wondering why we had sailed for two weeks, instead of one as predicted, and still believed that we were heading to Bali, you're not alone. With the benefit of hindsight I wonder the same thing myself almost every day of my life. All along we had planned on a one-week voyage that should have brought us within spitting distance of our goal. The distance wasn't great, and the sea and wind conditions had been as perfect as they could have been, so we should have realised that we had sailed too far. Maybe we were too happy on the boat and didn't bother to check, certainly Rick didn't. Or it's possible that none of us cared where we were, or how long it took to get there.

It's easy enough for me to justify the events that took place over the next forty-eight hours, simply by pleading ignorance. It doesn't make me feel any better about what happened, but at least I don't blame myself for the tragedy. We each took our chances when we first stepped aboard that boat in Singapore, and none of us were under any illusions over the dangers involved in such a voyage. Looking back, I think we were almost *unlucky* to have had two weeks of good weather because we were lulled into a false sense of security. But then, looking back, one can say a lot of things; it doesn't alter the facts. Nothing can change what's already happened.

I jumped into the ankle-deep water and waded across to the pump, picking up what looked like a T-shaped piston with about thirty feet of hose attached to it. After five minutes of inspection and testing, in which I tried everything conceivable to get the thing to pump, I threw it on the floor. 'Rick, it doesn't work.' I said, holding the hose.

No response. I'd forgotten that he was wearing headphones and couldn't hear me. 'Rick.' I tapped him on the shoulder and he jumped up.

'What?'

'The pump, it doesn't work.'

He looked at the hose in my hand and took off the headphones. 'You've got to put that outside.'

'I know, but the pump doesn't ... pump.'

'You've got to–'

'Look, just show me how to do it will you?'

He went across and picked up the T part, flicked a catch over and put it between his legs, a foot on top of each base plate. He brought the top T up and down a few times and I was startled as water spurted out the end of the hose. The jet of water shot across the room and soaked the radio.

There were no wisps of smoke or showers of sparks like in the movies, but when Rick rushed across and listened in the headphones, twiddling the dials, I knew it was busted. The expression on Rick's face and the acrid smell of electrics shorting out told me as much. I stood there like an idiot, one hand still holding on to the hose, still pointing it in the same direction. If it had been a comedy I would have looked down at the hose and said, 'Oops!' but it wasn't funny. I felt sick, partly because of the stinging smell and partly because of our predicament.

Rick put his head in both hands, dropping the headphones and allowing them to dangle by their cord like a pendulum under the boat's rocking motion. Without a word I took the end of the hose upstairs and out on to the deck.

Every time I went outside now it scared me; it seemed the sea was getting higher by the minute. Where once open ocean had been replaced by sheets of rain, now the sheets of rain were being rapidly replaced by waves. The wind was blowing with such force that even waves that didn't break against the side of the boat were blown on to us in a constant shower.

Dave looked terrified, as though he couldn't hold on to the wheel. 'Where's Rick?' he shouted as I emerged.

How should I answer that? I wondered. If I said 'down below' he would want to know what he was doing. I couldn't say 'operating the radio', because it was broken, and he would see the look of alarm in my eyes. For some reason I wanted to keep it a secret, so I tied the hose up and darted back down below with Dave calling behind me.

'Dave wants help,' I said, coming back inside. 'He looks shit scared to me.'

'I bet he does.' Rick looked up at me. 'What's it like out?'

I walked over and picked up the pump. 'Don't ask.'

'Oh, fooking hell.' He stood up wearily. 'I'll go back up, you have a go on that pump, and when its clear give me a shout.' He hesitated. 'No, when it's clear, get your valuables sorted like we said. I'll go and tell Dave to do the same.' He pushed open the hatch.

It took ages for the water to go down, and I continually put the hose to my ear to confirm that it was actually pumping. The piston hadn't been greased and had rust freckles all over it, so I guessed that it was much less efficient than it was designed to be. Also, every so often one of the handles would work its way loose and I'd have to stop and push it back into its socket, which was a real bind.

The heat in the confined space was terrible, made worse by the humidity given off by the amount of evaporating water. After ten minutes of pumping it felt as though there was no oxygen left in the room and I started to feel dizzy from the exertion. My body was prickly with sweat, and it poured so freely down my face that I had to keep my eyes closed to stop them from stinging.

The water eventually receded, I dropped the pump on the floor and flung myself on to one of the beds, exhausted, gripping the edges of the mattress to stop me from falling off. Even then the mattress started to slide off, and I had to turn around and place both feet flat against the wall to keep it steady. I drew the curtain back, using my toes as fingers, and stared at the porthole. It was completely submerged, only occasionally rising above the surface as we rose up, before going under again in a stream of bubbles. It was like being in a submarine, and I imagined fast swimming fish coming alongside and watching me with fishy eyes.

Still in that position, my legs at a right angle to my body, I heard a noise in the doorway and looked back. Dave appeared upside-down; his sad face a smile from where I was lying. Water ran from him and dripped on to the ceiling. 'Did Rick tell you about the radio?' I asked.

'Uh-huh. Don't matter, we wouldn't have got any help in this weather anyway.' He stumbled in and sat on the bed. 'John, man, I'm worried. I'm very fuckin' worried.'

'At least someone else is,' I said. 'The way Rick's behaving you'd think nothing was wrong.'

'He's worried too, it's just his way of dealing with it.' He punched the mattress. 'Fuck, man, why didn't he check our position? I can't believe he didn't double-check it.'

I watched little rivulets of water run from his afro on to his shiny forehead. 'Have you ever been in a storm like this before?' I asked after a pause.

'Yeah, but only on a ship. Not on anything this size.'

I sat up, shuffling along the mattress to his side. 'Be honest, Dave, what d'you think our chances are?'

He frowned as though going through the options in his mind, and said, 'Depends. Depends how long we're out here for, how long the storm lasts, whether or not it gets any worse than this. Depends on a lot of things. But the main thing I'm worried about is the condition of this boat. Some of those ropes,' he shook his head, 'they're old, and once they start to get wet they begin to fall apart, perish ... '

'But they've never been used. They all look brand new.'

'Exactly. They've never been used. Just lying around in the sun for a couple of years – they get brittle as shit. While we're under sail I reckon we'll be fine, but if those ropes start to go and we can't lash anything in place, we're gonna have problems. They're already showing signs of wear and tear.' He shook his head again. 'Rick bought a spare length with him but that'll only go so far.'

'And the good news?' A snort was about as close to a laugh as either of us could get. 'Did Rick tell you about waterproofing your valuables?' I asked, rolling off the bed to retrieve my bag from the wardrobe.

'Yeah, just gonna do that now. That's why I came down here. That and to help with the pumping.'

'Too late,' I said, opening the wardrobe door, 'I've already done it. Looks like you've escaped all the hard work.'

He pushed himself off the bed and stood in the doorway, looking into the galley. 'Yeah, you didn't do a very good job did you? Look at that.'

I pushed him aside and looked out into the galley, the butterflies in my stomach going wild. It had already refilled with water.

SIX

'Man the pumps!' I've always wanted to say that in earnest, though I never ever thought I would, and had never imagined I'd actually be doing it. I manned them; Dave had a go at manning them, and, eventually, so did Rick. We had to; it was just too much for one person to cope with.

The pumping went on non-stop for the rest of that day and through the night, with me doing the bulk of it for obvious unskilled reasons. At no other point during our whole voyage had I ever wished so much for a sea-faring skill that would have meant me being needed on another task other than down below. At least the other two could break up the monotony with long bouts at either the radio or on deck.

My shoulders were agony and my back felt like it was going to break. I had to stand in the same position: feet on the foot-plates, bent over almost double with both hands gripping the T-bar, and bring my arms up and down for hours on end. I tried every conceivable position, like the Kama Sutra of pumping: from sitting to kneeling to bending over, but whichever way I did it something gave. I even tried sitting on the bar and putting one hand between my legs to pull it up, rising and falling as though I was riding a horse. Rick came in, took one look at me going up and down and thought I was trying to get off on it!

The only time I could rest was during the brief period when the water had been pumped out and took fifteen minutes to seep back in again.

During this time I would just lie on the bed and inspect the blisters on my hands. After the first two hours the blisters had broken, and then I got blisters on blisters. The delicate new skin wasn't strong enough, and that too broke, leaving my palms and fingers bleeding non-stop. I wrapped them in bandages from the first aid box, but it did little to stop the pain.

To save my fingers from further damage I started to use different parts of my hands on the pump bar, working my way up each arm. I used the web between each finger, but that was too soft, splitting and leaving each membrane with a V-shaped slit in it. I had a go with my wrists, tying each hand to the push-bar with bandage. That lasted quite a long time but the problem was grip; whenever the boat rolled, the pump fell free and I had to dip my open wounds into the salt water to retrieve it.

Standing in water for so many hours made my feet look like pink brains. An intricate pattern of ridges and valleys, deep enough to stand a coin in on end, had formed all over them, right up to the ankles. My toes had turned pure white, and when I pinched the top of one to test for feeling, a piece of skin peeled off in one continuous strip like white sashimi.

At about five o'clock in the morning, during one of my fifteen-minute lulls, I fell asleep on the bed. The boat was being thrown all over the place as the swell picked up but I was too exhausted to care. Even when I was thrown on to the floor I just jammed myself in the gap between bed and wall and nodded off, my stinging hands cupped limply, one on top of the other in front of my face.

I don't know how long I slept for, half an hour, an hour at most, but when Rick woke me up I had a splitting headache and a mouth full of saline water.

'John, you OK?' he said, shaking me.

I felt like I was in a womb, protected by the warm fluid. Opening one eye I could see Rick's head looking over the edge of the mattress, water dripping from his soaked hair.

'John, the pump . . . '

I opened the other eye but couldn't see anything clearly through it, just a misty blue. The room was stifling, so, still lying on one side, I opened my mouth to suck in air and sucked in salt water instead. The shock was horrific, like drowning. I spluttered and pushed myself upright, my hands stinging in the water.

'The pump, John! What are you doing? The place is flooded.'

Still blinking the water from my eye, I got up on to the mattress. The bedroom too was now inches deep in water. I knew the bedroom door had a four inch threshold so it meant that the galley area must have filled to that level.

'Fucking hell, Rick, I can't take it any more.' I held my hands out in front of me. They had stiffened and I couldn't bend the fingers.

'Shit,' he gasped, and slumped back on the bed. 'I'd pump it out myself, but we need two people up top.'

We must have hit the crest of a wave at that moment as both of us were lifted off the bed for a second before being deposited heavily. I looked at him. 'Is it still bad outside?'

He nodded.

'What, worse or the same?'

'Worse.' He hesitated. 'Something's wrong. With the navigation, I mean. The swell's huge. Far too big for such a small sea.' He shook his head and looked down at the water swilling around his feet. 'I'll be honest with you, John, I haven't got a clue where we are now.'

'Great.'

'But I know one thing; these waves are too big to be caused locally. And they're coming in the wrong direction.'

'What do you mean, wrong direction?'

He put both of his hands out to clarify; one hand, on its edge, was the boat, the other represented the wind or waves. 'We're going that way, OK?' he said. 'The wind's still more or less behind us, but the swell's coming this way, against us. We're riding over an oncoming swell!'

I hesitated. 'So if we're heading south ...'

'Which we are.'

'The waves must be coming from the south.'

'Exactly.'

'But that's impossible. Bali is south, the islands are south, you said.'

'Which means either the compass is wrong, and we're heading north, east, or west which I doubt or–'

'Can you check it?'

He shook his head. 'How? There are no stars. I can't even see the end of the boat at times, the rain's so heavy.' There was a moment's pause. 'Or,' he continued, 'we've sailed into the Indian Ocean. Past Bali, or whichever islands we were near, and straight out into open water. We must have, even if the compass was wrong and we'd sailed away from the south, the swell would never be this big, or this regular. I've timed it: fourteen seconds apart.'

From my limited knowledge of sea swell, attained from trying to predict waves for surfing purposes, I got the basic drift of what he was saying. The bigger the body of water, the larger the waves that can be produced on it. The Mediterranean Sea, for example, produces relatively small waves, while the Pacific produces large ones. Every other sea or ocean wave lies somewhere in between, depending upon its size. The Java sea is smaller than the Med, and, even given a severe typhoon, it could never produce this kind of regular swell.

I paused, putting my head on to my stiff hands. 'So what now?'

'We luff.'

'In English.'

'Take down the sail and drift until we spot land. Or a boat. Or until the weather clears enough for us to take a bearing.'

I looked up. 'Isn't that a bit dangerous?'

'It's either that or we just keep flying along in the wrong direction.'

'Assuming that we are going in the wrong direction.'

'We are.' He stood up. 'Definitely.'

I watched him stagger to the doorway as a ripple of water from the pond that used to be the galley floor broke over the bottom of the door frame and slopped into the bedroom. 'I can't use the pump, Rick, my hands . . .'

He wadded a few steps and picked up the pump. 'I'll do this and then go back up with Dave to take the sails down.' He put both feet beside the pump to steady it, and was about to pull up the handle, when there was an almighty crash and the whole boat did what felt like a complete roll.

It's hard to tell exactly what happened next. I was thrown through the air and landed face down against the wardrobe door with such force that it broke through its frame, splintering the wood. My head smashed against the door and I slammed against the wall, turning over and over, my legs and arms totally out of control, like washing inside a tumble dryer.

In the confined space of the wardrobe I was protected more than harmed, hemmed in by three walls. I think I now know what it would be like to lie in a coffin and roll down a hill. I was scared but at the same time safe. Of course, it's easy to say that now, but at the time I didn't have a clue what was happening, I didn't even know which way was up and which was down.

At one point the weight of my body was supported on my neck, my head resting on what must have been the wardrobe ceiling. I gagged, trying to open my mouth as my chin was crushed against my chest and my back was bent double. Both knees bashed into my forehead, salt water raining down on me.

Just as abruptly, the pressure released and my body sprang back the other way under the force of gravity, sending me crashing down on the floor, landing painfully at the base of my spine. I immediately grabbed both sides of the wardrobe door frame to pull myself up, completely forgetting the pain in my hands, but the boat rolled the other way under its own momentum and I was launched out of the wardrobe.

If the bed hadn't been screwed to the floor I would have continued across the room and smashed my head against the opposite wall. In a rush of falling water and pieces of broken door, I landed against the bed with my thighs, my torso lying across the top at a right angle. The mattress had gone and my face was pressed hard against the plywood. The boat rolled back once more and I was left sitting upright in the wardrobe again.

I held on to the door frame, this time putting both feet hard up against the inner walls to stop myself being thrown out. The boat was being thrown everywhere at once now, and even from where I sat it was suddenly very apparent that we no longer had forward motion. Waiting no more than thirty seconds to see if we would roll again, and to catch my breath, I counted and listened. God knows why I was counting, I just did it. Maybe I thought I was going to die; I certainly felt as though I'd been to hell and back or maybe it was just an after-thought from the last thing Rick had said about counting the swell. I want to say that my whole life flashed before my eyes, but it didn't. I had flashes before my eyes, but that was more like a snowstorm of little lights in the darkness where my brain had banged against the skull. Squeezing my eyes tightly shut I saw a firework display of pulsating, popping colours and flares.

My name was called. 'Rick!' I shouted back.

'John!'

'I'm in here.'

He reached in and pulled me up with one hand. We were both thrown straight across the room, landing in a tumble on the bed and rolling against the other wall. We pulled ourselves apart and got to our feet, inspecting ourselves for damage. I had blood all over my chest and panicked, thinking that I'd been seriously wounded. Dabbing the spot with my fingers and feeling no pain, I quickly cupped a handful of water and threw it on to my chest. The blood washed away revealing unbroken skin.

'It's me.' I looked up and saw Rick's nose dripping with blood. 'It's OK,' he said, wiping the blood on to the back of his hand. 'We've got to get up to Dave.'

'Dave!' The name spurred me into life and we both sprinted to the door, running through the galley area and bouncing off the walls like pinballs.

Rick went outside first, pushing open the deck hatch and revealing a dull grey sky above. It was daylight outside, and the sudden brightness, even though it was dulled by the clouds and torrential rain, hurt my eyes. The water and fresh air felt beautiful as it rushed in through the hatch, and I soaked it up like a sponge. Rick jumped out on to the deck and I pulled myself out behind him.

From the moment I stepped out on to the deck nothing registered in my head except the steering wheel. I didn't notice the rain or the sky any more, the huge waves or the rising and falling of the boat. I paid no attention to the torn rigging, or the sail that was drooped over the side of the boat, half in the water like a huge white jellyfish. Even the smashed-in handrail and gunwale didn't attract my attention.

All I could focus on, like Rick, was the stainless steel steering wheel that was spinning around at the other end of the boat with no one there to hold it still.

SEVEN

We searched for hours. Alternating between tying a makeshift sail, steering the boat and pumping out the water, we squinted hard through the rain, trying desperately to spot his yellow life jacket bobbing up and down in the mountainous seas. We tacked backwards and forwards, going ten minutes one way then ten the other, until we had crossed and re-crossed the place where we estimated the accident to have occurred. Nothing.

The bottomless feeling in my stomach that I'd felt as soon I saw the unmanned wheel wouldn't go away. I felt sick but couldn't throw up. Even putting fingers down my throat didn't help, and all I could think about was Dave floating in the sea in a life jacket, drifting further and further away from us. When that thought occasionally subsided (it never went completely from my mind for months afterwards) it was replaced by the last image I'd had of him, when he'd come down to waterproof his gear: his ridiculous afro, that beaming smile and, most of all, his easy manner even though he said he was scared shitless. When that image faded my mind wandered further back, to Thailand.

Most of the morning we zigzagged back and forth, before eventually giving up and deciding instead to concentrate on pumping out the gallons of water. Something had hit the boat and there was a huge V-shaped crease in the side of the hull that ran from the gunwale down to a porthole, which had been smashed in. If I stood on deck and leaned over the buckled rail I could see inside the galley through the split. From inside, daylight and rain came in along with any sea water that hit us side-on. The split at the valley of the V was about as wide as a fist.

Rick took down what was left of the sail to stop us moving through the water, which inevitably caused the boat to dip into the swell and let water through the hole, while I plugged the gap with a rolled-up life jacket to keep out the worst. Water was still pouring in from an unknown source but at least we weren't adding to the chore of pumping it out.

According to Rick, we had most likely collided with a container that had fallen off a ship. The shape of the dent, and the yellow paint around the edges of the hole seemed to confirm his theory, and he said we were lucky that a wave hadn't carried it right up on top of us, smashing the boat to pieces.

I looked up at the life jacket stuffed into the hole and sighed, wiping the tears from my face. I'd been pumping water out for most of the afternoon and I knew that if we didn't come across help soon we were going to die. I just couldn't see how we were going to make it through another night.

The hatch opened and Rick's head came through. 'John, get up here quick, I can see something.'

I dropped the pump, which wasn't easy considering that my hands wouldn't open, and climbed up the steps, using my knuckles to get a grip.

The waves were still high outside but the rain had eased, and in the distance, to one side of us, I could see a dark line. I squinted, then closed my eyes and opened them again just to make sure I wasn't mistaken. 'It's land isn't it?' I said, almost breaking down with emotion. 'Oh, thank God. Where—'

Rick had already left my side and was steering the boat around. 'John, get over here.' I ran across. 'Hold the wheel. Don't turn it, just hold it, while I get the sail up.'

I waited until he'd finished before asking my question. 'Where are we, d'you think?'

'Indo maybe. Who fooking cares? It's land, so let's just go for it.'

The wind filled the sail, and within half an hour our field of vision was filled with a dark green hillside that sloped gently down to the sea before ending abruptly in a ragged cliff-face. The land ran out either side of us as far as we could see but there didn't appear to be a beach, just a mass of white water as the waves exploded against the rocks.

Rick swung the boat around. We started to run parallel with the shore when we must have hit the bottom. The boat dipped its nose so far down into the water that the next wave came right over the front, mast high, and over the two of us. I was instantly swept off the back and thrown into the sea, carried by a hill of water that spun me around and around. I fought against the surge, scrambling frantically one way and then the other, unsure which direction the surface was. Just as the air in my lungs was running out my head broke the surface and I gasped, sucking in lungfuls of air, before the next wave came from behind and I swallowed a mouthful and puked up.

'Ri-Rick!' I coughed and spun around one-eighty degrees. The up-ended hull of the boat appeared above the next wave and was already fifty feet away from me, its keel sticking up in the air like the dorsal fin of a white whale. The boat went into another trough of the swell, disappeared for half a minute, and then appeared again, this time at double the distance.

'John!'

Treading water frantically, I turned to my left just in time to see Rick's head bob up and then vanish behind a peak of swirling water. 'Rick, over here!' I started to swim in that direction, pulling hard against the water and the drag created by the life jacket. He appeared again, this time closer. 'Forget th-the boat,' I shouted between retches. 'Swim!'

I considered taking the life jacket off to get extra speed but decided against it. We were both going in the right direction now so it didn't seem to matter how long it would take to get there. The current created by the under-tow from the waves was horrendous but we were so close to the shore, and floating so high in the water due to the buoyancy aids, that the tops of breaking waves pushed us a little further in every minute.

There must have been a very shallow area in the sea bed because when I was twenty feet from Rick, a wave almost broke, lifting me up and throwing me forwards, almost landing on top of him. A second later we both got dragged backwards with the trough of the next wave and tumbled over and over as it propelled us forward again. Rick came up feet-first next to me, before righting himself and throwing up a gallon of water.

'We're gonna get smashed on the rocks,' I shouted between gasps, pointing at the boulders in front of us. 'Swim that way, there's a ledge.'

Just to our right the cliff-face had fallen in, leaving a huge U-shaped rent in the landscape about fifty-foot wide and fifty-foot high, where tonnes of boulders had cascaded down into the sea. It still looked sketchy as a landing place but it was all we had, and definitely a safer bet than a sheer wall of rock. I noticed that some of the boulders in that area looked as though they had been flattened by centuries of weathering, and although the waves still broke over them, they seemed to run up and down horizontally, not vertically.

It all happened at once. I swam perpendicular to the ledge and found myself suddenly, miraculously, standing waist-deep in water. Brilliant! I tried to walk forwards but was sucked off the rock, caught on the next wave and hurtled through the air. Flailing with both arms to keep upright, I did an involuntary somersault and landed back on my feet further up the ledge than where I'd started. When I say I landed on my feet, I mean my feet touched the ground first followed by the rest of me. The impact rammed a knee against my chin and I bit painfully into my tongue.

Choking on blood and sea water, I quickly crawled up the rock, not stopping until I was clear of where I thought the waves broke. When I looked back I could see Rick in the face of the next wave. There was an explosion of white-water, the ground shook, and his torn life jacket, minus Rick, was deposited right at my feet, the busted polystyrene buoyancy blocks floating around me. It was instantly sucked out in the next surge and disappeared.

Without even time to worry, there was a gasp and choking sound to one side of the rocks and Rick crawled up from a fissure in a huge slab of stone, bleeding heavily from the mouth. He spat out a shard of bloody tooth and lay beside me on the rock, nearly passing out from the effort.

We lay silent for ages after catching our breath, scarcely believing that we were both in one piece. I didn't even have the energy to check my legs and arms for breakages, and lay with my eyes closed for at least half an hour, only opening them briefly now and again to look at the cloudy sky. The clouds rolled quickly by, blown by the gale-force winds, and occasionally a brave bird would fly overhead, crabbing through the air in an attempt to cope with the gusts. A squawk in the rocks beside us gave me the horrible sensation that we were still on the islands where I'd seen the nesting bird, and I had to sit up to take a reality check.

I pulled a string of seaweed from my life jacket and looked down at Rick, lying next to me with his eyes closed, his hands behind his head. 'Rick.'

'Mmm?'

'It's going to be dark soon.'

'Mmm.' He opened one eye, still lying with his hands behind his head.

'Let's climb up and see what's over the top. We can't stay here.'

'Mmm.'

We clambered over the boulders, helping each other along until we reached the top of the cliff and found ourselves at the edge of a large expanse of grassland. I would call it a field but it wasn't cultivated; the word 'prairie' springs to mind, but that gives the impression of a field full of daisies swaying in the sunshine, like a scene from an American soap opera. Anyway, a windswept grassland greeted us, rugged and inhospitable, that reminded me of scenes from news footage of the Falkland Islands.

After debating which direction we should walk in, our minds were made up when we spotted a car on the horizon. It was obviously driving along a road, but from where we were at the bottom of the rising land it just appeared to be hovering on the grass.

'Run!' Rick shouted, and sprang forward towards the vehicle. 'Quick, John, before it goes.' Waving my life jacket above my head to attract attention, I ran after him, shouting at the top of my voice.

The car slowed, then turned and stopped, facing us and flashing its headlights.

'Fucking brilliant,' I shouted as we ran. 'Do you know any Indo, Rick?'

'Sudah kawin belum?' he panted.

'What does it mean?'

'"Are you married?" Titty taught me.'

There wasn't time to reply; I was too surprised at our good fortune at seeing the car. I'm surprised the guy didn't drive off; we must have looked like a pair of lunatics running across that field, waving a life jacket. Neither of us were wearing anything except shorts, and we were burnt to a crisp.

The driver wound down his window as we approached and leaned his elbow out, his large bearded face almost filling the space. He had so much facial hair that it was difficult to make out his features.

Rick held up a hand as we both doubled over, gasping to catch our breath. 'We are lost. Can you help us?'

The man turned around and smacked a dog that was slobbering all over the back seat before turning back to us. 'Where're you heading?'

'Great, you speak English,' I panted. 'Don't even know where we are.'

'Like that is it?' he chuckled. 'Well, come along with me if you want.' He reached over and opened the back door, shooing the hound to one side. 'Don't worry about him, he won't bitecha.'

'Whereabouts are you going?' Rick asked, stepping into the car.

'Just over there,' he replied. 'Darwin.'

F**K!

ONE

It took two days for the shock to wear off, and even then Rick and I walked around in a daze, continually shaking our heads in our shared disbelief. Whenever we caught each other's gaze during a quiet moment, we'd hold each other's eyes for a second before exhaling and saying, 'Unbelievable.'

Bob, the guy who'd given us a lift that first day, lived with his family in Darwin, in Australia's Northern Territories, and upon hearing our predicament, offered to put us up until we could sort ourselves out. He gave us some old clothes and we took full advantage of his offer to treat his home as our own, eating our way through the contents of his fridge.

During the daytime, while Bob was at work, Rick and I spent most of the first few days running over and analysing the events of the past weeks, trying to pin-point exactly how we had managed to get to Darwin. I don't think that either of us realised just how close Australia was to some of Indonesia's easternmost islands. Even though we'd been in possession of some excellent navigational charts, we had somehow blanked out the large land mass that looked like a blot of pink ink in the bottom corner of every sheet.

It was obvious to us now that the last bearing Dave had taken was correct, and that we had probably caught the storm somewhere around the cluster of islands near Damar. We had most likely sailed tantalisingly close to dozens of other islands without realising it; the rain being so heavy that we'd just passed them by. Within a few hours of leaving the reef that morning, our course had already taken us out of sight of land and into the Timor Sea, towards the north coast of Australia.

If Rick and I were not moping around looking at Bob's kid's atlas, we were moping around town wondering what to do next. We phoned the immigration at the airport with the intention of reporting everything and getting our passports stamped (Rick's waterproofing idea had worked) to make us bona fide entrants, but ended up arguing with the officials.

So, when it came to the interview with immigration, expecting no end of trouble convincing them what had happened, we didn't bother attending. It was quite likely that we would have had to explain about the boat, and one look at our passports would have shown that Singapore had been our last port of entry. All of this, despite the Dave factor, gave us little option but to forget the whole idea of getting an entry stamp, and with a last minute quip at the stern Aussie on the other end of the phone, Rick hung up. When I asked him what he'd said to the immigration officer, he replied: 'He asked me if I had a criminal record. So I said, "Why? Do you still need one to get into this country?"'

Talk about burning your boats!

We got to know Darwin pretty well over the time we spent at Bob's place. It was a bit like Milton Keynes, with flies. I'd always pictured it as some quaint outback town, with people riding around on horses, lassoing kangaroos, that sort of thing. A place where Aboriginal people sat around in dusty circles, either dancing or playing didgeridoos, waiting for dreamtime to begin. Instead what we found was a nondescript, medium-sized town with row upon row of newly-built semi-detached houses with front and back gardens and a car in every drive. The roads and streets were squeaky clean, and if you did't drink there was nothing else to do to pass the time but hang around the pedestrianised town centre watching drunkards abusing passers-by.

Bob showed us a few places that he considered to be of world-shattering significance, such as a nearby national park, but after travelling through Asia it paled by comparison: the 'wildlife' was just the odd lizard, while the 'great scenery' turned out to be not the huge canyons and stunning lakes that he had predicted, but rain-washed ravines and large ponds.

So, a few days later, when Bob told us that a friend of his was making the journey down into New South Wales and asked us if we wanted to go, we gladly accepted the offer. According to Bob it would soon be fruit-picking season in that part of the country, so we should easily be able to pick up work and earn ourselves enough to get sorted out. His friend was going to a place called Wagga Wagga, and said that he'd be passing by numerous orchards along the way, all of which were ready to start harvesting. The journey would take about three days if we shared the driving, and he promised to go through Alice Springs on the way so that we could all get to see Ayers Rock.

To my astonishment neither Bob nor his friend had ever been to Ayers Rock, and they said that neither had any other Australian. 'Who wants to stare at a fuckin' rock, mate?' 'Tourists?' I replied vacantly. I could see his point, though I felt like telling him that it could hardly be worse than his ponds and lizards.

The next morning we asked Bob's friend to drive us to Darwin's coast for one last look out to sea. It was a mistake. I should have known better than to gaze into the ocean, directly into Dave's watery eyes, filled with salt water and sad sea creatures, his lungs as much a part of the water as any gaping fish.

The expanse of wind-churned water in front of me slowly began to change into a bright blue Hat Rin day as my mind's eye opened and Dave came back to life. There he was, his ebony body jack-knifing off the rocks, resurfacing a moment later all white teeth and sagging afro. There he was, floating face-up, blowing fountains of water into the air and trying to catch them in his mouth, choking. Outside Bangkok airport, running around in the rain. Silent movies. I blinked, but he was still there, this time not alone but lying with me and Rick and the girls on the beach, all of us washed on to the shore like logs, giggling at one of his stupid comments, comments that were his way of telling a joke. Like all genuinely funny people he never actually told jokes.

I jumped as the car door slammed behind me, and I almost looked back, almost came back to the present but instead I only changed images. The realization hit me of just how reckless we had been, doing all these mad things with hardly a word to family or friends. How, absurdly, after so much time together, we didn't even know one another's personal details; no family address or contact numbers, nothing. I still didn't even know Rick's home address or phone number. Dave's poor mum and dad would grieve for years, expecting him to walk through their front door at any moment, going on believing he was having too good a time to call or write. Rick and I had anonymously informed all the appropriate authorities and had done everything possible, but with just a name we could only go so far.

I turned my head against the wind, first one way and then the other but it didn't work, the tears started to come again. Sniffing and turning away from Rick, but not before catching his gaze, I saw him trying to force his eyes wide open, the way children do to keep the tears where they don't belong. The weight of grief pressed down on our shoulders and I tried not to cry out, just letting some air escape in sickening, short, weak little breaths.

I don't know how long Rick and I stood there; maybe an hour, maybe more, long enough for me to go through all the emotions and back again.

'C'mon boys.' Bob's friend's hand slid over each of our shoulders.

Rick and I looked at each other, made a slit of the lips that wasn't a smile but a thought: shall we give in, go home to England? No, England wasn't home anymore and it would feel somehow wrong to Dave, as though we were throwing in the towel after only a token round or two. No fucking way.

We turned and stood, facing the retreating figure as he stepped into the car and fastened the seatbelt, and for a moment neither of us could move. I didn't dare look over my shoulder at the sea because I knew Dave was still there, and he'd be forced back up, back up inside me, tears waiting inside ducts.

The car engine whined into life.

Taking a deep breath, we stepped forward towards the car, wondering what lay ahead. I only knew one thing for sure: I didn't want to look out to sea again. Australia's barren outback should be just the ticket.

TWO

Pine Creek, Katherine, Tennant Creek, Alice Springs; all names that had sounded so romantic became nothing more than words on road signs or maps. Not because I didn't pay attention to the places we passed through, but because they were nothing more than names. Given a road atlas of Australia and seeing lots of dots along our route, I imagined that we would pass through towns, at least one of which I expected to satisfy my touristy eye. The dots and names, however, were nothing more than that: a creek or a single road-house surrounded by an expanse of waist-high green bushes that stretched as far as the eye could see. There wasn't even any desert to look at, not *real* desert.

Even Alice Springs, where we stayed overnight, was just like Darwin. We decided to forget Ayers Rock, and move on to a more civilised part of Australia. I think we must be the only foreigners to go though Alice without visiting the rock.

Eventually, after three days on the road, we neared Wagga Wagga and the countryside changed from one of extreme monotony to one which was only slightly less boring. Very similar to England in fact. Row after row after row of cultivated orchards stretching off to the next hillside like fields of corduroy.

'It's your choice boys,' Bob's friend shifted gear and crossed the small bridge over a picturesque stream as a tractor pulled out of a side lane, 'take your pick. You're in the heart of fruit-picking country now, so if your gonna get work it'll be around here somewhere.' He double-clutched and we shot past the tractor.

A road sign said *Batlow 2*, and I watched it pass before saying to Bob's friend, 'Where do you think?'

F**K!

'Well I'm going to Wagga, but there's not much there for you two blokes. You'd be better off around here.'

'Drop us off in the next village,' Rick said without looking from the window.

'Next place is Batlow, I think. That should do you, there are always plenty of orchard workers there. Just go to the RSL club, someone's bound to need help.'

Rick turned around and we both said, 'What's the RSL club?'

'Returned Servicemen's League. Sounds a bit militaristic, but it's not, it's really just a pub. There are hundreds of them all over the country.'

Rick looked at me and I shrugged. I just wasn't sure any more. To say I had doubts is an understatement; neither of us had any clothes to speak of, and I knew that the minute we got dropped off it would mean we would have to find a job or starve.

After five minutes of silent driving we turned off the main road and entered what looked like the main street of a village. There was a bank at one end, a few decrepit looking shops and houses along both sides and a large pub, before the road curved back out of town.

Bob's friend pulled up outside the RSL club. 'This is it, boys,' he said, and smiled awkwardly at us.

We thanked him and got out of the car. Instinctively I searched for my bag, and I noticed Rick doing the same, before realising we didn't have any. We looked at each other over the roof of the car and both made a frightened face, to cover the fact that we really were frightened, and I slapped the roof with the palm of my hand.

'Good luck,' Bob's friend shouted, and drove off, leaving us two staring after him.

Two minutes later we were standing at the other end of town, wondering if we had been dropped off in the wrong place by mistake.

'Fuck,' I said, looking in the window of a small supermarket at the clock on the wall, 'only three o'clock. Three more hours until that RSL place opens, Rick.'

303

'Mm,' he sat down on a wall, 'and there's no guarantee that we'll meet anyone who can give us work when it does. This place looks pretty dead to me.'

Apart from Bob's friend, and the woman at the checkout in the supermarket, we hadn't seen another person. One car had driven by, but otherwise the place was deserted.

I looked up and down the road, hoisting up Bob's trousers that were two sizes too big. 'Least it's not raining,' I remarked, and leaned against the plate glass shop window.

Rick thought for a moment, looking up at the sky as though checking the likelihood of rain. 'I don't like just waiting around for something to happen, do you? I feel better if I'm on the move.'

I nodded. 'Proactive, yeah. We could walk out of here and just go on to one of the orchards and ask for a job. It's got to be better than sitting here.'

He stood up. 'How much money have you got?'

I pulled out my passport, inside of which were ten Aussie dollars, and held it up.

'Ten. I've got five that's fifteen. Let me have it.' He took the money and disappeared into the supermarket, emerging a moment later with a two ounce packet of tobacco, cigarette papers and a box of matches. 'That's the last of the money gone. Let's get going.'

I was stunned. 'Shouldn't we have spent it on food?'

'Food?' He laughed. 'You're in the middle of about a million square miles of orchard!'

Within five minutes of leaving the village we were walking alongside vast open fields of fruit trees, each one sloping off gently either side of the road. Snatched glimpses of bright warm sunshine came and went as the clouds blew across the huge sky, making fast dark shadows on the rolling green hills. The weather was considerably colder than it had been in Darwin and I felt, for the first time since leaving England, what fresh air unladen with moisture, tasted like.

F**K!

For the first half an hour of walking the air actually hurt my lungs, and I wondered whether constantly breathing tropical air had turned them into saturated sponges. Rick said his hurt too, which made me feel better, so we decided that a roll-up was just what the doctor ordered, and smoked constantly, only occasionally stopping to eat a stolen apple.

A few cars passed us by as we walked, but none of them offered to give us a lift. One of them did stop, and when we enquired about the surrounding orchards, the occupants just shook their heads and said they only ate the fruit, they had no idea who or what picked it.

We kept on walking, and, for the first few hours at least, felt reasonably happy. As the sun got lower and lower in the sky, however, and the wind chilled, I began to wonder what we had done to deserve the punishment. My feet and legs started to ache, and what started out as a quick walk into the surrounding orchards was soon turning into a route march in which Rick and I both began to complain about Bob's friend. Although we had been walking beside orchards, there didn't appear to be any beginning or end to them, they just ran for mile after mile without any sign of an entrance gate or farm house.

I sat down on the roadside grass verge with a sigh, leaning against a fence post. 'D'you think we should turn back? I'm shattered.'

'Too late.' Rick looked back along the road that wound its way, seemingly, to infinity. 'Anyway, what'd be the point? We haven't got any money for a hotel room, and we can't even buy a beer in the pub.' He vaulted the wire fence and went into the orchard, disappearing from view.

I pulled off one of Bob's son's trainers to inspect my feet and got a nasty shock. What I'd taken to be sweat causing my foot to slide around in the shoe was in fact the pus from a huge blister on my heel that had burst. Seeing it made my feet feel worse and I regretted taking the sock off. The cool air felt nice on them though, so I took the other one off and wiggled my toes.

The fence post wobbled and Rick landed an inch from my foot, making me draw it back quickly. 'Get that down you,' he said, holding out a peach that was bigger than a cricket ball. When I held it, encircling it with both hands, the tops of my fingers and thumbs just managed to touch. It must have weighed about two pounds.

'That's deformed,' I said, bouncing it my palm. Inserting both thumbs into the dimple of the fruit, I split it in half. A huge grub fell on to my lap. 'Uggh! I don't know what fertiliser they use around here, but that's going to turn into a mother of a moth.' It crawled off into the grass and I stood up on one foot, splattering the peach on the road, thoroughly disgusted by the sight.

'There're people starving in India, John,' Rick said laughing, and bit into his own peach.

'Well they can eat it then. Fuck, that's disgusting. Trust you to find that funny.' I pulled on my sock and shoe, suddenly feeling drops of water on the back of my neck, and looked up. 'Oh no, please God, not now!'

'What were you saying about the weather?'

We quickened the pace to a cover of large trees at the top of the hill and took our bearings. Cows and sheep were dotted about for miles around, and in the bottom of the valley, about two miles away, was what looked like a small out-building of some kind. About half a mile further on we could see a house with smoke drifting up from a chimney, and, beyond that, another orchard with ant-sized people milling about. I could just see a track leading up to the house, but it seemed to go off in the opposite direction to us.

'What d'you reckon?' Rick asked, looking into the valley, apparently reading my thoughts.

'Definitely. It's either that or get wet.' I looked up at the sky. 'It's going to be dark in half an hour and I don't want to be stumbling around out here at night.'

'Poof.'

I shrugged.

'Let's get moving then, city boy. I'll show you how it's done.' He put his hands on a fence post. 'Just follow me.'

'We could be shot for trespassing you know?' I said, causing him to pause mid-vault.

Bob's flared trousers snagged on a wire twist and Rick was sent face first on to the ground on the other side, one hand sinking up to his wrist in cow shit. 'Fooking hell.'

'Maybe we ought to find the road into the place,' I said, looking down at him and suppressing a giggle, 'that way looks pretty dangerous to me.'

He pulled himself up, wiping the shit on to the fence. 'Come on. We could walk for hours looking for the entrance.'

We traipsed down the hill into the valley, towards the out-building, Rick trying to smoke himself into an early grave, while I tried hard to block out the cows in the field, all of which seemed to be staring menacingly at me.

'Rick, are you sure there are no bulls in this field?'

'It's all bull, John,' he said angrily, hunching up against the cold. 'Fooking hell, why didn't we stay in the tropics?'

The distance was deceptive. Either that or we underestimated how quickly the sun sets in the southern hemisphere. Before we'd even got halfway it was dark, and I couldn't tell the difference between cowpats and dips in the ground through the blackness. 'Rick, this is ridiculous,' I huffed, picking myself up for the umpteenth time. 'Where's that building we saw earlier?'

He stopped just ahead of me. 'Up that way, I think. Come on, just keep moving.'

The rain had slowed to a steady drizzle by the time we spotted the building again, and this time we just walked towards it, saying nothing to each other until we were standing outside. Without any moonlight it looked like a bungalow, but when I went up to it and rapped on the wall I realised it was only made of corrugated iron, and that it must indeed be some kind of out-building. 'A shed of some kind,' I said in a hushed voice.

'Why are you whispering?' Rick whispered back.

We circled it once and found that the building had a few windows but that they were either boarded over or smashed, and that the front porch was rank with accumulated cow shit, piled a foot deep on the floor.

'A cow shed?' Rick suggested, putting one hand on the doorknob.

'Or sheep,' I replied, pulling a tuft of wool from a jagged edge of the corrugated iron. I looked up the hillside to where I could just see lights flickering through the evening mist. 'Do you think we should go up to the house first and ask them if it's OK?'

'What, "Hello, I've got no money and nowhere to stay, please help me"?' He turned the doorknob and slowly pushed the door open. It creaked and groaned then fell off its hinges, crashing on to the wooden floorboards. Something flew out of the dark room, making us both leap sideways with a start. 'Shit, what was that?'

'A bat,' I said panting with fright, my heart thumping. 'Well, if there is anyone in here they've definitely heard us now.'

The building was sub-divided into four large rooms, all of which had corrugated iron walls, a sloping corrugated iron roof and boarded wooden floors. There were piles of fleeces everywhere, and we guessed that it must have been intended as living quarters for the shearers because the room we had first entered contained a brick fireplace.

After an initial recce under the light of a burning rolled-up newspaper that served as a cobweb burner as much as anything else, we pulled up a few floorboards from one of the rooms and built a fire. The room also contained a wooden table and some chairs, all of which ended up as fuel. We overdid it a bit, and soon we were both sitting as far away from the hearth as possible without actually leaving the room to escape the heat. Our clothes were laid out on the floor, steaming as they dried, while the pair of us sat there in our underpants and watched the flames as they licked up one of the chair legs.

'I hope no one lives here,' I said, hypnotised by the dancing flames.

Rick shrugged. 'Well if they do they won't have a table to eat off any more.'

THREE

The dreams came and went that night like butterflies flying in and out of an open window on a spring morning. I use the butterfly analogy simply because one of the dreams was about butterflies flying in and out of windows. Butterflies, a dream about cows with human heads, and one about maggots, no doubt inspired by the huge peach. John and the giant peach, Rick called it.

Rick also said that he'd dreamt a lot on that first night, though his were much, much weirder and harder to fathom than mine. In one of his nightmares he gave birth to a sheep, and the sheep, in turn, gave birth to him. I analysed it for him, saying that it meant that we had created a new episode in our travels, and that it indicated a new start for him, hence the second birth. He nodded wisely and said what a load of bollocks I talked, before throwing more chairs on to the fire and slithering back under a fleece.

We woke constantly through the night, only snatching the odd hour or two of sleep. We'd feed the flames until they were licking around the mantelpiece and slip back into a dream, only to find an hour later that the tinder-dry wood had burnt itself out and the room was freezing once again. Rick found two more battered old bug-infested fleeces that fell apart when he picked them up, but we gathered them together, along with all the other bundles of sheep's wool we could find, and made a kind of loose quilt. It stank to high heaven and made me scratch non-stop, but it was beautifully warm, and in the early hours I awoke again, this time in a pool of sweat.

Rick got the shock of his life when he woke to find a six-foot tall sheep walking around the room on its hind legs, lit only by the flickering orange glow of the fire. It couldn't have helped his state of mind much to have been halfway through the sheep dream at the time. I had got up to go to the toilet outside, and most of the sheep's wool was still stuck to the sweat on my body. Rick hadn't seen me go out but he later told me that the sound of the broken door being moved to one side had woken him from the dream. Still half-dazed he'd looked up to see this huge white, two-legged sheep staring back at him. He was about to jump up and run when the sheep turned around and had the decency to put the door quietly back into its hole, revealing very un-sheep-like boxer shorts. Putting another table leg on to the fire, I slipped back under the fleece, staring back at Rick's astonished eyes, his face a mask of perspiration. 'Thank God,' he gasped, turned over and went back to sleep.

There were a lot of creepy shadows in the shed too. Not just shadows created and brought to life by the flames, but other smaller, darker shadows that crept around in corners, or scurried across the floorboards. Bob had told us horror stories of the spiders that had their home in Australia, and New South Wales in particular. And, as if that wasn't particular enough, I remembered him saying that we'd never come into contact with any because it was unlikely that we'd ever live in an old out-building, which is where the most deadly species tended to nest. Great, I thought, of all the places to live we choose Black Widow Central. The wool made my skin crawl anyway, but the thought of spiders creeping on to my head while I was asleep filled me with horror. I harboured a nightmare scenario whereby one of them crawled up my neck and laid eggs in one of my ears. Two weeks later I'd be complaining of earache when suddenly, while shaving in a mirror, the side of my head would explode into an avalanche of tiny spiders.

Scared out of my wits by now, I decided to stay awake for the few remaining hours before dawn and went outside for a cigarette. The rain had stopped and the sloping field was knee-deep in white fog, as though someone somewhere had flicked a switch and turned on a dry ice machine. Just as the sky was brightening, the shed door was pulled aside and Rick emerged, rubbing sleep from his eyes, a plume of wool sticking out from the top of his sweater like the chest hair of an old man.

He leaned the door back against the opening, tutting loudly, and walked out into the misty early morning air, standing and looking back at the dramatic effect in the surrounding field. 'Wow.'

'Beautiful, huh?' I took in our surroundings. Behind the shed, in the direction we had walked from the previous night, the field sloped downwards for about a hundred metres until it hit what must have been a small stream. I don't remember having crossed a stream, but what else causes a valley? Perhaps 'valley' is a bit misleading because the slope was very gentle, only about ten degrees either side, so maybe it was just a base where two hills touched.

Anyway, geographic genesis aside, the opposite field then rose back up the other side for a mile to the road. Either side of the shed were yet more grassy fields, bordered with large trees that were either the start of a forest or just a boundary line; it was hard to tell from where we stood. At the base of the trees, and around various parts of the field, cows lay sleeping, their backs appearing like black and white boulders above the mist.

At the front of our shed was another hundred yards of field, hemmed-in by a wire fence, beyond which were orchards and the house we'd seen the previous night. Two houses in fact. Nobody seemed to be awake yet so we walked up to the fence and sat on the entrance gate. I didn't really want to be caught sleeping in someone's private property, so it seemed like a good place to wait, and Rick agreed . . . sort of.

'They know we're here already,' he said, concentrating on the cigarette he was rolling. 'Judging by the amount of wood we burned last night I should think that half of Australia knows we're here.'

There didn't seem to be much smoke coming from the chimney, but as he was from a relatively remote part of England where real fires were probably the norm, I didn't question his logic. 'Have you ever worked on a farm before?' I asked. He shook his head without looking up from his task. 'Do you think it's hard work?'

'Terrible. You have to get up at the crack of dawn.'

'I don't mind getting up the crack of Dawn.'

'Get up *at* the crack of dawn,' he corrected, 'milk cows, shovel shit, mend fences, repair tractors ...' he reeled off a list of labour-intensive jobs and ended by saying, 'and generally break your back.'

'And how much does one get paid for such Herculean effort?' I asked, knowing what the reply would be.

'Sweet FA. If you're lucky.' He put the finished cigarette between his lips. 'Aren't you glad you came?'

An engine started up and we both turned to see a cloud of white exhaust steam appear beside the house. 'You're right about the crack of dawn,' I said, looking up at the sky. 'Shit, it can't be five o'clock. What can he be doing at this time? It's hardly light enough to see.'

'Fooking farmers!'

More revving was followed by the crunch of wheels rolling over gravel, and a Land Rover came out from between the trees, free-wheeling slowly towards us. We both jumped down off the gate and watched as the car came down the track and pulled up beside us. The handbrake was put on and the driver got out. Grey-bearded and ruddy-faced, he looked a lot like Bob, only shorter. I was just about to apologise for using his shed when he spoke first.

'Morning,' he said brusquely. 'Had a good sleep?'

'Yeah,' we said in unison, 'thanks.'

His eyes shifted and looked over our shoulders, as though checking that we hadn't burnt down his property. He obviously knew that we had stayed in the shed, so he must know about the fire.

'A bit cold though,' I added.

'Got any blankets?' His voice was soft, matching his small build.

Shocked by his seeming benevolence, I hesitated. 'Um, no. We just used some of the wool that was inside the shed.'

He chuckled. 'You know that's fanny wool don't you?'

Rick and I looked at each other. 'What do you mean?'

'From around the sheep's hole, hee-hee. When the rams are in season we shave the holes of all the sheep for easy penetration, yeahh.' His tobacco-stained teeth stuck out like yellow talons from his uncontrolled facial hair every time he laughed, and he said 'yeahh' in all the wrong places, even when asking a question, making everything sound like a statement of fact. His Aussie drawl made the word sound like a car engine being switched off; starting high and ending low, or like gas escaping.

'Anyway,' he continued, rolling his small shoulders, 'it won't do you any harm. So, you boys need work do you? Well, I'll need more pickers now that the season's coming up, yeahh. Got a few of your lot already started but they're next to fucking useless, yeahh.'

His eyes wobbled in their sockets as though he was watching from a train window as the countryside flashed by, trying to focus on something steady. It was very unsettling to talk to someone whose eyes constantly moved so rapidly, but eventually we got the hang of it and said that we'd do whatever was required.

'What about food, yeahh, and money?'

We shook our heads.

'You got a tent? Most of our pickers are living in tents in the top field.' He pointed over towards the orchard. 'Got a toilet and shower block there, yeahh. Washing machine too.'

He reminded me of a leprechaun with his soft squeaky voice and small build. His grey eyebrows were arched and bushy through years of frowning, and the ends were twiddled slightly as though pointing and saying, 'they went thataway'. We shook our heads to the tent question.

'Well listen,' he said, 'you two blokes can use the shed; we've finished shearing. Just don't burn the fucking thing down, yeahh. As for food, I can give you some bread for today, and I suggest that you start picking with the others at seven,' he looked at his watch. 'That's one hour from now, yeahh. My wife will show you what to do and how the payment system works. We usually pay at the end of the week, but I'll pay you for what you pick today and then one of the blokes'll run you into town to get a stove and food. Get sorted out. OK?'

I nodded. 'OK.'

'OK.'

'Yeahh.'

FOUR

That first week in the orchard was the worst. The worst week in the orchard and probably the worst week of my life. After our initial meeting with Jack, the owner who'd met us that first morning, we were each given a big leather satchel and a ladder and directed to the rows of trees where we were to start picking.

To begin with, Jack's wife, Joan, gave us a demonstration of how to, and how not to pick apples and pears. She showed us how each fruit had to be carefully pinched at the top of its stalk, where it joined the branch, so that it remained attached to the fruit, which enabled them to get a better price at market. Apparently, the Japanese who bought the fruit liked to see the stalk still in it. Each one had to be carefully placed into the satchel so as not to bruise it against the others, and when the satchel was full it could be emptied into a bin.

'Bins' were in fact huge wooden crates, four feet long by three feet wide and four feet deep. Once Joan had filled her bag she climbed back down the ladder and, leaning over the ledge of the bin at a back-breaking angle, gently rolled the fruit into the bottom.

'Right,' she said airily to everyone standing around watching, 'no time to waste, let's get picking!' She turned to me. 'You can have this bin, I've already started it for you.'

I leaned over and looked in at the precious few apples huddled in one corner, lost against the cavernous walls of the crate, and said, 'How much money do we get for each bin?' I knew that everyone else was thinking the same thing so I thought I might as well ask.

As well as Rick and me, a few other backpackers had arrived from Sydney over the weekend and were also present at the demo. One of them was a Swede called Noel who, upon witnessing Joan's one and only attempt at fruit picking, immediately snatched a satchel and flew off into the orchard with a ladder before he'd even been told how much we would be paid.

'That's the spirit,' Joan enthused. 'Let's hope everyone's as keen as him. Now, what did you say?' She took the satchel from around her neck and hung it on the tree, as though any questions should come second to our love of working for her.

'How much per bin?' I repeated.

'Now, you can choose any row you want, but you must start at that end and work your way down, otherwise the guy laying out the bins'll get confused.' She took a ripe apple from the tree and began to polish it. 'The tractor driver brings out the bins and lays them at even spaces, as you see, so unless there're more apples on a tree than normal, there should be enough bins. If there isn't, just give me a shout and I'll get one down to you. Seventeendollarsabin. Any questions?'

As mumbled as the answer was, I extracted the relevant piece of information and was about to ask how long it would take to fill one bin, when she went on the defensive.

'But a good picker can fill a bin an hour, easy.' She reflected, gazing up lovingly at her trees. 'Huh, we've had professional pickers here that have done fifteen bins in a day, no worries. So you see, you really can earn quite a lot of money if you work hard.' She picked up her jacket, putting the polished apple into the pocket. 'I'll be walking around most of the day to see how you're getting on. Ladders are there, satchels in that bin. Good luck.' And she was gone.

That first day Rick and I, and the other newcomers, managed one bin each after four hours of work. We couldn't manage a full day, and gave up by lunchtime. Constantly climbing up and down a ten-foot ladder that often toppled sideways, throwing the picker painfully against the sharp branches, left my arms and legs torn to pieces, and my legs shaking from the exertion. And the weight of a bag full of apples hanging around my neck, pulling my head forward at such an unnatural angle for so many hours, and then having to bend over at right angles to empty them into the bin was back-breaking.

By one o'clock neither of us could walk, and we just went back to the shed and lay on the floor, silently wondering if we'd done something wrong in a past life to deserve such punishment. I had so many cuts and bruises I couldn't count them all. My legs and arms looked like a hundred cats had used them as a scratching post; a mass of thin red lines, each terminating in a tiny bead of blood. And, as if that wasn't bad enough, we were both covered in a thick layer of dust and grime that neither of us had the energy to get up and wash off. Instead, when it started to rain again that evening, we just stood outside and had a shower in the run-off from the corrugated iron roof.

We'd been given some bread and blankets as promised by Jack, and had re-lit the fire using wood that was scattered all over the surrounding fields and forest, so at least we were warm. We were offered a lift into town by one of the locals to spend our hard-earned seventeen dollars, but both of us were too tired to take him up on it and just fell asleep.

The rest of the week improved gradually, and by the weekend we were flat out at two bins each a day, though we were putting in six hours by that time. If anyone ever tells me that slavery was abolished at the turn of the century, I'd tell them to go to the orchards of Australia and see it for themselves. They should send school kids down as a sort of living history lesson.

The weather had also improved by the end of the first week, though that didn't help much, and instead of being cold at night and reasonably comfortable during the day, it was cold at night and hot and dusty during the day. The mornings were freezing cold, but by nine o'clock the sweaters would come off and we'd change among the trees into shorts and flip-flops for the day's slog under the burning sun.

One drawback to wearing shorts in the orchard, though, was the constant attack from March flies. These insects have the same anatomy as a normal house fly but are the size of a thumbnail, and on the end of their head they have a long stiff tube that they push through to break the victim's skin and suck out the blood. It's impossible to be vigilant while picking fruit, so the first you know of an attack is when you feel a sharp sting. Trying to shake them off doesn't deter them, and you have to actually flick them off, usually leaving a blob of blood behind, and sometimes the snapped-off proboscis with it.

Rick thought my fear of these flies bordered on paranoia, and taunted me cruelly, hiding in trees and flicking twigs at me, making me twitch and flinch all morning like someone with a nervous shake. He kept this up for a few days, skulking and sniggering among the trees, until one of them crawled up the leg of his shorts while he was picking and bit him on the scrotum.

The weird thing about the March flies was that they only appeared in the morning, and by the time the dew had dried on the grass at around ten o'clock they were gone. *They* were gone, but by ten-thirty they'd been replaced by clouds of normal flies and wasps that swarmed all over us, attracted by the sweet juice from the busted fruit that had been trampled underfoot. The best way around this problem was to get as close to the tree's trunk as possible, surrounding oneself in leaves.

On the home front, by the end of the first week we had secured the sheep shed and tried to make it a bit more liveable. All of the windows were now boarded up to stop the cold night wind from howling through, and we even managed to screw the front door back on its hinges. We found some old carpet in one of the rooms, another table, and some planks of wood that we balanced on piles of bricks and used as beds, to keep us off the ground and away from spiders.

We also now had a camping-style, single ring gas stove and two pots for cooking that we'd bought second-hand in Batlow's Oxfam shop. Our cheques from Jack were issued at the end of the week, and we went on a spending spree, buying, among other things: warm clothes, shoes, a pillow each, cups and anything else that we considered essential, but cheap. Toothpaste and razors were a luxury that we thought we could afford, and I even bought an air freshener for the sheep shed.

We celebrated that Friday night by going into town to the RSL club with two of the Aussie pickers from the orchard. One of them, Albert, who was a helpless alcoholic but had a beaten up old car that broke down every mile, managed to get us to the pub before closing time, and what we hadn't spent on food and clothes earlier was spent on drink. By the time we got back to the shed at midnight we'd forgotten all about fruit picking for the time being, and drifted happily to sleep by the fireside, imagining that we were lying on a beautiful tropical beach once again.

FIVE

A month or so after our arrival, Rick got the most sought-after job on the orchard (outside of Jack and Joan's); the job of driving the tractor that collected the bins. He was in heaven. Not only was it the only way of getting paid on the orchard without doing physical work, but he also got an hourly rate, which meant he could skive. The rest of us were sick with envy.

'How the fuck did you manage to get that job?' I shouted as he walked down between my row of trees, grinning and waving the keys to the tractor. I climbed down the ladder, already perspiring heavily in the mid-morning heat, wiping the sweat and dust from my face. 'It's not possible.'

He sat on the edge of my half-filled bin and looked in at the apples, taking one out to eat. 'Is that all you've done so far this morning? Tut tut tut.'

'I can't believe it. You? The cushiest job of all?' I took the satchel off my neck and threw it, apples and all, into the trees.

'Don't sulk.'

'Yeah, right.' I picked up an apple and pelted it against one of the other bins, exploding it into tiny, juicy segments. 'Fuck this for a game of soldiers. I can't do this job any more, not knowing that you've got it so easy.'

'Who says I've got it easy? Driving that tractor's hard work.' He rolled two cigarettes and handed one to me. 'It's a bit early for smoke, but seeing as how I'm in charge an' all . . . Only kidding.'

I took the cigarette and sat down. 'What happened to the other guy?'

'Had to go back to Sydney. His daughter's still here, though, but she can't drive. Reckon I might be in there.'

'Rather you than me.'

'Got a nice tent. All mod cons: TV, video, fridge. She makes a wicked dinner too, better than that stuff we've been living off. I'm pig sick of tinned stew.'

The cigarette tasted horrid so I flicked it away. 'What's the money like?'

'Hourly. Works out about the same as picking.'

'Yeah, except all you have to do is sit on a fucking tractor and smoke all day.' I leaned forward and rubbed my aching back. 'Just think how much pleasure you're going to get watching us suffer.'

'The thought had crossed my mind,' he said, turning the apple around in his hand.

'You've got the best job here and you're going to be shagging the only decent bird in the place. Bastard.' I brought my knees up to my chest and sighed. 'When d'you start?'

'Now. All I've got to do is take myself up to the top and pick up the tractor. I'll give you my bin, it's half full.'

I thanked him with appropriate sarcasm, and we finished another cigarette before he left. It didn't taste any better than the first so I stubbed it out on an apple and buried it under the rest in the bin. 'Rick,' I shouted after him as he walked back up the row, 'try to find out if there's any way of fiddling these bin tickets, so I can get the money without doing the work.'

'As far as I know Joan keeps the ticket book and stubs, but I'll check it out. See you back at the shed for lunch.'

I stood transfixed, watching as he swaggered down to the end of the trees and turned past the last, before screaming at the top of my lungs and punching the apples with anger.

When I started picking again, instead of pinching the apples at the stalk and removing them one by one, I just ripped off whole branches and chucked them into the bin, leaves and all, I was so angry. No longer caring about whether or not the fruit was bruised, and checking quickly that Joan wasn't spying on me, I gripped two of the largest branches on the tree and shook. A hundred apples fell to the ground. Astonished, I repeated the motion on a different side of the tree and got the same result. 'Fuck it,' I mumbled, and walked around the tree shaking until there wasn't a single fruit left hanging.

The whole lot was scooped up and the bin filled. Cleverly, or so I thought at the time, I spread a layer of the best apples over the top of the others to hide the bruised and unripe ones that weren't supposed to go in, and started on the next tree in the line.

Gossip is rife among the pickers of Australia, and what goes on in one orchard today is tomorrow's news in another orchard of New South Wales, and next week's news in a Northern Territory banana orchard. The gossip usually revolves around how easy it is to pick grapes compared to mangoes, and how much one can earn picking peaches as opposed to pears, and so on. If the discussion is based upon practices within the same region, say NSW, the comparisons are usually about the size of a particular fruit. This is a picker's bread and butter, because the bigger the apple, for example, the quicker he or she can fill each bin and the more they can make. Picking a bin full of small, tennis ball-sized Granny Smiths may require three hours hard slog, while working on large Red Delicious which are twice the size of the Grannies takes half that time.

In short it's vital to know which orchards have the biggest fruit, and whether the orchard you're working on has any large stuff at all. Most places grow different varieties to maximise profit, and it was this that formed the topic of conversation with the other pickers a few weeks later at the pub.

'You see,' Ted said, taking a sip of his bitter, 'you've got your Red

Delicious on all the orchards around these parts, and I say we-mmm-fuck off to another grower.' When Ted spoke he emitted a high-pitched hum, mid-sentence, higher than a bee and not unlike a mosquito. It was normally accompanied by him breaking wind.

Albert, who returned to Jack and Joan's every season, was on friendlier terms with them than the rest of us. He looked sceptical and took a sip from his beer. I listened intently. Rick sat and drank, never saying a word but listening nervously. He was in an awkward position now that he'd got the tractor job. He was still one of us, but his new line of work had brought him into greater contact with the management of the orchard, and some pickers had stopped talking to him. He was doing his best to stay neutral in any argument, but I think that just made people a little unsure, perhaps wondering whether what they said would get back to Jack.

Ted had no such doubts. 'I've picked fruit all over this country,' he continued, stabbing a forefinger on the table, 'from bananas to bloody oranges, and I've never earned so little as I'm getting now, and that's a fact. Jesus, I've never seen apples so-mmm-fucking small.'

I nodded.

'Look,' said Albert pleadingly, 'we've got Red Delicious on our orchard, they're just not ripe yet. When they are, we'll pick them.' He started to roll a cigarette. 'Every orchard's the same, they can't pick the fruit until it's ready, you should know that.'

'They've been telling us that for over two months now, Al.' I took up where Ted had left off. 'When I first came here Joan told me not to worry; the first week or so we'll be picking small fruit, waiting for the other stuff to ripen, and then we'll all be quids-in. It's just her bullshit.'

Albert looked embarrassed, suddenly realising that he sounded just like Joan, and hid behind his beer.

'I have to say, Al,' Rick said evenly, 'I think they're stringing it out a bit too far this time. Two months and they're still not ripe?'

'It takes time.'

'Then why did she tell me two weeks, max?' I took a sip of beer. 'I've got no intention of going to another orchard, but from what Ted's told me no one gets as little as seventeen dollars a bin for fruit that small.'

Albert looked dismissively at Ted. He went to take another sip of beer but Ted put his hand out, resting it in the crook of Albert's drinking arm.

'Matey, matey, matey, don't give me that "don't rock the fucking boat" mmm-cock and bullshit, please! You know as well as I do that you, me and every other fucking Aussie on that orchard is drawing dole money once a fortnight.' Albert's beer spilt so Ted took his hand away. 'It don't matter to us one way or the other if you pick reds, greens or fucking multi-coloureds. These blokes,' he stabbed a finger at me, 'these-mmm-backpackers are the ones who're being exploited.'

'He's right,' I said nodding. 'We've got no dole money and we've got no rights either. We're all working illegally. Every foreigner on that orchard, except those two Scottish girls, is working illegally. No one's got a work permit and Jack knows it. That's why he tells us to hide every time a car pulls up, in case it's the immigration doing a sweep, you know that Al. We all fill out tax forms with false names and addresses just as he tells us to so that he can claim the tax back, while us poor sods put in eight-hour days for a few measly dollars. It's bullshit!' I slammed a hand down on the table. 'I don't mind putting in the hours, but he's got to pay the going rate for the fruit, and from what I've heard he's not doing that. Seventeen bucks a bin for that fruit is too low, and I'm going to do something about it.' I gulped down my beer.

'I don't see what you can do,' Albert said nervously, 'there's no union for fruit pickers, least not illegal foreign ones.' He looked at Ted to see if it was worth chancing a drink before lifting the glass.

Ted put his hand out, stopping him again. 'That's exactly the kind of fucking attitude that's fucked this-mmm-country up. That's the reason I left here once before.'

'Can I drink my beer please, Ted?'

He released Albert's arm but put his hand back immediately as he thought of something else to say.'No, you're right, there is no union, but we can-mmm-sure as hell start one.' He sat back triumphantly and farted, wafting his hand in front of his face. 'Fuck me, been eating too many apples.'

Albert quickly seized the opportunity and gulped down the beer, emptying the glass. It was his round and he went up to the bar. A minute or two later he came back with the drinks and about twenty packets of crisps.

We tried to change the subject away from the slavery of the orchards on to something lighter, but the atmosphere was set. Whatever we talked about we either came back to the subject of wage rates and the rights of workers, or we thought about it. I could see by the look on everyone's face that their minds were elsewhere.

Unusually for a Friday night we left the RSL club at nine o'clock to make our way back to the orchard. Outside in the car park, a simple but very important split occurred that was subtle, yet as fundamental as anything that had been said in the bar. Rick and I had been driven into town, as usual, by Albert, but when we got outside I went over to Ted's car. I wasn't thinking, it just happened automatically.

'See you back at base,' I called over to the others.

Rick put a hand up and got into Albert's car.

Back at the orchard Ted asked me to go up to the main field with him for a night-cap, but I could see Rick waiting for me in the sheep shed field so I declined his offer, saying that the beer had made me feel tired. He dropped me off and I walked down to the shed.

When I got inside Rick was lighting the fire. I went over to the table to boil some water for tea. 'Hungry?' I asked.

'I've thrown the sausages away,' Rick called, reading my mind. 'They were fly-blown.'

'Fuck, nothing lasts in this place. Black and Gold tinned stew it is then.'

'None for me,' he said without looking away from the fire. Rick seemed uncharacteristically pensive, and was tearing off little strips of a cardboard box to get the wood started rather than putting the whole thing on as we usually did.

Rick lit the fire and sat on his bed. 'It's Ted you want to watch out for, John. He's a nice old bloke and all that, but I know what Jack's like; if anyone rocks the boat he'll give them the boot.'

I tutted. 'Oh leave it out, you're scaring me. You sound just like Joan. That job's gone to your fucking head.'

He looked at the fire. 'Do you want stay here, John? I don't. All I want to do is get enough money together so that we can get back into Asia again, or South America, that's all.' He looked around. 'Don't forget that. Don't start fighting for the rights of fruit pickers in Australia. Fook 'em. Fook 'em all. You and me have got our own dreams, and it's not living in this fooking shithole. If you get chucked out of here, then what?' I didn't reply. 'No, just keep your head down, save the money and let's get going. In two months the season'll be finished and we'll have enough for a flight out. One of the only things you saved from the boat was your pocket atlas, so I know you don't want to stay in one place.'

I slumped on the bed. 'They're taking the piss though, Rick. We can't earn any money. At this rate it'll take me forever just to get the price of a train ticket to Sydney, let alone a plane ticket!'

He sighed. 'Just steer clear of Ted, that's all I'm saying. He may sound very brave in the bar, but when Jack shows him the door on Monday he won't think it's so funny.'

'Gate,' I corrected.

'Whatever. He won't look so clever then. Albert's well in with Jack, and you can bet your bottom dollar that he's up at his house now telling him what was said in the pub.'

We didn't say much more that night, and after the gas bottle ran out I went straight to bed, hungry. At least I think it was hunger, I was still so angry about being cheated over the price of bins it was hard to tell.

As usual I dreamt a lot that night. I dreamt about beaches and girls, and I dreamt about being home in England, which was very unusual. But more than anything else, I dreamt about revolution.

SIX

The straw that broke the camel's back; salt sprinkled on already painful hand blisters is what came at the end of that week when, instead of being moved on to pick the Red Delicious as promised, we were all told to pick another variety. Far from going on to that huge, mythical fruit (where one apple could fill a whole bin!), we were guided, with our ladders, to an area of the orchard that none of us even knew existed. In this section of the field, the trees hadn't been pruned, making it harder to pick, and the fruits on those trees were not much bigger than walnuts.

There was a collective sigh from the dozen or so assembled pickers as we trudged off to our different row of trees (even the Swedish guy only jogged), each person's head hanging down at the prospect of having to work twice as hard for the same amount of peanuts. Jack and Joan didn't hang about. They knew they weren't flavour of the month and zoomed off on the bike before the inevitable griping started.

The noise of an engine sounded in the distance and slowly grew louder. Rick appeared beneath my tree, looking left and right, unable to see me in amongst the high branches. I picked an apple and dropped it squarely on to the top of his head, making him jump and bang his knee against the dashboard.

'Didn't see me did you?' I said, well satisfied at his shocked expression.

He switched off the engine. 'Come down.'

Using a thick branch as a swing, I dropped and propelled myself forward, landing in my empty bin.

'Haven't you picked any yet?' Rick said, rubbing his bruised knee.

'No. Why, what time is it?'

'Nine.'

That meant that I'd been daydreaming up the tree for well over an hour. I climbed out of the bin and slumped against the tree trunk, pointing up at the branches and sneering. Rick looked up and shook his head. 'They must be joking.'

'Seventeen bucks a bin still. No more, no less.'

He sighed. 'What do you think?'

'I can't do it, Rick, it's as simple as that. I've lost my momentum; putting us on to these trees after everything they said isn't funny. It'll take three or four hours just to fill one bin. Do you realise that works out to around five dollars an hour for working like a dog, under this sun? Christ, road sweepers get more than that.' I paused and threw an apple against the tractor wheel, ducking down as it rebounded and flew past me. 'No, either she raises the price or I'm off. It's an insult.'

'It's not left to Joan, it's Jack's decision how much you get per bin.'

I shrugged. 'Whatever.'

Rick got off the tractor and rolled us both a cigarette. 'How much money have you got saved?'

'Just enough for an airline ticket out.' Although the money we were earning was pathetic by any standard of the civilised world, our out-going expenses were minimal. Apart from the cost of food and tobacco there was little else to spend money on. We had no means of getting into town, except on a Friday when Albert took us in to get the week's supplies, and were therefore saved from ourselves as far as drinking was concerned.

One thing that did aggravate me though, was the ten dollars per week that all pickers had to pay back to Jack, supposedly for the use of electricity. Apart from one shower a day to wash off the dust, and the occasional use of the camp washing machine, there was no other use of electricity on the site. Everyone cooked on their own personal gas stoves. Ten Australian dollars may seem a petty amount to moan about, but to me it represented two hours of back-breaking work, and the more I thought about it, the more I boiled inside.

I stood up and took the satchel off, flinging it into the bin. 'I'm going to get the price raised,' I said firmly.

'Where are you going?'

'To talk to the others, see if they're as pissed off as I am.'

Rick took his hat off. 'John, he'll kick you out, you know he will. We're almost there, we've both got enough for a ticket, and in a few more weeks we'll have some spending money as well. Don't fuck it up!' he shouted.

'He can't kick everyone out. I'm going to start a union.' I began to walk down between the rows of trees. Behind me Rick switched on the engine and followed in the tractor.

'John, he won't give in, I know him, I know what he's like.' He trundled past and turned, blocking my path. 'Jack'll go into town and immediately find twenty other pickers to replace you. Where will it get you?'

'Pride,' I said, turning and ducking through the trees so he couldn't follow. 'I may need the money, but fair's fair.'

I spent the rest of the morning going from picker to picker in order to gauge their level of dissatisfaction, and to determine whether I had enough, if any, back-up in asking for the price per bin to be raised. It was all very well my going up to Jack and complaining, but unless he saw broad support he'd just give me the boot.

Out of the twenty or so pickers at the orchard, all of them complained bitterly about how difficult it was to fill a bin with such small fruit but only about half said they'd back me in any stand-off with the management. I tried to rally the others but they were vague, saying they needed time to think about it, which basically meant no.

I didn't even bother talking to some of them because I knew they were a completely lost cause so I decided to concentrate on the 'maybes'. With the help of the two Scots, who said that they could persuade people they were friendly with, we agreed to meet in our shed that night for a pow-wow, instead of going to the pub. Even those who didn't have the balls to stand up for themselves were welcome to come along if they wanted to, and were told to spread the word. We were to meet after dinner, and I made sure that Jack and Joan knew what was going on.

'Just ask him to raise the price per bin, that's all.' I stood beside the blazing fireplace and studied the assembled faces, all flickering and glowing orange from the flames, going through the same speech that I'd given Rick; the same one that Ted and I had gone over with Albert in the pub. Everyone asked the same questions and voiced the same concerns as before, and I went through the likely scenario as I saw it, dismissing their worries out of hand. I was getting good at this union stuff, and enjoying it too, ending as usual with my favourite line: 'They can't sack us all, there'd be no one left to pick the fucking fruit!'

To my utter astonishment Albert had come along with the others, and, although I thought he was nothing more than a spy for Jack, I let him sit in, pretending to welcome his presence. He, like Rick, sat on the periphery of the gathering, both physically and metaphorically. If Rick had been a picker he would have been standing where I was standing, but he had a cushy job and didn't want to lose it before he had earned enough money to get out of Australia. I didn't hold it against him, but wondered if I'd have behaved the same way in his position.

The upshot of the gathering was that I, as the representative, would ask Jack for the price per bin to be raised by three dollars. I was to approach him first thing Monday morning, while everyone else would stay in their tents and refuse to go to work. He would either bend under pressure or sack the lot of us.

As the gathering dispersed and people began to leave the shed, an old Sham 69 song came into my head. I'd only been a kid during the punk movement, but my elder brother had played this particular song non-stop. I used to sit in the bedroom with him, quietly inconspicuous in the corner, trying to understand the lyrics. Suddenly they all came flooding back to me now, and before the first person had left the shed I put up one fist and said, 'Remember, if the pickers are united they will never be divided!'

Everyone looked at me as though I was mad.

SEVEN

Jack and his wife looked concerned when I got to the top field, and were standing by the first row of trees, empty satchels at their feet. They were deep in conversation but broke off when they saw me walk out into the open, both looking in my direction. Jack immediately said something to Joan, kick-started his motorbike, straddled it and rode towards me.

'Shit,' I said through gritted teeth, but not wanting to appear afraid I kept on walking towards him. Out of the corner of my eye I could see movement around the tents, so I knew that some people hadn't gone to work. The two Scots were definitely there, but then that was to be expected, they had always supported the stand-off. I stopped near the edge of the field as Jack pulled up.

'So what's this all about then, John?' he said, pushing up the top of his sun hat, then putting his hand back on to the throttle and revving it impatiently.

'Nothing really. We, er . . . ' I hesitated slightly, wondering if 'we' was the correct word. 'That is, some of us think that this new fruit we're picking is pretty small. It's very hard to fill the bins.'

'Yeah?' he replied flatly.

I waited for him to continue but he didn't. 'So, um, we can't fill the bins,' I repeated. 'It's taking ages: three or four hours just to fill one.'

He looked around the field at the tents, which gave me a chance to do the same. Everyone who'd said they would stop work had, along with some who said they weren't sure, and were sitting in front of their tents watching us. It was only seven o'clock so they could have been getting ready to go to work, but the illusion of a show of support was a tonic, and I straightened up. 'Yep, that's it.'

Jack rolled his head as though massaging a tense muscle, and said, 'Yeahh. So, what do you want me to do about it? This is an orchard and those apples have got to be picked by someone, haven't they?'

His voice was a semi-tone lower, and, though not markedly different, I sensed less aggression in his manner. Renewed by this, and the apparent show of support, I hit him with our demands. 'We think the price per bin is too low, Jack. Those apples are so small.'

'Yeahh, well I'm a reasonable man.' He nudged the bike into gear. 'You lot get back to work and we'll discuss the possibility of raising the price. I'm only one of the owners here, yeahh. Got to talk to the other co-owners tonight and I'll let you know.' He turned the bike around and zoomed off towards his house.

One of the Scottish girls immediately came out of her tent to meet me. 'What did he say?'

'Reckons he's got to talk to the other owners before he raises the price. He'll let us know, probably tomorrow.'

She smiled and put a thumb up to her friend who was trying to light their gas stove. 'Well at least he's thinking about it, John, that's one thing.'

I nodded, unsure whether to be pleased or not. 'You making tea?'

'Uh-huh. Want a cup?'

'OK,' I said, moving towards the tent. 'We'll have one before we get to work.' I raised a fist. 'The pickers are united!'

When I reached the top field the following morning, one of the Scottish girls was waiting there for me. She came running over and kissed me on the cheek. 'We've done it, John. You've done it! Twenty dollars a bin instead of seventeen!'

'Yes!' I immediately broke into the Sham 69 song in which, after each verse, I either clapped twice or stomped my foot like the original:

'If the pickers (boom boom)
are united, (boom boom)
they will never (boom boom)
be divided. (boom boom)
If the pickers . . . (boom boom)'

I went around the whole orchard holding up one fist and shouting the words at the top of my lungs. Each person congratulated me from the branches of the tree they were perched in, and even Albert and the Swede said it was a job well done. Albert cautioned me against pushing Jack too far, saying that I'd better keep the noise level down, but I was too caught up in the victory to heed any warnings.

I should, however, have realised that something was wrong when, after leaving Rick at the tractor shed upon arriving at the top field, I had yet to see him doing his rounds. Normally he would be out and about delivering bins within ten minutes of the rest of us starting work. I'd been marching around the orchard for nearly an hour proclaiming victory and he still hadn't appeared. Joan, however, had.

'John!'

I looked down the avenue of apple trees to see Joan standing at the other end, waving.

'Can you come up to the house?' she called, 'Jack wants a word.'

The Aussie picker I'd been talking to slapped me on the back. 'Sounds ominous.' When I looked back Joan had gone, reappearing further up the hill. She was driving the tractor. Without another word, I picked up my satchel and walked after her.

Jack was sitting side-saddle on his bike outside his house when I arrived. He put the stand on, dismounted and came towards me, a cheque in one hand, cloth sun-hat in the other. 'There's the money for the work you've done up until yesterday,' he said, 'minus electricity and those fuckin' bins that were full of nothing but leaves, yeahh,' and handed over the cheque. 'Now get off of my land. You're nothing but fuckin' trouble.' He turned to walk away.

I looked at the amount written on the cheque. 'Seven dollars!'

'Yeahh,' he said, getting back on to his bike. 'Any problems, speak to the wife, she's the accountant. You've got till tomorrow to pack your gear and go. You and your fuckin' mate.'

'Rick?' I exclaimed. 'What's he got to do with it?'

Jack didn't reply, started his bike and rode off, leaving me to stare blankly at the cheque. 'Seven dollars,' I mumbled, shaking my head. Seven lousy dollars for what I remembered as being three bins picked the previous day. Even at the old rate of pay that should amount to fifty-one dollars.

I stormed off towards the shed, pulling down every branch and each and every apple within arm's reach along the way, continually muttering the words, 'Seven dollars.'

Rick was collecting firewood when I got back to the shed; unusual considering that it was still only nine o'clock in the morning. He dropped the logs by the front door when he saw me and started rolling a cigarette.

'Did you get the sack?' I asked, approaching him. He nodded without looking up from his task. 'Then why the fuck are you collecting wood?'

'Did you get paid?' he said, apparently ignoring my question.

'Yeah.'

'How much?'

'Seven shitty dollars. That twisting bastard! What about you?'

'Eight. Swizzled!' He did an 'up yours!' sign towards Jack's house, then sat down on the grass. 'So that's it now: eight dollars, plus the rest I've saved, that makes, well, enough to get going again.'

I sat down next to him, patting the ground first to see if the dew had dried. 'Yeah, but go where? Not another orchard?'

'No chance. I want to leave this country. I've got enough for a ticket out, but that's about all.'

'We've both got enough for a ticket but that's all. Great!'

'The alternative is to stay in Australia and get more of the four letter word, but neither of us want to do that.' He handed the completed cigarette to me and said, 'What about Hong Kong? Ted reckoned it's a great place.'

'That was during the Vietnam War. Things have changed a bit since he was last there.'

'Still a colony ... just. We don't need a visa to work; it's the only place we can get a job without hassle. Otherwise we stay here, or go back to England, and I'm not keen on that.' He paused to light his cigarette. 'Get your pocket atlas and let's have a look. I'm not even sure where Hong Kong is.'

I ran inside and came back out with the little book. 'It's the only way we're going to get enough money to travel again,' I said, handing the atlas to him, 'go there and work for six months, save our money, then leave. Do you think we'll have enough for the flight?'

Rick opened the atlas and ran his finger down the index page. 'Hong Kong,' He flicked to a small scale map and said, 'Yeah, it's not that far, look.'

I laughed at Rick's unwavering sense of humour in the face of adversity. 'How long did Jack say you can stay here for? Told me to be out by tomorrow.'

'Same here.' He closed the atlas and drew on the cigarette. 'We'll cash our cheques tomorrow morning in town and try to hitch a ride up to Sydney to buy our tickets, they'll be cheaper there. I don't think we should waste money going up by train. We'll leave here tonight.'

'Tonight?'

'Yep,' he flicked the cigarette on to the grass and stood up, bundling the logs under each arm, 'just after we burn this shed down.'

EIGHT

There was nothing of value in the shed, nothing worth taking anyway, but with nothing else to do I made another inspection, going from room to room just to make doubly sure that we were leaving nothing behind. I stopped in the sheep-shearing area and stood beneath a hole in the roof, a perfectly full moon shining down a beam of light on to my upturned face. It was so bright after the darkness of the other rooms that it hurt my eyes and made me look away.

We'd already packed our bags with what little gear we had, and Rick had gone off to the top field to give some of our household things to the Scots, promising to be back by midnight, the time we had set to leave. In addition to delivering the gifts, Rick was to hint at us leaving tonight, so that they wouldn't think that we had burned to death in the forthcoming fire. The two girls had said earlier that they were prepared to walk out in protest over our sacking but we told them to forget it, we were sick of Australia anyway. We'd already hinted at revenge so they shouldn't be too surprised to wake up the next morning and find a pile of ashes where our home used to be.

There was a noise outside and I looked back down through a gap in the wall. Rick was jogging down from the gate, huge puffs of white air floating up from his mouth like a steam train. I put an eye close to the crack in the corrugated iron to get a better view but a centipede moved out of its home, obscuring my slither of vision. I shivered and moved back into the warmth of our living room just as Rick came in.

'Shit,' he said excitedly, 'it's fooking cold out tonight.' He slammed the door behind him and went to the fire, rubbing his hands together briskly.

'We still going?'

'Definitely. Brrrrr. Just give me five minutes.'

I sat down on the wooden planks that used to be my bed and looked around the room, remembering how unlived in it had looked when we'd first arrived. Now, with the fire blazing and our two bags waiting by the door, I almost felt anxious, as though I was leaving home.

'Roll us both a cigarette,' Rick said, breaking my train of thought, 'my hands are too cold.'

Pulling the tobacco pouch from my pocket, I said, 'What about the two girls, did you tell them what we're going to do?'

'Didn't need to.' He looked up. 'D'you know, as soon as I got there they knew we were going to do something to get our own back. As I gave them the stuff, she said, "Oh-ho, leaving tonight huh? Interesting," and looked at me with one of those looks.' Rick squinted and turned back to the fire. 'They know all right.'

'You don't think they'll say anything?'

'No, not those two, they're OK. Albert would, but then he doesn't know anything about tonight, and by tomorrow morning it'll be too late.' I passed him the cigarette and he said, 'Wouldn't mind a cuppa before we go.'

'No stove.'

He swore, lit his cigarette from off the end of a length of burning wood and then pushed the flaming timber under my bed.

'Hold on!' I said, jumping up. 'What are you doing?'

'What?'

'Well . . . I'm not ready.'

And suddenly it all seemed to happen at once. I put my bag over one shoulder, took two pieces of blazing wood from the fire and ran around the room setting light to clumps of sheep's wool. Rick started laughing maniacally and, using a plank from the bed, put the windows through before using it to rake the whole fire out on to the wooden floor of the shed.

'OK,' he said, 'let's go through the other rooms and then leave by the back door.' We both shovelled up a plankful of glowing embers and walked through the shed from one end to the other, sprinkling the glowing coals on to the floor as we went, as though sowing seeds. Apart from making me sweat a lot, nothing seemed to be happening. The embers just sat there and glowed like huge rubies.

'They're not catching,' I remarked, looking back at the red trail.

'They will, just leave them. Ready?'

I looked around, said, 'OK,' and we both slid down the sheep chute at the back, landing on the wet grass. The sweat instantly froze on my skin as the cold night air engulfed me. 'Shit,' I gasped, partly at the chill and partly at how bright it was outside. It was like daylight. The trees, the grass, cows, everything was lit up with a silvery moonlight.

We ran across the open field in exactly the opposite direction to which we'd come five months earlier, and clambered up the slope towards the road, laughing and sweating the whole time. 'Don't look back until we get to the road,' Rick panted. 'It'll either be Guy Fawkes night in Batlow or as dead as a doornail.'

'I can't,' I gasped, sliding on the damp grass, 'I'm too excited. I've got to look.'

But I didn't, at least not until half an hour later, when I could see the fenced-off road up ahead. When we got to the top and did look around, I saw one of the most beautiful sights I think I've ever seen.

In the bottom of the valley a herd of cows were standing in a ring around the flaming shed, each one picked out in the orange glow as they stood warming their faces by the inferno. Some of them moved closer, but then retreated when they found that the fire was too hot, doing a sort of shimmy as they reversed. Occasionally they would turn to present their flanks or rear to the warmth.

The shed was still discernible as a building, but only just. The wooden floor and frame of the shed, tinder-dry no doubt from the recent lack of rain, was in full swing. The windows had already disappeared among the flames that were lapping up from the floor, and part of the corrugated wall on one side, having buckled under the heat, had fallen in. A mile-high column of smoke rose into the clear sky like a solid column of white wool, lit by the moon. As we watched, part of the roof silently fell in, sending a shower of sparks into the air that rose up the column like a swarm of fireflies. Even the trees, at least half a mile away, were blushing warmly under the orange light, as if embarrassed.

Another shower of sparks went up, and what remained of the roof and one whole length of wall fell in on itself, producing a black rectangle in a ring of fire like a square eclipse. Soon that too was on fire. A shriek in the trees heralded a flock of cockatoos that flew out, did a circle of the whole field before coming back to where they had started, content with their ringside seat.

It seemed that the whole place had come alive to watch the show, all except the humans. Neither Jack nor his neighbours, whose houses were only five minutes away, nor any of the pickers, who must have been able to smell the burning wood through their canvas walls, came out.

Two hours later, when the show had finished, without a word Rick and I started our long walk into town, never speaking. Both of us were happy in the knowledge that we had enough money to get us back to where we wanted to be, and that was all that mattered. The money we had would only get us there, after that we would be back at square one; we knew that, but it didn't matter. Hong Kong, like everywhere else we had been to, was completely unknown to us, and that was all we desired.

MAGNETIC NORTH

ONE

After we set fire to the sheep shed and walked back into Batlow, there wasn't much to do but wait until the next day and try to get a lift up to Sydney. It turned out to be much more difficult than we'd ever imagined, so rather than hang around, running the risk of being spotted by Jack or one of his cronies, we decided to buy a bus ticket to get us to the city. It cost more than either of us had wanted to pay, but Rick came up with a solution.

The cheques that Jack's wife had issued as our final payment, for seven and eight dollars, had been hurriedly filled out (no doubt she was eager to see the back of us), leaving room between the words, 'seven' and 'dollars' for us to put in a 'ty'. The amount in words would therefore read 'Seventy' dollars on mine and 'Eighty' on Rick's, and we easily put an extra zero in the box to make it all add up. The bank in Batlow knew our faces well, since we'd been cashing cheques for that amount every week for months, so there shouldn't be any problems. I didn't really like the idea of cheating anyone, but felt that it was more than justified considering that we'd been diddled out of what was rightfully ours. We sat in the pub and accurately forged Joan's handwriting, then went into the bank and cashed the cheques without a hitch.

Rick wanted to try to hitch a ride but I was so nervous, almost running out of the bank, that I went straight into the ticket office and booked us on to the next bus out. Before nightfall we were in Sydney.

We were the first customers in the travel agent when the woman opened the shutter at nine o'clock the next morning, and, according to her, the only people she'd ever seen waiting, cash in hand, for a seat on the next available flight out.

'What, tonight?' she exclaimed, rolling up the front shutter of her shop and looking back wide-eyed.

'Yes, tonight. If that's the next available flight.' I pulled out a wad of notes.

'Cash!'

'Yep.'

Rick and I followed her into the shop and pulled out all the money from our pockets, counting it out on her desk, while she went to one side to put the kettle on. 'Well, I don't know,' she said, spooning some coffee granules into a cup, 'I haven't even opened the safe yet, and . . . ' she turned and saw the money. 'Umm, OK then.'

It broke my heart to hand over that money. The cost of the ticket left me with a hundred dollars. 'One hundred dollars,' I said to Rick as we left the agent, holding up the remaining cash in one hand and a ticket voucher in the other. 'After five months of *very* hard work that's all I've got to show for it.'

'But we're heading to Hong Kong, John; the land of milk and honey.' Rick spread his arms wide. 'In a month's time you and me'll be millionaires!'

'You said that in Thailand.' I quickly stuffed the money back into my pocket, afraid that it might vanish or blow away in the breeze, 'And look what happened to us there!'

'This is different.' He held his plane ticket coupon up to the sky, angling it this way and that to catch the light. 'Hong Kong's just waiting for people like us.'

'Poor people you mean?'

'Entrepreneurs.'

We both laughed, and I asked, 'What about Chinese girls, what d'you think they'll be like?'

'Huh. Only the most beautiful women in the world, everyone knows that. You've seen those Bruce Lee films haven't you? A bit old now, but the birds are fantastic.' He put the coupon methodically into his pocket, trying not to fold or dent the edges, and winked. 'Suzie Wong and all that stuff. All walking about in those long sexy silk dresses.'

'Ooh, yeah: the harbour full of junks, bamboo houses, rickshaws ... I remember the books we had in geography class at school, they always showed pictures of Hong Kong with British policemen and Union Jacks flying everywhere. It looked pretty good.'

'You liked India, well Hong Kong is like that, only with a little more law and order. You know: things work properly, buses run on time, but it's still Asia.'

We continued walking and talking, and went down to the harbour to get a final, lasting impression of Australia. Our flight wasn't due to depart until midnight so we spent the rest of that day wandering around the Opera House, chatting and dreaming about being seduced by dozens of Chinese girls as soon as we stepped off the plane in Hong Kong. We were so consumed by our thoughts, and the talk of the wonders that awaited us, that when, months later, someone asked me what the Sydney Harbour Bridge and the Opera House were like, I couldn't recall ever having seen them.

TWO

'Sir. Excuse me sir.' Rick looked away from the window with a start. 'Would you put your seat belt on please sir, we'll be landing shortly.' The pretty Chinese stewardess smiled and leaned across me, pressing a button on Rick's armrest, bringing his seat upright and went away.

The plane banked gently on our side and we both fought to get our faces up against the plastic window. 'Fooking hell.'

'What can you see?' I asked eagerly, trying to look over his shoulder.

The back of his head shook. 'Buildings. Really horrible buildings.' He turned away from the window and stared at me. 'Is this a direct flight?'

'Let me see.' We changed seats. The early morning sun was shining its dull, polluted rays on to what looked like a ten-storey shanty town. Rust-stained concrete tenement-style blocks of flats stretched as far as I could see, in a wretched mass. It reminded me of pictures I'd seen in school textbooks of Hiroshima after the atom bomb had been dropped, where the buildings on the outskirts of the city had just about remained standing. I couldn't see any people, but as we descended it was possible to make out the lines of washing, row after row strung like dirty bunting on poles from every window. It looked as though a squadron of aircraft had flown over the city and carpet-bombed it with millions of tons of laundry.

'This can't be Hong Kong,' I said incredulously, still glued to the scene below. 'Where are all the bamboo houses, the junks?'

Behind me Rick was talking to a stewardess. 'Excuse me,' he said, 'is this a direct flight to Hong Kong, or are we going via somewhere else?'

She seemed a bit taken back by the stupidity of the question. 'We're landing in Hong Kong now, sir,' I heard her say assertively. '*Please* fasten your seat belt.'

Rick and I turned to each other at exactly and shrugged. 'This is it!'

Neither of us spoke until we cleared customs and went outside to catch the bus into town, we were so shell shocked by the overwhelming oppressiveness of the drab concrete cityscape. Rick wiped a trickle of sweat on to his T-shirt as we boarded the air conditioned bus. 'Jesus, it's fooking hot. And humid. Wow!'

'Fi'e dollar!' The bus driver looked angry and stabbed the money slot with his finger. 'More fi'e dollar.' I put in another five dollar coin in and he brushed me away aggressively with his hand.

'Welcome to Hong Kong,' I mumbled, and put my bag on a rack. We were still in Asia, weren't we?

The bus doors slid shut with a gasp of hydraulics and we moved off. A woman's recorded voice immediately welcomed us to Hong Kong in three languages (no doubt designed to dispel any lingering worries tourists may have that they had in fact landed in the wrong place). The English I understood, the second one sounded very aggressive, and the third, Mandarin, sounded like a record playing backwards. Every five minutes along the route the driver pushed a button and the voice started again, and every time we had to stifle our laughter at the Mandarin segment.

The streets were jam-packed with people to the point where there was no longer any space on the pavement and they were two or three abreast on the road. Cars, trucks and buses revved up clouds of black diesel fumes that mixed with the hot sticky air and hung like a dead weight. Young pedestrians dressed immaculately (and inappropriately for the suffocating heat) in Western-style suits held tissues over their mouths to avoid being choked under the blanket, while old men hanging around on street corners coughed up small blobs of yellow phlegm which they projected, like spoonfuls of mayonnaise, on to over-filled rubbish bins.

Nobody, I noticed, walked with a normal gait; everyone shuffled in little pigeon-steps, unable to get into a proper stride. They were like old lags whose legs have been in prison irons for so many years that, even when released they still can't get used to stretching them. I suppose years of walking along while being sandwiched between two people has much the same effect.

In amongst the boiling hot traffic, a butcher wound his way around the stationary vehicles, pushing a trolley that was loaded high with plucked chickens. The small trolley wheels hit a pot-hole and one of the wobbling poultry fell off on to the road. As he stooped to pick it up, the truck in front edged forward, unleashing its exhaust right on to the meat. He put the stray bird back on with the others and turned off into a nearby restaurant. At another butcher-shop, a man was blow-torching a dead pig. The carcass was hung up from a beam while the man circled it with the flame, blasting off the hairs in a blizzard of sparks. All these first impression we witnessed from the comfort of our air-con bus, like watching a film on a giant TV screen.

The two Scottish girls at the orchard had given us the names of a few guest houses, or at least the building that housed them, and half an hour later we jumped from the bus at what looked like the correct stop.

I checked the name of the road on the map against the one on the street sign, and we turned the corner into the busy main street, joining the flow of bodies. To stop meant becoming a boulder in the fast flowing river; thousands of people slammed into us and piled up, or slid either side in the slipstream and carried on out to sea.

'Should be around here somewhere.' A droplet of sweat splashed on to the sheet of paper, causing the ink to run. I wiped it off and lost half of the word. 'Chungking Mansions,' I said as soon as I noticed the decrepit block beside us, and pointed. 'This looks like it.'

'Here?' Rick exclaimed.

I nodded. 'That's what the girls wrote: "Chungking Mansions".'

There was a huge crowd on the steps leading up to the entrance, all pushing and shoving to see into the window of the adjacent shop. I pushed through the crowd to see what was so interesting and found that it was displaying the latest mobile phones. The look on the faces of the people in the crowd was one of complete and utter longing; the same way children look into a pet shop window at a cute puppy. We pushed past them into the entrance of the building and found ourselves in an old, mixed-use shopping arcade. We were instantly pounced upon by dozens of Indians, offering everything from tailored suits to 'the best Punjabi food in town'. Amongst other things we were also offered accommodation.

'Use stairs,' said the Indian boy, pulling me by the hand into a dimly lit stairwell, 'lift no good, wait one hour, many people.'

'What floor is your guest house on?'

He coughed out a word that sounded suspiciously like fifteen.

'Fifteen!' Rick shouted, 'You're kidding?'

'Early, sir, not too hot. Have shared shower in hotel for your washing selves.'

We slogged and panted our way up to the top floor of the building, weaving our way along open corridors piled to the ceiling with rotting rubbish and went into his 'hotel'. Basically it was a private flat that had been sub-divided into dormitories: one for females and two for males. The one we were shown to was twelve feet by six and had eight beds (four bunks) crammed into it. When the door was opened it banged against the foot of the nearest bunk, waking the occupant, and to get between the two rows of beds I had to turn sideways. I had to hold my nose; the smell of stale sweat and damp socks was so overpowering. Rick looked crestfallen, and dropped his bag on to the floor, nearly crushing a skinny cat that was licking at a stain. We looked at each other in despair before shaking our heads and walking out to find another.

The Indian boy wanted to show us to another hotel that belonged to his brother, so we went along to that one but it was even worse. After that it was the turn of his uncle's place on the seventh floor. It turned out to be nothing more than a bed in the corner of a rat-infested kitchen, and then we went to his friend's special rooms ('Shh, illegal, no tell other people!'), but that was just a large room full of Pakistani refugees and, though they seemed very welcoming, we declined.

Another hour or so went by in which we looked at every other illegal guest house in that building and the building next door, before we swallowed our pride and returned to the first one we had been shown.

'We'll get used to it,' I squeaked through pinched nostrils. 'We only need to sleep here, we'll spend the rest of the day out looking for work.'

'Which one do you want,' Rick asked, sliding between the metal frames of the bunks, 'top or bottom?'

'Don't mind.'

He threw his bag on to the bottom bed and sat down with a huff. My bed was so close to a pipe that ran across the ceiling that I couldn't sit up, and to get on to the bed I had to climb up and slither sideways.

'"Quaint bamboo houses. Rickshaws. Junks".' I slithered to the edge of the bed and hung my head over, 'I hope you're right about the girls.'

THREE

To save money, for the first few weeks we lived entirely on McDonald's hamburgers for breakfast, lunch and dinner, and although there are places where one can get inexpensive bowls of noodles, I didn't discover them until much later. Our days were usually taken up scanning the newspapers for jobs and generally mooching about doing anything to keep us out of the guest house until as late as possible. At night we would walk down to the harbour, look out at the lights of Hong Kong island and dream. 'Some day,' Rick would say to me, majestically sweeping his hand over the scene, 'all this'll be yours,' and then burst out laughing.

Two weeks later, we were both almost out of money and, although we knew it was wrong, we decided to cheer ourselves up by going into a pub for a drink. We couldn't afford it, but so what?

The night was spent under the influence of alcohol, blissfully ignoring our predicament, and at about three o'clock in the morning we staggered back to our hovel. The lift was empty for once and we were soon walking along the rat-infested, concrete walkway back to the room. We were so drunk that neither of us bothered to put our trousers up on the bed with our bags, where we usually kept our belongings for safety reasons, and instead just threw them on the floor.

The next day when we awoke, Rick's passport had been stolen. Not a big deal really, but we phoned the police nonetheless to report the incident, and to see what could be done to get it back.

'Please, sirs,' the India guest house owner pleaded, 'no need to phone police.'

'Really,' I said evenly, standing in the corridor with the phone in one hand, 'and why not?'

He babbled something in my ear about his own security guard, who was usually asleep on the hallway floor, but I'd already started to speak to the policeman on the other end and brushed him away with my hand.

After giving my name and that of the guest house, the inspector said they'd be there in five minutes.

One minute later the front doorbell rang and I opened it to twelve policemen. They came in, all twelve in uniform, and stood in the narrow corridor; twelve pens in twelve hands poised over twelve notepads. The sergeant at the front asked Rick what had happened, putting his hand across the Indian's mouth to stop him from speaking.

'My passport's been stolen,' Rick replied.

'Who by?' His English was reasonable but the idiocy of the question made Rick ask for a repeat. 'Who stole it?' the policeman said again.

'How should I know who stole it? We went out last night, and when I woke up this morning it was gone.'

The officer dropped his hand from the Indian's mouth to take a note but immediately replaced it when he started babbling again. 'When you first notice it was missing?'

'This morning, at about ten o'clock.'

There was moment's silence as the policemen thought of his next question. If his head had been made of glass I could have seen the cogs slowly turning as his brain tried to engage his voicebox. 'So, you have no passport?'

'Yep, that's about the size of it. Been stolen.' Rick shifted his weight, hands on hips. 'The passport, nothing else.'

'Can you show me your ID card please, sir?'

'ID card? I don't have one, I'm only a tourist.'

The policeman straightened, as though suddenly having been stuck with a great idea, and took a step forward. 'So, you have no passport *and* no ID?' His chin rose, having finally got to the bottom of the crime, and he said, 'Do you know it is an offence to enter Hong Kong without valid passport or ID, sir?'

Rick shrugged. 'I dare say it is, but my passport has been stolen, I had it last night, and this morning when I woke up it was gone. Stolen.'

The sergeant cleared his throat. 'It is an offence under the basic law of this territory to enter without valid travel documents,' he repeated and nodded self-satisfactorily to his men.

Rick's mouth opened. I could see that he was about to explode so I stepped in. The officer immediately put his hand in front of me. 'Do you have a passport, sir?'

'Of course I have,' I said, looking down at his hand on my chest. 'How d'you think I managed to get into the country?'

'Please show it to me.' He dropped his arm and turned back to Rick. 'You must come with us to the police station. Anything you say—'

'Now hold on,' I said, putting both hands up as though surrendering, 'this is going too—'

'Your friend is in Hong Kong without any form of ID and is therefore committing a crime.'

'How can he be? I phoned you, remember? If we wanted to break the law I wouldn't tell the police would I?'

He was unfazed. 'Can I see your passport please, sir?'

And so it went on like this for nearly an hour; all of us packed into that tiny corridor. They demanded to inspect the scene of the crime, so all of us tried to go for the world record for the number of human beings in a dormitory. It was like a scene from the *Keystone Cops*. Rick was eventually taken away to the police station for being an illegal immigrant, but returned three hours later without being charged. He had told them that his father was a friend of the governor, and that a distant relative, whose name he couldn't recall but who was only a phone call away, was an ex-commissioner of the Hong Kong police. The news had shaken them by the boots.

'They actually believed you?' I asked as he sat down on the bunk, exhausted. 'They're more stupid than I took them for.'

'I had to say something, otherwise those thick bastards would've charged me.' He stretched out on the bed with a sigh. 'Even I can't believe they fell for it, but they let me out.'

'Let you out? They shouldn't have taken you in there to begin with.'

'I'll tell you what, though, John, I'm glad I did go in. I met this Scottish guy in there . . . ' he trailed off as though thinking back, and began to laugh. 'What day is it today?'

I leaned across to the other bed and picked up the copy of the South China Morning Post that was lying there, and checked the date. 'Thursday,' I said, throwing it back, 'why?'

'Brilliant.'

'What is?'

He sat up. 'Saturday night there's a party and you and me are invited.'

'Party?'

'Not too busy are you?'

I shrugged.

'Believe me, you want to go to this party. The guy I've just been speaking to in the police station has organised some security for a party on Saturday night. But this is no ordinary party, John, this one's in the governor's residence.'

My mind went back to an article in the previous week's newspaper, in which there'd been complaints about the disuse of such a large property since the hand over of Hong Kong to China. The Chinese were apparently unwilling to use the colonial residence, supposedly because of bad feng shui, but it still didn't quite follow why there would be a party in the house. 'What's the party for?' I said with renewed interest, swinging my legs over the side of the bed.

'Some official function. This Scottish guy reckons the ex-governor's going to be in town so they're holding a party at his old house. They still use it whenever they can; usually for slap-up dinners or for visiting dignitaries, that sort of thing. They leave it to the kilt to organise the security.'

The questions were queuing up in my head. 'What's he doing in the police station then?'

Rick shrugged. 'Organising this inept police force, who knows?' He wasn't on my side of the bars though, I can tell you that. It was him who told me to say that I knew the governor, and him that put in a good word and got me out. According to him the police out here are hopeless; he has to order them about like robots.'

I pictured the ex-governor of Hong Kong arriving at the airport and being turned away because of invalid travel documents. 'But why the fuck would he invite a stranger?'

'I've thought about that.' He shuffled to the edge of the bed. 'He's been here thirty years, he told me. He was here in 'the good ol' days' as he put it, and now he's had enough. He's worked under one governor or another, and now it's all ended he couldn't give a shit. You should see the way he talks to those policeman,' Rick closed his eyes and tilted his head, 'unbelievable. They bow and scrape to him like shoeshines.'

'I'm not interested in that colonial power bullshit. Guys like him shouldn't be here. All that stuff makes me sick.'

He snorted. 'Right. You're not coming then?'

'Now I didn't say that.'

There was a pause in which we both shook our heads a lot without speaking, and Rick said, 'There's only one small drawback: we've got to wear suits.'

'Suits!'

'And ties.'

'Oh, Christ.' I lay down. 'Well that's that then. How can we afford suits when we've barely got enough money to eat?'

He scratched an imaginary beard. 'Yeah, that's a difficult one I know. We can hire one downstairs in the arcade, but I doubt if we can even afford that; even the crappy Indian ones are expensive.'

I looked around the room for inspiration, and for some reason finally settled my gaze upon the communal electric iron lying in the corner. 'I've got it!' I said, jumping down off the bunk. 'Have you paid for this room yet?'

'No, we don't have to until we leave, and . . .'

I smiled and Rick followed the line of questioning, breaking into a board grin. 'After all,' he said, 'they did steal my passport.' It was true that we had both suspected the Indian security guard, or another member of the staff, of carrying out the theft. All of the other guests in our room were known to us personally, and no one else had a key to the dorm. 'It's only fair.'

'And just.'

'What goes around . . .'

We wallowed in our self-righteousness for a moment, and I said, 'Where will we go to, though? We can't stay around here, all these Indians know each other.'

'There's a youth hostel on Hong Kong island, we could give that a try.'

'That's it then. We sneak out tomorrow morning as early as possible, without paying, and move over to the island side.' I clapped once and walked across to pick up the electric iron.

'What the fook are you doing?'

'Might need to iron a shirt,' I said, and stuffed it into my bag. 'Got to look smart on Saturday night.'

FOUR

The so-called security guard of our guest house was asleep on the corridor floor as usual when I peeped out of our room. 'So-called' because he was just another relative of the owner and his level of securing apparently involved nothing more extensive than a quick peek into the girls' dorm during the daytime. Most of the day he was out, and at night his vigilance amounted to sleeping at an angle across the floor, apparently believing that all Chinese burglars are unable to pick their feet up more than a few inches when they walk.

I turned to Rick and gave a thumbs up, whispering, 'OK,' but he came and took a look anyway. 'I've just told you it's OK,' I said curtly.

'I'm the stealth-master around here,' he whispered an inch from my ear. I tutted and moved from the door to let him past, a slither of light from the corridor window producing a thin, vertical white line like a scar the length of his face, crossing one eye. 'What time is it?' he said, closing one eye and observing the snoring guard.

'Two minutes after the last time you asked. Two minutes past seven.'

Most of the other people in the dorms were still asleep, but a few had jobs and would soon be stirring: making coffee in the hall, coughing up phlegm, going to the toilet. The previous night the owner had told us that he'd also suspected the security guard of the crime, which made us feel a little better about walking out.

We picked up our bags and stepped out into the hallway, tiptoeing silently over the body. The guard turned over in his sleep and snorted just as one of my feet was poised above his face. I froze in mid-air. Shit. Finding a comfortable spot on his side, he shuffled a bit and, to my amazement, put a thumb into his mouth and started sucking noisily.

Rick looked back, one hand on the front door latch and suppressed a giggle. 'Come on,' he mouthed. Allowing gravity to pull my front leg forwards, still holding my flip-flops in one hand, I crept over the body and joined Rick outside, where we immediately fell into fits of laughter.

In the street, Hong Kongers were already waking up to the bright warm sun of an early morning that would soon turn into another scorchingly hot and steamy day. It was already humid but the heat was still bearable; the traffic having not yet clogged the roads or the air.

The youth hostel Rick had spoken about was right at the far end of Hong Kong island, above a place called Kennedy Town. We caught the ferry, jumped on a tram for the remainder of the journey and walked up the hill to the hostel to save money on the cab fare.

At noon, having showered and met a few people, we had to walk back down again to find somewhere that hired out suits. Kennedy Town, we discovered, was next to useless for that sort of thing, while the central district was out of the question because of cost. Reluctantly, we caught the ferry back over to Kowloon and slipped into an Indian tailor back in Chungking Mansions, where we dispelled another of Hong Kong's myths.

I had always been led to believe that a trip to Hong Kong wasn't complete without a visit to one of the numerous tailors in Kowloon. Just go into any one of them, I imagined, get measured up and the next day return to collect a knockout, made-to-measure copy of the latest suit to go down the catwalks of Paris. And all for less than the cost of decent meal. Bollocks. If you don't mind paying double what you'd pay back in Europe, or anywhere else, for a suit of inferior quality, you'll find plenty of tailors in Kowloon willing to make one. You can get a suit at normal prices (not cheap) but it's made of crimplene and hangs off the wearer with all the panache of a tablecloth.

Luckily Rick and I didn't mind looking like extras in a B movie, and we persuaded the Indian tailor to rent two of them to us for forty-eight hours. He wrote on the deposit receipt the exact time that the suits were to be returned, or else we'd lose our money.

'What d'you think?' I asked Rick, looking in the mirror and laughing.

The Indian man butted in. 'Very good, sir, you both look so-fine-gentlemen.'

'Feels a bit funny.'

'No no no, sir.' He squatted and ran a hand up the inside of each leg. 'This fit perfect for you.'

'Too long aren't they?' Rick said, checking himself in the mirror and hoisting up his new trousers.

The Indian pinned up each bell bottom and took a step back. 'Ahhh,' he said, tilting his head to one side and clasping his hands in approval, 'that is lovely.'

'Flares though?'

Rick turned to look at me and started laughing again. 'Fook, I can see your balls.'

'Eh?' I looked down to check, but the fly was done up.

'No, the light from behind shines right through the material. There's a

352

silhouette of your nuts.' The Indian man just looked perplexed and started fumbling at the turn-ups again.

I felt the thinness of the material, 'Well it's all we can afford. I'll just have to stay away from bright lights, that's all.'

The agreed price for the hire included two shirts and ties that we were allowed to pick out from a suitably old-fashioned collection that the tailor assured us were pure silk. I said it didn't matter what they were made of, they were still twenty years out of date, but Rick actually thought they were the latest designs. 'Bloody northern redneck,' I goaded, trying one on.

'Southern poof.'

We had a short, good-natured slanging match over which half of England was the best to be born in, before both agreeing that it was all crap anyway in comparison with Asia, and admired our worldliness in the mirror. I tied the knot and squirmed. 'Feels horrible doesn't it? Wearing clothes, I mean.'

'Mmm. Feels like I'm in a straitjacket. Trapped in someone else's clothes or something.'

I nodded. 'It's not just that, it's the whole idea of being back in civilisation, I think. Do you realise, apart from Australia, we haven't worn clothes in two years?'

Rick looked disapprovingly at himself in the mirror. 'It's not the clothes, it's us. We'd look odd even in the best suits.'

Not for the first time since arriving back in modern civilisation I felt ill at ease. It's weird really, because I used to think the civilised world was where all the fun was, and although I could understand Rick's recent complaints about Hong Kong, being from London I'd have expected to fit right in. Hong Kong was a welcome change from the real Asia but I was beginning to feel that that's all it was: a novel change of scenery.

The person staring back from the mirror wasn't me; the transformation really was that remarkable. I leaned closer so that my nose touched the glass, filling my field of vision with two eyes, my body disappearing into the background, and John Harris emerged once more. Phew! It was just the clothes after all, I'm still inside there somewhere. We paid and left, carrying two large bags with *Best Tailors* printed on the sides in Olde Worlde lettering.

Throughout the whole journey back up to the youth hostel I caught myself walking with an unnatural gait, looking at my reflection in every shop window I passed. I'm not a vain person, I was just trying to see if the efficacy of the suit had worn off and to check if I was still me.

FIVE

Saturday night came around; Rick and I slogged our way up towards Government House dressed in our new suits, bell-bottoms swinging freely.

'Albert Road?' he asked.

I pulled out the scrap of paper and stopped beneath the street sign, wiping away the river of sweat that was obscuring my vision. 'That's what he said.' I had copied part of a street map from someone's guidebook back at the youth hostel but it seemed that the governor's residence had been replaced by a zoo. We had been around the place twice now. Using my rolled up silk tie as a swab I soaked up some of the sweat on my face and neck. 'It's got to be here somewhere,' I panted. 'I need a drink.'

Rick took the damp map from me, and was about to ask a passer-by when a black limousine drew up, the electric window sinking into the door. 'Hello again.' A man's head poked out of the window. 'Lost? It's just up ahead. Keep going around the curve in the road and it's on the right, 'K?' The pane of glass emerged from the door and slid back up as the car moved off.

'Fooking hell,' Rick fumed, staring at the car's vanishing tail lights.

'Is that the Scottish guy you met in the police station?'

'Yeah. Could have given us a fooking lift.'

After resting and sweating a few more pints, we walked off in the direction the car had gone. We were arguing about whose fault it was that we'd taken the wrong road earlier, when the Scot stuck his head out through a small iron gate in a twenty-foot high perimeter wall. 'In here boys.'

We shrugged and followed him, accompanied by a policeman, through some bushes and out on to an immaculate floodlit lawn, beyond which was a huge house thronging with people. Black limos were pulling in through the large entrance gates and stopping on the circular drive, while press cameras flashed as local celebrities and dignitaries stepped out in dinner suits, accompanied by their gowned women.

'Now,' the Scotsman said in a croaky voice that sounded like a posh version of Sean Connery's, 'as you know, gwailos are a little thin on the ground at the moment,' he broke off as we ducked under a conifer and then continued, 'so I'd like you two to remain in the picture but in the background. Give the old hoose a bit of white presence, if you catch my drift, hmm?'

'What the fuck's a gwailo?' I whispered to Rick.

'Dunno. Don't ask.'

We all walked in single file around the manicured flowerbeds and in through a side door that led into a long, dimly lit corridor. We were told to get washed and smartened up in one of the toilets, before being taken into the main entrance hall where all the action was.

By 'action' I mean a lot of dreary looking fat Chinamen in suits, all smoking cigars and looking like they were about to have a heart attack. I'd never seen a fat Chinese person before, and it was quite a shock after having spent so much time in parts of Asia where people are lean and healthy, especially the men. These guys were all bloated and ashen-faced, but accompanied by the most stunning women I'd ever seen. Up until that point I hadn't seen an ugly Chinese woman in Hong Kong, but these women took my breath away.

'Right,' said the Scotsman, suddenly appearing through a side door, 'I want you two to just stand here against this wall, like soldiers. Straight, man, straight! Don't talk to anyone, don't look at anyone, just stand there and smile, 'K? You'll be paid later, and then you can get back to wherever it is you came from.' He turned and went across to the other side.

'What?' I moved forward but Rick held my arm. 'What's all this "go back to where you came from" shit?'

'That Scottish prick.'

'Pick up that vase and hit him over the head,' I said through clenched teeth, grabbing the rim.

'No. I've got a better idea.' He put his hands on my shoulders and turned me towards an open doorway on the other side of the hall. In the room a lot of people were sipping cocktails and eating hors d'oeuvres.

'See it? Just to piss him off let's go straight in there and mingle with the crowd.'

Without hesitating or even replying, I looked back at the Scotsman to see if he was watching, and when he started to speak to one of the dignitaries in the crowd we walked quickly but casually across the hall and into the room. I walked straight up to the sea of faces and held out my hand to the first person nearest the door. 'Good evening. John Harris,' I said at the top of my voice.

The Chinese man broke off the conversation he was having with a middle-aged woman and turned to me, putting on the most fake smile I'd ever seen. 'Evening,' he said shaking my hand. 'Glad you could-ahh-come. My wife.' He gestured to the woman and I shook her hand before kissing it.

Rick was beside me in an instant, and I turned to him, catching a glimpse of a fuming Scotsman in the background. 'This is Sir William George Garthrick Jenner.'

'Helloo.' Rick tried an upper-class accent but he just sounded gay. 'Pleased to make your acquaintance.'

'Ahh-good evening,' the man said in his croaky voice. 'My wife.'

'Helloo, my name's Sir William, so pleased to meet you.' This time his voice sounded like John Merrick, the elephant man.

The man snapped his fingers in the air and a tray of drinks was brought over. We took a glass of champagne each and said cheers before the man and his wife moved off to another person, 'Ahh if you'd excuse me?' The second he left our side we both took a step further into the room and struck up a conversation with another couple. As Rick introduced himself I looked behind to see the Scotsman standing in the doorway. Brilliant! What a nice twist; he invited us here and even he's not allowed into the room. I lifted my glass to him and tipped an imaginary hat before turning around and being struck by lightening.

I wouldn't like to say that I didn't believe in love at first sight up to that point because it's hard to dispel something like that. How can one say there's no such thing when the only way of knowing is to fall in love at first sight! It's like, no one believes in ghosts until they see one, but then it's too late not to believe.

As I moved closer she began to blush, her milky-white skin turning the colour of one of Jack's Red Delicious as she lowered her eyes. I think I even blushed when I introduced myself.

Two almond-shaped eyes looked up at me, the edges turned up slightly in that beautiful Asian way. Her small button nose and full red lips gave her such an extreme amount of sex appeal that, mixed with a childlike beauty I'd never seen before, I think I actually gasped out loud. Her blue-black hair hung straight down on to tiny shoulders that were exposed from the top of her ball-gown so invitingly that I almost kissed them there and then. Further down, her small breasts gave a gentle bulge to her top half, while her sides curved into the smallest waist and most perfect bum I'd ever seen.

'Hi,' she peeped, holding out her delicate hand, 'I'm Apple.'

I shook her hand and laughed. 'Apple?'

'Yes,' she said a little more sternly, 'Apple', and proceeded to spell it for me.

'That's a fruit,' I said, trying to keep my eyes off her cleavage. 'You weren't named after a fruit were you?'

A blank expression. 'Prease speak more srowry, thank you.'

'Why are you called Apple? That's not a Chinese name.'

'No, not Chinese name. Eve'yone have Chinese name but also have Engrish name.'

Her femininity was a shock. She spoke and carried herself in a way that I'd never seen before, in a way that Western women have long since forgotten.

I watched her sip her orange juice before saying that I'd just arrived in Hong Kong and was looking for work.

'My boss is gwailo, I work in gwailo company,' she said. 'Many gwailo.'

'What's a gwailo?'

'You are gwailo. Gwailo white man.'

The penny dropped. 'What do you do for your boss?'

She giggled. 'I am sec'etaly, but boss not here. On'y me. I win competition to wisit government house,' she screwed up her face, 'but don't like it.' She told me that she worked for a huge property company and thought that they may have a job to suit me. Not being involved in the business dealings herself, she gave me her boss's name and number and said that I should phone the following Monday morning.

After we had chatted for about ten minutes someone banged a gong and announced that dinner would be served shortly.

'Will you sit next to me?' she asked coyly. 'I'm aflaid.'

'I'm not invited,' I said, surprised at my own honesty. 'But I want to see you again. Can I have your phone number?'

She blushed and pointed to the card she'd given me.

'But that's work,' I said looking up. A few people started to leave the room to go to dinner and I suddenly panicked, thinking that I'd never see this girl again. I really panicked. 'But can I–'

'John,' Rick was standing behind me tapping my shoulder, 'the game's up.'

Most of the people had left the room, and the Scotsman was coming towards us, straightening his bow tie while he stretched his neck, a look of grim determination on his face. 'What about tomorrow,' I asked, turning back to Apple. 'It's Sunday. What do you do on Sundays?'

'John, come on, let's go.' Rick was impatient.

'Hold it, Rick. What's the number of the youth hostel?'

'I don't know. Come on!'

'Apple?'

'Monday.'

The Scotsman arrived. 'Excuse me, miss,' he said sternly, 'you need to go into the dining hall now.' She blushed again and was taken out by one of the waiters.

He turned and said something to me too, but I was too preoccupied with Apple's wiggle to notice. Her wiggle, her hair, her . . . everything.

SIX

I knew there was something wrong with me because I spent the whole of Sunday walking around the youth hostel in a daydream. People, their faces and actions came and went but all I could think about was Apple's eyes, and lips and the way she spoke. Rick kept talking to me but all I did was nod mechanically and say, 'Mmm, what?' He'd repeat the question or statement but before the sentence was finished I was off to dreamland once again.

Things that would normally have made me laugh seemed insignificant too, and I'd just snort obligingly at the joke and nod while staring into space. For example, the TV in the hostel was switched to one of the Chinese channels that night, and was showing a kind of Miss World contest, only instead of being Miss Hong Kong it was called Miss Factory, China. One by one the workers came up to the interviewer, dressed only in their bikinis, and had to utter a few rehearsed words into the microphone. According to one of these girls, when asked what she wished for should she be crowned Miss Factory, she replied, 'I would like to eat lamb chops, that is my dream.' Everyone in the hostel roared with laughter. Except me. I seemed to be staring right through the TV set.

I wondered where Apple was and if she had a boyfriend or not.

After two sleepless nights, Monday morning came around, and at nine o'clock I was on the phone to a Mr Leiky, Apple's boss. She had yet to arrive at the office so he was answering the early calls. I told him the story of my meeting with his secretary (with a few necessary aversions) and he asked me to come along for an interview.

I phoned up Best Tailors to say that I'd be a day late returning the suit, and by 9.30 a.m. I was in a McDonald's restaurant toilet changing out of my shorts and flip-flops. With borrowed clothes on my back and a borrowed briefcase in my hand that held only my ragged beachwear, I strode into the company's plush reception area and was shown into the office by Apple.

To cut a short story even shorter, I got the job. The interview was nothing like the ones I was used to in England where three or four people sit and grill you for half an hour, trying their hardest to catch you out. This was a one to one in which we basically just chatted about everything, from the part of London we both came from to what it was like to live and work in Hong Kong. Apple's boss seemed more interested in whether or not I was an accomplished footballer than a good worker, and I soon forgot all about my earlier worry of how to hide the fact that I'd spent the past two years fucking about on beaches instead of working. There was a minor sweat when I knocked over the briefcase and one of my flip-flops slid out, but I hurriedly kicked it back in without him noticing.

On the way out, I asked Apple if she wanted to go out to the pub that night, and to my complete delight she agreed. 'Tonight,' I repeated, unsure if she was aware what she had consented to.

'Yes, I do understand Engrish you know?'

Her boss came out and found me sitting on the edge of her desk. 'You don't waste any time, John,' he said, and I quickly jumped off. 'Apple, could you get this typed up before lunch. Thanks,' and he went back into his office.

'What time shall we meet then?' I asked, moving back in and leaning over her computer.

She smiled, her brilliant white teeth flashing like the flesh of an apple against the red peel that was her lipstick. She didn't know any of the pubs by name so we agreed to meet at the bottom of a street called Lan Kwai Fong at seven and go from there. Even with limited funds, over the past few weeks I had come to know the area quite well and I thought I could easily impress her with my knowledge of its nightlife.

Lan Kwai Fong is what Wan Chai used to be in the fifties: the centre of Hong Kong's nightlife. Wan Chai is still there, and still has bars, but with its decrepit old brothels and downbeat discotheques it has categorically refused to reinvent itself, and consequently repels the younger generation rather than attracts it. In any case, anyone wanting to pay for sex would go to Tsim Sha Tsui where the really beautiful Chinese girls are employed, and not Wan Chai where the dregs from the rest of Asia are gamely worked.

Lan Kwai Fong is a small, comfortable street full of bars, without a red light in sight. I sat in one of them, alone, sipping a beer before Apple arrived. Most of the people sitting around the bar were foreigners, and I began to think that I could be sitting in any bar anywhere in the world when someone tapped me on the shoulder. I looked round.

'Hi,' said the Chinese girl in an American accent. 'Just finished work?'

'No,' I said, turning around on the stool, 'haven't started. Tomorrow's the big day. You?'

She held up her briefcase. 'With anyone?'

'Um . . . ' I hesitated.

What I'm about to say may not sound like much to most people, but for me it was a big deal. A *very* big deal. I actually said 'yes' to that girl's question, and it wasn't until later, thinking back, that I realised how significant it was for me to say it. She was stunningly beautiful, and as she walked away I almost couldn't believe what I'd said.

When Apple came we went off to another pub up the street to avoid any embarrassment, and sat at the bar. 'You look beautiful, Apple,' I said, 'really beautiful. I think–' I was cut off mid-sentence by the sight of the same girl from the other pub appearing over Apple's shoulder. She had obviously followed me. 'I–I think we should go . . .' My concentration was completely thrown as the girl came in and sat beside us, so close that if I said anything personal she would overhear it.

Apple looked at me and frowned. 'John?'

I began to sweat. Shit, I thought, what am I so scared of? I haven't done anything wrong. 'I, um, I'm just going to the toilet. Back in a minute.' The barman directed me to a door in the corner and I went in. I did want to go the toilet anyway but seeing the girl had made the urge stronger. I felt as though I was trying to hide something from Apple. Wrestling with these weird new feelings, I started to wash my hands when there was a crash and a scream from outside.

Apple and the American girl were on top of each other when I came out, rolling around on the floor pulling each other's hair out. Bar stools and Cantonese expletives went flying as their bodies crashed into everything in their way. I couldn't understand what was being said but by the look on Apple's face she was about to kill the other girl. Her claw-like fingernails came out and raked across tender skin, accompanied by the American girl's animal cry.

With the help of the barman I managed to separate them, and the American fled, clutching her briefcase in one hand and her scratched cheek in the other. Apple immediately ran into the toilet with her handbag before I could really get a look at her face. She emerged two minutes later looking as beautiful as before.

'What happened?' I asked as she sat down.

'That girl call me prostitute,' she panted, immediately standing again and going red in the face. 'She says I only with you because you are gwailo, and . . . '

'OK, OK,' I placed a calming hand on her shoulder and looked over the bar at the barman, who seemed as interested in the subject as I was.

He nodded, 'It's true, I heard her say it.'

'I never have gwailo boyfriend before,' she said sitting down, a tear welling in her eye.

I couldn't help myself and leaned across, kissing her once on the lips, while the barman turned away and pretended to polish some glasses.

She said that one kiss was enough for our first date because we were really only supposed to swap phone numbers and, maybe, after one week we could hold hands in public. 'It is Chinese custom.'

I shrugged. 'That's OK, I'm not Chinese,' I said, and leaned forward and kissed her again.

SEVEN

It was on a Friday that Rick gave me the news. I know that because it was the same day that I received my first pay cheque from work and I had been intending to meet him in Lan Kwai Fong to celebrate. As it turned out, he called me and we ended up celebrating for a totally different reason.

It was midday when the phone rang at work and I was startled out of my usual eight-hour daydream. Rick asked me what I was doing at lunchtime and said he'd like to see me down at the hot dog shop in Lan Kwai Fong where he worked. I said I didn't mind coming down but wanted to know if anything was wrong. 'Far from it,' he replied, and put the receiver down. Weird, I thought.

Over the few weeks since meeting Apple, Rick and I hadn't seen each other very much at all. He'd got himself a job as manager of a Western-style hot dog shop so both of us were at work during the day, and my passion for Apple meant that I rarely saw him at night. Occasionally we'd bump into each other just before or after going to bed because he had the bottom bunk in the hostel, but otherwise nothing. Not such a bad thing really considering that we had virtually lived in each other's pockets in the past and hadn't not seen one another on a single day since meeting in Thailand. Neither of us had broached the subject of living apart, but I sensed a subtle change in our direction, mainly because of Apple. It was probably too subtle for Rick to pick up on, but it was there nonetheless.

It was with these thoughts in mind that I left my office in Sheung Wan at midday and made the ten-minute walk to Central.

Sheung Wan is one of the few remaining places in Hong Kong where one still has the feeling of being in the Far East. Small hole-in-the-wall style Chinese seafood traders still display huge sharks' fins on stalls outside their shops, while vendors of traditional medicine proclaim to the millions of passers-by that they have a cure for their husbands' impotence, and hold up a tiger's penis. And, like everywhere else in Hong Kong, Sheung Wan has dozens of won ton shops. Every lunchtime between twelve and two, these tiny places ('restaurant' seems like the wrong word) are frantic with action as half a dozen cooks cram themselves into a corner and cook up noodles and won ton at the rate of a bowl a minute. Anyone who thinks that McDonald's invented fast food should visit the won ton shops of Hong Kong.

I turned off Des Voeux Road and walked up the hill, or rather pushed my way through the crowd and shuffled up the hill, to the hot dog shop, where Rick was sitting outside, smoking, his face angled up to the sun.

Taking out my first pay-cheque, I approached him, pulling both ends to make a sharp *snap* sound. 'Guess what I've got?'

He looked at me with a start. 'You've been paid?'

'Uh-huh.' I walked up to him and showed him the sum written on it. 'For two weeks' work. That's the same amount I earned picking fruit in five months!'

He took the cheque from me, bit it and said, 'Unbelievable,' before standing and pulling another office chair from a heap of builder's rubble, brushing it off for me to sit down. 'Do you want me to put some paper down to save your trousers?'

'No, I can afford to buy some more now,' I said, sitting and putting the cheque back into my pocket. 'What's for lunch?'

'What do you want? We've got dog hot dog, cat hot dog, rat–'

'Don't say that, I'm starving. Let me try the, um, cat. What's the cat like?'

'Supposed to be chicken,' he said walking into the little shop and calling back, 'but I've got doubts.'

'Chicken? How can you have a chicken hot dog? I thought they were supposed to be made of pork or something.'

His head came around the corner, grinning. 'This is *Chino's Dogs*, John,' he said, pointing to the sign above the shop. '*"Dogs Make Your Day"*.'

I looked up and squinted at the sign. 'OK then, I'll have dog hot dog. Go on, make my day.'

'Sure? I don't want to start cooking fine food only to have you change your mind.'

'Positive.'

He vanished and came back a moment later with a tiny steaming sausage that was lost in the bun. 'Your dog, sir.'

'What,' I exclaimed, 'is that?'

'Hot dog. Chinese have got smaller bodies, they don't need so much.' He sat down. 'We tried serving Western-sized ones but people just ate half and threw the rest in the bin. Take it, it's burning my hand.'

'Christ, no wonder they're small if they're living off these.' I took it and bit the end off, scalding my tongue. 'So, what do you want to tell me?'

Of all the things that might have happened to either Rick or I that would put a stop to our travels, what he told me next was the last thing I would have come up with. On the way to meet him I'd briefly thought about what he wanted to say, and all I could think of was that he'd had enough of Hong Kong and was going to suggest that we leave as soon as possible. That seemed unlikely considering that we had never planned on staying long anyway, and it certainly wasn't a reason to ask me around at midday. Maybe he'd won the lottery.

'I'm getting married,' he said matter-of-factly. 'Mustard?'

I immediately choked on the food and with one firm cough the mangled, doughy ball of bread and pork flew out and landed on the pavement. 'You what?'

'D'you want mustard on that?'

The coughing fit brought water to my eyes and I had to put the hot dog down to wipe them on my sleeve. Rick patted me on the back. 'Ahem, I'm OK, I just don't think I heard you right.'

'You did. I'm getting married.'

'You're get– Who to?'

'A girl I met here yesterday.'

I put a hand up to stop him patting my back, but also to stop him from talking. 'Wait a minute, Rick, just wait one minute. Rewind a second. Take it slowly for me, please, from the beginning. You–'

'You think I'm crazy, right?'

'You met a girl here yesterday,' I shouted, swivelling the chair to face him, 'and you're going to get married?'

'Yep. I asked her and she said yes. She's beautiful, John, you've got to see her.'

'Hold it. You met her yesterday and proposed to her, when, last night?' I swallowed. 'Too fucking right I think you're crazy. You must be mental.'

He seemed slightly offended. 'You're the same with Apple. You told me how you knew when you first saw her that it was love at first sight, remember? Well, I took the piss then but now I have the same feeling about Laura.' He sat back.

I was struck dumb for a few seconds by the name, and the way it suddenly personalised what I was saying. I felt as though I'd insulted someone that I hadn't met. Finally I said, 'Yeah, but I didn't agree to marry her the same bloody day! Why the fuck do you want to marry her? Just go out with her, that's enough isn't it?' I found my hands waving about in the air, pleading, and quickly put them down. 'Arrgh, Rick! Why?'

'You think I'm doing the wrong thing don't you?'

I bowed my head and looked at the floor. 'Yeah, I do. I'm not saying she's not nice, or that she's not the right one for you, I'm just saying that you should think about it a bit longer. One day!'

He hesitated. 'I have thought about it, John. I've been thinking about it all night, and it's right.' He went into the shop and came back holding two cups of coke. 'I've got to wait two weeks anyway; it takes that long for the registry here to check that I'm not already married in England.' He gave me the drink. 'I want you to be best man.'

'Course I will, you don't need to ask, you know that.' I took a sip, thinking about our situation. 'You know, this is so funny, you and me, here, living in a hostel ...'

He shook his head. 'Not any more, we've been kicked out.'

I pulled the cup from my lips. 'What?'

'We refused to do our daily chores, and you've been going around telling the others that they don't need to do theirs either.' He took a drink. 'You know what that old witch who runs the place is like.'

The reason the youth hostels in Hong Kong are able to offer cheap accommodation is because their operating costs are much lower than normal guest houses. They achieve this by issuing a work rota whereby all guests are required to carry out a daily task, such as cleaning the toilets or dorms and tidying the mess hall, thus saving on cleaner's wages. Over the past few weeks I'd fallen out with the manager and told everyone that they didn't need to do any work because they were all paying guests.

I sighed. 'How long has she given us?'

'Until tomorrow morning.'

'Have you got any more bombshells you want to drop, or is that it for now? I don't think I can take any more.'

He sniggered. 'Nothing else. I don't think. Oh, I might need to borrow some money for a wedding ring.'

'No problem. Anything else? Where are you going to live?'

He shrugged. 'Haven't really thought about it. I get paid at the end of this month so we should be able to rent a shoe box.'

I nodded and sipped the coke, occasionally gazing up at the square of sky that was visible between the buildings. We sat and talked things over for nearly an hour, and Rick described his fiancée to me in detail. Among the things that came out was her catholic religion, and I wondered if he wasn't marrying her just to get her into bed.

'She won't sleep with me out of wedlock, John,' he giggled in answer to my question as I stood up to make my way back to work. 'I've got to marry her to get her knickers off.'

'I hope you're joking, Rick. Don't fall for the oldest trick in the book.' I slapped him on the back and started to walk away. 'I'll see you later.'

'Aren't you going to congratulate me?' he called after me.

'Congratulations', I shouted back. 'I'll see you tonight.' I went away down the busy street, dreaming and bumping into people more than usual. I tried to picture what the needle on a compass looked like, and wondered whether or not it was a two-edged sword.

EIGHT

A certificate of non-impediment; that's what Rick and Laura had to obtain before they could be married, Rick's from England, Laura's from the Philippines. As the best man, I saw it as my duty to protect the groom-to-be, and that's why I spent the two weeks it took for the necessary clearance to come through trying to dissuade my best friend from taking the plunge. And, unlike the previous month, I spent almost all of my evenings with Rick, either in the company of Apple or, more usually, alone with him.

It wasn't that I thought he was a condemned man waiting on death row, or that I thought he shouldn't get married (who am I to say what's right for him?), I just wanted him to put the brakes on a little. The fact was that, financially speaking, their future didn't look rosy, and when, after being chucked out of the youth hostel, I rented a room, Rick moved in with me temporarily. It would have to be temporary because it was a single room just large enough for one single and one put-me-up bed. Basically, a flat had been converted into five rooms, three of which (mine included) had no windows at all, just four formica walls. When my alarm clock woke me at eight o'clock every morning, it was impossible to tell whether it was day or night. The noise coming from the queue of people waiting to use the communal toilet at the end of the hall was my only confirmation that it was in fact morning.

I made enquiries with the landlord as to whether or not other rooms would become vacant over the next few weeks but drew a blank, adopting, like Rick, a 'cross that bridge when we come to it' attitude. If he didn't mind running the risk of having no bed to sleep in on his wedding night, why the hell should I?

Apple, I think, was the most ecstatic of all over the prospect of going to a wedding. The Chinese generally seem to love ceremonies, add to that the influence of Hollywood love stories that flood Hong Kong and you have a nation of girls obsessed with romance. For the two weeks before the big day she questioned me non-stop, constantly bobbing up and down with excitement trying to pry a little more information out of me.

During that time I learned a whole repertoire of sounds that Chinese girls make when showing emotion. 'Yerrrrr!' or 'Yieew!' with a stamp of the foot was Apple's reaction to a negative answer; I learned that on the Friday evening before the wedding when I tried to explain what a stag night was. Apparently Chinese men don't have them, and she insisted that the only reason I didn't want her along was because I was going out to meet other women. I was going to say, 'Yes, of course, that's what a stag night is for!' but decided that Chinese culture wouldn't understand, and kept quiet instead. 'It's just a night out in which the best man and the groom go over last minute details of the wedding,' I pleaded, kissing her. 'See you tomorrow morning.'

The barmaid asked us to come down off the tables so we both jumped together, landing heavily in the crowd.

It was still only ten o'clock in the evening but Rick and I were already slurring words and dancing on the tables. The pub's band were just setting up their equipment in the corner but we were too excited to sit around and wait. The anticipation of tomorrow's wedding combined with tequila shots had given us all the guts we needed, and more.

Rick held on to the barmaid's arm as he landed. 'You know I'm getting married tomorrow?' he said as quietly as the juke box and crowd would allow.

'Ri', why you tell me?' she replied, putting her hands on her hips.

'This is your last chance to kiss me.' He grabbed her around the waist and clamped his mouth on to her soft face.

I ordered two more tequilas and offered one to Rick, allowing the girl a chance to pull from the embrace. 'Typical!' he said, gesturing to the whole room. 'As soon as you say you're getting married the girls start falling over themselves to get at you. Fooking typical.'

'She was hardly falling over herself, Rick.' I passed him the tiny glass of clear liquid. 'Still got time to change your mind you know. Never too late.'

He hesitated for a moment, watching the beautiful girl as she threaded her way through the mass of customers to get to the bar where another tray of drinks were waiting to be handed out. She wore only a singlet and I could see the side of her breasts, shiny with perspiration, every time she lifted her arms to collect a glass. 'I need a woman, John,' Rick said dreamily, still staring at the girl.

'Chat one up then, there're plenty to choose from in here.'

Apparently ignoring my comment, he looked around the bar and said, 'One last woman – before I get married . . . '

'You mean . . . a woman?' I wasn't following him.

'A woman, John, not a girl. I need a woman tonight. These girls are all very pretty, but I don't want to spend the whole night chatting them up and then find myself going home alone. Too risky.'

'Ahh, you mean a *woman*.'

'*Yes*. One who can take me in hand and give me a good seeing to. A real woman.'

We clinked glassed and drank the fiery liquid. 'So, ahem, where to next then?'

'Wan Chai?'

I shook my head. 'Kowloon side's better. My contractors always talk about the clubs in Tsim Sha Tsui being the best in Hong Kong. They reckon it's what Wan Chai used to be like thirty years ago.' Someone at another table dropped a glass and it shattered on the floor. I looked around briefly before I said, 'I know roughly where they are. One of them is called Club Paris, everyone's heard of it. All we have to do is jump into a cab and ask the driver, he'll know.'

He raised his eyebrows, mulling over the possibility of a good time on his last night of freedom as a single man. 'Club Paris,' he echoed, 'sounds exotic.'

'Hundreds of girls, I mean women, all waiting to give you a good seeing to. Don't worry about the money, it'll be my wedding gift to you.'

'Wedding gifts are supposed to be for the both of us, aren't they? What does Laura get out of it?'

I shrugged, 'Aids probably.'

We went out and hailed a cab and, as expected, the driver knew the club in question. Within twenty minutes we had crossed the harbour and were sitting in a small room surrounded by half a dozen girls wearing only underwear. The room had karaoke and a TV in one corner, and a long sofa that curved around the walls. The girls giggled and fed us fruit from bowls that were arranged on a glass coffee table in the middle, while Rick and I tried to look dignified and not tear off their skimpy lingerie.

I was trying to get a word of English out of a Shanghai girl who seemed to be overly obsessed with the hair on my chest, while Rick was buried under the other five in the corner. He managed to breathe for long enough to let out a giggle before another tongue shot into his mouth and cut him off. His crotch was hidden beneath a pile of hands, all massaging one another. He looked like he was beneath an octopus in lace.

'Shouldn't have told them you were getting married tomorrow,' I giggled. 'Now you'll be here forever fighting that lot off.'

'Mmm! Mmm!'

The mama-san, the woman in charge, eventually came in to take orders for more drinks and fruit platters. She clapped her hands and the girls got up and scurried out, to be immediately replaced by a different six. After half an hour of this turn around system I'd completely forgotten what the first girls had looked like and couldn't decide which one was the most beautiful. They were all stunning.

The woman came in again and clapped, but I put up a hand in protest. 'No more please. Too many, I can't remember them all.'

She laughed and sat on the sofa between Rick and I. 'Which one you like?'

'Rick?' I said, unwilling to make the first move. I'd never done this sort of thing before and I still felt uneasy.

'They're all fooking lovely,' he said with delight, 'all thirty-six of 'em.'

'How do you know there are thirty-six?' I slurred.

'Six changes, six in each batch, that equals thirty-six.'

'You should be an accountant.'

'In a brothel.'

The woman stood up to leave. 'So what happens now?' I asked, standing up with her.

'You must choose one. I bring in new girl, one for you and one for you.' She wagged a finger. 'Very beautiful girls from Peking, only for special customer. Wait.' She left and a moment later reappeared with two models. They were both six feet tall and had huge silicone breast implants that meant they had to walk leaning backwards, as though they were going uphill. Rick and I agreed that the search was over and, after a few minutes of discussion in which the mama told us the paying arrangements, we paid for the drinks and left, a Chinese version of Barbie on each of our arms.

We were led through the brightly lit streets by the girls, like two poor donkeys on ropes, towards a pre-arranged 'love hotel' where rooms were rented out by the hour. I almost ran, I was so ashamed to be seen with the girl; she couldn't have looked more like a prostitute if she'd tried. In the club she had been wearing only underwear and I had expected her to put on jeans and a T-shirt before we left. Instead she just slipped on a plastic rain-coat that only came down to the bottom of her buttocks, leaving the tops of her long, stockinged legs visible. Every step she took caused the plastic coat to ride up over her bum and reveal her frilly knickers.

With barely concealed relief, the four of us entered the love hotel, booked into a room each, and I shut the door behind us.

The girl immediately started to ask for double the price that had been agreed with her boss. 'You pay now!' she insisted. I slumped on the huge bed and looked at my reflection in the mirrored ceiling. I closed my eyes briefly but the room started to spin from the effect of the tequilas so I opened them again. My double was still staring back at me. 'He says I shouldn't pay you so much,' I said, pointing at my reflection, 'him and your boss.'

She didn't follow the English. 'You pay now.'

'"You pay now, you pay now." Can't you say anything else?'

'You pay now!' She held up two fingers. 'Two.'

'One. Your boss say one, not two.' I rolled off the bed and she instantly took the key out of the door and popped it into her handbag.

'Two!' she shouted, and pushed herself against the door in a crucifix, her huge tits bursting through the V-neck of the raincoat. All of the innocent, smiling beauty that had so radiated from her face before was suddenly replaced with a look of sheer rage, born out of greed.

'This is stupid,' I said appeasingly, trying to calm her down, 'your mama told me the price, and now you've changed it.' I stood up and walked to the door. 'Let's just forget the whole thing, shall we?' We stood face to face, staring into each other's eyes, almost touching noses, before she moved her head to one side and went over to the phone. I tried the door but it was locked. 'Give me the key,' I demanded, slightly panicky. 'Who are you calling? Phone your boss,' I said, thinking that she already was, 'good idea. Phone your boss and she'll tell you that I'm right.'

'Police.' She pointed at the phone and started speaking Mandarin.

'Police!' I huffed. 'Prostitution is illegal in Hong Kong, or don't you know that?' Any sexual desire in me that hadn't been killed by the alcohol was now well and truly doused by this woman's sudden change in behaviour. I watched her talk for a moment, speculating on how quickly she would change back to being nice if I offered her the money she was asking, and went into the toilet, locking the door behind me.

Above the toilet was a small window with flimsy aluminium bars across it. I pondered over the reasoning behind them for a second before giving them an exploratory yank. The whole lot, frame and all, came off, sending chunks of plaster and screws rattling into the bathtub. Quickly zipping up my fly, I opened the window, and without thinking about what I was doing, threw the bars on to the floor and climbed out into the warm, humid night air.

I didn't remember coming upstairs to the room, but when I looked down into the street below I could see that we were at least a floor up above pavement level. 'Shit.' I held on to the window frame and edged forwards, trying to gauge whether I was one or two storeys up, when there was a laugh from the next room along from mine. I could hear Rick's voice and the sound of a shower being turned on, and then a shadow passed by the frosted glass.

'Sir?'

I started and almost lost my footing on the ledge before looking back into my bathroom. There was a knock on the bathroom door and a man's stern voice the unmistakably stony voice of a policeman. 'Sir? Could you come out please, sir? This woman says you've cheated her out of some money.'

I leaned my head in and shouted, 'Yeah, just a minute, I'm having a shit,' and shuffled along the ledge to Rick's room, rapping on the glass. The glow from the neon street sign bathed the whole wall in light, and when Rick opened the window his shocked face was a beautiful soft purple. 'Good evening,' I giggled, 'window cleaning service.'

'What the fook are you doing out there? Get in.'

'Just came to say goodnight.'

He leaned out and looked down on to the street; left then right. 'What happened to the girl?'

'She's otherwise engaged. A bit like you really,' I said, pointing behind him at the girl clutching a towel to her breasts. 'I'm off.' I turned around to face the street and said, 'I'll see you tomorrow morning. You've got to be at the registry by eleven, remember, so don't be late.' And before he could reply, I crouched down and jumped into thin air.

NINE

'B-b-b-beep, b-b-b-beep, b-b-b-beep.'

I leaned out of bed and swept my hand blindly over the floor until it came into contact with the cheap plastic alarm clock. Picking it up and depressing the button, I checked the luminous dial hovering magically in the pitch-black room. Ten o'clock. Ten?

'*Ten o'clock*! Rick! Rick!' Still leaning over, I shook his camp bed to wake him but it just slid across the floor without the weight of a body to hold it down. 'Rick?' As soon as my legs swung over the side of the bed and my feet touched the floor I winced in pain, and the memory of the previous night's jump from the window came flooding back.

'Shit!' I paused, one hand still holding the clock, before stepping gingerly on to the floor to test my ankles.

Just as I hobbled to the door and switched on the bedroom light, the front doorbell rang. 'Thank God for that.' Heaving a sigh of relief, I opened the door and made my way down the hall, opening the front door without looking through the spy-hole. It was Apple, looking radiant in her best designer gear. She kissed me and came in. I swore.

'You don't want me come today?' Her eyes flicked down to the floor, hurt.

'No. I'm sorry. It's not you.' I returned the kiss and shut the door behind her. 'It's Rick.' I quickly ran over a story in my head to explain away the previous night to a suspicious Chinese mind. 'He's, umm . . .'

'He is leady?'

'Well, that's sort of the problem.' I said, ushering her over to our room and pushing open the door to present the empty bed, ' . . . he's not here.'

'Oh shit,' she said, looking at her watch. 'Where?'

'I don't know. We got drunk last night and I left him in the bar. I thought he'd be back by now.'

'This not good for wedding celemony. Chinese say bad luck if late: late for wedding mean man beat wife.' She shook her head morbidly.

'And what about if the woman is late for the wedding?' I asked, momentarily distracted by this new Chinese logic.

'This good, no have probrem.'

At that moment there was the sound of a key turning in the front door lock and we both spun around to watch Rick come bursting through. He shut the door and looked up. 'Ready?'

'Thought you'd changed your mind,' I said releasing my breath.

'Course not, I'm getting married at eleven o'clock. Let's get moving!'

'Talk about cutting it fine. Fucking hell. Do you know what time it is?'

He looked around and shrugged. 'Tennish?' He clapped his hands and seemed to notice Apple for the first time. 'OK, Apple? You look pretty today.'

'Thank—'

'Never mind that crap, Rick,' I walked briskly over to the telephone, 'get your gear on. Where's your shirt and stuff?'

Rick went into the bedroom without replying, and I phoned one of my Chinese building contractors. I didn't know him very well, but the previous week when I'd told him that a friend of mine was getting married, he put his Rolls Royce and driver at my service with the brassy disregard for cost that characterises Hong Kong's comparatively well-off. I thought it stupid to refuse. The driver answered the car-phone in Cantonese and Apple gave directions and times.

'He come ten for'y fi'e,' she said, putting the receiver down.

We went back into the bedroom to find Rick buttoning up a brand-new white granddad shirt, with the clear plastic strip that's used to keep it in shape sticking out from the neck. 'Where did you get that from?' I asked.

'Bought it in Central yesterday,' he said without looking up. 'Cost me a packet.'

'Why the fuck did you buy a collar-less shirt? How are you going to wear a tie if the shirt's got no collar?'

He looked up and then down at his chest.

'Have you even got a tie?'

'Oops.'

'Jacket?'

'Got trousers ... Fook,' he said, holding the neck of the shirt with both hands, 'I never thought about needing a collar.'

I went over to the wardrobe and pulled out one of my white shirts for him. It was three sizes too big, and made him look like he was ready for bed, but there was nothing else. I gave him my only black jacket, and he tried it on.

'What do you think?' he said, checking the inside pocket for cash.

Apple burst out laughing. 'Look like Charie Chaprin.'

He rolled up the foot or so of sleeve that hung off the end of his hands and looked in the mirror. 'Bit on the long side ...'

'Rick, you can't wear that, it looks like a trench coat. You'll have to buy one in town.' I checked Apple's watch again. 'If the driver comes early we should have enough time.' Apple said that there were numerous boutiques in Central, all within a stone's throw of the registry office in City Hall, so we shouldn't have a problem buying a jacket.

We both got dressed, Rick in my shirt and tie, me in my own black jacket, and the three of us descended the narrow staircase down into the street, where the driver was already waiting.

TEN

The metallic-blue convertible Rolls Royce pulled off the elevated roadway and joined the steady stream of traffic that wound its way slowly into Central. The sunlight glinted off a rear windscreen, so I closed one eye and turned towards my beautiful Chinese girlfriend. 'Ask the driver to drop us outside the shops,' I said, blinking hard against the dazzling light. 'You wait in the car with him and we'll run in and buy a jacket.'

Apple leaned forward and spoke to the driver. He shook his head and then jabbered away for a moment before abruptly turning off the main road. 'He say cannot stop on main road,' she said, turning back to me, 'too many traffic.'

I swore under my breath. 'What time is it?' She held up her watch. 'Ten to eleven, we'll never make it.'

Rick looked back from the front seat. 'Don't worry, City Hall's just over there. The shops are down there,' he said, pointing ahead. 'We can buy the jacket and run back. It'll be quicker anyway; all the roads around here are one-way and he'd have to drive right around the block again.'

'We'll never get there in time, look at the traffic.' We had come to a standstill behind a bus, and without thinking I slapped the driver on the back, said thanks and jumped from the car without bothering to open the door. Rick and Apple followed behind. 'The present!' I shouted to Rick, and he leaned into the car and plucked the little wooden box off the front seat.

We ran across Chater Gardens, into Des Voeux Road where the shops were and literally dived into the first doorway that had men's clothes displayed in the window.

'Jackets!' Rick shouted as we ran into the shop.

'Excuse me, sir?'

He stared at the shop assistant and held up the lapel of my jacket, repeating the word.

'And what style would you like to see, sir?'

'Anything, just hurry up.'

The girl motioned towards a rack-full. 'Over here we have the latest in–'

'That'll do.' We all brushed past her and started frantically pulling the jackets off their hangers, holding them up to see which one matched Rick's trousers. 'This one!' I shouted, holding out a fairly standard black job.

'No, no, this better.' Apple passed one to Rick and he tried it on. 'OK?'

'OK?' he asked me.

'OK.' I turned to the shop girl. 'How much?' It was extortionate. 'What time is it, Apple?'

She held up her wrist. 'I will buy you watch.'

'Shit. No time to argue. Buy it or we'll never make it in time. No bag, thanks, he'll wear it.'

We puffed and panted our way back out and down the street towards City Hall. On the way, while still jogging, I pulled off the price tag and manufacturers labels from Rick's back, and as we ascended the stairs into the main hall of the building Apple straightened his tie.

'How do I look?' Rick said, dabbing his forehead with a tissue.

'Fine,' she replied.

'Sweating like a pig,' I added, 'but fine.' I pulled the shirt from my skin to allow the sweat to dry and scanned the hall for a sign of Laura.

Someone called out Rick's name from a reception counter and we went over. Laura had already signed in, and I could see her and her friends waiting in a sort of ante-chamber next to the registry office.

'You're a little late, Mr Jenner,' the woman behind the counter said in a hushed but firm voice, 'but we can hardly start without you.' She handed him the pen to sign in, and as he bent forward looked him over inquisitively. 'Is it raining outside?'

Two minutes later, a dozen or so people came out of a room and we were asked to go in. A sign above the door read, *Please Do Not Throw Confetti Inside The Building – Max Fine $1,000.* I nudged Rick and pointed. 'Romantic, huh?'

'Very,' he said, not really listening, and walked in behind Laura, nervously turning my gift over in the palm of his hand.

Velvet walls; that's what I remember about the marriage hall. Green velvet walls like an upper-class padded cell. Four rows of seats for the guests, while at the front of the room the Chinese registrar and his assistant sat stony-faced behind a large desk, numbed into madness, no doubt by the piped wedding march that played non-stop.

We all sat down and the registrar's assistant handed a printed plastic card to Rick. He read the single line sentence, handed the card to Laura, who did the same, and the registrar pronounced them man and wife. They exchanged rings and we all cheered. That's it. The whole thing took less than five minutes. There was a minor hiccup when Laura couldn't say Rick's full name but otherwise she read the sentence like a pro.

Standing side by side at the top of the stone steps that led down into the little garden of City Hall, Rick and I squinted out into the bright sunshine of the harbour. We stood like that for a while, looking blankly into space and cogitating, before I elbowed him gently in the ribs. 'You can open it now if you want.'

He looked down as if suddenly realising where he was. 'What? Oh, yeah . . .'

Apple shouted up from the bottom of the steps that she wanted to get some film of Rick and Laura together, and that I should get out of the frame.

'Just take one of me and John first,' Rick said, untying the ribbon from the gift. Laura moved to one side, while the other guests walked down to the bottom of the steps. He put the ribbon into his pocket, opened the lid of the box and started laughing.

'Thought you wouldn't be able to use yours any more . . . ' I said, and patted his back.

He held the little antique compass at arm's length and we both peered at the delicate needle as it spun around, seemingly out of control.

I looked at him. 'D'you think it's broken?'

He brought it up to his face. 'No, just confused.'

'Confused?'

'Yeah. You know when you bring two poles together they repel, well it's the same with compasses.' He sighed that recently-married-man sigh (the one that comes from deep inside and tells of lost freedom), and looked sideways at me. 'Let's jump.'

'What?'

'Jump. Down the steps. Come on!' He held my arm and we both took two steps back before running forward and leaping into the air, clearing the four steps into the garden.

As we went, both of us held up our fists, legs spread wide, while Apple aimed the video camera and pressed *RECORD*.

'like Alex Garland's *The Beach*, dog-eared copies are sure to be falling out of backpacks in airports the world over.' FHM

MARK MANN

THE GRINGO TRAIL

summersdale *travel*

The Gringo Trail

Mark Mann

'...there I was in the middle of Bogotá, coked up to my eyeballs, in a hallway holding two machetes, while some drunk Colombians argued about whether or not to blow up a bar with a live hand-grenade...'

Asia has the hippie trail.
South America has the gringo trail.

Mark Mann and his girlfriend Melissa set off to explore the ancient monuments, mountains and rainforests of South America. But for their friend Mark, South America meant only one thing...drugs.

Sad, funny, shocking. The Gringo Trail is an On The Road for the Lonely Planet generation. A darkly comic road-trip and a revealing journey through South America's turbulent history.

Drama and discovery. Culture and cocaine.
Fact is stranger than fiction.

Paperback

For a current publishing catalogue and full listing of
Summersdale travel books,
visit our website:

www.summersdale.com